Handling Priority Inversion in Time-Constrained Distributed Databases

Udai Shanker
Madan Mohan Malaviya University of Technology, India

Sarvesh Pandey
Madan Mohan Malaviya University of Technology, India

A volume in the Advances in Data Mining and
Database Management (ADMDM) Book Series

Published in the United States of America by
IGI Global
Engineering Science Reference (an imprint of IGI Global)
701 E. Chocolate Avenue
Hershey PA, USA 17033
Tel: 717-533-8845
Fax: 717-533-8661
E-mail: cust@igi-global.com
Web site: http://www.igi-global.com

Library of Congress Cataloging-in-Publication Data

Names: Shankar, Udai, 1963- editor. | Pandey, Sarvesh, 1994- editor.
Title: Handling priority inversion in time-constrained distributed
  databases / Udai Shankar and Sarvesh Pandey, editors.
Description: Hershey, PA : Engineering Science Reference, an imprint of IGI
  Global, 2020. | Includes bibliographical references and index. |
  Summary: "This book explores technologies that can enable high
  performance atomicity, consistency, isolation, and durability in
  time-constrained distributed databases"-- Provided by publisher.
Identifiers: LCCN 2019040392 (print) | LCCN 2019040393 (ebook) | ISBN
  9781799824916 (hardcover) | ISBN 9781799824923 (paperback) | ISBN
  9781799824930 (ebook)
Subjects: LCSH: Distributed databases. | Real-time data processing. | Ad
  hoc networks (Computer networks)
Classification: LCC QA76.9.D5 H35 2020 (print) | LCC QA76.9.D5 (ebook) |
  DDC 005.75/8--dc23
LC record available at https://lccn.loc.gov/2019040392
LC ebook record available at https://lccn.loc.gov/2019040393

This book is published in the IGI Global book series Advances in Data Mining and Database Management (ADMDM)
(ISSN: 2327-1981; eISSN: 2327-199X)

British Cataloguing in Publication Data
A Cataloguing in Publication record for this book is available from the British Library.

All work contributed to this book is new, previously-unpublished material. The views expressed in this book are those of the authors, but not necessarily of the publisher.

For electronic access to this publication, please contact: eresources@igi-global.com.

Advances in Data Mining and Database Management (ADMDM) Book Series

David Taniar
Monash University, Australia

ISSN:2327-1981
EISSN:2327-199X

MISSION

With the large amounts of information available to organizations in today's digital world, there is a need for continual research surrounding emerging methods and tools for collecting, analyzing, and storing data.

The **Advances in Data Mining & Database Management (ADMDM)** series aims to bring together research in information retrieval, data analysis, data warehousing, and related areas in order to become an ideal resource for those working and studying in these fields. IT professionals, software engineers, academicians and upper-level students will find titles within the ADMDM book series particularly useful for staying up-to-date on emerging research, theories, and applications in the fields of data mining and database management.

COVERAGE

- Enterprise Systems
- Data Analysis
- Data Mining
- Educational Data Mining
- Customer Analytics
- Quantitative Structure–Activity Relationship
- Neural Networks
- Data Quality
- Information Extraction
- Predictive Analysis

IGI Global is currently accepting manuscripts for publication within this series. To submit a proposal for a volume in this series, please contact our Acquisition Editors at Acquisitions@igi-global.com or visit: http://www.igi-global.com/publish/.

Titles in this Series

For a list of additional titles in this series, please visit: https://www.igi-global.com/book-series/advances-data-mining-data-base-management/37146

Feature Extraction and Classification Techniques for Text Rcognition

Munish Kumar (Maharaja Ranjit Singh Punjab Technical University, India) Manish Kumar Jindal (Panjab University Regional Centre, Muktsar, India) Simpel Rani Jindal (Yadavindera College of Engineering, India) R. K. Sharma (Thapar Institute of Engineering & Technology, India) and Anupam Garg (Bhai Gurdas Institute of Engineering and Technology, India)

Engineering Science Reference • © 2020 • 300pp • H/C (ISBN: 9781799824060) • US $225.00

Neutrosophic Graph Theory and Algorithms

Florentin Smarandache (University of New Mexico, USA) and Said Broumi (Faculty of Science Ben M'Sik, University Hassan II, Morocco)

Engineering Science Reference • © 2020 • 406pp • H/C (ISBN: 9781799813132) • US $245.00

Handbook of Research on Big Data Clustering and Machine Learning

Fausto Pedro Garcia Marquez (Universidad Castilla-La Mancha, Spain)

Engineering Science Reference • © 2020 • 478pp • H/C (ISBN: 9781799801061) • US $285.00

Big Data Analytics for Sustainable Computing

Anandakumar Haldorai (Sri Eshwar College of Engineering, India) and Arulmurugan Ramu (Presidency University, India)

Engineering Science Reference • © 2020 • 263pp • H/C (ISBN: 9781522597506) • US $245.00

Trends and Applications of Text Summarization Techniques

Alessandro Fiori (Candiolo Cancer Institute – FPO, IRCCS, Italy)

Engineering Science Reference • © 2020 • 335pp • H/C (ISBN: 9781522593737) • US $210.00

Emerging Perspectives in Big Data Warehousing

David Taniar (Monash University, Australia) and Wenny Rahayu (La Trobe University, Australia)

Engineering Science Reference • © 2019 • 348pp • H/C (ISBN: 9781522555162) • US $245.00

Emerging Technologies and Applications in Data Processing and Management

Zongmin Ma (Nanjing University of Aeronautics and Astronautics, China) and Li Yan (Nanjing University of Aeronautics and Astronautics, China)

Engineering Science Reference • © 2019 • 458pp • H/C (ISBN: 9781522584469) • US $265.00

701 East Chocolate Avenue, Hershey, PA 17033, USA
Tel: 717-533-8845 x100 • Fax: 717-533-8661
E-Mail: cust@igi-global.com • www.igi-global.com

Editorial Advisory Board

Table of Contents

Detailed Table of Contents

Section 1
Issues With Modern Databases

Chapter 1

Sarvesh Pandey, Madan Mohan Malaviya University of Technology, India
Udai Shanker, Madan Mohan Malaviya University of Technology, India

The problem of priority inversion occurs when a high priority task is required to wait for completion of some other task with low priority as a result of conflict in accessing the shared system resource(s). This problem is discussed by many researchers covering a wide range of research areas. Some of the key research areas are real-time operating systems, real-time systems, real-time databases, and distributed real-time databases. Irrespective of the application area, however, the problem lies with the fact that priority inversion can only be controlled with no method available to eliminate it entirely. In this chapter, the priority inversion-related scheduling issues and research efforts in this direction are discussed. Different approaches and their effectiveness to resolve this problem are analytically compared. Finally, major research accomplishments to date have been summarized and several unanswered research questions have also been listed.

Chapter 2

Shruti Jadon, Motilal Nehru National Institute of Technology, India
Rama Shankar Yadav, Motilal Nehru National Institute of Technology, India

For a hard real-time multicore system, the two important issues that are required to be addressed are feasibility of a task set and balancing of load amongst the cores of the multicore systems. Most of the previous work done considers the scheduling of periodic tasks on a multicore system. This chapter deals with scheduling of aperiodic tasks on a multicore system in a hard real-time environment. In this regard, a multicore total bandwidth server (MTBS) is proposed which schedules the aperiodic tasks with already guaranteed periodic tasks amongst the cores of the multicore processor. The proposed MTBS algorithm works by computing a virtual deadline for every aperiodic task that is arriving to the system. Apart from schedulability of aperiodic tasks, the MTBS approach also focuses on reducing the response time of aperiodic tasks. The simulation studies of MTBS were carried out to find the effectiveness of the proposed approach, and it is also compared with the existing strategies.

Ashish Ranjan Mishra, Rajkiya Engineering College, Sonbhadra, India
Neelendra Badal, Kamla Nehru Institute of Technology, India

This chapter explains an algorithm that can perform vertical partitioning of database tables dynamically on distributed database systems. After vertical partitioning, a new algorithm is developed to allocate that fragments to the proper sites. To accomplish this, three major tasks are performed in this chapter. The first task is to develop a partitioning algorithm, which can partition the relation in such a way that it would perform better than most of the existing algorithms. The second task is to allocate the fragments to the appropriate sites where allocating the fragments will incur low communication cost with respect to other sites. The third task is to monitor the change in frequency of queries at different sites as well as same site. If the change in frequency of queries at different sites as well as the same site exceeds the threshold, the re-partitioning and re-allocation are performed.

Manipriya Sankaranarayanan, National Institute of Technology, Tiruchirappalli, India
Mala C., National Institute of Technology, Tiruchirappalli, India
Samson Mathew, National Institute of Technology, Tiruchirappalli, India

The advancements of several real-time system applications enable us to provide better solutions to day-to-day problems. One such real-time systems that has significantly enhanced its efficiency in aiding travelers to make commutation pleasant is the intelligent transportation system (ITS). There are several aspects of an ITS application that make it efficient and resourceful, but the major significant factor is its capability to provide services within a time constraint. This chapter aims to provide the basic concepts, background, and importance of dependability on distributed real-time systems in ITS using two applications for efficient traffic management. A novel automated traffic signal (ATS) is proposed that manages traffic flow by enumerating vehicle density of road segments using image processing techniques. The other proposed work involves the estimation of congestion rate (CONGRA) for given target area using the proposed hybrid vehicular ad hoc network (VANET). The details of the modules, implementation, and result analysis of the applications are discussed and presented.

Prakash Kumar Singh, Rajkiya Engineering College, Mainpuri, India

In broadcasting, schemes are widely used in a wireless environment. In this chapter, a heuristic broadcasting scheme is proposed that directly affects the concurrency of database transactions. The proposed broadcasting scheme is suitable for real-time transactions. A heuristic scheme is developed in a mobile environment to enhance system performance. Further simulation results in the chapter show that the proposed broadcasting scheme is suitable to improve transaction processing in a wireless environment.

Chapter 6

The demand for scalability in replicated distributed real-time database systems (RDRTDBS) is still explorative and, despite an increase in real-time applications, many challenges and issues remain in designing a more scalable system. The objective is to improve the scalability of the system during system scale up with new replica sites. Existing research has been mainly conducted in maintaining replica consistency between different replicas via replication protocol. However, very little research has been conducted towards improving scalability and maintaining mutual consistency and timeliness. Consequently, the ultimate aim of this chapter is to improve scalability in RDRTDBS such that performance of the system does not degrade even though new replica sites are added.

Section 2
Databases and Interdisciplinary Expansions

Chapter 7

Cloud computing has revolutionized the IT world by its benefits. Cloud users can take relational and non-relational databases in the form of services or can run their own database on computing resources provided by the cloud. With evolution of cloud, new challenges are emerging, and the responsibility of the professional is to provide solution to these challenges. Dynamic pricing of computing resources in the cloud is now widely acceptable by its users. But in the current market of cloud, reverse auction (a mechanism to implement dynamic pricing) is not getting the attention from professionals that it deserves. This work is an effort to identify the facts in the cloud market that are responsible for current condition of reverse auction. In this work, from the identified limitations of current cloud market and case study on existing model for reverse auction in cloud, one can observe that coalition of small cloud providers with common interoperability standard in reverse auction is a feasible solution to encourage cloud market for adapting reverse auction-based resource allocation.

Chapter 8

The cloud-based computing paradigm helps organizations grow exponentially through means of employing an efficient resource management under the budgetary constraints. As an emerging field, cloud computing has a concept of amalgamation of database techniques, programming, network, and internet. The revolutionary advantages over conventional data computing, storage, and retrieval infrastructures result in an increase in the number of organizational services. Cloud services are feasible in all aspects such as cost, operation, infrastructure (software and hardware) and processing. The efficient resource management with cloud computing has great importance of higher scalability, significant energy saving, and cost reduction. Trustworthiness of the provider significantly influences the possible cloud user in his selection of cloud services. This chapter proposes a cloud service selection model (CSSM) for analyzing any cloud service in detail with multidimensional perspectives.

Chapter 9

Pawan Kumar Chaurasia, Mahatma Gandhi Central University, Motihari, India

This chapter conducts a critical review on ML and deep learning tools and techniques in the field of heart disease related to heart disease complexity, prediction, and diagnosis. Only specific papers are selected for the study to extract useful information, which stimulated a new hypothesis to understand further investigation of the heart disease patient.

Chapter 10

V. Punitha, National Institute of Technology, Tiruchirappalli, India
C. Mala, National Institute of Technology, Tiruchirappalli, India

The recent technological transformation in application deployment, with the enriched availability of applications, induces the attackers to shift the target of the attack to the services provided by the application layer. Application layer DoS or DDoS attacks are launched only after establishing the connection to the server. They are stealthier than network or transport layer attacks. The existing defence mechanisms are unproductive in detecting application layer DoS or DDoS attacks. Hence, this chapter proposes a novel deep learning classification model using an autoencoder to detect application layer DDoS attacks by measuring the deviations in the incoming network traffic. The experimental results show that the proposed deep autoencoder model detects application layer attacks in HTTP traffic more proficiently than existing machine learning models.

Chapter 11

Sneh Garg, Chandigarh College of Engineering and Technology, India
Ram Bahadur Patel, Chandigarh College of Engineering and Technology, India

With the advancements in technology, wireless sensor networks (WSNs) are used almost in all applications. These sensor network systems are sometimes used to monitor hostile environments where human intervention is not possible. When sensing is required to be done in areas that are hostile, there is need for autonomous/self-managing systems as it is very difficult for the human to intervene within such hostile environmental conditions. Therefore, in such systems, each node is required to do all functionalities and act like autonomous decision taking node that performs both data forwarding and network control. Therefore, introducing a self-management for large-scale distributed wireless system is a highly tedious task due to resource constrained nature of these nodes. It is very difficult to achieve required quality of service by large systems as a huge amount of energy is dissipated by systems in radio communication. Owing to resource constraint as well as vulnerable nature, developing a self-managing system for distributed WSN is a very challenging and demanding task.

Santosh Kumar, National Institute of Technology, Kurukshetra, India
Awadhesh Kumar Singh, National Institute of Technology, Kurukshetra, India

Numerous research articles exist for backbone formation in wireless networks; however, they cannot be applied straightforward in cognitive radio networks (CRN) due to its peculiar characteristics. Since virtual backbone has many advantages such as reduced routing overhead, dynamic maintenance, and fast convergence speed, the authors propose a backbone formation protocol in CRN. In this chapter, a backbone formation protocol is proposed using the concept of minimum spanning tree. The protocol is based on non-iterative approach, thus leading towards limited message overhead. The proposed algorithm first forms the minimum spanning tree, and second, the nodes having more than one neighbor are connected together to form the backbone.

Pavan Kumar Pandey, Dr. A. P. J. Abdul Kalam Technical University, Lucknow, India
Vineet Kansal, Institute of Engineering and Technology, Lucknow, India
Abhishek Swaroop, Bhagwan Parshuram Institute of Technology, Delhi, India

Over the past few years, there has been significant research interest in field of vehicular ad hoc networks (VANETs). Wireless communication over VANETs supports vehicle-to-vehicle (V2V), vehicle-to-infrastructure (V2I) communication. Such innovation in wireless communication has improved our daily lives through road safety, comfort driving, traffic efficiency. As special version of MANETs, VANETs bring several new challenges including routing and security challenges in data communication due to characteristics of high mobility, dynamic topology. Therefore, academia and the auto mobile industry are taking interest in several ongoing research projects to establish VANETs. The work presented here focuses on communication in VANETs with their routing and security challenges along with major application of VANETs in several areas.

Joy Christy A, School of Computing, SASTRA University (Deemed), India
Umamakeswari A, School of Computing, SASTRA University (Deemed), India

Outlier detection is a part of data analytics that helps users to find discrepancies in working machines by applying outlier detection algorithm on the captured data for every fixed interval. An outlier is a data point that exhibits different properties from other points due to some external or internal forces. These outliers can be detected by clustering the data points. To detect outliers, optimal clustering of data points is important. The problem that arises quite frequently in statistics is identification of groups or clusters of data within a population or sample. The most widely used procedure to identify clusters in a set of observations is k-means using Euclidean distance. Euclidean distance is not so efficient for finding anomaly in multivariate space. This chapter uses k-means algorithm with Mahalanobis distance metric to capture the variance structure of the clusters followed by the application of extreme value analysis (EVA) algorithm to detect the outliers for detecting rare items, events, or observations that raise suspicions from the majority of the data.

This chapter presents an overview of spam email as a serious problem in our internet world and creates a spam filter that reduces the previous weaknesses and provides better identification accuracy with less complexity. Since J48 decision tree is a widely used classification technique due to its simple structure, higher classification accuracy, and lower time complexity, it is used as a spam mail classifier here. Now, with lower complexity, it becomes difficult to get higher accuracy in the case of large number of records. In order to overcome this problem, particle swarm optimization is used here to optimize the spam base dataset, thus optimizing the decision tree model as well as reducing the time complexity. Once the records have been standardized, the decision tree is again used to check the accuracy of the classification. The chapter presents a study on various spam-related issues, various filters used, related work, and potential spam-filtering scope.

The quality of retrieval documents in CLIR is often poor compared to IR system due to (1) query mismatching, (2) multiple representations of query terms, and (3) un-translated query terms. The inappropriate translation may lead to poor quality of results. Hence, automated query translation is performed using the back-translation approach for improvement of query translation. This chapter mainly focuses on query expansion (Q.E) and proposes an algorithm to address the drift query issue for Hindi-English CLIR. The system uses FIRE datasets and a set of 50 queries of Hindi language for evaluation. The purpose of a term ordering-based algorithm is to resolve the drift query issue in Q.E. The result shows that the relevancy of Hindi-English CLIR is improved by performing Q.E. using a term ordering-based algorithm. The outcome achieved 60.18% accuracy of results where Q.E has been performed using a term ordering based algorithm, whereas the result of Q.E without a term ordering-based algorithm stands at 57.46%.

Foreword

Research in the domain of Time-Constrained Database has a rich history of around three decades which has led to the most relevant and important developments in the field of Computer Science and Engineering discipline. Mostly, database technologies, architectures and conceptual frameworks have been discussed in last few decades. Moreover, database management has evolved in such a way that databases have become a key component at the heart of current computing environments and modern information systems. This has provoked a deep impact and significant change in the way organizations and institutions operate and make their business decisions. It is worthwhile mentioning few facts that have promoted such a growth: the ubiquity of powerful and easy-to-use personal computer database management products, new modeling techniques and tools, the emergence of client-server processing, the decreasing price of hardware and software, availability of BIG data, and the imperious need to properly and efficiently manage huge amounts of information.

The design of database applications is a crucial factor in the success of information systems in any organization. Data is one of the most valuable assets to an organization whose validity, consistency, availability and accuracy are vital. A database management systems (DBMS) greatly contributes with these purposes by providing data persistence, efficient access guarantees by integrity constraints. Current database systems offer the SQL query language standard, which has become the query and manipulation language standard. By isolating the conceptual schema from the implementation schema, database systems guarantee data independence from storage techniques. Also, by means of the management of users and their privileges, the DBMS can provide secure controlled access to data. While the control of concurrent access to data is managed through different protocols of transaction scheduling and varied locking techniques, backups and database recovery strategies allow the database recovery after hardware and software failures. This has happened in such a way that database knowledge has become an essential part of the education and research fertinity related to computer science.

The growth of database effectiveness is accompanied by a huge increase of users and user profiles. The need of users for information sources has naturally and extensively grown. I believe this edited book will help to close the gap between both aspects. Other new and powerful issues of database research are programming languages, active databases, temporal databases, spatial databases, multimedia databases, and databases related to the Web.

Leading specialists in each area, researchers with profuse publications on the topics covered, practitioners with a vast experience in the development of database systems in organizational environments, and teachers with accumulated experience teaching graduate and undergraduate courses have contributed articles on their field of expertise related to databases im this edited book.

The potential audience of this book is widely diverse. This book is intended for computing students who have some knowledge on databases, for teachers giving not only introductory but advanced courses on databases, for researchers with concerns about specific concepts in their area of interest, and for practitioners facing database implementation choices. Inexperienced readers and students will also find this book a valuable resourse to increase their knowledge about databases, in addition to the main issues and applications related to the field. Experienced teachers will discover a comprehensive compendium of teaching resources. On the other hand, this database book is also a valuable reference book for professionals, designers, application programmers, researchers and database practitioners. This important new publication brings together a discussion of a wide spectrum of database issues, giving researchers, scholars, students, and professionals the access to the latest knowledge related to database science, technology and the trends in this promising and continuously evolving field. The main endeavor of this book has been to grant access to essential core material for education, research, and practice on database systems.

The current effort of edited book is broader than most database books that links to current technologies. It offers a sound grounding and state of the art foundations of database technology and also provides solid ideas about current trends and evidence on how this field is likely to develop in the near future. Many articles offer an analytical approach, so that the concepts presented can be applied not only to the wide variety of actual databases but also can be used as a fundamental stone to build future systems.

Topics covered by this work include the time-constrained databases, machine learning, cloud computing, and the development of challenging database applications. Many articles have numerous examples on how to apply the available techniques. Conventional and current database systems are (and typically have been designed and optimized for On-Line Transaction Processing (OLTP)) explored. In this sense, the current databases can manage huge quantities of transactions, executing, concurrently modifying or reading generally small and changeable amounts of data. However, recently applications in the context of the management of a complex enterprise require a far-reaching, overall view of all aspects of its activities.

Fundamental issues of database technology such as transactions, concurrency control, reliability, and recovery are explored into a set of entries, with emphasis on distribution, replication and parallelism. The purpose of these writings is to offer the reader not only the state-of-the-art knowledge in databases but also to disseminate the knowledge and challenges associated with the scale-up of distributed databases.

The emergence of powerful portable computers and the development of fast reliable networks have promoted the birth and growth of a new dimension in data processing and communication known as mobile computing. Mobility and portability have created a new repertory of applications and have produced a deep impact in the data management field. In this sense, mobile database systems have emerged as a paradigm bringing support to transactions provided by mobile clients and creating a broad and promising research field in the past decade. Entries exploring mobile databases focus on data dissemination over limited bandwidth channels, location-dependent querying of data, and concurrency control and recovery mechanisms.

In summary, this edited book offers a unique and exciting opportunity to find out, not only about the state of the art of fundamental database concepts, but about current trends, novel technology, and challenging applications to meet the needs of current data management system students, faculty and researchers.

It is in fact state-of-the-art compilation of fundamental and current topics in database research!

Lalit Kumar Awasthi
National Institute of Technology, Jalandhar, India

Preface

On reading the title of this book, *Handling Priority Inversion in Time-Constrained Databases*, a sudden impression that may come in reader's mind is that this book is all about discussing the advancement in algorithms related to databases with prime focus on real time constraints. Yes, it is right to some extent, but we have included a miscellaneous set of chapters to present the larger picture when almost all aspects of computer science research are somehow connected with databases.

There are total of 16 chapters in this edited book. In a clearer word, this book is written with an interdisciplinary orientation. For that reason, the book is divided into two sections. The first section, titled "Issues With Modern Databases," consists of the topics that are largely related to database research community. In this section, the applications of real time database systems and related concepts are discussed, reviewed and explored. This section includes following six chapters. These chapters are briefly described over here to provide a glimpse of what this book has to offer to its wider set of readers.

CHAPTER 1: CAUSES, EFFECTS, AND CONSEQUENCES OF PRIORITY INVERSION IN TRANSACTION PROCESSING

The problem of priority inversion occurs when a high priority task is required to wait for completion of some other task with low priority as a result of conflict in accessing the shared system resource(s). This problem is discussed by many researchers covering wide range of research areas. Some of the key research areas are real-time operating systems, real-time systems, real-time databases and distributed real-time databases. Irrespective of the application area, however, the problem lies with the fact that priority inversion can only be controlled with no method available to eliminate it entirely. In this book chapter, the priority inversion related scheduling issues and research efforts in this direction are discussed. Different approaches and their effectiveness to resolve this problem are analytically compared. Finally, major research accomplishments to date have been summarized and several unanswered research questions have also been listed.

CHAPTER 2: SCHEDULING OF APERIODIC TASKS ON MULTICORE SYSTEMS

For a hard real time multicore system, the two important issues that are required to be addressed are feasibility of a task set and balancing of load amongst the cores of the multicore systems. Most of the previous work done considers the scheduling of periodic tasks on a multicore system. This chapter deals with scheduling of aperiodic tasks on a multicore system in a hard real time environment. In this regard, a multicore total bandwidth server (MTBS) is proposed which schedules the aperiodic tasks with already guaranteed periodic tasks amongst the cores of the multicore processor. The proposed MTBS algorithm works by computing a virtual deadline for every aperiodic task arriving to the system. Apart from schedulability of aperiodic tasks, the MTBS approach also focuses on reducing the response time of aperiodic tasks. The simulation studies of MTBS were carried out to find the effectiveness of the proposed approach and it is also compared with the existing strategies.

CHAPTER 3: LOCALIZATION OF DATA SET IN DISTRIBUTED DATABASE SYSTEM USING SLOPE-BASED VERTICAL FRAGMENTATION

This chapter explains an algorithm which can perform vertical partitioning of database tables dynamically on distributed database systems. After vertical partitioning, a new algorithm is developed to allocate that fragments to the proper sites. To accomplish this, three major tasks are performed in this chapter. The first task is to develop a partitioning algorithm which can partition the relation in such a way that it would perform better than most of the existing algorithms. The second task is to allocate the fragments to the appropriate sites where allocating the fragments will incur low communication cost with respect to other sites. The third task is to monitor the change in frequency of queries at different sites as well as same site. If the change in frequency of queries at different sites as well as the same site exceeds the threshold, the re-partitioning and re-allocation is performed.

CHAPTER 4: SIGNIFICANCE OF REAL-TIME SYSTEMS IN INTELLIGENT TRANSPORTATION SYSTEMS

The advancements of several real time system applications enable to provide better solution to day to day problems. One of such real time systems that have significantly enhanced its efficiency in aiding travelers to make commutation pleasant are from Intelligent Transportation Systems (ITS). There are several aspects of an ITS application that makes it efficient and resourceful, but the major significant factor is its capability to provide services within a time constraint. This chapter aims to provide the basic concepts, background and importance of dependability on distributed real time systems in ITS using two applications for efficient traffic management. A novel Automated Traffic Signal (ATS) is proposed that manages traffic flow by enumerating vehicle density of road segments using image processing techniques. The other proposed work involves the estimation of Congestion Rate (CONGRA) for given target area using the proposed hybrid Vehicular Adhoc Network (VANET). The details of the modules, implementation and result analysis of the applications are discussed and presented.

CHAPTER 5: A BROADCASTING SCHEME FOR TRANSACTION PROCESSING IN WIRELESS ENVIRONMENT

In Broadcasting, schemes are widely used in a wireless environment. In this chapter, a heuristic broadcasting scheme is proposed which directly affects the concurrency of database transactions. The proposed broadcasting scheme is suitable for real-time transactions. A heuristic scheme is developed in a mobile environment to enhance system performance. Further, simulation results in the chapter show that the proposed broadcasting scheme is suitable to improve transaction processing in a wireless environment.

CHAPTER 6: IMPROVING SCALABILITY IN REPLICATED DRTDBS

The demand for scalability in replicated distributed real time database system (RDRTDBS) is still explorative and, despite an increase in real time application, many challenges and issues remain in designing a more scalable system. Our objective is to improve the scalability of the system during system scale up with new replica sites. Existing research has been mainly conducted in maintaining replica consistency between different replicas via replication protocol. However, very little research is conducted towards improving scalability, maintaining mutual consistency, and timeliness. Consequently, the ultimate aim of this chapter is to improve scalability in RDRTDBS such that performance of the system does not degrade even though new replica sites are added.

The second section, titled "Databases and Their Interdisciplinary Expansions," dips into the theory, the technology, and the tools that reshape what links modern databases with cloud computing, machine learning and natural language processing. The applications and issues resulting due to their win-win handshake are discussed, reviewed and explored. This section includes ten chapters. Again, these chapters are briefly described over here to provide a glimpse of what this book has to offer to its wider set of readers.

CHAPTER 7: FEASIBILITY OF PROVIDERS' COALITION IN REVERSE AUCTION-BASED CLOUD MARKET

Cloud computing has revolutionized the IT world by its benefits. Cloud users can take relational and non-relational databases in the form of services or can run its own database on computing resources provided by the Cloud. With evolution of cloud, new challenges are emerging, and responsibility of professional is to provide solution of these challenges. Dynamic pricing of computing resources in cloud is now widely acceptable by its users. But in current market of cloud, reverse auction (a mechanism to implement dynamic pricing) is not getting attention from its professional that it deserves. This work is an effort to identify the facts in the cloud market which are responsible for current condition of reverse auction. In this work, from the identified limitations of current cloud market and case study on existing model for reverse auction in cloud, one can observe that coalition of small cloud providers with common interoperability standard in reverse auction is a feasible solution to encourage cloud market for adapting reverse auction based resource allocation.

CHAPTER 8: A CLOUD TRUSTING MECHANISM BASED ON RESOURCE RANKING

The cloud-based computing paradigm helps organizations to grow exponentially through means of employing an efficient resource management under the budgetary constraints. As an emerging field, Cloud computing has a concept of amalgamation of database techniques, programming's, network, and internet. The revolutionary advantages over conventional data computing, storage and retrieval infrastructures result into the increase in the number of organizational services. Cloud services are feasible in all aspects such as cost, operation, infrastructure (software & hardware) and processing. The efficient resource management with cloud computing has great importance of higher scalability, significant energy saving and cost reductions. Trustworthiness of the provider significantly influences the possible cloud user in his selection of cloud services. This chapter proposes a Cloud Service Selection Model (CSSM) for analyzing any cloud service in detail with multidimensional perspectives.

CHAPTER 9: PARADIGMS OF MACHINE LEARNING AND DATA ANALYTICS

From last one decade, digital computers have changed the views in almost every segment of life. Our daily life has seen dramatic changes after emergence of data analytics. Industrial revolution brought significant changes in our daily occurrence as well as social occurrence. One day machine would be able to learn and take decisions itself by using artificial intelligence, big data and machine learning. Today, most of the industries use ML, AI and Big Data for implementation of various applications. Large amount of data provides computational analysis of similar data by finding the patterns in that data. This chapter is focused on to conduct study on a critical review on ML and Deep Learning tools and techniques in the field of heart disease with related to heart disease complexity, prediction and diagnosis. Only specific papers are selected for the study to extract useful information which stimulated new hypothesis to understand further investigation of the heart disease patient.

CHAPTER 10: A DEEP LEARNING APPROACH FOR DETECTION OF APPLICATION LAYER ATTACKS IN INTERNET

The recent technological transformation in application deployment, with the enriched availability of applications induces the attackers to shift the target of the attack to the services provided by the application layer. Application layer DoS or DDoS attacks are launched only after establishing the connection to the server. They are stealthier than network or transport layer attacks. The existing defense mechanisms are unproductive in detecting application layer DoS or DDoS attacks. Hence, this chapter proposes a novel deep learning classification model using an autoencoder to detect application layer DDoS attacks by measuring the deviations in the incoming network traffic. The experimental results show that the proposed deep autoencoder model detects application layer attacks in HTTP traffic more proficiently than existing machine learning models.

CHAPTER 11: SELF-MANAGED SYSTEM FOR DISTRIBUTED WIRELESS SENSOR NETWORKS – A REVIEW

With the advancements in technology, Wireless sensor networks (WSNs) are used almost in all applications. These sensor network systems are sometimes used to monitor hostile environments where human intervention is not possible. When sensing is required to be done in area that is hostile, then there is need for autonomous /self- managing systems as it is very difficult for the human beings to intervene in such a hostile environment conditions. Therefore, in such systems, each node is required to do all functionalities and acts like autonomous decision taking node that performs both data forwarding and network control. Therefore, introducing a self-management for large scale distributed wireless system is highly tedious task due to resource constrained nature of these nodes It is very difficult to achieve required quality of service by a large systems as huge amount of energy is dissipated by system in radio communication. Owing to resource constraint as well as vulnerable nature, developing a self-managing system for distributed WSN is very challenging and demanding task.

CHAPTER 12: A BACKBONE FORMATION PROTOCOL USING MINIMUM SPANNING TREE IN COGNITIVE RADIO NETWORKS

Numerous research articles exist for backbone formation in wireless networks; however, they cannot be applied straightforward in cognitive radio network (CRN) due to its peculiar characteristics. Since, virtual backbone has many advantages such as reduced routing overhead, dynamic maintenance, and fast convergence speed, it intends to propose a backbone formation protocol in CRN. In this chapter, a backbone formation protocol is proposed using the concept of minimum spanning tree. The protocol is based on non-iterative approach, thus leading towards limited message overhead. The proposed algorithm first forms the minimum spanning tree and second, the nodes having more than one neighbors are connected together to form the backbone.

CHAPTER 13: VEHICULAR AD HOC NETWORKS (VANETS), ARCHITECTURE, CHALLENGES, AND APPLICATIONS

Over the past few years, auto mobile industry has triggered significant research interest in field of vehicular ad hoc networks (VANETs). Wireless communication over VANETs supports Vehicle to Vehicle (V2V), Vehicle to Infrastructure (V2I) communication. Such innovation in wireless communication has improved our daily life a lot through road safety, comfort driving, traffic efficiency etc. As special version of MANETs, VANETs bring several new challenges including routing and security challenges in data communication due to characteristics of high mobility, dynamic topology etc. Therefore, several academia and automobile industries are heavily taking interest in several ongoing research projects to establish VANETs. Work presented here focuses on communication in VANETs with their routing and security challenges along with major application of VANETs in several areas.

CHAPTER 14: PERFORMANCE ENHANCEMENT OF OUTLIER REMOVAL USING EXTREME VALUE ANALYSIS-BASED MAHALONOBIS DISTANCE

Outlier detection is a part of data analytics that helps user to find discrepancies in working machine by applying outlier detection algorithm on the captured data for every fixed interval. An outlier is a data point that exhibits different properties from other points that are due to some external or internal forces. These outliers can be detected by clustering the data points. To detect outliers, optimal clustering of data points is important. Problem, which arises quite frequently in statistics, is identification of groups or clusters of data within a population or sample. The most widely used procedure to identify clusters in a set of observations is K-Means using Euclidean distance. Euclidean distance is not so efficient for finding anomaly in multivariate space. This chapter uses K-Means algorithm with Mahalanobis distance metric to capture the variance structure of the clusters followed by the application of Extreme Value Analysis (EVA) algorithm to detect the outliers for detecting rare items, events or observations which raise suspicions from the majority of the data.

CHAPTER 15: SPAM MAIL FILTERING USING DATA MINING APPROACH – A COMPARATIVE PERFORMANCE ANALYSIS

This chapter presents an overview of the spam email as a serious problem in our Internet world and create a spam filter that reduces the previous weaknesses and provides better identification accuracy with less complexity. Since J48 decision tree is a widely used classification technique due to its simple structure, higher classification accuracy and lower time complexity, it is used as a spam mail classifier here. Now, with lower complexity, it becomes difficult to get higher accuracy in the case of large number of records. In order to overcome this problem, Particle Swarm Optimization is used here to optimize the spam based dataset, thus optimizing the decision tree model as well as reducing the time complexity. Once the records have been standardized, the decision tree is again used to check the accuracy of the classification. This chapter presents study on various spam related issues, filters used, related work and potential spam filtering scope.

CHAPTER 16: TERM ORDERING BASED QUERY EXPANSION TECHNIQUE FOR HINDI-ENGLISH CLIR SYSTEM

The quality of retrieval documents in CLIR is often poor as compared to IR system due to (a) query mismatching, (b) multiple representations of query terms and (c) un-translated query terms. The inappropriate translation may lead to poor quality of results. Hence, automated query translation is performed using the back-translation approach for the improvement of query translation. This chapter mainly focuses on Query Expansion (Q.E) and proposes an algorithm to address the drift query issue for Hindi-English CLIR. The system uses FIRE datasets and a set of 50 queries of Hindi language for evaluation. The purpose of a term ordering based algorithm is to resolve the drift query issue in Q.E. The result shows that the relevancy of Hindi-English CLIR is improved by performing Q.E. using a term ordering based algorithm. The result of Q.E. with a term ordering based algorithm stands at 60.18% accuracy. The result of Q.E without a term ordering based algorithm stands at 57.46% accuracy.

Overall, in this book, we have carefully selected and included the chapters by considering their relevancy towards the applications of databases in various computer science domains. Various graphical illustrations, images, diagrams, and tables which are included in each chapter will make these chapters easy to understand. We strongly believe that our enormous effort taken to bring these chapters together in the form of valuable book will help the Academicians, Research scholars, Industrial experts, Scientists, post graduate students who are willing to work / working in the field of Time-Constrained Modern Databases.

Udai Shanker
Madan Mohan Malaviya University of Technology, India

Sarvesh Pandey
Madan Mohan Malaviya University of Technology, India

Acknowledgment

First and foremost, we would like to thank the God. In the process of putting this book together, we realized how true this gift of writing is for us. You have given us the power to believe in our passion and pursue our dreams. We could never have done this without the faith we have in you, the Almighty.

Editing a book is harder than we thought and more rewarding than we could have ever imagined. None of this would have been possible without the support of expert members of the advisory board of this book. Our heartily thanks go to all of them for their active contributions and suggestions. We cannot possibly repay you all. Also, the best way to thank all the authors for their contributions submitted as book chapter is to keep them informed of the outcome and we promise to do that. Meanwhile, most of them have also played such an important role as reviewers and their help would not be forgotten. We are indebted to all the external reviewers for their thoughtful and thorough reviews. We believe their time and contribution to the critical evaluation of submissions made our book more balanced. They all have no idea how much their help has meant for us.

We would like to express our deepest appreciation to everyone on the publishing team. Special thanks to IGI Global for sharing their expertise in guiding and organizing this project. Their professional support really made the production of this book in a very smooth way.

Nobody has been more important to us in the pursuit of this book than the members of our families. We wish to express a deep appreciation to our family members, to whom this book is devoted, for providing us the needed inspirational resources to balance our careers and family trajectories.

Udai Shanker
Madan Mohan Malaviya University of Technology, India

Sarvesh Pandey
Madan Mohan Malaviya University of Technology, India

Section 1
Issues With Modern Databases

Chapter 1
Causes, Effects, and Consequences of Priority Inversion in Transaction Processing

Sarvesh Pandey
https://orcid.org/0000-0002-3014-9792
Madan Mohan Malaviya University of Technology, India

Udai Shanker
https://orcid.org/0000-0002-4083-7046
Madan Mohan Malaviya University of Technology, India

ABSTRACT

The problem of priority inversion occurs when a high priority task is required to wait for completion of some other task with low priority as a result of conflict in accessing the shared system resource(s). This problem is discussed by many researchers covering a wide range of research areas. Some of the key research areas are real-time operating systems, real-time systems, real-time databases, and distributed real-time databases. Irrespective of the application area, however, the problem lies with the fact that priority inversion can only be controlled with no method available to eliminate it entirely. In this chapter, the priority inversion-related scheduling issues and research efforts in this direction are discussed. Different approaches and their effectiveness to resolve this problem are analytically compared. Finally, major research accomplishments to date have been summarized and several unanswered research questions have also been listed.

DOI: 10.4018/978-1-7998-2491-6.ch001

INTRODUCTION

Today, the systems/ applications are not only supposed to provide correct results, but these results should also come on or before some predefined time. Consequently, it has become very critical to design application-specific and time-constraint aware scheduling algorithms. The problem of priority inversion is a most talked about topic which requires wider researchers' attention as there are not vital solutions proposed till date to resolve this problem completely. It is a situation where task with high priority has been put on hold so that a low priority task may finish its execution. In the beginning of the research in this direction, priority inheritance approach was tried to resolve this problem. However, this approach does not actually eliminate the priority inversion completely but reduces its negative impact to some extent on the system by reducing the duration of it.

Let us suppose that two tasks are involved in a priority inversion problem. One is low priority task and another one is high priority task. Low priority task is currently holding the shared resource which is being requested by the high priority task. High priority task is waiting for completion of low priority task since low priority task is already holding the required resource. This is the case of priority inversion. It is done by upgrading the priority of low priority task to that of high priority task. The debate on usefulness of priority inheritance approach as a solution to the priority inversion problem is more than three decades old. Interestingly, researchers still do not agree and come to a conclusion whether this approach has a potential to address the ever-changing today's complex system requirements or not. More specifically, in some environments, this approach was proven to be an effective one while in others the completely contrary results were obtained.

Real-time computing systems are vital to a wide range of applications such as in the control of nuclear reactors & automated manufacturing facilities, in controlling & tracking air traffic, in advanced aircraft and in communication systems etc. All such systems control, monitor or perform critical operations, and must respond quickly to emergency events in a wide range of embedded applications (Rajkumar, 1989). They are, therefore, required to process tasks with stringent timing requirements and must perform these tasks in a way that these timing requirements are guaranteed to be met. Real-time scheduling algorithms attempt to ensure that system timing behavior meets its specifications, but typically assume that tasks do not share logical or physical resources. Since resource sharing cannot be eliminated, synchronization primitives must be used to ensure that resource consistency constraints are not violated.

Later, Lui Sha et al. analyzed the general priority inheritance class and proposed two protocols — the basic priority inheritance protocol and the priority ceiling protocol (Sha, Rajkumar, & Lehoczky, 1990). The objective of both the protocols was to solve the uncontrolled priority inversion problem. It has been claimed that the priority ceiling protocol solves this uncontrolled priority inversion problem particularly well and reduces the worst-case task blocking time to at most the duration of execution of a single critical section of a lower-priority task. This protocol also prevents the occurrences of deadlocks.

In software systems using preemptive scheduling based on task priorities, it is desirable to include a priority inheritance mechanism. This is an arrangement by which a task's priority is temporarily increased when it is blocking a task of higher priority. Although, it is easy to work out the time and way to increase a task's priority, the subsequent reduction of that task's priority involves some hidden traps. It is shown that the "obvious" solutions are flawed, in that they can reduce the priority either too early or too late (Moylan, Betz, & Middleton, 1993).

The criticalness of the priority inversion problem can better be explained through discussing what we experienced because of this problem in past. One true instance happened in late nineties with NASA Mars mission. The Mars path finder incident happened due to a concurrent software glitch after landing on July 4, 1997 (Reeves, 1998). The trouble experienced by the Mars Pathfinder lander is a classic example of problems caused by priority inversion in real time systems. This incident happened because of the problem of priority inversion. During the initial days of the mission, in just a period of 10 days (from July 5 to July 14, 1997), four computer resets experienced by the path finder when it started gathering metrological data from mars because of the above priority inversion problem. To resolve this problem, this problem was virtually reproduced at its ground control station in NASA and corrected with the help of logging and debugging functionality. On July 21, patching of the software was performed to enable the priority inheritance feature. This incident made computer researchers to rethink and to resolve the priority inversion problem in a better and more advanced manner.

In some cases, priority inversion can occur without causing immediate harm—the delayed execution of the high priority task goes unnoticed, and eventually the low priority task releases the shared resource. However, there are also many situations in which priority inversion can cause serious problems. If the high priority task is left starved of the resources, it might lead to a system malfunction or the triggering of pre-defined corrective measures.

Priority inversion can also reduce the perceived performance of the system. Low priority tasks usually have a low priority because it is not important for them to finish promptly (for example, they might be a batch job or another non-interactive activity). Similarly, a high priority task has a high priority because it is more likely to be subjected to strict time constraints—it may be providing data to an interactive user or acting subject to real time response guarantees. Because priority inversion results in the execution of a lower priority task blocking the high priority task, it can lead to reduced system responsiveness, or even the violation of response time guarantees. A similar problem called deadline interchange can occur within earliest deadline first scheduling (EDF).

In real-time systems with threads, resource locking and priority scheduling, one may face the problem of priority inversion. This problem can make the behaviour of the threads unpredictable and the resulting bugs can be hard to find. The Priority Inheritance Protocol is implemented as a solution in many systems for solving this problem, but the correctness of this solution has never been formally verified in a theorem prover. The limitations, dangers, and performance costs of the priority inheritance scheme in dealing with priority inversion are studied and criticized by some researchers (Yodaiken, 2004). On the basis of these criticisms, it has been claimed that priority inheritance is a poor choice of design for most real-time projects.

The original informal investigation of the Property Inheritance Protocol has presented a correctness "proof" for an incorrect algorithm. The problem of this proof is fixed by making all notions precise and implementing a variant of a solution was proposed earlier (Zhang, Urban, & Wu, 2012). The scheduling problem is also generalized to the practically relevant case where critical sections can overlap. The formalization in Isabelle/HOL was based on Paulson's inductive approach to protocol verification. The formalization facilitated in efficiently implementing the priority inheritance protocol.

Some other approaches to handle priority inversion problem are priority abort approach, priority ceiling approach, lender-borrower approach etc. The priority abort approach is a simplest and straightforward approach to resolve the priority inversion problem in which the conflict is resolved immediately in favour of task with high priority by aborting all the low priority tasks that had previously locked the conflicting data item. The priority of a data item is equal to the priority of highest priority task from among the tasks that have requested access to it. The priority ceiling approach is a non-preemptive approach in which priority is assigned to both data and task which require to access the data. The Lender-Borrower approach is an optimistic approach which allows the low priority task to access the dirty data even when it requires to access it in conflicting mode by creating a dependency among the tasks involved in any such conflict. Though, the above approach is a most suitable one for hard Real Time Systems (RTS), this comes at a cost of the uncontrolled and larger resource wastages. All the above approaches have their own pros and cons and there is no clear winner in efficiently resolving the problem of priority inversion. These approaches are discussed in detail in subsequent part of this chapter.

Rest of the book chapter is organized as follows. The differences between real time systems and conventional database systems are discussed. Moving forward, the requirements demanded by the environment concerning real time database systems are also formulated. The types of transactions in real time database systems and their unique nature is examined. Later, the importance of data access scheduling algorithms and their influence on the system performance is pointed out. Then after, various concurrency control protocols and commit protocols are examined reflecting research efforts in this field.

BACKGROUND & RELATED WORKS

A research in the direction of real time systems (RTS) is actively going on since last more than three decades. The environments required to run the real time applications are becoming more and more complex with continuously changing user requirements. Today, not only the correctness and timeliness but the characteristics like volume of the data also need to be considered to meet user expectations.

In the past, priority inversion problem and its solutions are discussed in detail in so many contexts (Carlow, 1984) (Pandey & Shanker, 2019c). Application of priority inheritance protocols in solving the problem of unbounded priority inversion is widely studied by researchers in the RTS domain. The basic priority inheritance and priority ceiling are two widely studied priority inheritance protocols. Though the Real-Time Specification for Java (RTSJ) supports both the protocols, it is initially assumed that only one protocol can be utilized at a time. In today's context, with larger RTSs, this assumption may not stand valid. This has motivated to come up with the mixture of the above two protocols. The Technical Interpretation Committee for the RTSJ has proposed a new version of the priority ceiling emulation protocol that will enable it to work in harmony with basic priority inheritance (Wellings, Burns, Santos, & Brosgol, 2007).

Some key research applications facing the above priority inversion problem are critical space missions, RTS, real time database systems (RTDBS), distributed real time database systems (DRTDBS), mobile distributed real time database systems (MDRTDBS), active distributed real time database systems (ADRTDBS) etc. Before going in detail of these research fields, the first point responsible to prompt the research community to move from conventional database-based applications to real time applications deserves a thorough discussion.

Table 1. Comparison of task and transaction

Terminology Parameters	Task	Transaction
Environment	Real Time Systems	Database Systems & its other various types
Schedulable Resource	CPU	Data
Preemption	Allowed	Not Allowed
Requirement of Consistency	No	Yes
Focus	Task Centric	Data Centric

Real-Time versus Conventional Database Applications

RTS differ from database systems (DBS) in many aspects. Some of the promising aspects are time requirements, data characteristics, consistency criteria, scheduling & resource allocation strategies, basic schedulable unit property, performance metrics, correctness criteria, conflict resolution policies and overload management (Graham, 1992). However, this work focuses only on time constraints.

Although, the performance of any computer system depends on several factors such as the system architecture, speed of its components etc., it is primarily determined by the scheduling policy to access the system resources for a given system configuration (Haritsa, Carey, & Livny, 1993). The basic schedulable unit for RTS is CPU to be allocated for the execution of a task. It is characterized by various parameters such as arrival time, deadline, criticality, worst-case execution time, resource requirements etc. These parameters are assumed to be known a priori. A comparative study of task and transaction has been given below in table 1.

Summing up, although characteristics of both RTS and DBS differ significantly, RTDBS inherit features and advantageous points of RTS namely timing constraints, time-driven scheduling and resource allocation etc. Likewise, any database system, RTDBS must also ensure logical consistency, correctness & integrity constraint, efficient data access & management techniques and guarantee the correct execution of transaction in spite of concurrency and failures (Ramamritham, 1993).

Priority Inversion in Transaction Scheduling

In conventional DBS, no timing constraints are associated with transactions. However, it is prime concern in RTDBS. On the basis of consequences of missing a deadline, three categories of transactions can be distinguished in RTDBS: hard-deadline, soft-deadline and firm deadline transactions. Hard-deadline transactions are those, for which, missing deadlines may be equivalent to a catastrophe. They deliver constant values if computed before their deadlines, but large negative values if their deadlines are missed. They are primarily for life-critical applications. Transactions have soft deadlines if their results are still valuable after missing the deadline (although the value is reduced) and may run up to their completion. The outcomes of firm-deadline transactions have no value if the deadline is missed. Manufacturing and financial applications are usually either soft or firm-deadline RTDBS. The performance goals for firm-deadline RTDBS are to minimize the percentage of transactions that do not meet their deadlines, and for soft-deadline systems to minimize total tardiness, mean tardiness and mean weighted tardiness of transactions. For a given system configuration, data resource scheduling policies have greater influence on the overall system performance. If some transactions have to be aborted and restarted, the service already received from the hardware resources is lost. Hard deadline RTDBS require meeting all timing constraints and may be achieved using real-time task scheduling techniques assuming a priori knowledge concerning transaction parameters. For soft/firm-deadline RTDBS, several concurrency control algorithms have been proposed. Most of them have been developed for firm-deadline RTDBSs. The experiences with firm-deadline RTDBS provide a foundation for more complex soft-deadline systems.

Removing Priority Inversion in the Concurrency Control Protocol

In the RTDBS, to eliminate the priority inversion, in the perspective of the execute-execute conflict, the 2PL with High Priority (2PL-HP) protocol is proposed which decides that the requesting cohort will be either blocked or permitted to lock the data item (s) (Abbott & Molina, 1992), (Haritsa, Carey, & Livny, 1992). The requesting cohort is blocked if a data item requested by it is already held by some other executing cohort with higher priority. However, to ensure the uninterrupted execution of the requesting cohort, the lock-holding cohort may get aborted if its priority is lower than the priority of the lock requesting cohort. Further, in case of multiple read requests followed by multiple write requests on the same data item, a new incoming cohort intending to read can join the group of lock-holding reader cohorts only if its priority is higher than that of all the cohort waiting for the write lock (Haritsa, Carey, & Livny, 1990) (Abid, Mhiri, Salem, Bouazizi, & Gargouri, 2017). The 2PL-HP is free from the ill effects of priority inversion resulting due to execute-execute conflict. However, it may cause wastage of system resources due to unnecessary abort (Haritsa, Carey, & Livny, 1992).

The static 2PL with priority inheritance (S2PL-PI) protocol (Pandey & Shanker, 2017b) is proposed for DRTDBS. It specifically minimizes the resource wastage by avoiding unnecessary abort of transactions through the use of priority inheritance policy in an optimal way and also overcomes the starvation problem associated with lengthy transactions only to some extent. This protocol is developed for parallel DRTDBS framework. Through avoiding the deadlock with the help of controlled locking and reducing the negative effect of starvation with fair resource allocation strategy, the Controlled Avoidance of deadlock and starvation causing Resourceful Conflict resolution between Transactions (CART) protocol has been proposed in (Pandey & Shanker, 2018b) which minimizes the miss percentage of transactions. It is basically achieved by reducing resource wastage. A sequential distributed transaction execution model has been considered for assessment of the performance of the CART protocol and comparison has been made with other available previous protocols.

Removing Priority Inversion in the Commit Protocol

The researches on developing efficient real-time variants of the classical 2PC are still an open question in the study of the DRTDBS (Pandey & Shanker, 2016). Ramesh Gupta et al. first proposed a real-time variant of classical 2PC protocol named OPT (Gupta & Haritsa, 1996) (Gupta, Haritsa, Ramamritham, & Seshadri, 1996); this protocol is specifically proposed to fulfil the consistency and deadline requirements of the DRTDBS by reducing the negative impact of execute-commit conflict and inherent priority inversion problem. The OPT protocol permits a high priority cohort to borrow/access the uncommitted data item(s) held by prepared low priority cohort. Such lending by a prepared cohort creates a dependency among cohorts. The fate of borrower distributed real time transaction (DRTT) depends on the final outcomes of DRTTs from whom it had borrowed the data items — if final outcomes of all the lender

DRTTs are 'commit', then only the borrower DRTT can start its commit processing. Thus, the OPT makes the borrower to be blocked till lenders complete their execution. This optimism is advantageous only when lenders successfully complete their executions. While the policy of using uncommitted data items may result in the chain of dependencies responsible for the cascading aborts, the OPT protocol restricts the length of chain to only one by not allowing the borrowers to simultaneously become lenders. Therefore, it doesn't suffer from a cascading abort problem. It provides a significant performance improvement over 2PC.

Moreover, two variants of the OPT is also suggested: Healthy-OPT and Shadow-OPT (Gupta, Haritsa, & Ramamritham, 1997) (Gupta, Haritsa, & Ramamritham, 1997). In Healthy-OPT, every executing transaction is assigned a health factor (HF) and a transaction can become lender only when its HF value is greater than or equal to some threshold value. Obviously, the performance of the system heavily varies with change in the chosen threshold value. In Shadow-OPT, the cohort originates a shadow (replica of itself) at the instance it borrows some uncommitted data item. Moreover, the original version of the cohort continues its execution as usual even after borrowing uncommitted data item while the shadow cohort is blocked right after being forked off as a separate cohort. In case lenders successfully commit, the shadow cohorts are discarded since optimistic borrowing has done its job well. Otherwise, if any of the lenders (who has a dependency with this cohort) aborts, the shadow cohort is activated, and the executing cohort is aborted. Thus, the Shadow-OPT saves the cohort from restarting and provides a feature so that the cohort can resume the processing from the point the borrowing is done in case of an unsuccessful lending-borrowing event. The detailed simulation results showed that the Healthy-OPT performs reasonably fairer than the Shadow-OPT. Later, the 'Permits Reading of Modified Prepared Data for Timeliness' (PROMPT) protocol is proposed; it is an extension/ integration of the work done in the OPT protocol and its variants (Haritsa, Ramamritham, & Gupta, 2000). The PROMPT provides features like controlled optimistic access to uncommitted data, active abort, silent kill, and healthy lending. Though PROMPT protocol remained the standard for a long time to assess the implementation-performance of other real time commit protocols that came after it, several shortcomings of this protocol are raised by researchers with time. Some key developments are discussed below.

To reduce data inaccessibility and priority inversion duration, the Double Space Commit (2SC) protocol exhibits two properties (Qin & Liu, 2003). The 2SC protocol, unlike PROMPT, has two main features: (i). permits a non-healthy prepared transaction to lend the data, that is earlier locked by it in shared mode to the transactions that lead to commit dependency with it. (ii). in case of the abort of the prepared lender transaction, transactions from its abort dependency set are aborted. Such abort does not affect the execution of transactions that are in the commit dependency set of the prepared lender transaction. The 2SC protocol performs fairer than the PROMPT protocol. The 'Static two-phase locking and high priority based, Write-update type, Ideal for Fast and Timeliness commit protocol' (SWIFT) protocol (Shanker, Misra, & Sarje, 2006) analyzed all type of dependencies that may happen during execute-commit conflicts. The SWIFT divides the execution phase of the cohort into two phases: (i). locking phase and (ii). processing phase. Here, the cohort sends an early message named as WORK-STARTED message just after the completion of the locking phase. This leads to a situation in which the WORKDONE message need not be sent after the completion of the processing phase of executing cohort. The changed scenario leads to an improved system performance since the delay involved in sending the WORKDONE message is eliminated; it has been done through overlapping the send event of WORKDONE message and the processing time involved in executing a cohort. The SWIFT protocol enhanced the system performance as compared to PROMPT and 2SC protocol by reducing transaction miss percentage up to 10%. The Extended SWIFT protocol proposed by Ankit Aakash et al. discussed the database inconsistency problem resulting due to Read-Read access in the DRTDBS. It also uses the Lender-Borrower approach to deal with the priority inversion.

ACTIVE protocol (Shanker, Agarwal, Tiwari, Goel, & Srivastava, 2010) categorizes borrowers as following; (i). Commit dependent borrower and (ii). Abort dependent borrower. To reduce the data inaccessibility, the commit dependent borrowers are further allowed to lend their uncommitted data. Here, a metric named 'borrowing factor' is formulated and computed for each borrower distinctly. This ensures that the lock can be granted to a second step abort dependent borrower fruitfully by a first step commit dependent borrower. In PERDURABLE protocol (Shanker, Vidyareddi, & Shukla, 2012), a lender writer cohort that has already provided access to uncommitted data to an abort dependent borrower cohort can provide access to the same data in shared mode to other borrowers. It further improves the data item availability by allowing all the locks that were not required during the processing phase to be released before the start of the commit phase. As a part of one more advancement in this direction, an Improved Data Lending based Distributed Real-Time Commit (IDRC) protocol (Pandey & Shanker, 2017) has been developed; it lessens the effect of the Executing-Committing conflict on the DRTDBS performance by providing the better data accessibility in comparison with earlier protocols. It does so by allowing the commit-dependent first-step borrower (who has already provided access of uncommitted data item to the second step abort dependent borrower) to lend the same data item in shared mode to numerous other second step borrower cohorts.

Most of the above discussed protocols, extending the PROMPT protocol, specifically reduce data inaccessibility to achieve their common goal. As a successor of them, the proposed Early Data-Lending based Real-Time Commit (EDRC) protocol provides a feature to start the lending process just after the completion of the data processing task during the processing phase obviously after locking phase (Pandey & Shanker, 2019a). As a result of allowing lending to happen even before the voting phase of a cohort, the EDRC reduces the transaction deadline miss percentage.

In (Haritsa, Ramamritham, & Gupta, 2000), the Priority Inheritance Commit (PIC) protocol is also been discussed as an alternative approach to increase data accessibility and reduces the negative effects of priority inversion. It does so by allowing all the cohorts and a coordinator of conflicting low priority transaction to execute at the highest priority (highest priority is a priority value which is highest amongst the priority values of all the high priority cohorts blocked by conflicting prepared low priority cohort). After completion of low priority transaction, its inherited priority value reverts to original priority value, and data item(s) locked by it get released. Thus, the high priority transaction blocked by some low priority transaction will get the required data items somewhat earlier. It has been said that the performance results with PIC protocol are equivalent to that of with 2PC protocol.

As an extended version of the PIC protocol, a 1-Phase PIC (OPPIC) protocol (Pandey & Shanker, 2018a) is proposed. The OPPIC protocol is, in principle, opposite to the PIC protocol in terms of the dissemination of PRIORITY-INHERIT message between participants of the distributed transaction, at least one of whose cohort encountered a priority inversion problem. In this case of occurrence of priority inversion, the conflicting low priority cohort sends the PRIORITY-INHERIT message parallelly to all its other sibling cohorts as well as to coordinator. It is beneficial in dealing with priority inversion as it notably reduces the overall completion time of the firm DRTT that has suffered from execute-commit conflict.

The role of priority assignment heuristics' is also vital in time-constrained databases from the transaction scheduling perspective (Pandey & Shanker, 2019b). Though assignment of priorities to transactions affects the overall system in terms of issues such as real-time constraints, data contention level, cyclic restarts and deadlock. All these issues indirectly result into a larger number of priority inversions. Several studies suggested that contention level directly depends on the selection of priority heuristics. Increased data contention leads to a larger number of data conflicts. Increase in data conflicts mostly result into the increase in number of priority inversions.

CRITICAL DISCUSSION ON FUTURE RESEARCH DIRECTIONS

As discussed in the above sections, further research efforts in the direction of coming up with more efficient solution to the problem of priority inversion as it is severely affecting the system performance even beyond the boundary line of real-time database-based applications. The pin-pointed critical discussion on what need to be done next is provided below.

1. The data conflicts and possible priority inversion because of them are one of the main reasons for degraded system performance. Therefore, existing transaction scheduling algorithms need a fresh look from the perspective of efficiently resolving data conflicts.
2. The existing priority assignment heuristics do not give promising performance results under today's rapidly growing complex database environment. More enhanced priority heuristics need to be developed by considering both the time constraints and the data contention.
3. Today with the natural extension of RTDBS to distributed RTDBS, it has become extensively complex to design separate concurrency control and commit protocols as it has created inter-dependencies between these two protocols. For instance, during concurrent execution of transactions, the executing-committing conflict may occur which requires a coordination between the above two protocols.
4. The research in the direction of mobile distributed real time databases can be a logical extension of our work as there are many applications that we used today are based on mobility of devices (Singh and Shanker, 2018a)(Singh and Shanker, 2018b)(Singh and Shanker, 2019a)(Singh and Shanker, 2019b).

CONCLUSION

The continuous research efforts are being made in multi-disciplinary research areas to solve the problem of priority inversion. The study performed in this book chapter is of limited nature as it only discusses the impact of priority inversion problem on transaction scheduling protocols in detail. Some of the key transaction scheduling schemes discussed here are lock based concurrency control mechanisms and commit protocols with centre of attention on complex real time environments and associated issues particularly priority inversion problem The traditional transaction scheduling protocols such as 2PC and 2PL are not suitable for real-time applications since they do not take time constraint of transaction into consideration. The transaction scheduling protocols are discussed for both the environments — centralized RTDBS & distributed RTDBS. Most of these protocols use either priority inheritance or lender-borrower approach to improve system performance. However, considering the critical nature of the above discussed problem and users' requirement, there is a need to further improve the above two approaches or even to come up with some other innovative alternative to resolve this problem.

REFERENCES

Abbott, R. K., & Molina, H. G. (1992). Scheduling real-time transactions: A performance evaluation. *ACM Transactions on Database Systems*, *17*(03), 513–560. doi:10.1145/132271.132276

Abid, W., Mhiri, M., Salem, M., Bouazizi, E., & Gargouri, F. (2017). A feedback control scheduling architecture for real-time ontology. In *12th International Conference on Intelligent Systems and Knowledge Engineering (ISKE)*. IEEE.

Carlow, G. (1984). Architecture of the space shuttle primary avionics software system. *Communications of the ACM*, *27*(09), 926–936. doi:10.1145/358234.358258

Gupta, R., & Haritsa, J. (1996). Commit Processing in Distributed Real-Time Database Systems. *Proc. of National Conf. on Software for Real-Time Systems*. 10.1109/REAL.1996.563719

Gupta, R., Haritsa, J., & Ramamritham, K. (1997). Revisiting commit processing in distributed database systems. *SIGMOD Record*, *26*(2), 486–497. doi:10.1145/253262.253366

Gupta, R., Haritsa, J., Ramamritham, K., & Seshadri, S. (1996). Commit Processing in Distributed Real-Time Database Systems. *Real-Time Systems Symposium*, 220-229. 10.1109/REAL.1996.563719

Haritsa, J., Carey, M., & Livny, M. (1990). On being optimistic about real-time constraints. *Proceedings of the ninth ACM SIGACT-SIGMOD-SIGART symposium on Principles of database systems*, 331-343. 10.1145/298514.298585

Haritsa, J. R., Carey, M. J., & Livny, M. (1992). Data Access Scheduling in Firm Real-Time Database Systems. *Real-Time Systems*, *04*(03), 203–241. doi:10.1007/BF00365312

Haritsa, J. R., Ramamritham, K., & Gupta, R. (2000). The PROMPT real-time commit protocol. *IEEE Transactions on Parallel and Distributed Systems*, *11*(02), 160–181. doi:10.1109/71.841752

Moylan, P., Betz, R., & Middleton, R. (1993). *The Priority Disinheritance Problem*. Technical Report EE9345, University of Newcastle.

Pandey, S., & Shanker, U. (2016). Transaction Execution in Distributed Real-Time Database Systems. *Proceedings of the International Conference on Innovations in information Embedded and Communication Systems*, 96-100.

Pandey, S., & Shanker, U. (2017a). IDRC: A Distributed Real-Time Commit Protocol. *Procedia Computer Science*, *125*, 290–296. doi:10.1016/j.procs.2017.12.039

Pandey, S., & Shanker, U. (2017b). On Using Priority Inheritance Based Distributed Static Two Phase Locking Protocol. *Proceedings of the International Conference on Data and Information System (ICDIS)*, 179-188.

Pandey, S., & Shanker, U. (2018a). A One Phase Priority Inheritance Commit Protocol. *Proceedings of the 14th International Conference on Distributed Computing and Information Technology (ICDCIT)*. 10.1007/978-3-319-72344-0_24

Pandey, S., & Shanker, U. (2018b). CART: A Real-Time Concurrency Control Protocol. In *22nd International Database Engineering & Applications Symposium (IDEAS 2018)*. ACM.

Pandey, S., & Shanker, U. (2019a). *EDRC: An Early Data Lending based Real-Time Commit Protocol. Encyclopedia of Organizational Knowledge* (1st ed.). Administration, and Technologies.

Pandey, S., & Shanker, U. (2019b). MDTF: A Contention Aware Priority Assignment Policy for Cohorts in DRTDBS. In Encyclopedia of Organizational Knowledge, Administration, and Technologies, 1st Edition. Academic Press.

Pandey, S., & Shanker, U. (2019c). Transaction Scheduling Protocols for Controlling Priority Inversion: A Review. *Journal of Computer Science Review*.

Qin, B., & Liu, Y. (2003). High performance distributed real-time commit protocol. *Journal of Systems and Software*, *68*(02), 145–152. doi:10.1016/S0164-1212(02)00145-0

Rajkumar, R. (1989). *Task synchronization in real-time systems*. Ph. D. Dissertation.

Reeves, G. (1998). What Really Happened on Mars? *Risks Forum, 19*(54).

Sha, L., Rajkumar, R., & Lehoczky, J. P. (1990). Priority Inheritance Protocols: An Approach to Real-Time Synchronization. *IEEE Transactions on Computers*, *39*(9), 1175–1185. doi:10.1109/12.57058

Shanker, U., Agarwal, N., Tiwari, S., Goel, P., & Srivastava, P. (2010). ACTIVE-a real time commit protocol. *Wireless Sensor Network, 2*(3).

Shanker, U., Misra, M., & Sarje, A. K. (2006). SWIFT - A new real time commit protocol. *Distributed and Parallel Databases*, *20*(01), 29–56. doi:10.100710619-006-8594-8

Shanker, U., Vidyareddi, B., & Shukla, A. (2012). PERDURABLE: A real time commit protocol. *Recent Trends in Information Reuse and Integration*, 1-17.

Singh, P. K., & Shanker, U. (2018a). A New Priority Heuristic Suitable in Mobile Distributed Real Time Database System. In *International Conference on Distributed Computing and Internet Technology* (pp. 330-335). Springer. 10.1007/978-3-319-72344-0_29

Singh, P. K., & Shanker, U. (2018b). A Priority Heuristic Policy in Mobile Distributed Real-Time Database System. In *Advances in Data and Information Sciences* (pp. 211–221). Singapore: Springer. doi:10.1007/978-981-10-8360-0_20

Singh, P.K., & Shanker, U. (2019a). Transaction Scheduling Heuristics in Mobile Distributed Real Time Database System. *Recent Advances in Computer Science and Communications*.

Singh, P.K., & Shanker, U. (2019b). Priority Heuristic in MDRTDBS. *International Journal of Sensors, Wireless Communications and Control*.

Wellings, A., Burns, A., Santos, O., & Brosgol, B. (2007). Integrating priority inheritance algorithms in the real-time specification for java. *Proceedings of the 10th IEEE International Symposium on Object and Component-Oriented Real-Time Distributed Computing (ISORC' 07)*, 115-123. 10.1109/ISORC.2007.40

Yodaiken, V. (2004). *Against Priority Inheritance*. Technical report, Finite State Machine Labs (FSMLabs).

Zhang, X., Urban, C., & Wu, C. (2012). Priority inheritance protocol proved correct. *Proceedings of the 3rd Conference on Interactive Theorem Proving (ITP)*, 7406, 217–232. 10.1007/978-3-642-32347-8_15

ADDITIONAL READING

Bernstein, P., & Newcomer, E. (2009). *Principles of transaction processing* (2nd ed.). San Francisco, CA: The Morgan Kaufmann Series in Data Management Systems.

Elmasri, R. (2016). *Fundamentals of database systems. Pearson Education India* (7th ed.). University of Texas at Arlington.

Gray, J. (1981, September). The transaction concept: Virtues and limitations. In VLDB, 81, 144-154.

Gray, J., & Reuter, A. (1992). *Transaction processing: concepts and techniques* (1st ed.). The Morgan Kaufmann Series in Data Management Systems Elsevier.

Gupta, S., & Sadoghi, M. (2019). Blockchain Transaction Processing, Encyclopedia of Big Data Technologies.

Kim, Y. (1995). *Predictability and consistency in real-time transaction processing*. Doctoral dissertation, University of Virginia.

Nakamoto, S. (2008). Bitcoin: A peer-to-peer electronic cash system. https://bitcoin.org/bitcoin.pdf

Ramamritham, K., Son, S. H., & Dipippo, L. C. (2004). Real-time databases and data services. *Real-Time Systems*, 28(2-3), 179–215. doi:10.1023/B:TIME.0000045317.37980.a5

Sadoghi, M., & Blanas, S. (2019). Transaction Processing on Modern Hardware. *Synthesis Lectures on Data Management*, 14(2), 1–138. doi:10.2200/S00896ED1V01Y201901DTM058

Shanker, U. (2008). *Some Performance Issues in Distributed Real Time Database Systems*. PhD Thesis. Indian Institute of Technology Roorkee.

Yu, P. S., Wu, K., Lin, K., & Son, S. H. (1994). On Real-Time Databases: Concurrency Control and Scheduling. *Proceedings of the IEEE*, 82(01), 140–157. doi:10.1109/5.259432

KEY TERMS AND DEFINITIONS

Distributed Real-Time Database System (DRTDBS): The DRTDBS consists of multiple data sites that are connected through an underlying computer network specifically used to run applications based on distributed real-time transactions.

Earliest Deadline First (EDF): As per the EDF heuristic, priority of a task is inversely proportional to its deadline. So, the highest priority is assigned to the task with the earliest deadline.

Firm Distributed Real-Time Transaction (Firm DRTT): The firm DRTT is killed in case it misses its deadline because its outcome has no value after deadline miss.

Hard Distributed Real-Time Transaction (Hard DRTT): The hard DRTT must be finished before its deadline; otherwise, it may lead to potentially catastrophic consequence.

Priority Assignment Heuristic: Act as a base for all other DRTT processing components (i.e., concurrency control and commit processing); therefore, largely affects the DRTDBS performance.

Real-Time Commit Protocols: Ensure that either all the effects of the DRTT persist or none of them irrespective of any such failure.

Soft Distributed Real-Time Transaction (Soft DRTT): The soft DRTT is not killed/aborted in case of its deadline miss because the result has some value (obviously degrading) even after the deadline miss.

Chapter 2
Scheduling of Aperiodic Tasks on Multicore Systems

Shruti Jadon
Motilal Nehru National Institute of Technology, India

Rama Shankar Yadav
Motilal Nehru National Institute of Technology, India

ABSTRACT

For a hard real-time multicore system, the two important issues that are required to be addressed are feasibility of a task set and balancing of load amongst the cores of the multicore systems. Most of the previous work done considers the scheduling of periodic tasks on a multicore system. This chapter deals with scheduling of aperiodic tasks on a multicore system in a hard real-time environment. In this regard, a multicore total bandwidth server (MTBS) is proposed which schedules the aperiodic tasks with already guaranteed periodic tasks amongst the cores of the multicore processor. The proposed MTBS algorithm works by computing a virtual deadline for every aperiodic task that is arriving to the system. Apart from schedulability of aperiodic tasks, the MTBS approach also focuses on reducing the response time of aperiodic tasks. The simulation studies of MTBS were carried out to find the effectiveness of the proposed approach, and it is also compared with the existing strategies.

INTRODUCTION

Real time systems have been widely used in a variety of devices across a wide range of applications such as mobile phones, electronic game devices, motor vehicles, medical equipments, avionic products, etc. In real time systems, there are two types of tasks or events: periodic events and aperiodic events. The periodic events repeat themselves after a particular interval of time; whereas, the aperiodic events never repeat themselves. The main concern of any real time system is to schedule the periodic as well as aperiodic events with no miss of their deadlines. In this regard, several algorithms had been proposed previously for scheduling of periodic tasks or inclusion of aperiodic tasks together with periodic tasks

DOI: 10.4018/978-1-7998-2491-6.ch002

on single core systems. However, very few research works have been proposed to accommodate the aperiodic tasks together with the periodic tasks for the case of multicore systems.

This chapter is an extension of the previous work reported (Jadon et al. 2018) to accommodate the case of aperiodic tasks when the periodic tasks are already allocated on the cores of the multicore system. In the previous reported work, the periodic tasks for multicore systems were considered and they are applicable for the applications which work only on periodic arrival pattern tasks. However, there are applications that have combination of both periodic as well as aperiodic ones. For example, in an aircraft control system, the instances of parameters like vibration levels on wings, altitude, atmospheric pressure and temperature, engine fuel burn rate and thrust etc. are measured periodically after regular intervals of time. These parameters are checked on the basis of signals accomplished by periodic events. However, if the system signals an air pressure drop, then the jobs that are executed to raise such randomly occurred events are aperiodic jobs. The periodic tasks are scheduled in offline approach using different approaches and algorithms, whereas online approach is required to check the feasibility of aperiodic tasks. The scheduling of aperiodic tasks over periodic ones is the main concern of this chapter.

Based on the above concern, this chapter deals with scheduling of aperiodic tasks that may arrive randomly in the system such that they can be feasibly scheduled on the cores of the system without disturbing the feasibility of already guaranteed periodic tasks on the cores. In this chapter, hard real time system is assumed therefore, the aperiodic tasks with hard deadlines are considered as those were considered like in case of periodic tasks. Thus, it is important for the system to accommodate all periodic as well as aperiodic tasks' within their respective deadlines.

The present chapter deals the case of periodic task set where each task has relative deadline not lesser than its period is considered for inclusion of aperiodic tasks. Further, while dealing with the periodic tasks are scheduled using earliest deadline first approach and the aperiodic tasks are scheduled using total bandwidth server (D. Duy et al. 2017, K. Tanaka 2013, S Kato et al. 2008). The rest of the chapter is organized as follows. The next section provides the study related to the basic understanding of periodic tasks in real time systems. Further sections discuss the preliminaries for this chapter and deals with the scheduling of aperiodic tasks with periodic tasks having relative deadlines not lesser than their respective periods, through total bandwidth server followed by an example to illustrate the effectiveness of proposed multicore total bandwidth server. The simulation experiments for this part of work along with its result analysis are also being carried out in this section. Finally, the chapter concludes. The next section discusses about periodic tasks in real time systems.

PERIODIC TASKS IN REAL TIME SYSTEMS

Real Time Embedded Systems (RTES) have become pervasive and indispensable in our daily life that is, from mobile phones to digital recorder, transportation to industry controls and medical instruments to home appliances, as such these systems affect almost every aspects of our day to day routine. Typical applications of real time embedded systems include smart phones, electronic gaming devices, robotics, space navigation and guidance, weapon monitoring and delivery, aviation and aircraft engine control, nuclear power plant control, medical monitoring and equipments, multimedia systems, anti-lock breaking systems etc. (Liu 2000, Burns 1991, Burns 1995, Haritsa et al. 1993, Kuo et al. 2002, Baruah 1998, Hoyme et al. 1992, Philippou et al. 1998, Buttazzo 2006, Agrawal 2008, Kuo et al. 2017, Macchelli et al. 2002). In Real Time Systems (RTS), the correctness of the system depends not only on the logical results obtained but also on the timeliness of results produced by the system (Liu 2000, Ravi 2012). The timeliness of the results produced can be critical and in concern with the safety and usability issues, this timing constraint needs to be guaranteed. A late response, even coming with a logical correct result, can be catastrophic or have a degraded Quality of Service (QoS).

From perspective of deadlines, real time embedded system can be classified as hard or soft (Ramanathan et al. 1995, Chantem et al. 2008). Hard real time systems require a guarantee that all the tasks deadlines are met and even a single miss in deadline can lead to catastrophic consequences in the form of mission failure. Whereas, in soft real time systems few incomplete deadlines can be tolerated with reduced quality and system is accepted. However, missing more number of deadlines may lead to mission failure in soft real time systems. Further, system requirements could be of fixed pattern, termed as periodic in nature (Chaturvedi et al. 2010, Thomadakis 1999) whereas aperiodic nature of requirement incurred in case of dynamic systems (Kato et al. 2008, Lee et al. 2004). The set activities related to fixed pattern is termed as periodic task whereas aperiodic task is used for the case of dynamic arrival pattern. For the case of periodic task, full guarantee can be given which is decided offline whereas only prediction can be made for the aperiodic one. Further, it is noted that aperiodic tasks are more critical in nature and missing of its deadline could be of catastrophic effect.

Periodic Tasks

The periodic tasks tend to be released after a certain interval of time. For example, the status of an aero traffic system is monitored after a defined time period and is updated accordingly. A periodic task T_i can be defined with four parameters: release time (r_i), worst case execution time (e_i), period (p_i) and relative deadline (d_i). If $r_i = 0$ then absolute deadline is equal to relative deadline else absolute deadline is summation of release time and relative deadline (Baruah et al. 2008, Chantem et al. 2008). The time required by a task to complete its execution during run time, actual execution time, may be less than the worst case execution time. However, the execution time can be affected by various factors like looping, branching etc. (Babamir 2012) and to provide offline guarantee the worst case time is considered that takes care of all these factors by providing an upper bound to the execution time. Let us discuss the description of some keywords used in regard of periodic tasks.

- **Release Time (r_i^j)**: It is the time instance at which the release of a task is ready for its execution. For a task T_i, release time of jth instance of task T_i would be $j *$ period of task T_i.
- **Absolute Deadline (D_i^j)**: It is the time instant by which a task release must complete its execution. It is the summation of relative deadline and release time. For the first job of a task, release time is zero and hence, absolute deadline is the same as of relative deadline. Thus, absolute deadline of jth job of task T_i is given by,

$$D_i^j = r_i^j + d_i \tag{1}$$

where, r_i^j is the release time of job T_i^j and d_i is the relative deadline of task T_i.

- **Task's Utilization (U_i):** The utilization of the task is the ratio of task's execution time and task's period. For a task T_i with execution time e_i and period p_i, it is given as below.

$$U_i = {e_i}\Big/{p_i} \tag{2}$$

  Utilization of Task set (U_T): The total utilization of the task set T is the summation of utilization of every task in the task set and is given as below.

$$U_T = \sum_{i=1}^{N} U_i \tag{3}$$

- **Utilization of Core (U_{Ci}):** In case of multicore systems, when the tasks are allocated to cores of the multicore processor then the utilization of a particular core C_i is summation of utilization of all the tasks assigned to that core and is calculated as given below.

$$U_{C_i} = \sum_{T_i \in C_i} U_{T_i} \tag{4}$$

- **Total System Utilization (U_{tot}):** The total utilization of the multicore system is summation of utilization of all the cores, where utilization of each core is calculated using equation (1.4). System utilization is calculated again as given blow.

$$U_{tot} = \sum_{j=1}^{M} U_{Ci} \tag{5}$$

Real Time Scheduling for Periodic Tasks

As discussed previously, the periodic tasks tend to repeat themselves after a certain interval of time. In order to schedule these periodic tasks, the priorities of the tasks are to be assigned. These priorities can be static or dynamic. In this regard, depending on the area of application, priority-based scheduling policies, like Earliest Deadline First (EDF), Rate Monotonic Scheduling (RMS), and Deadline Monotonic Scheduling (DMS) are of special interest and are having a great importance (Andersson et al. 2000). These scheduling policies are discussed as follows.

- **Earliest Deadline First Scheduling (EDF):** EDF is a preemptive dynamic priority scheduling algorithm, where the tasks are assigned priorities during run time (Andersson et al. 2000). Whenever, a new event is released, the EDF check for the priority of absolute deadlines between the events releases and the tasks already executing on the system. The EDF scheduling strategy selects the tasks to execute on the system for which the deadline is closest (Stankovic et al. 1998). In this manner, even if the task is of lower priority but if its deadline is closest, the EDF scheduler assigns a higher priority to this task and proceeds with this task's execution. EDF is an optimal scheduling strategy (Stankovic et al. 1998). This means that a task set feasible by any other scheduling algorithm will also be schedulable by EDF. But if EDF fails to schedule a task set then no other scheduling strategy can schedule this task set.

- **Rate Monotonic Scheduling (RMS):** The rate monotonic scheduling strategy is a static scheduling algorithm that assigns static priorities to the periodic tasks based on their periods or rate of occurrences. The higher the period is, the lower priority will be assigned to the tasks (Stankovic et al. 1998). The RMS scheme is simple and efficient. However, it is difficult for RMS to incorporate aperiodic or sporadic tasks together with periodic tasks being assigned on the system. Also, RMS strategy is an optimal static priority algorithm in the cases where the deadline of the tasks is equal to their periods. If the deadline and period of the tasks differ, RMS is no more an optimal static scheduling strategy.
- **Deadline Monotonic Scheduling (DMS):** As discussed above that for tasks whose deadline and period are different, RMS is no longer an optimal scheduling strategy. For such cases, the DMS strategy turns out to be more efficient than RMS. The DMS scheme is similar to RMS scheme except that DMS assigns priorities to the tasks on the basis of their relative deadlines. Smaller the deadline, highest is the priority being assigned to the tasks (Yao et al. 1995). Also, for the cases of aperiodic tasks, DMS turns out to be more supportive and progressive than RMS.

A number of variants of EDF, RMS and DMS (Jinchao et al. 2016, Hassan et al. 2016, Wang et al. 2011) are also available as proposed by many researchers. Others than these three real time scheduling strategies, there are few more scheduling strategies that can be used to schedule real time periodic tasks like least laxity first, shortest job first etc. However, EDF, RMS and DMS have been used extensively in the area of scheduling with other design parameter of an application like feasibility analysis, minimizing load imbalance etc. (Quan et al. 2010, Abdelzaher et al. 2004).

REAL TIME SCHEDULING FOR MIXED ARRIVAL PATTERN TASKS

The key concern of any real time system is to schedule aperiodic tasks and periodic tasks together. As discussed in the previous section, the feasibility for periodic tasks can be checked priory as all the information regarding such tasks is already known to the system before the occurrence of periodic tasks. However, in any real time systems, the external events may occur at any instance of time on the occurrence of some events or conditions. When such situation arises, the system runs a set of tasks which aims to deal with the generated events successfully and allow the system to work in an undisturbed manner. Since, such events may occur at any random time instants due to which the release time of such tasks or events cannot be known priory. These tasks are called as aperiodic tasks and from the name itself it is very clear that this type of tasks is not periodic in nature. For the case of periodic task, full guarantee can be given which is decided offline whereas only prediction can be made for the aperiodic one.

Periodic tasks scheduling strategies have already been discussed in previous section. But, for the case where aperiodic tasks are considered together with the periodic tasks, the approaches used are as follows.

- **Background Approach:** Background scheduling (Liu 2000) approach was the first scheduling in this regard. In this approach, the aperiodic tasks are allowed to execute only when there are no periodic tasks left for execution. Even though this strategy is easier to implement, however, it is not suggested to use. The reason is that this approach provides no guaranteeing of the aperiodic tasks and also it may lead to infinite long responses of the aperiodic tasks. To rectify this requirement, slack stealing and polling server approaches came into existence.

- **Slack Stealing Approach:** This approach can be easily used to reclaim the unused time of the processors (Azhen et al. 2017, Syed et al. 2018). The slack stealing approach tries to execute the aperiodic tasks ahead of the periodic task, wherever slack is available without maintaining servers. This approach aims to shift the available slack either before or after the execution of periodic tasks such that deadlines of periodic tasks are not missed. The aperiodic tasks are then made to run in these accumulated slack slots. Many variants of slack stealing and slot shifting approaches are also available (Schorr 2015, Vestal 2007, Theis 2015, Syed et al. 2018). The main drawback of these approaches is that they require a significant large amount of memory to keep a track of every time instant status. This may lead to large scheduling overhead on the system.

- **Polled Server Approach:** The polling server (Spuri et al. 1996) serves like a periodic task together with the other periodic task in the system. In polling server, the server is provided with an upper bound of execution time (budget) and a time period after which the server is replenished and repeated again for execution. Whenever the server is ready for execution, the job queue is checked for any aperiodic tasks. If aperiodic task exists, the server's budget is used to execute them else the budget is exhausted at the end of server's period. If suppose the aperiodic task arrives just after exhaust of the budget, it has to wait till its next replenish period. Thus, the poling server may lead to the loss of bandwidth.

- **Bandwidth Preserving Server Approach**: To overcome the limitation of polled servers, bandwidth preserving servers' (Spuri et al. 1996) were proposed. The main aim of this approach is to preserve the budget of the server if the job queue is empty, so that, if an aperiodic task arrives later, the correctness of the schedule is not affected. Many variants of bandwidth preserving servers are available. In these scheduling servers, the consumption rule of polling server is modified in such a way that the budget is preserved till the next replenishment time. The remaining budget is exhausted only at the next replenishment period.

The next section deals with assumptions, system model and symbols used in this chapter.

PRELIMINARIES

This section discusses the assumptions which are considered in this work, system model of the proposed approach and symbols which are used in this part of work and were not discussed in the introductory section.

Figure 1. System model of the proposed approach

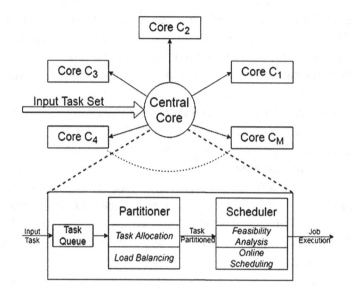

Assumptions

Following considerations are used in this research.

- Assume a multicore system with a set of independent periodic tasks and aperiodic tasks arriving randomly to the system.
- The periodic task set assigned to a core is fixed and it remains feasible after inclusion of aperiodic tasks.

System Model

In this work, centralized multicore system is considered. The task set is available with central core also termed as scheduler, which is responsible for performing feasibility analysis and partition the task set correspondingly to assigned cores and dispatch jobs of periodic tasks released time to time on application core processor where jobs are executed on assigned cores. The application core is also termed as core and it is used as independent core in literature (Langston et al. 2007, Blake et al. 2009). The model used is centralized model is shown in Figure 1.

The main responsibilities of the centralized core are to perform feasibility analysis to allocate the tasks on different cores and maintain queue corresponding to the tasks assigned on each core. Here, each core has an independent queue. The jobs arrivals corresponding to periodic task are sent to the cores assigned and join the queue maintained at assigned application core. The queue maintained at each application core is priority queue where priority is assigned based on task's absolute deadline. The priority assignment policy used is earliest deadline first (EDF).

There are N independent periodic tasks $T_1, T_2, \ldots, T_N$ which are already partitioned among M processing cores of the multicore system. Further, each periodic task has parameters execution time, relative deadline and period. This work considers periodic tasks with relative deadline no lesser than their respective periods. As discussed previously, aperiodic tasks may arrive to the system at any time instant on occurrence of certain conditions and parameters are known only after its arrival. An aperiodic task AP_j is defined as $\left(A_j, E_j, D_j\right)$ where A_j is the arrival time instant at which the aperiodic task AP_j arrives to the system, E_j is the worst case execution time required by the aperiodic task AP_j and D_j is the absolute deadline associated with AP_j. Since, the deadline associated with the aperiodic as well as the periodic tasks are hard in nature which means that all the tasks should complete their execution within their respective deadlines. In the next subsection, the symbols and keywords used in this proposed work are discussed.

Symbols and Keywords Used

The symbols used in this chapter are worst case execution time (e_i), relative deadline (d_i), period (p_i), task utilization (U_i) and system utilization (U_{tot}) with respect to periodic tasks, which were already discussed in introductory section. In addition to these already defined symbols, some new keywords that consider aperiodic task parameters are included. These new symbols are briefly discussed below.

- **Arrival Time (A_i):** It is the time instant at which a task arrives to the system.
- **Finish Time (F_i):** The time instant at which a task finishes its execution is called as the finish time. In order for a task T_i to meet its deadline, finish time should be less than or equal to the task's deadline.
- **Utilization of Server:** The remaining unutilized capacity of a core that is used in execution of aperiodic tasks only.

In the next section, the proposed work for inclusion of aperiodic tasks with periodic tasks which are already allocated on the cores of the multicore system and are having relative deadline no lesser than their respective periods is discussed.

PROPOSED MULTICORE TOTAL BANDWIDTH SERVER FOR SCHEDULING OF APERIODIC TASKS WITH PERIODIC TASKS HAVING $d_i \geq p_i$

In a multicore system having a mixed task set where both periodic as well as aperiodic tasks exists, the proposed multicore total bandwidth server approach deals with the assignment and scheduling of aperiodic tasks on the cores of the multicore system with already guaranteed periodic tasks. The multicore bandwidth server is an extension of total bandwidth server used for single core in a multicore scenario. Further, the criterion for selecting deadlines of aperiodic task after assigning virtual deadline on the basis of proposed approach has been modified followed by detailed description of proposed total bandwidth server on multicore system. The next subsection discusses the total bandwidth server in detail.

Total Bandwidth Server

Total bandwidth server approach is used to assign aperiodic tasks with the periodic tasks such that the response time of aperiodic tasks can be improved. The name total bandwidth server comes from the fact that whenever an aperiodic request arrives to the system, the total bandwidth of the server is immediately assigned to it, whenever possible, for its execution. The total bandwidth server works by computing a deadline of the aperiodic task based on the bandwidth of the server, task's execution time and this new computed deadline is termed as virtual deadline. Now, aperiodic task have two deadlines, one is the assigned deadline at the time of creation of tasks by application and the other one is computed one. If the computed deadline is smaller than the actual deadline of the aperiodic task, then it is considered that the aperiodic task is feasible with the periodic tasks assigned on the core, else, it is infeasible. If the virtual deadline is smaller than original then it is considered as the deadline for scheduling by earliest deadline first scheduling policy with the other periodic tasks assigned on the system.

For a given core C_x, the server is denoted as T_x^{ser} which has a bandwidth of U_x^{ser}. When the kth aperiodic task AP_k arrives to the system at time instant A_k with execution time E_k and absolute deadline D_k then the virtual deadline $VD_{k,x}$ of the aperiodic task AP_k for core C_x is calculated as equation (1.6),

$$VD_{k,x} = \max\left(A_k, VD_{k-1,x}\right) + \frac{E_k}{U_x^{ser}}$$

(6)

Here, $VD_{k-1,x}$ is the virtual deadline for (k-1)th task assigned on core C_x. From equation (1.6), it is clear that virtual deadline of aperidioc task AP_k is calculated by taking the maximum of arrival time of aperiodic task AP_k and the virtual deadline of predecessor arrived aperiodic task AP_{k-1} allocated on core C_x. The ratio of aperiodic task's execution time and bandwidth of the server has assured that the virtual deadline will never demand more than the server utilization during interval $[A_k, VD_{k,x}]$. That is, all aperiodic tasks assigned on a core never demand more time than that provided by server corresponding to the core for the execution of aperiodic tasks.

Once the virtual deadline of the aperiodic task AP_k is calculated against the core and compared with the actual deadline, the aperiodic request is added to the core's queue along with the periodic tasks already present. All the tasks periodic as well as aperiodic tasks will be schedulable if the total utilization of core is less than one. Same fact gets supported from lemma 1.1 and theorem 1.1 given below (Azhen et al. 2017).

Lemma 1.1. In each interval of time $[t_1, t_2]$, if E_{ap} is the total execution time demanded by aperiodic requests arrived at t_1 or later and served with deadlines less than or equal to t_2, then

$$E_{ap} \leq \left(t_2 - t_1\right) U_{ser}$$

Theorem 1.1. Given a set of N periodic tasks with a system utilization U_x and a total bandwidth server with utilization of U_x^{ser}, the whole task set is schedulable if and only if

Figure 2. Periodic tasks schedule

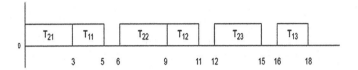

$$U_x + U_x^{ser} \le 1$$

Thus, in order to make the whole task set feasible, the utilization of server can be calculated as per equation (1.7) using theorem 1.1.

$$U_x^{ser} = 1 - U_x \tag{7}$$

The working of total bandwidth server approach for assigning aperiodic tasks can be easily understood with an example. Consider a periodic task set T having two periodic tasks, $T_1 = (2, 8, 8)$ and $T_2 = (3, 6, 6)$ with their execution times, relative deadlines and periods. The two periodic tasks are scheduled as shown in Figure 2. The total utilization is given below.

$$U_x^{ser} = 1 - \left(\frac{2}{8} + \frac{3}{6} \right) = 0.25$$

Suppose, the first aperiodic task $AP_{x,1}$ arrives to the system at time, $A_{x,1} = 2$ having an execution time, $E_{x,1} = 2$ and absolute deadline, $D_{x,1} = 14$, the virtual deadline for this aperiodic task $A_{x,1}$ will be calculated as written below.

$$VD_{x,1} = \max \left(A_{x,1}, VD_{x,0} \right) + \frac{E_{x,1}}{U_x^{ser}}$$

$$VD_{x,1} = \max \left(2, 0 \right) + \frac{2}{0.25} = 10 < D_{x,1} = 14$$

The aperiodic task $A_{x,1}$ is then added in the system queue with the periodic tasks. Since, the arrival time of $A_{x,1}$ is 2, therefore the total bandwidth server algorithm now checks if the system can be provided to task $A_{x,1}$. At time instant $t = 2$, periodic task T_2 is executing and it has a deadline of 6 which is earlier than that of the virtual deadline assigned to aperiodic task $A_{x,1}$. Therefore, the periodic task T_2 will continue with its execution while the aperiodic tasks will wait in the system queue. Similarly, a second aperiodic request $AP_{x,2}$ enters the system with parameters, $A_{x,2} = 8$, $E_{x,1} = 1$ and $D_{x,2} = 16$. The virtual deadline of $AP_{x,2}$ is as follow.

Figure 3. Combined schedule of periodic and aperiodic tasks

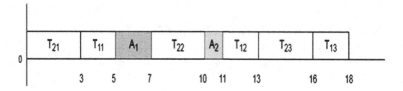

$$VD_{x,2} = \max\left(A_{x,2}, VD_{x,1}\right) + \frac{E_{x,2}}{U_x^{ser}}$$

$$VD_{x,2} = \max\left(8,10\right) + \frac{1}{0.25} = 14 < D_{x,2} = 16$$

At time instant $t = 8$, periodic task T_1 has to start its execution. But the deadline of aperiodic task $AP_{x,2}$ is less than the deadline periodic task T_1, i.e., $14 < 16$. Therefore, the aperiodic task $AP_{x,2}$ will start its execution and the periodic task will wait in the system queue. The final schedule is depicted in Figure 3.

Thus, in total bandwidth server the aperiodic requests are queued into the system queue and are treated by earliest deadline first scheduling policy as any other periodic instance of a task. In the next subsection, the proposed total bandwidth server which is used to schedule the aperiodic in a multicore system is discussed.

PROPOSED TOTAL BANDWIDTH SERVER IN MULTICORE SYSTEMS

The multicore total bandwidth server is an approach for scheduling aperiodic tasks in a multicore system where M processing cores are available in the system. In the proposed work, the periodic tasks are already allocated to the cores and assignment of aperiodic tasks to a core whose arrival pattern is not known is planned, amongst different cores of the system. In this approach, each core is using a server of its own, comprising of a total of M servers. The bandwidth allotted to each core's server is the respective unused utilization of every core. Whenever an aperiodic task arrives to the multicore system, it is assigned to the core for which the aperiodic task has minimum response time and all tasks assigned on that core are guaranteed.

In the proposed work, the aperiodic tasks with hard deadlines are considered. Here, also the virtual deadline for aperiodic task is being calculated against M servers. Out of these computed virtual deadline, which are calculated as per the available bandwidths of the servers, the proposed approach selects one server for allocation of aperiodic task for which the computed virtual deadlines is least. The aperiodic task corresponding to the least virtual deadline have least response time than compared to other virtual deadlines of the aperiodic task corresponding to its assignment on other servers. In case no virtual deadline is less than or equal to the actual deadline of the task, it is considered infeasible. This process is repeated for each aperiodic task one by one based on the shortest arrival time.

Consider a task set T of independent periodic tasks $T = \{T_1, T_2, \ldots, T_N\}$ where each periodic task is already allocated on M processing cores of the system making M feasible partitions of the periodic tasks. Each core in the multicore system works as a server for execution of aperiodic tasks and each server is treated as a total bandwidth server. Therefore, for M cores, there are M servers, $U_1^{ser}, U_2^{ser}, \ldots, U_M^{ser}$. The bandwidth assigned to i^{th} server C_i, with their respective server utilization, U_i^{ser}, is calculated as equation (1.8).

$$U_i^{ser} = 1 - U_{C_i} \qquad (8)$$

where U_{C_i} is the utilization of server C_i. For an aperodic task AP_j, the virtual deadlines calculated for M servers will be $VD_{j,1}, VD_{j,2}, \ldots, VD_{j,M}$. The proposed approach now compares the computed virtual deadlines $VD_{j,1}, VD_{j,2}, \ldots, VD_{j,M}$ calculated for aperiodic task AP_j against M cores with the actual deadline of aperiodic task AP_j, which is D_j and selects only those servers as candidate servers for allocation of aperiodic task on servers whose virtual deadlines are smaller than the D_j. The server corresponding to least virtual deadline is selected for assignment of the aperiodic task. In case two or more virtual deadlines of an aperiodic task is same as is of least, the server which has least total utilization, due to periodic tasks assigned on that server, is selected as candidate server. Let V be the set of virtual deadlines of aperiodic task AP_j corresponding to candidate servers. That is, for an aperiodic task AP_j, $V = \{VD_{j,1}, VD_{j,2}, VD_{j,3}, VD_{j,x}, VD_{j,h}\}$. The selected server corresponding to virtual deadline of task AP_j is $VD_{j,x}$ such that,

$$VD_{j,x} = \min\left(VD_{j,1}, VD_{j,2}, VD_{j,3}, VD_{j,x}, VD_{j,h}\right) \qquad (9)$$

This means that $VD_{j,x}$ is the minimum of all virtual deadlines selected for task AP_j which are not more than the actual deadline of aperiodic task and the aperiodic task is allocated on that server. Henceforth, the jth aperiodic task, AP_j, assigned on server C_x is denoted by $AP_{j,x}(A_{j,x}, E_{j,x}, VD_{j,x})$, where $A_{j,x}$ is its arrival time and $E_{j,x}$ is its worst-case execution time and $VD_{j,x}$ is the virtual deadline of aperiodic on server C_x. The above steps of proposed approach are framed as algorithm 1, Multicore Total Bandwidth Server (MTBS) where P is the M periodic partitions.

Lines 1 to 5 calculate the virtual deadlines for every aperiodic task against M cores in order to find the available cores where the aperiodic task can be made feasible. Once the feasible cores are chosen, the MTBS algorithm then selects the virtual deadline with minimum value if more than one virtual deadline is present in set V which is mentioned in line 6. Finally, lines 7 and 8 assign the aperiodic task to the selected core combination where aperiodic tasks are executed with periodic tasks already executing on that using earliest deadline first scheduling policy. In the next paragraph, an example for better understanding for functioning of multicore total bandwidth server is illustrated.

Algorithm 1. MTBS (*T,N,M,P*)

1. For each aperiodic task AP_j that arrives to the system
2. Calculate the virtual deadlines against M cores using equation (1.6)
3. For each M virtual deadline
4. Check if $VD_{j,x} \leq D_j$
5. Add to chosen set V
6. Select the minimum deadline from V, (say $VD_{j,p}$)
7. Assign aperiodic task AP_j to core C_p
8. Schedule aperiodic and periodic tasks using earliest deadline first policy

Consider a multicore system with two cores C_1 and C_2. The periodic tasks assigned on core C_1 are: $T_1 = (3,6,6), T_2 = (2,8,8)$ and that on core C_2 are: $T_3 = (1,4,4), T_4 = (5,15,15,)$ with their execution times, relative deadlines and periods. Two aperiodic tasks arrive to the system: $AP_1 = (2,2,11)$ and $AP_2 = (1,7,14)$ with their execution times, arrival times and deadlines. The server for core C_1 is U_1^{ser} and that for core C_2 is U_2^{ser}.

Bandwidths of the two servers are given below.

$$U_1^{ser} = 1 - \left(\frac{3}{6} + \frac{2}{8}\right) = 0.25$$

$$U_2^{ser} = 1 - \left(\frac{1}{4} + \frac{5}{15}\right) = 0.58$$

The periodic jobs are executing as shown in Figure 4. However, at time instant $t = 2$ aperiodic task AP_1 arrives to the system when periodic task T_1 is executing on core C_1 and task T_4 is executing on core C_2.

The virtual deadline of aperiodic task AP_1 against core C_1 is:

$$VD_{1,1} = \max\left(A_1, VD_{0,1}\right) + \frac{E_1}{U_1^{ser}}$$

$$VD_{1,1} = \max\left(2,0\right) + \frac{2}{0.25} = 10$$

Since, the actual deadline of aperiodic task AP_1 is 11 while the virtual deadline for core C_1 is 10, which means that the aperiodic task AP_1 is feasible on core C_1, therefore minimum deadline with value 10 is considered as the deadline of AP_1. Now, the virtual deadline of aperiodic task AP_1 against core C_2 is calculated. The virtual deadline of aperiodic task AP_1 against core C_2 is given below.

$$VD_{1,2} = \max\left(A_1, VD_{0,2}\right) + \frac{E_1}{U_2^{ser}}$$

$$VD_{1,2} = \max\left(2,0\right) + \frac{2}{0.58} = 6$$

Again, the actual deadline of aperiodic task AP_1 is 11 but the virtual deadline for core C_1 is 6, which makes AP_1 feasible on core C_2 also, therefore, consider minimum value 6. The virtual deadline of aperiodic task AP_1 against core C_1 and C_2 is 10 and 6 respectively, therefore, $V = \{10,6\}$. Since the virtual deadline against core C_2 is smaller therefore, the proposed approach chooses core C_2 for assignment of aperiodic task AP_1. Now, the virtual deadline of aperiodic task AP_2 against core C_1 and C_2 is calculated.

The virtual deadline of aperiodic task AP_2 against core C_1 is given below.

$$VD_{2,1} = \max\left(A_2, VD_{0,1}\right) + \frac{E_2}{U_2^{ser}}$$

$$VD_{2,1} = \max\left(7,0\right) + \frac{1}{0.25} = 11$$

The actual deadline of aperiodic task AP_2 is 14 but the virtual deadline for core C_1 is 11, therefore, consider minimum value as 11. Now, the virtual deadline of aperiodic task AP_2 against core C_2 is calculated.

The virtual deadline of aperiodic task AP_2 against core C_2 is given below.

$$VD_{2,2} = \max\left(A_2, VD_{1,2}\right) + \frac{E_2}{U_2^{ser}}$$

$$VD_{2,2} = \max\left(7,6\right) + \frac{1}{0.58} = 9$$

Figure 4. Periodic schedules on cores C_1 and C_2

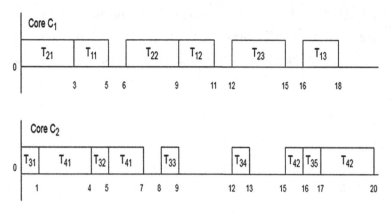

Figure 5. Final schedules on cores C_1 and C_2 with periodic and aperiodic tasks

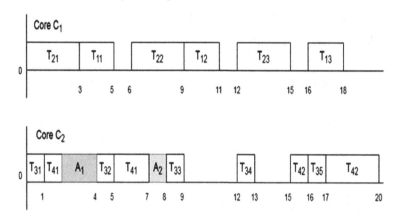

Similarly, the actual deadline of aperiodic task AP_2 is 14 but the virtual deadline for core C_2 is 9, therefore consider minimum value as 9. The virtual deadline of aperiodic task AP_2 against cores C_1 and C_2 is 11 and 9 respectively, therefore, $V = \{11,9\}$. Since the virtual deadline against core C_2 is smaller therefore, the proposed approach chooses core C_2 for assignment of aperiodic task AP_2. The final schedule after assignment of aperiodic tasks is shown in Figure 5. In Figure 5, at time instant $t = 2$, periodic task T_{41} is executing and aperiodic task AP_1 arrives with a virtual deadline of 6 which is smaller than that of periodic task.

Therefore, aperiodic task AP_1 will preempt the execution of task T_{41} and finishes its execution at $t = 4$. At $t = 4$, higher priority periodic task T_{32} will execute and completes its execution at $t = 5$. At $t = 5$, periodic task T_{41} resumes its execution as it has remaining execution time of 3 units. But at $t = 7$, aperiodic task AP_2 arrives with deadline of 9 which is smaller than the deadline of periodic task T_{41}, which is 15. Therefore, T_{41} is preempted by an aperiodic task AP_2. In the next section, the effec-

Table 1. Simulation parameters

Parameters	Description
Periodic task's utilization	In range of [0.1, 1.0]
Periodic load	50% and 70% of system load
Aperiodic load	15%, 30%, 45%, 60% of unused periodic load
Guarantee ratio (GR)	Ratio of the number of aperiodic jobs which are finished before their deadlines to the total number of aperiodic jobs.
Acceptance ratio (AR)	Ratio between the task sets that are scheduled by the total number of task sets, including both periodic and aperiodic task sets, considered during the experiments.

Figure 6. Average guarantee ratio when periodic load = 50%

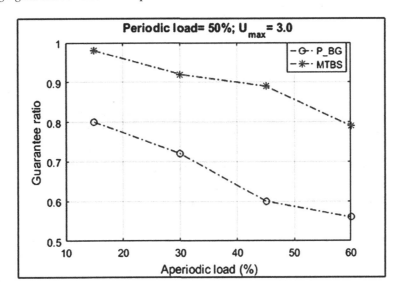

tiveness of multicore total bandwidth approach is discussed in concern with the number of periodic and aperiodic tasks that are accepted by the system which means the deadlines of the tasks are met.

SIMULATION RESULTS

This section discusses the effectiveness of proposed total bandwidth server approach in multicore scenario (MTBS) under simulation setup. To evaluate the performance of proposed MTBS algorithm, it has been compared to Preemptive Background scheduling approach (P_BG) (Syed et al. 2018). The periodic task sets used for simulating the results are generated randomly on the basis of execution, deadline and period range. The execution time of tasks ranges from 1 to 50 whereas the deadline and period of the tasks ranges from 1 to 100. Similar parameters along with values were also taken by researcher (Syed et al. 2018). The simulation parameters are discussed in table 1.

Figure 7. Average guarantee ratio when periodic load = 70%

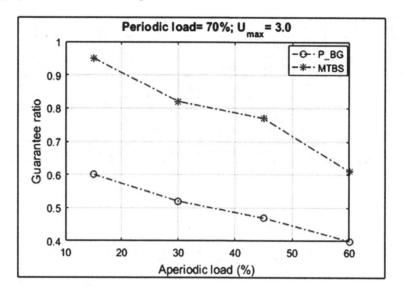

Simulation results are obtained as average of result obtained in running the simulation for 500 task sets generated randomly. From table 1, it can be noted that the utilization of periodic task may vary from 0.1 to 1.0. Two periodic loads are simulated, by setting the periodic load as 50% and 70% of the total system load. The aperiodic load for these simulations is varied across 15%, 30%, 45% and 60% of the unused utilization of periodic tasks. The simulations studies are carried out to measure the effect of system load on guarantee ratio of aperiodic tasks, response time of aperiodic tasks and performance of the proposed approach MTBS. These studies are discussed under following points.

Effect of System Load on Average Guarantee Ratio of Aperiodic Tasks

The Figures 6 and 7 show the average guarantee ratios of the aperiodic tasks for a variation of 15%, 30%, 45% and 60% against periodic load of 50% and 70%. It can be seen from figures that the average guarantee ratio of the proposed total bandwidth server approach in multicore scenario (MTBS) is more as compared to the background processing. When the aperiodic load is 15%, in concern with guarantee ratio of the system, the MTBS approach gives improvement of 23% and 59% over preemptive background approach, when periodic load is 50% and 70% respectively. However, when the aperiodic load is increased to 60%, the MTBS approach provides 40% and 53% better guarantee ratios over preemptive background approach, when periodic load is 50% and 70% respectively.

Effect of System Load on Performance for Periodic Load Of 70% and Aperiodic Load of 60%

The performance of MTBS can be measured in terms of acceptance ratio as shown in Figures 8 and 9. It can be seen from figures that the acceptance ratio is high when system load is less which means that the task sets having periodic as well as aperiodic one are more feasible whereas when the system load is increased, the chance of accepting every task set reduces. When the system has three cores, periodic

Figure 8. Performance of MTBS for M = 3

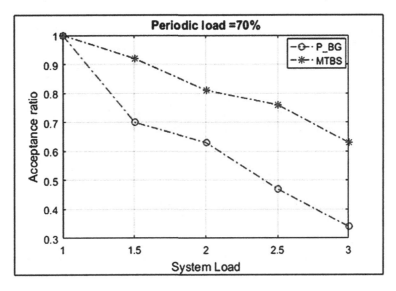

Figure 9. Performance of MTBS for M = 8

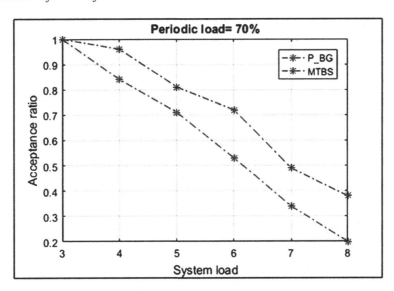

load is 70% of the system load and aperiodic load is 60% of the unused periodic load, MTBS approach provides 85% better performance than preemptive background approach as shown in Figure 8.

Figure 9 shows the effect on acceptance ratio when the number of cores is increased to eight and system load is varied from 3 to 8 with a step size of 1. It is very much clear from Figure 9 that when the system load is 3 then both the approaches has acceptance ratio of one which means that system is accepting all the tasks and all the tasks are feasible. But as the system load increases, this acceptance ratio decreases. However, it can be observed that the proposed MTBS approach has a greater acceptance ratio as compared to P_BG approach. This means that on increasing the system load, MTBS approach has more number of feasible task sets as compared to that of P_BG approach.

CONCLUSION

The real time applications include mission critical applications, medical equipments, multimedia applications etc. Depending on the system requirements, these applications may have two types of tasks, tasks that arrive after every certain interval of time periodically and tasks that may arrive at any random time to the system. For the case of periodic tasks, full guarantee can be provided offline whereas, in case of randomly arriving aperiodic tasks, only predictions can be made. These tasks are generated as a result of some condition incurred within the system and raise an unpredicted system requirement. The proposed work is an extension of previous reported work for inclusion of aperiodic tasks with already guaranteed periodic tasks amongst the cores of multicore systems. For this, total bandwidth server had been used in multicore scenario. Here, with respect of every core in the multicore system, a server was maintained to assign the aperiodic tasks amongst the core of the system. The proposed multicore total bandwidth server (MTBS) algorithm computed a virtual deadline for every aperiodic task that arrived to the system. This virtual deadline of an aperiodic task on a core was calculated on the basis of arrival time of aperiodic task, virtual deadline of previously assigned aperiodic task, execution time of aperiodic task and the bandwidth of the server of the that core. The aperiodic task was then assigned to that core where response time of the aperiodic task was minimum and deadline of all the periodic as well as aperiodic tasks were met. The effectiveness of the proposed MTBS algorithm was measured on the basis of parameters: guarantee ratio and acceptance ratio and was compared with preemptive background approach (P_BG). It can be concluded from results that for an aperiodic load of 60% of unused periodic load, the MTBS approach has provided 40% and 53% better results than P_BG approach against a periodic load of 50% and 70% respectively.

REFERENCES

Abdelzaher, T. F., Sharma, V., & Lu, C. (2004). A utilization bound for aperiodic tasks and priority driven scheduling. *IEEE Transactions on Computers*, *53*(3), 334–350. doi:10.1109/TC.2004.1261839

Agrawal, S. (2008). *An efficient scheduling algorithm for reliable energy aware real time system with arbitrary deadline* (Ph.D. Thesis). Motilal Nehru National Institute of Technology, Allahabad, India.

Andersson, B., & Jonsson, J. (2000). *Fixed-priority preemptive multiprocessor scheduling: To partition or not to partition*. Real-Time Systems and Applications.

Azhen, P., Ruifeng, G., Haotian, W., Changyi, D., & Liaomo, Z. (2017). Adaptive real-time scheduling for mixed task sets based on total bandwidth server. *IEEE International Conference on Intelligent Computation Technology and Automation*, 11-15. 10.1109/ICICTA.2017.10

Babamir, S. M. (2012). *Real-Time Systems, Architecture, Scheduling, and Application*. In-Tech. doi:10.5772/2344

Baruah, S., & Fisher, N. (2008). Global fixed-priority scheduling of arbitrary-deadline sporadic task systems. *International Conference on Distributed Computing and Networking*, 215-226. 10.1007/978-3-540-77444-0_20

Baruah, S. K. (1998). A general model for recurring real time tasks. *IEEE Real Time Systems Symposium*, 114-122. 10.1109/REAL.1998.739736

Blake, G., Dreslinski, R. G., & Mudge, T. (2009). A survey of multicore processors. *IEEE Signal Processing Magazine*, *26*(6), 26–37. doi:10.1109/MSP.2009.934110

Burns, A. (1991). Scheduling hard real time systems: A review. *Software Engineering Journal*, *6*(3), 116–128. doi:10.1049ej.1991.0015

Burns, A., Tindell, K., & Wellings, A. (1995). Effective analysis for engineering real-time fixed priority schedulers. *IEEE Transactions on Software Engineering*, *21*(5), 475–480. doi:10.1109/32.387477

Buttazzo, G. (2006). Special Issue on Major International Initiatives on Real-Time and Embedded Systems. *ACM SIGBED Review*, *3*, 1–10. doi:10.1145/1164050.1164052

Chantem, T., Dick, R. P., & Hu, X. S. (2008). *Temperature-aware scheduling and assignment for hard real-time applications on MPSOCS*. Design, Automation and Test in Europe.

Chantem, T., Wang, X., Lemmon, M. D., & Hu, X. S. (2008). Period and deadline selection for schedulability. *Euromicro Conference on Real-Time Systems*, 168-177.

Chaturvedi, V., Huang, H., & Quan, G. (2010). Leakage aware scheduling on maximal temperature minimization for periodic hard real-time systems. *International Conference on Electronic Spectroscopy and Structure*, 1802-1809.

Driscoll, K., & Hoyme, K. (1992). The airplane information management system: An integrated real time flight-deck control systems. *Real Time Systems Symposium*, 267-270. 10.1109/REAL.1992.242654

Duy, D., & Tanaka, K. (2017). An effective approach for improving responsiveness of Total Bandwidth server. *International Conference of Information and Communication Technology for Embedded Systems*, 1-6. 10.1109/ICTEmSys.2017.7958777

Golnaraghi, F., & Kuo, B. C. (2017). *Automatic Control Systems*. New York: Mc Grew Hill Education.

Haritsa, J. R., Canrey, M. J., & Livny, M. (1993). Value-based scheduling in real-time database systems. *The VLDB Journal*, *2*(2), 1993. doi:10.1007/BF01232184

Hassan, H. A., Salem, S. A., Mostafa, A. M., & Saad, E. (2016). Harmonic segment-based semi-partitioning scheduling on multi-core real-time systems. *ACM Transactions on Embedded Computing Systems*, *15*(73).

Jadon, S., & Yadav, R. S. (2018). Load balancing in multicore systems using heuristics based approach. *International Journal of Intelligent Systems and Applications*, *12*(12), 56–68. doi:10.5815/ijisa.2018.12.06

Jinchao Chen, F. X., Du, C., & Lin, B. (2016). *Allocation and scheduling of strictly periodic tasks in multi-core real-time systems*. Embedded and Real-Time Computing Systems and Applications.

Kanaka, H.-H., Lee, I., Choi, J.-Y., Sokolsky, O., & Philippou, A. (1998). Symbolic schedulability analysis of real-time systems. *IEEE Real Time Systems Symposium*, 409-418.

Kato, S., & Yamasaki, N. (2008). *Scheduling aperiodic tasks using total bandwidth server on multiprocessors*. IEEE Embedded and Ubiquitous Computing. doi:10.1109/EUC.2008.28

Kato, S., & Yamasaki, N. (2008). Portioned Static-Priority Scheduling on Multiprocessors. *IEEE International Symposium on Parallel and Distributed Processing*, 1-12.

Kuo, T.-W., Yang, W.-R., & Lin, K.-J. (2002). A class of rate-based real-time scheduling algorithms. *IEEE Transactions on Computers*, *51*(6), 708–720. doi:10.1109/TC.2002.1009154

Langston, J. W., & He, X. (2007). *Multi-core processors and caching: A survey*. Citeseerx.

Lee, C.-H., & Shin, K. (2004). On-line dynamic voltage scaling for hard real-time systems using the EDF algorithm. *Real Time Systems Symposium*, 319-335.

Liu, J. (2000). *Real-Time Systems*. Prentice Hall.

Macchelli & Melchiorri. (2002). A real-time control system for industrial robots and control applications based on real-time linux. *IFAC, 35*, 55-60.

Quan, G., & Chaturvedi, V. (2010). Feasibility analysis for temperature-constraint hard real-time periodic tasks. *IEEE Transactions on Industrial Informatics*, *6*(3), 329–339. doi:10.1109/TII.2010.2052057

Ramanathan, P., & Hamdaoui, M. (1995). A dynamic priority assignment technique for streams with (m, k)-firm deadlines. *IEEE Transactions on Computers*, *44*(12), 1443–1451. doi:10.1109/12.477249

Ravi. (2012). *Embedded system and its real time applications*. Electronic Hub Tutorial. Retrieved from https://www.electronicshub.org/embedded-system-real-time-applications/

Schorr, S. (2015). *Adaptive real-time scheduling and resource management on multicore architectures* (Ph.D. Thesis). Technische Universität Kaiserslautern.

Spuri, M., & Buttazzo, G. (1996). Scheduling aperiodic tasks in dynamic priority systems. *Real-Time Systems*, *10*(2), 179–210. doi:10.1007/BF00360340

Stankovic, J. A., Spuri, M., Ramamritham, K., & Buttazzo, G. (1998). *Deadline scheduling for Real-Time* (Vol. 460). Systems, The Springer International Series in Engineering and Computer Science. doi:10.1007/978-1-4615-5535-3

Syed, A., Pérez, D. G., & Fohler, G. (2018). Job-Shifting: An algorithm for online admission of non-preemptive aperiodic tasks in safety critical systems. *Journal of Systems Architecture, 85*, 14–27. doi:10.1016/j.sysarc.2018.01.005

Syed, A., Pérez, D. G., & Fohler, G. (2018). Job-Shifting: An algorithm for online admission of non-preemptive aperiodic tasks in safety critical systems. *Journal of Systems Architecture, 85*, 14–27. doi:10.1016/j.sysarc.2018.01.005

Tanaka, K. (Ed.). (2013). Adaptive total bandwidth server: Using Predictive execution time. In Embedded Systems: Design, Analysis and Verification. Berlin: Springer.

Theis, J. (2015). *Certification-cognizant mixed-criticality scheduling in time-triggered systems.* Ph.D. Thesis.

Thomadakis, M. E., & Liu, J.-C. (1999). On the efficient scheduling of non-periodic tasks in hard real-time *systems. IEEE Real Time Systems Symposium*, 148-151. 10.1109/REAL.1999.818836

Vestal, S. (2007). *Preemptive scheduling of multi-criticality systems with varying degrees of execution time assurance.* Real Time Systems Symposium. doi:10.1109/RTSS.2007.47

Wang, J., Han, S., Lam, K., & Mok, A. K. (2011). On least idle slot first co-scheduling of update and control tasks in real-time sensing and control systems. *IEEE International Conference on Parallel and Distributed Systems*, 684-691. 10.1109/ICPADS.2011.86

Yao, F., Demers, A., & Shenker, S. (1995). A scheduling model for reduced CPU energy. *IEEE Symposium on Foundations of Computer Science*, 374-382. 10.1109/SFCS.1995.492493

Chapter 3
Localization of Data Sets in Distributed Database Systems Using Slope–Based Vertical Fragmentation

Ashish Ranjan Mishra

Rajkiya Engineering College, Sonbhadra, India

Neelendra Badal

Kamla Nehru Institute of Technology, India

ABSTRACT

This chapter explains an algorithm that can perform vertical partitioning of database tables dynamically on distributed database systems. After vertical partitioning, a new algorithm is developed to allocate that fragments to the proper sites. To accomplish this, three major tasks are performed in this chapter. The first task is to develop a partitioning algorithm, which can partition the relation in such a way that it would perform better than most of the existing algorithms. The second task is to allocate the fragments to the appropriate sites where allocating the fragments will incur low communication cost with respect to other sites. The third task is to monitor the change in frequency of queries at different sites as well as same site. If the change in frequency of queries at different sites as well as the same site exceeds the threshold, the re-partitioning and re-allocation are performed.

INTRODUCTION

Today, the world is witnessing rapid growth in all domains of science and technology, health, agricultural, transportation, manufacturing, commerce etc. All these domains are frequently using the database technology due to the ease of storage of the data. Earlier, when database technology was in its initial stage, the structure of data was very simple and size was very small. So, it is possible only to store the data at the local site. The data can be retrieve and update locally only. Processing of simple data at lo-

DOI: 10.4018/978-1-7998-2491-6.ch003

cal site leads to faster Query Response Time (QRT). QRT of the database is dependent on how fast the data is retrieved from the database repository. As the time passed, the structure of data is evolved to be more complex and size of data has become larger. The user needs the big size of complex data at a higher velocity rate.

The data is often stored in the secondary storage, such as disks. When the database size is smaller, the time spent on reading/writing data from/to disk and operating on the data is usually small. Thus, impact of small sized database on QRT may not be very critical. But, the today database size is getting bigger and bigger. If the database is not organized properly, this will lead to the unacceptable QRT because it takes too much time to search the data in large size databases.

Further the development of distributed system, where group of related people at multiple sites work together to achieve a task, leaded to development of distributed database systems (DDBS). In DDBS, instead of storing the data at single site, data is either fragmented or replicated and stored at various sites. A proper fragmentation and allocation of partitions to proper site can increase the QRT in distributed environment.

There are two partitioning approaches for a relation. First one is horizontal partitioning and second is vertical partitioning. Horizontal partitioning partitions the relation in the smaller relations on the basis of rows. Each smaller relation contains the same number of columns but fewer rows. Horizontal partitioning involves putting different rows into different relations. A horizontal fragment of a relation contains all the rows which satisfy the condition (predicate) applied on relation. Vertical partitioning is a process of dividing the table on the basis of different columns. Vertical partitioning divides a relation into multiple relations that contains fewer columns. In fact, normalization is process of splitting the columns of the table to reduce the redundancy and ease of readability but vertical partitioning is beyond that concept and partitions columns even when they are normalized.

A query does not require the entire attributes of a relation at the same time. Only few attributes of the relation is needed by the queries. So, the vertical partitioning is more effective in improving the QRT rather than horizontal partitioning. Therefore, an attempt has been made here to develop a new slope based vertical partitioning algorithm.

In distributed database, optimal allocation of fragments to the sites also plays a crucial role in improvement of QRT. Queries in distributed database system access the same fragment from many sites. The fragments should be stored in such a way that maximizes the localization of data in the system. The fragments must be allocated to the sites to minimize the amount of the data transfer during the processing of the queries.

The outline of this chapter is organized into as the sections given ahead. Introduction section deals with statement of the problem. It also describes the issues related to vertical partitioning in distributed database. Section 2 describes the previous work related to the vertical partitioning as well as issue and problem of allocation. The chapter describes the previous work in three stages. These are static database vertical partitioning, dynamic database vertical partitioning and dynamic database vertical partitioning. In this section 3, proposed vertical fragmentation model and allocation model have been described. This section 4 describes the performance evaluation of the developed concept. The comparison is made between proposed model and centralized model. At last Section 5describes the conclusions and scopes for future research works.

BACKGROUND

Different scientists and researchers have given different methods for vertical partitioning of the database table and allocation of the partitions in the distributed environment. In this section, some of these previous methods for the vertical partitioning of the database table as well as for the allocation of the partitions to distributed system have been described briefly.

Vertical Partitioning

In this section, previous methods for vertical partitioning have been categorized in two parts; the first one is known as static database vertical partitioning and second is dynamic database vertical partitioning. Further, the dynamic partitioning is divided into two categories. Those are dynamic partitioning on single computer and dynamic partitioning on distributed system.

Static Database Vertical Partitioning

The Bond Energy Algorithm

The first algorithm for clustering was developed in the 1972 with the name of Bond Energy Algorithm (BEA) by McCormick (1972, 20(5)).The purpose of this algorithm is to identify the clusters in the complex database table. This is an attribute affinity based algorithm. A two dimensional array is used to show the relation between row variable and column variable. This task is accomplished by shuffling the rows and columns of the relation in order to push the numerically lager data element together. The block with the dense value in the relation is considered as the cluster. The limitation of this algorithm is that it is hard to implement without human's interpretation. Sometimes blocks may overlap and some elements may not belong to any block. So, the clustering is not efficient as the user point of view.

The Navathe's Vertical Partitioning Algorithm Based on Frequency of Queries

After the BEA, Navathe (1984, 9(4)) has developed Navathe's Vertical Partitioning (NVP). This clustering algorithm considered the frequency of queries first time and reflects the frequency in the attribute affinity matrix on which clustering was performed. This algorithm performs repeatedly the Binary Vertical Partitioning (BVP) on the larger fragments which is taken from the previous BVP to form two fragments. This process does not stop until the partition of the fragment is not possible. A function checks which fragment should be chosen and whether its partitioning is further possible or not. The complexity of this algorithm is $O(2^n)$ time, where n is the number of times the binary partitioning repeated. The complexity can be increased if overlapping is allowing.

The Branch and Bound Based Optimal Binary Vertical Partitioning Algorithm

The optimal binary vertical partitioning algorithm given by Wesley (1993,19(8)) uses the branch and bound to make a binary tree whose nodes represent the query. The left branch of the node represents the attributes that are queried by the query and are put in a reasonable cut (a reasonable cut is a binary cut that partitions the attributes into two sets; in these two sets at least one of them is a contained fragment which is union of a set of attributes that the query accesses). The right branch of a node represents the remaining attributes. A query is not considered as the child of the current node if all attributes of this query are contained in the fragment of the current node. This algorithm reduces time complexity compared to the Navathe's Vertical Partitioning algorithm but it does not consider the impact of query frequency and also its run time still grows exponentially with the number of queries.

The Graph Traversal Vertical Partitioning Algorithm

The Graph Traversal Vertical Partitioning was also proposed by Navathe (1989). This is a graph theory based clustering technique. In this technique, a similarity graph is created from the attributes that are usually queried together. A vertex represents an attribute and an edge represents how frequently the two attributes connected by this edge will appear together in the same query. Then, the algorithm will traverse the graph and divide the graph into several sub graphs; each of which represents a cluster. In this algorithm, the frequent queries and infrequent queries are given the same priority.This may lead to inefficient partitioning results. The reason for this is that the attribute, that are usually accessed together in infrequent queries but are not accessed together in frequent queries, may be put in the same fragment.

The Eltayeb's Optimized Scheme for Vertical Partitioning Algorithm

Eltayeb's Optimized Scheme for Vertical Partitioning algorithm has been given by Abuelyaman (2008,8(1)). It is based on the attribute affinity matrix. This algorithm starts with a vertex V that satisfies the minimum degree of reflexivity and then finds a vertex with the maximum degree of symmetry among V's neighbors. Once, the neighbor is found; both the vertex are grouped together and put in a subset. V's neighbor becomes the new V. The process continues to find neighbors of the most recent V recursively until a cycle is formed or no vertex is left. The next step is to compute the hit ratio of partition. If the partition hit ratio is less than predefined threshold then find the attribute with the minimum hit or miss ratio and move it to a different subset. In the above graph based vertical partitioning algorithm, infrequent queries are treated same as frequent queries.

The Autoclust Vertical Partitioning Algorithm

The increase in the processor's speed and use of sophisticated software make the database cleaver and more powerful than ever before. Researchers realized that database systems can also help developer in the physical design of distributed database. It gives the researcher to work in a new direction for designing the physical database design. Papadomanolakis (2007) gave a new idea of using the query optimizer for automated design of database. The selection of query execution plan among the multiple query execution plans is done using query optimizer. A query optimizer can gather useful statistics information for system views and perform *what if* calls to help the database systems to make a decision on the selection of the best query execution plan among multiple query execution plans without running the query.

The AutoClust algorithm is based on query optimizer to generate the partitions. There are five steps in AutoClust algorithm. In the first step, Attribute Usage Matrix (AUM) is calculated on a query set indicating which attribute is used by which query. In step second, Closed Item Sets (CIS) are identified. An item set is called closed if it has no super set having the same support which is the fraction of the queries in the data set where the item set is appears as subset. CIS can tell us which attributes are frequently used by the same query. Attributes, that are frequently used by the same query, are tried to put in the same cluster (partition as much as possible). In step third, augmented closed item sets (ACIS) are created. An ACIS is the combination of the CIS and the primary key. After this, duplicate ACIS are removed. In step four, an execution tree is generated where each leaf represents a candidate attribute clustering. In step five, the solution are submitted to query optimizer to estimate the query cost and solution with the best estimated cost chosen as the vertical database partitioning solution.

Dynamic Database Vertical Partitioning

All above partitioning algorithm reviewed yet is based on the fixed query set. These types of algorithms consider the fixed query set to be very similar to the query set used in the future. If the future query set changes then the future partitioning solution generated by the algorithms will not be accurate. Inaccurate partitioning results in performance degradation. So, Static Database Vertical Partitioning algorithms are not suitable for today's database systems. This is the reason for the use of Dynamic Database Vertical partitioning.

The DYVEP Vertical Partitioning Algorithm

The DYVEP vertical partitioning algorithm is presented by Amossen (2010). This is a dynamic vertical partitioning algorithm. DYVEP monitors queries and gathers the relevant statistics for the vertical partitioning process. DYVEP analyzes the statistics to determine whether a new partition is needed or not. If yes, it triggers a Vertical Partitioning Technique (VPT) to generate a new partitioning solution. After that it checks whether the new partitioning solution has better result than the one in place or not. This algorithm depends on the VPT used and the set of rules that it develops to decide when to trigger the VPT. This algorithm gives a way how to re-run an existing VPT automatically.

The Autostore Vertical Partitioning Algorithm

AutoStore is a self-tuning data store that has recently published by Jindal (2011). This algorithm is able to collect the queries automatically and partitions the data at checkpoint time interval. When the enough queries have been collected by the algorithm, the algorithm updates old Attribute Affinity Matrix (AAM) and does permutation on AAM matrix to make the matrix to have the best quality. After that, algorithm performs clustering on the new generated matrix using the greedy approach. Once the best partitioning solution is found, the costs of building the new partitions and the estimated benefit by the new partitions will be calculated separately. If the benefit is larger, the re-partitioning action will be triggered; otherwise, re-partitioning will not be triggered.

Database Partitioning on Distributed System

Online Analytical Processing (OLAP) queries are heavy weighted and ad-hoc. Thus, OLAP queries require high storage capacity and processing power. How to improve Query-Response-Time (QRT) is still an open problem. Now a day, distributed systems are widely used to solve such a problem and partitioning of database table on distributed system has attracted the interest of researchers. Various partitioning algorithms have been developed for distributed database designs in distributed systems. Some of these algorithms are database table label algorithms and some of them are database schema level algorithms.

It has been evaluated that distributed databases greatly improve the performance and satisfy the business requirements on distributed systems. Thus, distributed database has widely used and has become a hot research topic to find ways to improve their physical database design. This section reviews the existing database partitioning algorithms for distributed system.

The ElanTras Algorithm

The ElanTras Algorithm on distributed system was introduced by Das (2009). This algorithm is based on database schema level partitioning algorithms. The key idea behind the database schema level partitioning is that for a very large number of database schemas and applications, queries access only a small number of related rows which can be potentially spread across a number of database tables. ElanTras Algorithm takes the root database table of the tree structure database schema as primary partitioning database table. The other nodes of the tree are as secondary partitioning table. The primary partitioning table is partitioned independently. Then, all partitions are spread across several transaction managers which own one or more partitions and provide transactional guarantee on them. This algorithm is generally used for static partitioning purpose.

The Finder Algorithm

This algorithm is presented by Garcia (2012)with an aim to find optimal distribution for set of database tables for a given workload. It assumes that the workload is given and future workload will be very similar to the present workload. So, it is called static algorithm. Given a set of database tables T= {T_1, T2....T_T}, this algorithm can find the distribution policy D= {X_1, X2....X_T} where X_I is set of attributes and T_I is distributed based on X_I. The tuple of the table is assigned to different segments according to the hash value of X_I.

Allocation of Partitions

In this section, the previous methods proposed for allocation of partitions of the database table in distributed systems have been described. Various algorithms have been proposed by various scientists and researchers for allocation of partitions in distributed database. Some of these algorithms are described as follows.

Ismail O. Habebeh's Allocation Algorithm:

Ismail O. Habebeh's Allocation Algorithm is designed for allocating the fragments in the DDBs. This algorithm shows a way of grouping the sites to which the fragments would be allocated. This algorithm describes a method which minimizes the transaction communication cost by distributing the database fragments over the DDBs sites, increases the data availability and integrity by allocating the multiple copies of the same database fragments over the sites where ever it is possible, and minimizes the Query Response Time.

Grouping sites into the clustered has several advantages. It increases the system I/O performance and reduces the storage overhead. It reduces the communication cost between the sites during data allocation. It is a fast way to determine the data allocation to a set of sites rather than the each site. Two sites are grouped into a cluster if the communication cost between them is less than Communication Cost Range (CCR).

In this algorithm, initially the fragments are allocated to all the clusters having query or set of queries using that fragments. A decision value (D) of allocating a fragment to a cluster is calculated as logical value for the difference between the cost of not allocating the fragment to a cluster and cost of allocating a fragment to a cluster. If the cost of not allocating a fragment to the cluster is greater than or equal to the cost of allocating a fragment to a cluster then the decision value is true and the fragments are allocated to the cluster. If the cost of not allocating a fragment to the cluster is less than the cost of allocating a fragment to a cluster then the decision value is false and the fragments are removed from the cluster.

Hasan I. Abdalla's Allocation Algorithm

Hasan I. Abdalla's Allocation Algorithm (June 2012, 5(2)) is described. This is a data re-allocation model for distributed database systems. In this method, some information is needed to analyze well in advanced to derive the cost formula. This information includes database information, query information, site information and network information. In database information, the size of each fragment needs to be predefined. Retrieve matrix and update matrix are also needed to be defined in advance. Retrieve matrix and update matrix describe the retrieval and update behavior of all queries. Site information describes the site information and fragment limit to store. Network information defines the communication cost between two sites.

Initial allocation is done with the help of retrieve matrix. If a site retrieves fragments, that fragment must be store to that site. In initial allocation, all the retrieve queries will execute locally. But in the case of update queries, the overhead in communication will increase. In this method, a dynamic data reallocation model for replicated and non-replicated DDBS is proposed according to a given fragment update matrix and distance cost matrix. Then, the migration decision is made by selecting a site that has the highest query update cost for the fragment to be chosen as candidate site to store that fragments.

VERTICAL FRAGMENTATION MODEL

Before partitioning a table vertically, it is required to have some knowledge about the queries that run against distributed database. Since the vertical partitioning places together the attribute that are accessed together very frequently, there is a need of some technique through which this *"togetherness"* can be measured. This measure is the affinity of attributes indicating how closely attributes are related. This is a tedious task for the user or designer of the database to easily specify these values. Here, a method is presented from which affinity can be calculated from the primitive data. For the fragmentation, major data required are the frequency of queries at different sites and the attributes used by those queries represented by Frequency Matrix (FM) and Attribute Usage Matrix (AUM).

Table 1. Attribute Usage Matrix

Query	Attribute			
	A_1	A_2	A_3	A_4
Q_1	1	0	1	0
Q_2	0	1	1	0
Q_3	0	1	0	1
Q_4	1	0	0	1

Attribute Usage Matrix (AUM)

The Attribute Usage Matrix is used to indicate the attributes used by a query. A query Q_K may use one or more attributes $\{A_1, A_2...A_N\}$ of a relation R. The entire row represents usage of attributes by a query. Let $Q = \{Q_1, Q_2...Q_Q\}$ be the set of user queries that will run on set of attributes $\{A_1, A_2...A_N\}$. then for each query Q_I and each attribute A_J, an attribute usage value is associated and denoted as USE (Q_I, A_J) and assigns the value to USE (Q_I, A_J) as following.

$$USE\left(Q_I, A_J\right) = \begin{cases} 1, if\ Attribute\ A_J\ is\ referenced\ by\ query\ Q_I \\ 0, otherwise \end{cases}$$

In the AUM, row refers to query and column refers to attribute. The value in AUM indicates whether the attribute is used by the query or not. If the matrix element contains the value 1, it indicates that the attribute is used by the corresponding query; however, the value 0 indicates that the attribute is not used by the corresponding query.

Frequency Matrix (FM)

Partitioning of attributes in a relation as fragment cannot be done on the basis of attribute usage values because these values do not represent how frequently the attributes are accesses by the queries. A query may be fired more than one time from a site. For this purpose, Frequency Matrix (FM) is included which indicates the number of times a query is fired from a site. Each site $S = \{S_1, S_2... S_M\}$ executes a set of queries $Q = \{Q_1, Q_2...Q_Q\}$. Each Query Q_K can be executed from any site with a certain frequency. The execution Frequency of Q queries at M sites is represented by a matrix of size $Q \times (M+1)$ known as Frequency Matrix, where, $(M+1)^{th}$ column represents the query access.

$$query\ access = \sum_{at\ all\ sites} access\ frequency\ of\ a\ query$$

Table 2. Frequency matrix

Query	Site			
	S_1	S_2	S_3	*Query Access*
Q_1	15	20	10	45
Q_2	4	0	0	4
Q_3	25	25	25	75
Q_4	2	0	0	2

Attribute Affinity Matrix (AAM)

The rows of the AAM represent the attributes and columns of the AAM and attributes as well. The element of Attribute Affinity Matrix denotes the Attribute Affinity Value (aff) between two attribute A_I and A_J. Attribute Affinity Value between two attribute A_I and A_J is calculated as the number of times these two attributes are used together with respect to a set of queries $Q = \{Q1, Q2..., Q_Q\}$. The definition of Attribute Affinity Matrix measures the strength of an imaginary bond between the two attributespredicated on the fact that attributes are used together by queries.

The attribute affinity value between two attributes A_I and A_J of a relation $T[A_1, A_2... A_N]$ with respect to the set of queries $Q = \{Q1, Q2..., Q_Q\}$ is defined as follows.

$$aff\left(A_I, A_J\right) = \sum_{\text{all queries that access } A_I \wedge A_J} query\ access$$

Attribute Affinity Value between attributes A_1 and A_3 can be measured by identifying those Queries that uses both attributes A_1 and A_3. From the above Attribute Usage Matrix, it is found that only Query Q_1 uses both the attributes A_1 and A_3. Now from Frequency Matrix, query access for Q_1 is calculated.

$$aff\left(A_1, A_3\right) = \sum_{Q_1} query\ access = 45$$

The rest of the Attribute Affinity Value can be calculated in the same way as mentioned above. Finally, the Attribute Affinity Matrix is generated as below.

Clustering Algorithm

The primary focus in this section is to make the cluster of attributes of database table on the basis of contribution. In 1975 (Hoffer, & Severance, 1975), it has suggested that the Bond Energy Algorithm (BEA) should be used for this purpose. The Bond Energy Algorithm takes Attribute Affinity Matrix as input, permutes its rows and columns, and generates a Clustered Affinity Matrix (CAM). Before explaining the Bond Energy Algorithm in detail, here some quantities are needed to be defined.

Table 3. Attribute affinity matrix

Attribute	Attribute			
	A_1	A_2	A_3	A_4
A_1	47	0	45	2
A_2	0	79	4	75
A_3	45	4	49	0
A_4	2	75	0	77

Table 4. Bond matrix

Attribute	Attribute			
	A_1	A_2	A_3	A_4
A_1	4238	330	4320	248
A_2	330	11882	512	11700
A_3	4320	512	4442	390
A_4	248	11700	390	11558

Table 5. Clustered affinity matrix with two columns

Attribute	Attribute			
	A_1	A_2		
A_1	47	0		
A_2	0	79		
A_3	45	4		
A_4	2	75		

Bond Matrix

The Bond Matrix is used to show the bond between two attributes. The Bond Matrix shows that how strongly the two attributes are connected to each other. The bond between two attributes can be measured by making the product of corresponding elements of the attributes in AAM. The bond between two attributes A_x and A_y can be expressed mathematically as below.

$$Bond\left(A_X, A_Y\right) = \sum_{J=1}^{n} aff\left(A_J, A_X\right) aff\left(A_J, A_Y\right)$$

The following Matrix shows the bond between the two attributes A_X and A_Y.

Bond Energy Algorithm

Bond Energy Algorithm (BEA) has been used for clustering of attributes based on Attribute Affinity Value in AAM. Bond Energy Algorithm makes the cluster of those attribute which has high Affinity Value and other cluster of those attributes which has low Affinity Value. It can be done by ordering of attributes such that the Global Affinity Measure (GAM) is maximized.

The above conditions show the boundary conditions when the attributes are placed to the leftmost or to the rightmost of the Clustered Affinity Matrix. Clustered Affinity Matrix (CAM) is generated by Bond Energy Algorithm in three steps.

- **Initialization:** In the initialization step, first two columns of the AAM is placed directly to the respective columns in the Clustered Affinity Matrix.
- **Iteration:** After the initialization step, the remaining attributes (n-i) are picked one by one and try to place them in remaining positions (i+1) Clustered Affinity Matrix. The placement is done on the basis of greatest contribution to the Global Affinity Measure. This process is continued until no more columns attribute remains to be placed.
- **Row Ordering:** Once the column ordering is determined, the order of row attributes should also be changed accordingly, so that, their relative positions match the relative positions of the columns attribute.

Now, the above three steps are explained as follows. In the initialization step, first and second columns of the Attribute Affinity Matrix are placed to the first and second columns of the Clustered Affinity Matrix respectively. So Attributes A_1 and A_2 are placed to the first and second columns of the Clustered Affinity Matrix respectively. The column ordering after the placement of the two attribute A_1 and A_2 is as follows.

In the Iteration step, all the remaining attributes are picked one by one and are placed to the position where contribution of the GAM is the greatest. For example, Attribute A_3 is picked and can be placed to the one of the three positions. These positions are to the left of A_1 (leftmost), between A_1 and A_2, to the right of A_2 (rightmost).

The total contribution to the global affinity measure of placing A_3 to the left of A_1

Contribution $(A_0, A_3, A_1) = 2 \times \text{bond} (A_0, A_3) + 2 \times \text{bond} (A_3, A_1) + 2 \times \text{bond} (A_0, A_1)$

$= 0 + 8640 + 0 = 8640$

The total contribution to the global affinity measure of placing A_3 in between A_1 and A_2

Contribution $(A_1, A_3, A_2) = 2 \times \text{bond} (A_1, A_3) + 2 \times \text{bond} (A_3, A_2) + 2 \times \text{bond} (A_1, A_2)$

$= 8640 + 1024 - 660 = 9004$

The total contribution to the global affinity measure of placing A_3 to the right of A_2

Contribution $(A_1, A_3, A_{N+1}) = 2 \times \text{bond} (A_1, A_3) + 2 \times \text{bond} (A_3, A_{N+1}) + 2 \times \text{bond} (A_1, A_{N+1})$

Table 6. Clustered affinity matrix with three columns

Attribute	Attribute			
	A_1	A_3	A_2	
A_1	47	45	0	
A_2	0	4	79	
A_3	45	49	4	
A_4	2	0	75	

Table 7. Clustered affinity matrix with column ordering

Attribute	Attribute			
	A_1	A_3	A_2	A_4
A_1	47	45	0	2
A_2	0	4	79	75
A_3	45	49	4	0
A_4	2	0	75	77

Table 8. Clustered affinity matrix

Attribute	Attribute			
	A_1	A_3	A_2	A_4
A_1	47	45	0	2
A_3	45	49	4	0
A_2	0	4	79	75
A_4	2	0	75	77

$=1024+0+0=1024$

Since the largest contribution is gained by placing the column A_3 to in between A_1 and A_2, Attribute A_3 must be placed to the in between A_1 and A_2. So, the column ordering is given below.

This step is repeated until no more attribute remains to be placed. After completion of this step, the following column ordering is found.

In the third step, row ordering is performed such as the column ordering. Since AAM is a symmetric matrix, so the row ordering is same as the column ordering as performed above. Finally, the Clustered Affinity Matrix generated by using the above three steps of the Bond Energy Algorithm is given below.

Figure 1. Two Clusters of attributes

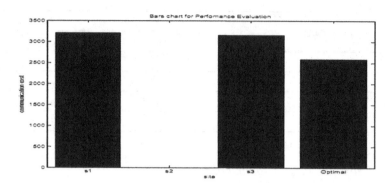

Table 9. first Row of clustered affinity matrix

Attribute	Attribute			
	A_1	A_3	A_2	A_4
A_1	47	45	0	2

Partitioning Algorithm

The objective of partitioning algorithms is to extract set of attributes that are frequently accessed by distinct set of queries. If two attributes A_I and A_J are accessed by query Q_K only and Attributes A_M and A_N are accessed by queries Q_O and Q_P, it is obvious to keep A_M and A_N in one fragment while partitioning. Hence, in this section, it is required to design an algorithmic method that can identify these groups.

In the previous section, if the CAM is observed carefully two sets of attributes are identified. One set of attributes $\{A_1, A_2...A_I\}$ is found at top left corner and denotes as TLC and another set of attributes $\{A_{I+1}, A_{I+2}...A_N\}$ is found at bottom right corner denotes as BRC.

Slope Based Partitioning

In this section, a new vertical partitioning algorithm is presented. This algorithm is named as "Slop Based Partitioning Algorithm". This algorithm takes Clustered Affinity Matrix as input and produces the two partition of the given database table. This algorithm tries to find out the most suitable diagonal point for fragmentation in Clustered Affinity Matrix. The Slop Based Partitioning Algorithm calculates the slop between each neighbour attributes in the Clustered Affinity Matrix. The Slop between the neighbour attribute may be either increasing or decreasing in nature. Now, the Slop Based Partitioning Algorithm searches for the point where the slop diminishes very rapidly. In the proposed algorithm, the point, where the slop diminishes very rapidly, is considered as the splitting point.

Table 10. First fragment of clustered affinity matrix

Attribute	Attribute	
	A_1	A_3
A_1	47	45
A_3	45	49

Table 11. Second fragment of clustered affinity matrix

Attribute	Attribute	
	A_2	A_4
A_2	79	75
A_4	75	77

To calculate the split-point using Slop Based Partitioning Algorithm, first row of the Clustered Affinity Matrix is required, and then the slop between the neighbour attributes is calculated. The point where the slop diminishes very rapidly is considered as split-point. First row of the Clustered Affinity Matrix is taken below.

In the first row of Clustered Affinity Matrix, it is shown that the slop diminishes rapidly between A_3 and A_2. Hence point between A_3 and A_2 is considered as splitting point. Therefore, Clustered Affinity Matrix is divided into two clusters. One cluster contains the attributes $\{A_1, A_3\}$ and the second cluster contains the attributes $\{A_2, A_4\}$.

Each of the attributes in a cluster has largest contribution and they are used together very frequently by the queries in distributed database system. Two clusters of Clustered Affinity Matrix are given below.

Slope Based Partitioning Algorithm(SBPA)

The objective of Slope Based Partitioning Algorithm is to find a set of attributes that are frequently accessed by distinct set of queries. Using the Slope Based Partitioning Algorithm, the user makes the fragments of a relation on the basis ofCAM, which is calculated by AUM and FM. The first row of CAM is taken for fragmenting the clusters from a relation. The point between the neighbor attributes of the CAM is considered as Split-point if slop diminishes between these attributes very rapidly. The pseudo code for the SBPA is given below.

```
Algorithm: SBPA
Input: CAM: Clustered affinity matrix
Output: F: set of two fragments
Begin
{Initialization of the variables}
X [1, 1…..N]; //used to store the value from 1 to N of loop in corresponding
index
```

```
Y [1, 1…..N]; // used to store the value of slop
Smallest=0; // used to store the smallest slop value
Split-point=0; // used to store the point from where to fragment the table
{Determine the Split-point}
For i←1 to n do
If (I = = 1) then
Y [1, i] ←CAM (1, i);
Else
Y [1, i] ←CAM (1, i)-CAM (1, i-1);
End-If
X [1, i] ←i;
End-For
Plot (X, Y);
Smallest←Y [1, 1];
Split-point=1;
For i←2 to n
If (Smallest< Y [1, i)] then
Split-point is recorded as X [1, i]
Smallest←Y [1, i]
End-If
End-For
End-Begin
```

Allocation Model

Like fragmentation, allocation is also considered as an important design issue that has the great impact on database performance. The data localization in database is highly dependent on its design issues i.e. fragmentation and allocation model used. For the efficient working of distributed database system, it is required to allocate the fragment across the sites in such a way that reduces the communication between the sites while processing a query. In this chapter, the main focus is on minimizing the total amount of data transmitted during the query processing over sites.

For an efficient allocation, it is required to find out the number of times the queries retrieve and update the attributes. The minimum distance between the sites is also used as an allocation factor in proposed allocation model. The retrieval and updating of the attributes by queries can be shown using Attribute Read Matrix (ARM) and Attribute Write Matrix (AWM). The minimum distance between the sites can be shown using the Minimal Communication Matrix (MCM).

Allocation Model Description

Allocation problem assumes that the fragment of the database table is known well in advance. The proposed method for fragments allocation assumes that there is a fully connected network containing sites $S = \{S_1, S_2..., S_M\}$. Each site has a storage capacity (SC), fragment limit (FL) and a local database. Let, S contains a set of fragments $F= \{F_1, F_2...F_P\}$. Between the two sites S_I and S_J, there is a link which

Table 12. Fragment size

Fragments	F_1	F_2
Size	12	12

represents the cost of the unit of data transfer between the sites denoted as $CDTM_{IJ}$. The focus of this chapter is to find the optimal allocation of F to S.

According to dowdy and foster, the definition of optimality can be given by two measures.

- **Minimal Cost:** The total cost of the distributed database system is the sum of the cost of querying fragment F_I at site S_J, cost of storing fragment F_I at site S_J, cost of updating fragment F_I at all the site where it is stored and the cost of data communication. Minimizing the any of the cost stated above reduces the total cost.
- **Performance:** The allocation scheme should be designed in such a way that maintains the performance metric. Two well-known metric are as minimize the response time and maximize the system throughput at all the sites.

In the proposed model, minimal cost is chosen for optimality measurement. In this model, optimality problem can be defined as minimization of communication cost while allocating a fragment F_I to site S_J.

Information Requirements

For the allocation of fragments to the appropriate sites, quantitative data about the database, communication network, queries the processing capabilities and storage limitation of each site is known priori. All these information are described in the next subsections.

Database Information

While fragmentation, a large and global database table is fragmented into many partitions. Each of these partitions has a size that must be known well in advance as it plays a key-role in computing the communication cost. In the proposed model, size of each of the cell in database table is considered as one unit.

Size (F_I) = number of cell in F_I where I= 1, 2...p

Number of cell = row (F_I) × col (F_I)

Query Behaviour Information

Any query can either retrieve or update the data in fragmented database table. The access behaviour of queries, whether the query is update query or retrieve query, can be defined by two access matrix Update Matrix (UM) and Retrieve Matrix (RM). The elements RM_{IJ} of Retrieve Matrix gives the frequency

Table 13. Attribute read matrix

Query	Attribute			
	A_1	A_2	A_3	A_4
Q_1	2	0	2	0
Q_2	0	1	1	0
Q_3	0	3	0	1
Q_4	1	0	0	2

Table 14. Attribute write matrix

Query	Attribute			
	A_1	A_2	A_3	A_4
Q_1	3	0	2	0
Q_2	0	2	1	0
Q_3	0	1	0	3
Q_4	2	0	0	2

of retrieve whereas elements UM_{IJ} of Update Matrix gives the frequency of update of fragments F_I by query Q_J.

In this proposed Allocation Model, RM and UM are calculated by ARM and AWM respectively.

$$ARM_{IJ} = \begin{cases} \geq 1, if\ Q_I\ retrieves\ A_J \\ 0, otherwise \end{cases}$$

$$AWM_{IJ} = \begin{cases} \geq 1, if\ Q_I\ updates\ A_J \\ 0, otherwise \end{cases}$$

Site Information

In the proposed method, site information is represented as site constraints. System knows well in advanced the Storage Capacity (SC) and Fragment Limit (FL) constraints that represent the maximum size and the number of fragments at each site. The constraints are presented as below.

Each fragment must be allocated to all the sites in the system in initial allocation phase. A site can store more than its capacity of storage. A site can handle less than or equal to its Fragment Limit. The fragment will be allocated to only one site after the re-allocation phase.

Table 15. Site Constraint Matrix

Site	Site Constraint	
	Storage Capacity	Fragments Limit
S1	26	2
S2	15	1
S3	24	2

Table 16. Cost of data transfer matrix

Sites	Sites		
	S1	S2	S3
S1	0	5	9
S2	5	0	3
S3	9	3	0

Table 17. Minimal communication matrix

Sites	Sites		
	S1	S2	S3
S1	0	5	8
S2	5	0	3
S3	8	3	0

Network Information

In the proposed model, the network is assumed to be fully connected. The link between two sites S_I and S_J has the positive integer value which represents the cost of unit data transfer between them ($CUDT_{IJ}$). To make the model more simplified, CDTM matrix is given as symmetric matrix. The cost of unit amount of data transfer between S_I to S_J is same as cost of unit amount of data transfer between S_J to S_I. Cost of unit amount of data transfer within the same site is considered as zero.

After applying the min function on CDTM, the Minimal Communication Matrix (MCM) is found as below.

Table 18. Retrieve matrix

Query	Fragment	
	F1	*F2*
Q1	4	0
Q2	1	1
Q3	0	4
Q4	1	2

Table 19. Update matrix

Query	Fragment	
	F1	*F2*
Q1	5	0
Q2	2	1
Q3	0	4
Q4	2	2

DESCRIPTION OF COST MODEL

The proposed model is based on the assumption that information about fragment size, Retrieve Matrix, Update Matrix, Capacity and Fragments Limit of the site, Cost of Unit Data Transfer (CUDT) is known well in advance. This model is divided into two phase; initial phase and re-allocation phase.

Initial Phase

Initially, the fragments are replicated to all the sites. This is called the initial allocation phase. In this phase, all the queries at a site get the requested data locally. So, the cost of retrieval is zero. But due to the full replication, this site sends the update to all the other sites. This increases the cost of Update. The Optimal allocation is one which involves the minimization of total cost of update in the entire network without violating the site constraints.

Re-Allocation Phase

In the re-allocation phase; Retrieve Matrix, Update Matrix, Frequency Matrix and Minimal Cost Matrix are used to calculate the cost of allocation. Here, it is assumed that retrieval query has a half weightage in communication cost as compare to update query if the fragment needed by query is not found at the local site.

Table 20. Weightage matrix

Query	Fragment	
	F1	*F2*
Q1	5	0
Q2	0	4
Q3	0	6.5
Q4	4.5	2

Table 21. Cumulative weightage matrix

Site	Fragment	
	F1	*F2*
S1	84	182.5
S2	100	162.5
S3	50	162.5

Step 1- Calculate Retrieve Matrix (RM) and Update Matrix (UM) from Attribute Read Matrix (ARM) and Attribute Write Matrix (AWM) Respectively

RM and UM are used to find the number of times a query update a fragments. In this model, RM and UM are calculated by ARM and AWM. The element of Retrieve Matrix RM_{IJ} is calculated as sum of elements of ARM whose attributes belong to the attributes of corresponding fragment for that element in RM. The element of Update Matrix UM_{IJ} is calculated as sum of elements of AWM whose attributes belong to the attributes of corresponding fragment for that element in UM.

Step 2- Calculate the Weightage Matrix (WM)

WM is used to find the weight of communication cost due to query Q_I on fragment F_J. The element of the WM_{IJ} can be calculated as sum of the half of element of retrieval matrix and update matrix.

Step 3- Calculate the Cumulative Weightage Matrix (CWM) at All the Sites

TWM is used to find the weight of storing the fragment at a site. The element of CWM_{IJ} can be calculated as the product of FM and WM.

$$CWM_{IJ} = \sum_{k=1}^{Qrynum} FM_{KI} \times WM_{KJ}$$

Where

Table 22. Allocation cost matrix

Query	Fragment	
	F1	*F2*
S1	900	2112.5
S2	570	1400
S3	788	1947.5

Table 23. Fragment re-allocation matrix

Query	Fragment	
	F1	*F2*
S1	0	0
S2	1	0
S3	0	1

$1 \leq I \leq$ Sitenum // Sites

$1 \leq J \leq 2$ // Fragments

$1 \leq K \leq$ Qrynum // Queries

Step 4- Calculate the Allocation Cost Matrix (ACM) at All the Sites

ACM is used to find the cost of storing the fragment at a site. The elements of ACM_{IJ} can be calculated as the product of DM and CWM.

$$ACM_{IJ} = \sum_{k=1}^{Sitenum} DM_{KI} \times CWM_{KJ}$$

Where

$1 \leq I \leq$ Sitenum // Sites

$1 \leq J \leq 2$ // Fragments

$1 \leq K \leq$ Sitenum // Sites

Step 5-Re-Allocation of Fragments to the Sites

The above matrix shows the cost of allocation of a fragment to the site. The fragments are re-allocating to the site which results in the lowest update cost while keeping the constraint in the mind. In the above matrix, fragment F_1 is allocated to the site S_2 because it results in the lowest update cost. Fragment F_2 must be allocated to the site S_2 but Fragment limit at S_2 is one. So, fragment F_2 must be allocated to the site which results in the next higher update cost. Since, the next higher update cost occurs at site S_3, the fragment F_2 is allocated to the site S_3.

PERFORMANCE EVALUATION

The performance of the proposed distributed database design method on distributed system is compared with performance of centralized database in distributed system. In the proposed model, performance evaluation is done by the incurred cost of communication at site.

Performance of Centralized Allocation

In the case of centralized allocation in distributed system, the whole database is stored on the single computer. As given constraint matrix in previous section 5.4.3, it is clear that we can store the whole database table either to the Site S_1 or Site S_3. These two cases are checked one by one.

CASE 1: When the database table is stored on site S_1.

Incurred communication cost at site S_1= 900+2112.5= 3012.5

CASE 2: When the database table is stored on site S_3.

Incurred communication cost at site S_3= 788+1947.5= 2735.5

Performance of Proposed Allocation Model

In distributed database, the fragments of the database may be stored on more than one computer. Each fragment is stored to site where the cost of allocation (communication cost) is low. In the proposed partitioning model, two fragments are created. As given constraint matrix in chapter 5 section 5.4.3, it is clear that one fragment is stored at site S_2 and another one is stored at site S_3.
    Incurred communication cost in proposed Model= 570+1947.5=2517.5

Performance Boost

In this section performance boost is calculated. Performance boost can be calculated as percentage of communication cost reduced due to allocation of fragment according to proposed allocation model and centralized Allocation of database.

Figure 2. Bar chart of communication cost at each site

TOP LEFT CORNER	
	BOTTOM RIGHT CORNER

$$PERFORMANCE\ BOOST = \left(\left(ICCA - ICPA\right) \div ICCA\right) \times 100$$

Where

//ICCA= Incurred Communication Cost in Centralized Allocation.

// ICPA= Incurred Communication Cost in Proposed Allocation.

CASE 1: When the centralized database table is stored on site S_1.

Performance Boost= ((3012.5- 2517.5)/3012.5) ×100= 16.43

CASE 2: When the centralized database table is stored on site S_3.

Performance Boost= ((2735.5- 2517.5)/2735.5) ×100= 7.96

The Performance Bar Chart for the Above Calculation is given in Figure 2.

CONCLUSION

A new technique for designing of distributed database has been studied in this work. The designing of distributed database has implemented in two steps. In first step, database table has been vertically fragmented. A new algorithm SBPA has been used to partition the fragments from the database table. In the second step of the distributed database design, fragmented clusters have been stored to the proper sites where incurred cost of communication has been very less. After storing the fragments to the proper sites, the performance evaluation has been done. It has been achieved by comparing the amount of incurred cost of communication at each site which is capable of storing the whole database to the amount of incurred cost of communication in proposed allocation model. While evaluating the performance, it has been found that the incurred cost of communication in proposed allocation model is always less than or equal to the incurred cost of communication at each site which is capable of storing the whole database.

REFERENCES

Abdalla, H. I. (2012, June). A New Data Re-Allocation Model for Distributed Database Systems. *International Journal of Database Theory and Application*, *5*(2).

Abuelyaman, E. S. (2008). An Optimized Scheme for Vertical Partitioning of a Distributed Database. *International Journal of Computer Science and Network Security*, *8*(1).

Amossen, R. (2010). Vertical partitioning of relational OLTP databases using integer programming. *Data Engineering Workshops (ICDEW) of IEEE 5th International Conference on Self Managing Database Systems (SMDB)*. 10.1109/ICDEW.2010.5452739

Chu, W. W., & Ieong, I. (1993, August). A Transaction-Based Approach to Vertical Partitioning for Relational Database Systems. *IEEE Transactions on Software Engineering*, *19*(8), 804–812. doi:10.1109/32.238583

Das, S., Agrawal, D., & Abbadi, A. E. (2009). ElasTraS: an elastic transactional data store in the cloud. *Proceedings of the conference on Hot topics in cloud computing*.

Duan, S., Thummala, V., & Babu, S. (2009, August). Tuning Database Configuration Parameters with iTuned. *Proceeding of Very Lagre Data Bases*, *2*(4), 1246–1257.

Garcia-Alvarado, C., Raghavan, V., Narayanan, S., & Waas, F. M. (2012)Automatic Data Placement in MPP Databases. *Data Engineering Workshops (ICDEW) of IEEE 28th International Conference on Self-Managing Database Systems (SMDB)*.

Habebeh, I. O. (n.d.). A Method for Fragment Allocation Design in Distributed Database System. *The Sixth Annual U.A.E. University Research Conference*.

Horowitz, E., & Sahni, S. (1978). *Fundamentals of Computer Algorithms*. Rockville, MD: Computer Science Press.

Jindal, A., & Dittrich, J. (2011). *Relax and Let the Database Do the Partitioning Online*. Business Intellignce for Real Time Enterprize.

Li, L., & Gruenwald, L. (2012). Autonomous database partitioning using data mining on single computers and cluster computers. *Proceedings of the 16th International Database Engineering & Applications Sysmposium (IDEAS)*, 32-41.

McCormick, W. T. Jr, Schweitzer, P. J., & White, T. W. (1972, September). Problem Decomposition and Data Reorganization by A Clustering Technique. *Operations Research*, *20*(5), 993–1009. doi:10.1287/opre.20.5.993

Navathe, S., Ceri, S., Wierhold, G., & Dou, J. (1984, December). Vertical Partitioning Algorithms for Database Design. *ACM Transactions on Database Systems*, *9*(4), 680–710. doi:10.1145/1994.2209

Navathe, S., & Ra, M. (1989). Vertical Partitioning for Database Design: A Graph Algorithm. *ACM Special Interest Group on Management of Data (SIGMOD) International Conference on Management of Data*.

Papadomanolakis, S., Dash, D., & Ailamaki, A. (2007, September). Efficient use of the query optimizer for automated physical design. *Proceeding of the 33rd international conference on* Very Large Data Bases *(VLDB)*.

Pasquier, N., Bastide, Y., Taouil, R., & Lakhal, L. (1999). Efficient mining of association rules using closed itemset lattices. *Information Systems, 24*(1).

Rao, J., Zhang, C., Megiddo, N., & Lohman, G. (2002). Automating physical database design in a parallel database. *Proceedings of the* ACM SIGMOD international conference on Management of data, 558-569.

Rodd, S. F., & Kulkarni, U. P. (2010). Adaptive Self-Tuning Techniques for Performance Tuning of Database Systems: A Fuzzy-Based Approach. *International Journal of Computer Science and Information Security, 8*(1).

Schnaitter, K., Abiteboul, S., Milo, T., & Polyzotis, N. (2012). On-line index selection for shifting workloads. International workshop of self-managing database systems, 459-468.

Schnaitter, K., & Polyzotis, N. (2012). Semi-Automatic Index Tuning: Keeping DBAs in the Loop. *Proceeding of Very Lagre Data Bases, 5*(5), 478–489.

Severance, D. J., & Hoffer, J. A. (1975). The use of cluster analysis in physical database design. *Proceedings of the 1st International Conference on Very Large Data Bases*.

Chapter 4
Significance of Real–Time Systems in Intelligent Transportation Systems

Manipriya Sankaranarayanan

🆔 https://orcid.org/0000-0002-0973-2131

National Institute of Technology, Tiruchirappalli, India

Mala C.

National Institute of Technology, Tiruchirappalli, India

Samson Mathew

National Institute of Technology, Tiruchirappalli, India

ABSTRACT

The advancements of several real-time system applications enable us to provide better solutions to day-to-day problems. One such real-time systems that has significantly enhanced its efficiency in aiding travelers to make commutation pleasant is the intelligent transportation system (ITS). There are several aspects of an ITS application that make it efficient and resourceful, but the major significant factor is its capability to provide services within a time constraint. This chapter aims to provide the basic concepts, background, and importance of dependability on distributed real-time systems in ITS using two applications for efficient traffic management. A novel automated traffic signal (ATS) is proposed that manages traffic flow by enumerating vehicle density of road segments using image processing techniques. The other proposed work involves the estimation of congestion rate (CONGRA) for given target area using the proposed hybrid vehicular ad hoc network (VANET). The details of the modules, implementation, and result analysis of the applications are discussed and presented.

DOI: 10.4018/978-1-7998-2491-6.ch004

INTRODUCTION

The technological advancements in the field of computer science and communications network have become extremely immense in order to make a stress free living. These advancements and improvements are focused on developing applications that are easy to use in real-time with co-ordinated system (Sumit Mallik 2014). Today, such applications are innumerable and developed in every field possible. One such highly developing application is in the field of road traffic management. Applications and services that are managed in real time in the field of transportation to provide a smart, safe and co-ordinated use of transport networks are the Intelligent Transportation Systems (ITS). It is a broad area of research which combines information and technologies to solve day to day transportation related problems. The developments in this field have been drastically significant over the past decade. Initially, only few countries such as United States and European Union had proposed and implemented ITS concept (Alam Muhammad et al., 2016). However now, they have raised up against various issues which have subdued its success, such as systems not having enough expertise, not being properly integrated, not establishing appropriate master plan, or importantly, financial restrictions. The most common issues, that have been experience so far, are the compatibility and integration of the applications and concepts across nations due the difference in the environmental impacts, data acquisition, traffic rules and regulations etc. (Mashrur Chowdhury et al., 2017).

Several applications and innovations are developed in field of ITS to make hindrance free travelling experience to commuters (Fayaz, Danish 2018). The need to work effectively in real time must be addressed by these applications. The future of ITS and the way forward in the future have become a hot topic of research (Agachai Sumalee et al., 2018, A. B. Nkoro et al., 2018). In this chapter, two ITS applications that work efficiently in real time are explained in detailed way. Each application is an example from diverse area of implementation and technology. Both the applications work towards providing solution to traffic management.

The first application involves traffic management through traffic signal. In developing countries at present, the traffic signal works as per fixed phase time and time requires manual labor to operate it. Therefore, there is a need to develop a traffic control system by evaluating all the criteria necessary to properly manage traffic imitating experts in the field of transportation. This work proposes a unique algorithm for automated traffic signals using surveillance camera feed for controlling traffic in intersection. Such applications are already existing using image processing. (Prakash et al., 2018, Akoum Al., 2017, Prashant Jadhav et al., 2016). All the existing work proposes a new infrastructure to fit into their proposed work and provide solution specific to a location or scenario. The major uniqueness of the work is utilizing existing infrastructure, robust method of detection of vehicles and the algorithm proposed for Green phase of traffic signal. This chapter explains how the traffic signal function can be made fruitful by using real time information of exiting vehicle density to control traffic efficiently. The details of the work are discussed in the subsequent section.

The other application is aimed as future technology of a real time application involving the estimation of congestion information of roads using smart vehicles. Seamless transportation is a necessity for our societal and economic sustainability. The congestion occurs due to two major problems: one is due to the limited capacity of the road and the other is lack of traffic assistance information to travellers. In order to resolve this congestion problem, new facilities and infrastructure needs to be developed to provide travelers prior traffic information about the route. Therefore, it is important to detect where the congestion occurs and to estimate the CONGestion Rate (CONGRA). A common solution to this is to use Intelligent Transportation System (ITS) that involves the use of cameras, detectors, and environmental sensors to collect traffic related parameters. There are several sensors that are involved in such communication of information (Guerrero-Ibáñez J et al. 2018). Several conventional estimating strategies are available in control centers to monitor the vehicular traffic related predictions and estimations. These strategies implicate the use of cameras, detectors and some environmental sensors to record the traffic related parameters in real time. Most commonly recorded parameters include speed, density, flow, demand, queue length, flow-speed, low-density and speed-density. These parameters play a major role in making optimal decisions to traffic related problems such as waiting time, travel cost, congestion and accidents (Amudapuram Mohan Rao et al. 2012, V. Pattanaik et al. 2016). Apart from Image Processing technique, the new technology that has received significant attention in ITS is the Vehicular Communications by using Vehicular Ad-hoc Network (VANET). There are various proposed works that involve developing strategies to control and regulate traffic using VANET (Heba El-sersy et al. 2015, Mushtaq Ahmad et al. 2018, Lanlan Rui 2018). In this chapter, a real time cost effective and reliable Hybrid Infrastructure to dynamically estimate the CONGRA using fuzzy logic for target area is proposed. The traffic CONGRA or the jamming rates are estimated from parameters obtained from Image Processing and VANET based Infrastructures.

The rest of the chapter is structured as follows. The discussion begins with general overview of ITS section comprising of modules, applications and working of ITS. The next section comprises of two real time application in ITS. The detailed explanation of the Automated Traffic Signal and Hybrid Infrastructure for Congestion Rate Estimation applications are discussed in the subsections. It also provides implementations information and performance analysis. Finally, the chapter is summarized with conclusion followed by references.

OVERVIEW OF ITS

The several components and applications of ITS are discussed in detail. All the applications under the banner of ITS are always interdisciplinary combining various technologies and techniques.

Modules of ITS

The overall architecture for ITS technology is shown in Figure 1 and the details about each module are discussed below.

Data Acquisition

Several technologies are available for traffic data acquisition that include wide range of sensors and sensing devices such as simple loop detector embedded in the road surface, Video Image Detectors(VID), CCTV cameras, etc. The purpose of a data acquisition system is to obtain the traffic parameters like dimension of vehicle, lane occupancy, oil pressure, flow rate, vehicle speed, fuel level, engine temperature etc.

Figure 1. ITS Information Chain
Source: Jarasuniene 2007

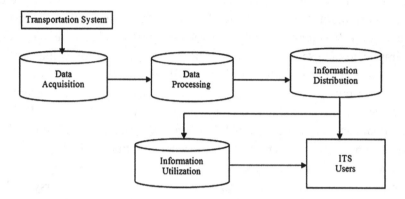

Data Communication

Data acquired through detectors and sensors are transmitted to the transport center for processing and converting that into information to be transmitted to the users. The mode of communications like static and dynamic are used for this purpose. The cost of communication increases with band width required in terms of frequency or bits per second.

Data Processing

In order to generate the information for decision making, the acquired data through communication lines are processed. The traffic parameters are processed for which specific decision support systems like intelligent algorithms, software and techniques are created. This processed data is converted as information of common man understandability and communicated either to transport center operators or to the users. The entire processing in this phase is done either in a centralized or distributed manner. Recent technologies have improved drastically in such a way that the device themselves do such processing.

Information Distribution and ITS Users

The information from the processing center is communicated via various transmitters and receivers. The users of ITS technology vary from daily common transport users to research professionals. Information needed by the user is conveyed by fixed terminals like radios, televisions, websites, computers, VMS boards etc. and mobile terminals like cellular phones, car radios, laptop or car mounted computers, pagers, handheld digital services. Based on the user's need, the ITS technology delivers information.

Information Utilization

Information generated is utilized by the users and intelligent and coordinated decisions are made to support traffic and vehicle controls. On utilizing such information, it helps in regulating, reducing and eradicating the list of problems faced in transportation.

Figure 2. Examples of ATMS[12]

APPLICATIONS OF ITS

Applications in ITS can be classified into two categories (Lelitha Vanajakshi et al. 2010): (i) based on area of application (ii) Technology used in the application

Classification of ITS Application based on Area of Implementation

Applications are classified based on the area of usage and comprises of the following categories.

1. Advanced Traffic Management Systems (AMS) or Arterial Management System
2. Advanced Traveler Information Systems (ATIS)
3. Commercial Vehicle Operations (CVO)
4. Advanced Vehicle Control Systems (AVCS)
5. Advanced Public Transportation Systems (APTS)
6. Advance Rural Transportation Systems (ARTS)

Advanced Traffic Management Systems (ATMS)

ATMS include technologies that manage traffic along arterial roadways employing traffic detectors, traffic signals and various means of communicators to travelers. Information is collected by different technologies such as CCTV cameras, induction loop detectors, real-time detector graphics, microwave detection, video detection etc. This information is processed to circulate real time data based on the application. For example, dynamic traffic control systems respond to the changing traffic condition across different habitation and types of roads by routing drivers around alternate route where possible. Some of the latest ATMS applications include incident management, traffic light control, electronic toll collection, congestion prediction and congestion-ameliorating strategies.

Advanced Traveller Information System (ATIS)

The main principle behind the technologies under the ATIS is 'uncertainty' while travelling. Technologies with real time traffic, information are available to users in order to make smart and compatible traveling decisions. ATIS applications include travel conditions on Variable Message Signs (VMS), traffic congestion maps, alternate route guidance, special event signing and information about transit operations. For

Figure 3. Sample Images Traveller Information System[34]

Figure 4. Images from public Transportation Information Systems[56]

travellers' convenience, most of the applications are accessible over the Internet from home to work, in vehicle navigation systems, mobile phones and other communicators.

Advanced Public Transportation Systems (APTS)

APTS applications are specific in improving the efficiency and user friendliness of public transport services. The applications include information systems that offer timetable, fare and ride sharing information more conveniently to users through the internet and other media. The other most common applications include automated fare collection systems, vehicle location systems, exact arrival time of public transport etc.

Advanced Vehicle Control Systems (AVCS)

AVCS combine sensors, computers and control systems in vehicles infrastructure that warns and assist drivers and also intervene the driving task by means of improving the information about the driving environment. The ultimate goal of the AVCS function is to enable "hands off" driving under certain conditions, where the vehicles would operate safely under complete automatic control. Some applications include anti-collision warning and control, driving assistance, automatic lateral/longitudinal control, long-run plans of automatic driving, automated parking assistance, steering assistance, traffic jam assistance, night vision monitoring, speed limit identification, pedestrian detection, and automatic highway system.

Advance Vehicle Safety System (AVSS) is another main sub category of AVCS. AVSS includes technologies that help in improving the safety of the passengers and the vehicle. Some applications include blind spot detection systems, lane departure warning systems, enhanced visibility, rear view

Figure 5. Prototype Image of an Autonomous Car[7]

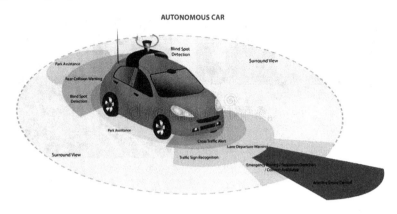

Figure 6. Sample model of Commercial Vehicle applications[8]

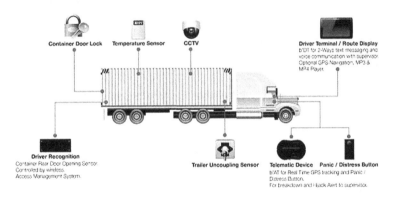

camera, reverse backup sensors, automatic braking, forward collision avoidance system, side view assist and stability control.

Commercial Vehicle Operating Systems (CVOS)

CVO applies the technology of ATMS, ATIS and AVCSS in commercial vehicle operation such as trucks, buses, taxis and ambulances in order to improve efficiency and safety. Vehicle identification, automatic vehicle monitoring, fleet management, computer scheduling and electronic payment are some of the applications of CVO technologies. Another popular application is the Automatic Vehicle Locations (AVL) systems to instantly determine the location of any vehicle in order to manage their fleet more efficiently.

Advanced Rural Transportation Systems (ARTS)

ARTS represent applications of ITS to rural transportation environment. Unique characteristics of rural travel, such as longer trip lengths, uneven terrain in some locations, unfamiliar routes, more hazardous conditions during bad weather, animal hazards and poor lighting, medical facilities during accidents

Figure 7. Example Images of ARTS Implementation[9]

all contribute to safety and essential component of information to travelers. Therefore, the applications are classified into four categories, i.e., safety and incident detection, traveler information, medical and emergency services and public transportation.

Classification of ITS Application based on Technology Used

The technologies that are deployed in these systems comprises of three level

1. Vehicle Level
   a. Technologies are that are deployed within the vehicle such as sensors, processors & display units used for providing useful information to the driver.
2. Infrastructure Level
   a. All the sensors that aid in collecting traffic data and tools that help in communicating traffic related information e.g. GPS, Sign board, Signals etc.
3. Co-Operative Level
   a. Smart vehicles are that cooperatively communicate among themselves and to the infrastructure. It is a combination of the above two levels.

OVERALL WORKING OF ITS

The working of any application in ITS is shown in Figure 8 below. In infrastructure and co-operative level of applications, the major sector of operation is the Traffic Management Centre (TMC) which comprises of several processing units that receive and communicate information through a network to execute set of activities in a distributed manner (Alam, Muhammad et al.., 2016, Mashrur Chowdhury et al., 2017). Traffic monitoring systems, travel time predictions, congestion detection, e-parking, Vehicular Adhoc Network (VANET) applications are few examples of distributed systems of ITS. All the applications require a communication network to transfer information from one processing unit to the other to make the system/application work in real time efficiently. Similarly, the applications under vehicle level are centralized in nature. For example speed detection, vehicle Auto parking, driver mood detection, auto vehicle driving system, collision avoidance system etc. Unless the vehicle level applications are designed to communicate with distributed systems based applications, it remains to work in a

Figure 8. Working of ITS[10]

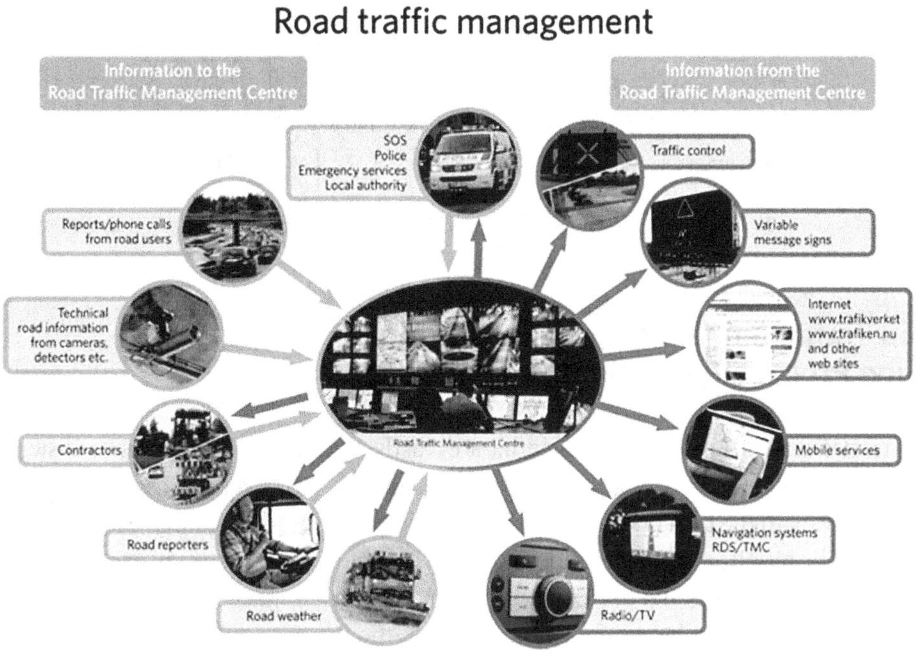

centralized mode. Irrespective of the type of application of ITS, all the systems are real time systems. All applications depend on the efficiency of computation that aids in achieving appropriate behavior within time constraint and not to miss its deadline.

REAL TIME SYSTEMS IN INTELLIGENT TRANSPORTATION SYSTEMS

The several aspects that make ITS work effectively in real time are further discussed with the aid of two popular applications. The first application involves an efficient traffic management system of ITS using a novel Automated Traffic Signal using Real Time Multilevel Parallel Video Image Processing. The other real time application discussed in detail is the Hybrid Infrastructure for Estimation of Congestion Rate (CONGRA) in Vehicular Ad-Hoc Network.

Traffic Management in Intelligent Transportation System

In this chapter, the importance of real time systems are explained by means of an ITS application in the area of ATMS. This category of applications ensures to utilize the existing infrastructures such as cameras, roadside unit sensors, etc., to collect traffic data and communicate through a network to management centre. This requires several integration processes with time constraints to manage the road traffic effectively. One of the popular real time service providers using this technique is Traffic Signal Management. An innovative system is proposed in this chapter: Automated Traffic Signal (ATS) using Real Time Multilevel Parallel Video Image Processing (R-MPVIP) from S.Manipriya et al. (2016).

Figure 9. Modules of automated traffic signal management

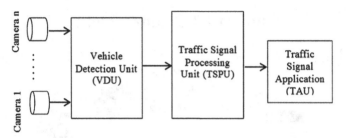

Automated Traffic Signal using Real Time Multilevel Parallel Video Image Processing (ATS using R-MPVIP)

The existing traffic controlling systems in India are vastly relying on human labor instead of system hardware due to random traffic throughout the day. As a result, detection and assessment of traffic congestion are obtained with the concentration of the human operator. Additionally, area under surveillance may be too large to be monitored by a few operators and number of cameras may exceed their monitoring capability. This situation forces the use of more personnel, which makes it even more expensive in an era of technological equipment being much cheaper than the human resource.

The prime aim of the Automated Traffic Signal (ATS) Management is to make the system robust and automated and also to make maximum possible comfort for travelers. The prime component that makes this system efficient in real time is the collection of data which is done by the surveillance cameras installed few meters before the traffic signal. The main reason to use surveillance or any camera based method for a traffic signal inspite of other sensors is that (i) it can easily handle a broad area with multiple lanes (ii) possible to adjust the area of detection (iii) it has a rich array of data for easy visual analysis (iv) it is possible to integrate and link the information from one camera to other (v) it is easy for any result analysis, and (vi) the results can be utilized to other application.

The major modules in this real time application are given below.

- Vehicle Detection Unit (VDU)
- Traffic Signal Processing Unit (TSPU)
- Traffic signal and other Application Integration Unit (TAU)

Vehicle Detection Unit (VDU)

This unit comprises of all operations and processing of live video from cameras and detecting the vehicle of the respective road segment progressing towards the traffic signal. ATS management system can work for junction comprising of two or more roads intersecting. The traffic signal phase is modified based on the number of vehicles progressing towards the intersection. It requires atleast one feed from the camera to be communicated in real time without any loss of information to the TMC for processing the content. If more than one camera is used for detecting vehicle, then the integration of the results needs to be done within time constraint in order to make sure that the traffic signal operation has no hindrance and does not increase congestion or bring any type of irritability to the travelers. There are several techniques of using image processing techniques for vehicle detection (Ishaan Gulati et al. 2019)

The initial step to this real time application is to identify the vehicles passing across the region of interest. To reduce unwanted computation, only a region of the frame is selected and represented as SRF. Since, all the image processing techniques are carried out in an outdoors environment, the illumination changes are better represented in HSV color model and represented as Converted Selective Region of the Frame (CSRF). Instead of losing the color information (Manipriya Sankaranarayanan et al.. 2014 and S. Manipriya et al..2016), all the three color models are processed in parallel. The changes in the consecutive frames of acquired images of the traffic scene over time by a static camera are detected using background subtraction. The images are compared with background image that is updated using running average. The most advantageous process of this work is that an optimal balance between computational cost and accuracy in detection is achieved using Buff-S Module from S. Manipriya et al.,(2016). It ensures all vehicles are detected by skipping unwanted frames that have similar content and prominently meets deadline. The Updated Background Frame and the CSRF are compared with Threshold (Th) pixelwise. The corresponding Resultant Frame pixel ($RF_{(x,y)}$) are given a value 0 or 1 (black or white), 1 represents the candidate of a moving vehicle as in Figure 10. The selected region of interest in RF is converted to single row and multiple columns of virtual sections called boxes. Vehicle classification and density estimation are done using two parameters. One is the width of the vehicle (WV) corresponding to number of boxes and the other is the time (TV) for which the boxes are candidates of moving vehicle respectively. Using thresholds($Th_{Btw}, Th_{BFW}, Th_{BFW}, Th_{Ttw}, Th_{Tfw}$), the candidate vehicles are classified as Two wheeler(TW), Four wheeler (FW) and other categories.

Algorithm 1: Vehicle Detection Unit

```
Begin Background Subtraction Module
      Select Region of Interest
      SRF→CSRF
      For each CSRF
          Buff-S Module(CSRF)
          Generate UBF
```

$$RF_{(x,y)} = \begin{cases} 1 & if\left(UBF - CSRF\right) > Th \\ 0 & Otherwise \end{cases}$$

```
      End For
    Return RF
End
Begin Vehicle Count Module
    For each RF
          WV= No of Boxes(RF)
          TV= Time of Boxes(RF)
```

Figure 10. Resultant Frame of VDU

$$Counter = \begin{cases} TW++ & if\,WV \leq Th_{Btw}\,,\; TV \geq Th_{Ttw} \\ FW++ & if\,Th_{BFW} \leq WV \leq Th_{Bfw}, TV > Th_{Tfw} \\ Others++ & Otherwise \end{cases}$$

```
    End For
    Return TW,FW,Others
End
```

The complete technical detail of detecting and classifying vehicles from live video feed are incorporated from Manipriya.S et al.., (2015). The overall pseudocode is in Algorithm 1. Figure 10 shows the detection of vehicles from the VDU using the proposed Algorithm 1.

Traffic Signal Processing Unit (TSPU)

The traffic signals timers or phase cycles are fixed over a period to switch traffic between different directions. This leads to increased waiting time for vehicles even when there is less traffic density. If the phase cycle time can be adjusted or manipulated according to the varying traffic density, the problem of congestion can be significantly reduced. The proposed ATS adjusts the phase cycle time based on the results obtained from VDU. The aim in this work was to improve the traffic control system by using an improved and accurate method of identifying vehicle density and also make the real time operation consistent and to mimic the operation of any traffic analysing expert. This adjustment will result in the change of traffic density patterns and optimizes the delay in transit of vehicles in odd/peak hours of the day.

The major advantage of the work is that the number of roads and the number of direction based on the geometry of the intersection can be altered. The prerequisite for this work is the number of roads involved in the traffic signal operation that has to be provided with the camera. There are four major entities that are involved (i) integration of the outcomes of VDU in real time (ii) Processing the outcomes to alter the green band of phase cycle, and (iii) distribution of green band variation to the location.

The algorithm requires a distributed architecture with several VDU and each one representing a separate processing unit that communicates through a network to cooperate and exchange information to TSPU. For any traffic signal automation, the green band of each phase cycle is consistent. Based on the traffic density approaching the signal location, the green band is altered. The entire algorithm works for both homogenous and heterogeneous traffic condition. In India, the direction of flow of vehicle can be altered frequently due to several reasons. Hence, the algorithm provides the flexibility to modify the number of direction for each road segments. The VDU units deliver the vehicle density information at regular interval less than the green band time. Based on the vehicle density, the traffic lights are modified.

$$T = l_l + h.N \tag{1}$$

where, T is the time required to clear N vehicles through signal, l_l is the start-up lost time, and h is the saturation headway in seconds as in Tom V Mathew (2014). The algorithm works as follows.

Step 1: Initially one of the roads has been given default green phase which can be altered by experts or the operator. The current and previous Green Band time is represented as GB_{curr} and GB_{prev} respectively.
Step 2: There are four cases possible from the vehicle density information: (i) High density (ii) Medium intensity (iii) Very high traffic density with static vehicles, and (iv) Low vehicle density. The headway is calculated based on the four cases of intensities.
Step3: The highest density using VDU is identified and the time T from Equation 1 is calculated. The Variation in Green band time (V_{GB}) is calculated using Equation 2.

$$V_{GB} = T - GB_{prev} \tag{2}$$

Step 4: The GB_{curr} is bounded within a minimum and maximum time limit as GB_{min} and GB_{max} respectivetly. This condition makes sure that irrespective of the traffic density (very high or no traffic), all other road intersections get the opportunity and not wait till time T.

$$GB_{curr} = GB_{min} + V_{GB} \tag{3}$$

Step 5: In order to overcome the last two cases of vehicle density where the VDU will deliver nil result for ($Low_{Traffic}$), two conditions are specified in the algorithm. In both the cases when $T < Low_{Traffic}$ than GB_{curr} is given value of GB_{Min}. The average of previous K green phase cycle of the respective road are stored and analyzed. If the average value of $T > Th_{GB}$ then GB_{curr} is set to average of K green band cycle else it is set to GB_{min}. If the $Low_{traffic}$ condition for a long time then it indicates that there is no traffic else in the next few phase cycle, the value of T will definitely increase.
Step 6: The value of GB_{curr} is calculated for other roads in junction by the descending order of the vehicle density obtained from VDU.

Performance Analysis

This algorithm is simulated in Matlab2010 and the screenshot of the result is shown in the Figure 11. The corresponding vehicle density in each phase cycle is also displayed within the video window.

Sample Green Band time for very high traffic and medium traffic video simulated for a three road intersection using proposed ATS is shown in Figure 11. The figure shows the phase cycle for a road segment that has the highest vehicle density among three of them. The comparison of the Green Band time (GB_{curr}) against the Time (T) for clearing N vehicles is shown in the Figure 12. It can be seen from the graph that GB_{curr} fulfils approaches to T in almost all phases. During high traffic video, the algorithm make

Figure 11. Simulation of ATS using R-MPVIP

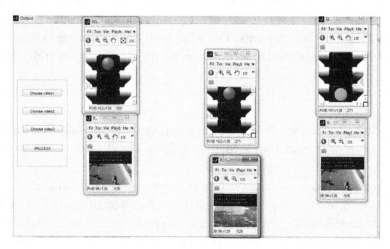

Figure 12. Simulation of green band for high and low traffic using ATS

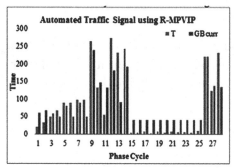 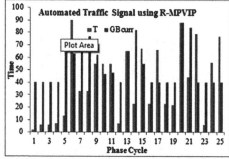

sure that the maximum vehicle density road segment is assigned the green phase. Also, in high traffic condition when at times the traffic is below the low density of traffic, the default GB_{curr} time is assigned irrespective of the minimal traffic. Similarly, in medium traffic video, the low traffic is maintained by assigning GB_{curr} constant. It should be noted that the GB_{curr} is calculated for all the road segments and assigned green phase as per the descending order of density. This ATS makes sure that the waiting time is reduced drastically. From simulation, it is also calculated that the overall waiting time for traffic signal with the ATS model is 23secs for high traffic and 12 secs for low traffic. The computation complexity of the algorithm is drastically reduced due to the Buff-s Algorithm. The speed up of algorithm comes upto 56 frames per second for detection of vehicles. The proposed work therefore shows better performance in minimizing computation as well as reducing traveller waiting time. Both these elements of the work provide the ideal description for a practical application in real time.

Traffic Signal and Other Application Integration Unit

The communication of information to any application is inherently distributed as they are physically apart to exchange information and cooperate to achieve the goal of efficiently handle traffic. In order to ensure the precise behaviour of a typical distributive system, the application is made available, maintainable, reliable and easy to integrate as described in Alam Muhammad et al.., (2016). Moreover, this type of application has high probability to provide continuous services to assure that the real time activities are not affected and performed with in stringent bound. It is also possible to integrate several other applications with the single VDU system such as speed detection, congestion detection, flow patter analysis etc.

Vehicular Communication using Vehicular Adhoc Network (VANET) in Intelligent Transportation System

The first generation ITS include standalone applications such as driver assistance, traffic management, electronic toll collection etc. It does not neither share nor communicate any information among travellers. A new subset of applications in which participants communicate and exchange information to facilitate or advise are under research focus. This set of applications are from Cooperative Intelligent Transportation System (C-ITS) and the network in which these communication occurs are Vehicular Adhoc Network (VANET). The information exchanged is regarding traffic jam, accidents, road hazards etc. The applications in this section are categorised into three major sections as Alam Muhammad et al., (2016)

* Road/ Traffic Safety
* Traffic Efficiency
* Other value added application

In this section, estimation of Congestion Rate (CONGRA) as one of the value added application in ITS using VANET is described. Vehicular communications are inherently distributive due to high mobility, link condition and dynamic network. The communication can be either based on the Vehicle to Vehicle (V2V) or Vehicle to Infrastructure (V2I) communications. Road Side Unit (RSU) is the major component for a VANET infrastructure with reasonable communication range. They are communicating devices located on roadside, to provide support for the passing vehicles and act as a wireless access point to share messages (e.g., traffic, road information, and safety messages). When the vehicle is in the communication range of RSU, the vehicles communicate information to it, else information is communicated from one vehicle to the other through wireless medium as in (Rahul Kala, 2016). The former method of communication is V2V and the latter is V2I communication. In estimation of CONGRA, a strong real time constraint exists as the congestion information when received with sufficient time in advance aids in avoiding highly dense location and avoid unnecessary delays (Manipriya Sankaranarayanan et al., 2017).

Proposed Hybrid Infrastructure for Estimation of Congestion Rate (CONGRA)

This section proposes the Hybrid Infrastructure and the methods used for better assessment of traffic parameters to estimate *CONGRA* at a target geographic area. The target area considered comprises of road segments and sub road segments. Optimal number of infrastructure units required for the area is evaluated and deployed in order to overcome the undesirable expenses. The main objective is to provide

Figure 13. Proposed hybrid infrastructure

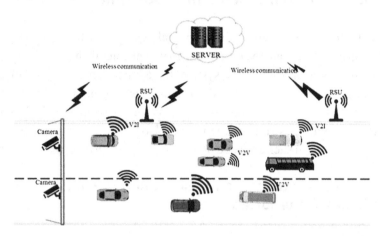

any user to access the estimated information for their travel and get a better insight well in advance to avoid congestion and to minimize the transit delay in the target area.

Figure 13 proposes the Hybrid Infrastructure used for estimation of *CONGRA*. This infrastructure comprises of IMaGe PROcessing based (IMGPRO) Infrastructure and Vehicular Ad hoc Network (VANET) Infrastructure. The IMGPRO Infrastructure comprises of cameras fixed before the target area and uses Image Processing techniques to process the images and to calculate the parameter values. In VANET Infrastructure, all vehicles are equipped with wireless communicating equipment and Global Positioning System (GPS) that are synced in time. In this infrastructure, the vehicle periodically broadcasts beacons, also known as CAM (Co-operative Awareness Message) to announce their presence and status information (speed, location, timestamp etc.,) to the neighboring vehicles or RSU's. Few parameters such as speed, type of vehicle etc., are obtained from IMGPRO Infrastructure and other parameters required for estimation of *CONGRA* are obtained from the VANET Infrastructure.

The parameters from both the infrastructures are communicated to the distributive server in TMC through wireless communication. The physical topology of a network is determined by the capabilities of the network access devices, level of control or fault tolerance desired, and the cost associated with cabling or telecommunications circuits. Once the parameter value reaches TMC, Congestion Rate (CONGRA) is estimated using fuzzy logic controllers in real time. The estimated result and parameter values from Hybrid Infrastructure are communicated to several decentralized servers and RSUs which acts as access points to make CONGRA values accessible from any location. Travelers demanding congestion information of a target area can get it from the nearest decentralized servers to their access points.

1.   CONGRA estimation is done using the following modules
2.   Determination of Influential Parameters for CONGRA
3.   Estimation of CONGRA using Fuzzy logic
4.   Communication of CONGRA to Travellers On Demand

Determination of Influential Parameters for CONGRA

Parameters such as Average Speed, Queue Length, Average Waiting Time, Time of Day, Type of Day, Arrival Rate, Type of Vehicle and Occupancy that influence the congestion in a road and their respective methods and equations by which they are calculated are discussed in this section (Manipriya Sankaranarayanan et al., 2017).

Average Speed (AS)

The speed of vehicles is estimated for vehicles entering the target area of interest from the IMGPRO Infrastructure. This parameter helps in contributing to the perspective of how fast the vehicle is approaching the target destination using Image Processing Techniques. Using the individual vehicle speed, the AS of vehicles that are captured in the video are estimated. The space mean speed method is best suited for such average calculation and given in Equation 4

$$AS = \frac{n}{\sum_{i=1}^{n} 1/s_i} \tag{4}$$

where, n is the total number of vehicles captured in the video for which the speed is calculated and s_i is the speed of the ith vehicle covering the distance D.

Queue Length (QL)

Traffic will depend on the number of vehicles that are already in the area waiting (*QL*) to move from the current location to their respective destinations. All information is communicated to the RSU's by vehicles about their respective status such as time stamps, location, vehicle id etc. From this status information, the vehicle at the tail of the queue is determined. The distance from Head of Vehicle Queue (HVQ) to Tail of Vehicle Queue (TVQ) is the total length or distance of the vehicles in queue or Queue Length Distance (QLD). When the target area is found to have a straight road segment $Ax + Bx + C = 0$ (with *A, B* and *C* are coefficients), then the Queue Length Distance (QLD) is calculated using Equation 5.

$$QLD = \frac{|Ax_0 + By_0 + C|}{\sqrt{A^2 + B^2}} \tag{5}$$

where, (x_0, y_0) is the location of the TVQ. If there is a curving road segment, then QLD is calculated as arc length. QL is calculated by Passenger Car Unit (PCU) for the QLD from the projected area of the vehicle and the dimension of the road (single lane or multilane). Finally, the Queue length parameter is estimated in terms of PCU for dynamically varying *QLD*.

Average Waiting Time (AWT)

The time for which the vehicles are waiting to enter the target area is another parameter influencing the CONGRA and obtained from VANET infrastructure. The waiting time is calculated from the data segments of consecutive RSU's (RSU_i and RSU_{i+1}) available along the side of the road using the Equation 6. The status information of vehicle received in RSU_i and the RSU_{i+1} are transmitted to the centralized server. The waiting time is calculated by the time stamp and distance travelled by the vehicle obtained from the GPS trackers of the vehicle.

$$AWT = \begin{cases} H & if\,(D < Th_d) \\ \dfrac{\sum_{k=1}^{n}(T_{RSU_{i+1}})_K - (T_{RSU_i})_K}{n} & Otherwise \end{cases} \qquad (6)$$

where $(T_{RSU_{i+1}})$ and (T_{RSU_i}) is the time stamp of the kth vehicle to the RSU_{i+1} and RSU_i respectively. The average waiting time of vehicles entering the target area is estimated for every k vehicles reaching RSU_{i+1}. H is the default minimum waiting time of kth vehicle whose distance travelled is less than a threshold distance Th_d.

Time of Day (TiD)

The above three parameters are required by default to estimate congestion. Time of day has a significant appeal in this scenario because vehicular traffic and dispersion time at different time of the day varies. TiD is obtained from the timer from the centralized server used for processing. For our evaluation, the value chosen for parameter vary from early morning to night.

Type of Day (TyD)

TyD is a sub-category of TiD which plays a vital role. The congestion pattern will vary during the weekday or weekend for a specific region. For instance, the congestion seen in a shopping area during weekend is not same as in weekdays. The special cases of such parameters are holidays and emergency situations. Hence the parameter value of TyD for our consideration is categorized into weekend and weekday.

Arrival Rate (AR)

From the above mentioned parameters, it is evident that the number of vehicles arriving at a specific region depends on various factors such as the type of area, time of the day, type of day etc., To analyze the outcome of diverse scenarios based on the number of vehicles arriving per unit time, it is necessary to take account of arrival distribution. In some of the target areas, the arrival of individual vehicle is independent and random in nature. For a target area, the probability of arrival of vehicle with Poisson distribution is given by

Figure 14. Membership Function for input and output parameters

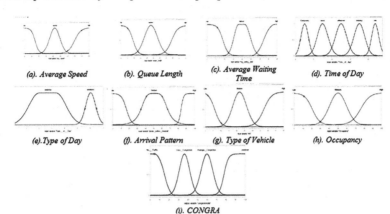

i. $p\left(x;u\right) = \dfrac{\mu^{x}e^{-\mu}}{x!}$ (7)

Similarly, arrival with Binomial Distribution is given by

$$b\left(x;n,p\right) = \frac{n!}{x!\left(n-x\right)!} \times p^{x} \times \left(1-p\right)^{n-x} \qquad (8)$$

where, x is the actual number of successes of arrival that result from the experiment, *e* is approximately equal to 2.71828 and p is the probability of success of vehicle arrival.

The function *FI* for CONGRA estimation is based on the above mentioned parameters and is given by the relation in Equation 9

FI= F (AWT, QL, AS, TiD, TyD, AR)   (9)

where, F is the function of the five estimated parameter from above methods. Though, the parameters from Equation 6 contribute a lot in the congestion estimation, the heterogeneous nature of the vehicular traffic acts as a hindrance to this estimation. For instance, let the number of two wheelers and heavy motor vehicles are X and Y respectively. The congestion caused by X is not equivalent to the congestion caused by Y both being same value (X=Y). This is due to the fact that the area occupied by each class of the vehicle is not unison. Hence, two more parameters such as Type of Vehicle and Occupancy are included to improve the value calculated from Equation 9.

Type of Vehicle (TV) and Occupancy (Occ)

The classified count of vehicles provides a better comprehensive composition of the heterogeneous traffic condition. Similarly, the occupancy rate governs the number of vehicles occupied for a unit distance over a time period. Analogous to *AS* calculation, both parameters are obtained from the IMGPRO Infrastructure. The different class of vehicles such as Two Wheeler (TW), Four Wheeler (FW), Three

Figure 15. Rule base implication

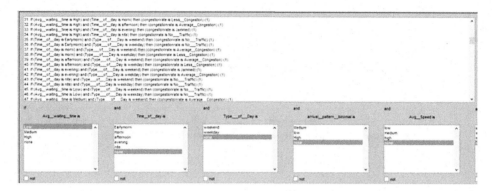

Wheeler (3W) and Heavy Motor Vehicle (HMV) are estimated for Type of Vehicle. The number of vehicles occupying unit area is calculated as the average occupancy rate.

From the new set of parameters, the new function *F2* for estimating *CONGRA* is given by the Equation 10

$$F2 = FI + F\ (TV,\ Occ) \tag{10}$$

where, *FI* is the function from Equation 9 and *F2* is *FI+* Function Type of Vehicle (TV) and Occupancy (Occ).

Estimation of CONGRA using Fuzzy Logic

The proposed hybrid architecture using fuzzy logic and control methods to estimate *CONGRA* does the following:

1. Calculates the input parameters from Hybrid Infrastructure and communicates them to the distributed server.
2. In the distributed server, the membership functions are defined in fuzzy logic controllers as in Figure 14.
3. Human based "if-then" rules are applied to input parameters and processed as in Figure 15.
4. The results from all the individual rules are averaged and weighed into one single output fuzzy set.
5. The crisp output result of *CONGRA* is estimated.
6. The input and output parameters are communicated to travelers on demand.

Table 1 shows the set of parameters (X) and their corresponding fuzzy sets ($\mu(X)$) used in the proposed fuzzy system.

Communication of CONGRA to Travelers on Demand

CONGRA in a geographical area can be communicated to any potential traveller/third party on demand to make their travel plan decisions. The input parameters from Hybrid Infrastructure and resultant

Table 1. List of fuzzy sets

	X	μ(X)
Input Parameter	Average speed	Low, Medium, High
	Queue Length	Low, Medium, High
	Average Waiting Time	Low, Medium, High
	Time of Day	Early Morning, Forenoon, Afternoon, Evening, Night
	Type of Day	Weekday, Weekend
	Arrival Pattern	Low, Medium, High
	Type of Vehicle (TW,3W,FW,HMV)	Low, Medium, High
	Occupancy	Low, Medium, High
Output Parameter	*CONGRA*	No Traffic, Less Congestion, Average Congestion, Jammed

Figure 16. Analysis of CONGRA with other parameters

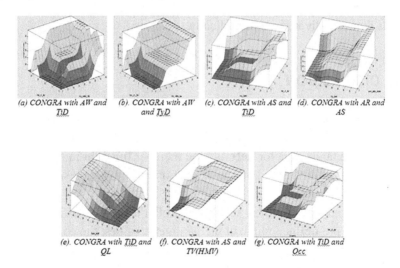

(a). CONGRA with AW and TiD

(b). CONGRA with AW and TyD

(c). CONGRA with AS and TiD

(d). CONGRA with AR and AS

(e). CONGRA with TiD and QL

(f). CONGRA with AS and TV(HMV)

(g). CONGRA with TiD and Occ

CONGRA enumerated in the server are distributed and communicated to travelers with minimal delay to the RSU and the decentralized servers. The number and position of decentralized servers are decided based on two criteria.

- Maximum distance between two servers that minimizes delay in communication
- No. of users accessing information

When the request for *CONGRA* information is near to the target area, RSU broadcasts this information to the neighbouring RSUs to provide the required information on a real time scenario. In case, the request of information is few kilometres away from the target area, the decentralized server acts as an

Figure 17. Comparison of estimated CR with actual congestion

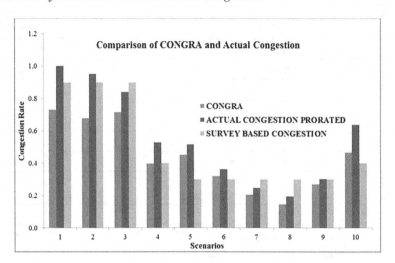

access point and provides the information via a wireless communication network. The CONGRA and other related information are also available at the RSU and decentralized server of the hybrid infrastructure which avoids overloading of the server. The information is available few kilometres from the target area which in turn is dynamically revised periodically.

RESULTS AND DISCUSSION

The influence of parameters for a sample location simulated in Vissim and integrated with MATLAB. Since, the parameter values encountered in each of the target area will certainly not be the same, the range of fuzzy sets in each of the target area for defining the member function in MATLAB varies. The rule base of the fuzzy system is defined based on the dispersion rate of vehicles, i.e., how fast the vehicles propagate from one point to the other.

Once the rules are defined for each fuzzy set, the controller is ready to estimate the congestion in the area (*CONGRA*). With the pre-defined range of the parameter values, the congestion is estimated. Two parameter value ranges and their corresponding congestion rates are analyzed from the Figure 16(a)-(g). From the Figure 16(a) and (b), it is seen that the value of *CONGRA* increases as the waiting time of the vehicles increases. The *CONGRA* values due to waiting time show that the movements of vehicles in this area are not usually rapid. In Figure 16(b), the weekends are found to have more congestion than the weekdays. Similarly in Figure 16(b), (c), (e) and (g), it is found that it is crowded during evening than morning time of the day. Figure16.(c), (d) and (f) show that when average speed of vehicle increases, the traffic is said to be gradually minimized due to the inverse proportionality. When the average speed of vehicles is zero, it is considered that the vehicles are waiting in the queue to move to other location. Hence at zero speed, the congestion of vehicle is found to be high. Figure 16(d) shows that the queue length of vehicles have significant role than other parameters. In shopping area, even during off peak hours when the queue length is beyond a threshold value, the *CONGRA* is found to be high. When the rate of arrival of vehicle increases, the congestion also increases as shown in Figure 16(d). The Figure

16(f) and (g) show that the values of Type of Vehicle and Occupancy are directly proportional to *CON-GRA* values. The movement of vehicle from one point to other depends on the Time of Day and Type of Day. Hence, both the parameters play an important role in this target area as all other parameter values depend on it. The estimated CONGRA value helps in deciding various alternatives the driver or traveler can choose based on the congestion at the desired location in real time. The proposed methodology can be implemented in any desired location due to its dynamicity. The parameter values estimated from the hybrid infrastructure is also provided to the end users. This mainly helps in planning the travel according to the congestion beforehand.

Figure 17 shows that CONGRA value corresponding to the actual congestion prorated and survey based congested rate for different scenarios. The actual prorated values were calculated manually using visual data of traffic. It shows that all the estimated *CR* values are closer to the actual congested value. Though, the congested value approximation may vary based on individual, the fixed fuzzy based controllers estimate the value near to the actual value.

From the above two applications, it is evident that real time systems have significant role in ITS. However, in India most of the application cannot be integrated but the proposed two applications are designed to integrate any type of traffic (homogenous or heterogeneous) conditions. Both the applications follow the time constraint delivery of information. Since, the information shared if missed does not raise any hazardous condition hence both the application falls under soft real time systems. Since, hard real time systems are application based and mostly concern with the safety related applications, it requires fine tuning of algorithm or addition of modules that ensures authenticity, confidentiality, error free and consistency of information in order to guarantee real time constraints within stringent bounds.

CONCLUSION

Intelligent Transportation Systems (ITS) refers to initiatives that apply data, communication and sensor technology to vehicles and transportation infrastructure to provide real-time information for road users and transportation system operators to make better decisions. ITS aims to improve traffic safety, congestion, air pollution and energy efficiency and use comprehensive strategies to achieve the above mentioned objective. ITS recent development emphasizes the use of dedicated short-range communications in wireless vehicle-to-vehicle and vehicle-to-road communications called as Vehicular Ad-hoc Network (VANET). In this chapter, two real time applications that aim to manage traffic efficiently are discussed in detail. Initially, a novel Automated Traffic Signal using Real Time Multilevel Parallel Video Image Processing (R-MPVIP) is proposed that effectively manages traffic flow. It enumerates vehicle density for the road segments of intersection for traffic signal controller. The detection process is robust that it can handle any type of video and does not depend on any complexity of road layout or camera feed. The result shows drastic improvements during very high traffic with minimal waiting time. Later application involves estimation of Congestion Rate (CONGRA) for given target area using hybrid Vehicular Adhoc Network (VANET). The CONGRA estimation requires parameters such as speed, queue length, time of the day, type of day, arrival rate, type of vehicle and occupancy to be calculated. The enumeration process is done by Image Processing of video and also from information communicated in VANET from the respective location. The results indicate promising results when compared with human interpretation. This chapter therefore provides an overview of the fact that strong real-time constraints are present in any application of ITS.

REFERENCES

Ahmad, M., Chen, Q., & Khan, Z. (2018). Microscopic Congestion Detection Protocol in VANETs. Journal of Advanced Transportation. doi:10.1155/2018/6387063

Akoum, A. (2017). Automatic Traffic Using Image Processing. *Journal of Software Engineering and Applications*, *10*(09), 765–776. doi:10.4236/jsea.2017.109042

Alam & Ferreira. (2016). *Introduction to Intelligent Transportation Systems*. doi:10.1007/978-3-319-28183-4

Chowdhury, M., Apon, A., & Dey, K. (2017). *Data Analytics for Intelligent Transportation Systems*. Elsevier.

El-sersy & El-sayed. (2015). Survey of Traffic Congestion Detection using VANET. *Communications on Applied Electronics, 1*(4), 14-20.

Fayaz, D. (2018). Intelligent Transport System-. *RE:view*.

Guerrero-Ibáñez, J., Zeadally, S., & Contreras-Castillo, J. (2018). Sensor Technologies for Intelligent Transportation Systems. *Sensors (Basel), 18*(4), 1212. doi:10.339018041212 PMID:29659524

Gulati & Srinivasan. (2019). Image Processing In Intelligent Traffic Management. *International Journal of Recent Technology and Engineering, 8*(2), 213-218.

Jadhav, P., Kelkar, P., Patil, K., & Thorat, S. (2016). *Smart Traffic Control System Using Image Processing. International Research Journal of Engineering and Technology, 3*, 1207–1211.

Jarasuniene. (2007). *Research Into Intelligent Transport Systems (Its) Technologies and Efficiency*. Academic Press.

Kala, R. (2016). *On-Road Intelligent, Vehicles*. Butterworth-Heinemann Publications.

Mallik, S. (2014). Intelligent Transportation System. *International Journal of Civil Engineering Research, 5*(4), 367-372.

Manipriya, S., & Gitakrishnan, V. V. (2015). Grid- Based Real Time Image Processing (GRIP) Algorithm for Heterogeneous Traffic. In *IEEE International conference on Communication Systems and Networks*. IEEE Publications.

Manipriya, S., & Mala, C. (2016). Real Time Multilevel Video Image Processing for VANET. *Proc. 5th international Conference on Computing, Communication and Sensor Network*.

Nkoro, A. B., & Vershinin, Y. A. (2018). Current and future trends in applications of Intelligent Transport Systems on cars and infrastructure. *17th International IEEE Conference on Intelligent Transportation Systems (ITSC)*, 514-519.

Pattanaik, V., Singh, M., Gupta, P. K., & Singh, S. K. (2016). *Smart real-time traffic congestion estimation and clustering technique for urban vehicular roads. In IEEE Region 10 Conference* (pp. 3420–3423). TENCON.

Prakash, U., Thankappan, A., & Balakrishnan, A. (2018). *Density Based Traffic Control System Using Image Processing*. doi:10.1109/ICETIETR.2018.8529111

Rao, A. M., & Rao, K. R. (2012). Measuring Urban Traffic Congestion – A Review. *International Journal for Tra-c and Transport Engineering*, *2*(4), 286–305. doi:10.7708/ijtte.2012.2(4).01

Rui, L., Zhang, Y., Huang, H., & Qiu, X. (2018). A New Traffic Congestion Detection and Quantification Method Based on Comprehensive Fuzzy Assessment in Vanet. Ksii Transactions On Internet And Information Systems, 12(1), 41-60.

Sankaranarayanan, Mala, & Samson. (2014). *Performance Analysis of Spatial Color Information for Object Detection Using Background Subtraction*. Elsevier Publications.

Sankaranarayanan, M., Mala, C., & Samson, M. (2017). Congestion Rate Estimation for VANET Infrastructure using Fuzzy Logic. In *International Conference on Intelligent Systems, Metaheuristics & Swarm Intelligence*. ACM Digital Library.

Sumalee, A., & Ho, H. W. (2018). Smarter and more connected: Future intelligent transportation system. *IATSS Research*, *42*(2), 67–71. doi:10.1016/j.iatssr.2018.05.005

Tom, V. (2014). Design Principles of Traffic Signal. *Transportation System Engineering*, 34.1-34.13.

Vanajakshi, L., Ramadurai, G., & Anand, A. (2010). *Centre of Excellence in Urban Transport IIT Madras Intelligent Transportation Systems Synthesis Report on ITS Including Issues and Challenges in India*. Tamil Nadu, India: IIT Madras.

ENDNOTES

[1]   Retrieved from: http://www.qualix.co.in/rising-need-advance-traffic-management-system/
[2]   Retrieved from: http://nissen-uk.com/
[3]   https://www.apshire.com.au/electronic-sign-hire/variable-message-signs-vms
[4]   https://pioneer-india.in/buy/car-entertainment-car-stereos-navigation-av-systems/
[5]   https://mvixdigitalsignage.com/blog/transit-digital-signage-enhances-business/
[6]   https://www.my-media.tv/2017/11/outdoor-digital-signage-kiosk/
[7]   https://www.dreamstime.com/stock-illustration-autonomous-driverless-car- automobile-sensors-use-self-driving-cars-camera-data-pictures-radar-lidar-image69822822
[8]   http://ptdhs.com/?page_id=210
[9]   https://www.pcb.its.dot.gov/eprimer/module10.aspx
[10]   http://www.trafikstockholm.com/docs/en/trafikledning_en.html

Chapter 5
A Broadcasting Scheme for Transaction Processing in a Wireless Environment

Prakash Kumar Singh

Rajkiya Engineering College, Mainpuri, India

ABSTRACT

In broadcasting, schemes are widely used in a wireless environment. In this chapter, a heuristic broadcasting scheme is proposed that directly affects the concurrency of database transactions. The proposed broadcasting scheme is suitable for real-time transactions. A heuristic scheme is developed in a mobile environment to enhance system performance. Further simulation results in the chapter show that the proposed broadcasting scheme is suitable to improve transaction processing in a wireless environment.

INTRODUCTION

In recent few years, the use of portable mobile devices has their key role in technological development. The wireless technology depends very much on these fast processing portable devices. In near future, it may be realistic that everybody will store and share their information using these wireless devices. The various daily life applications using these devices run transactions to complete their tasks on time. Admin at server end controls all the mobile devices connected using these wireless networks. Data consistency during transaction execution is the key issue in the database (Gray, 1978). Real time application like satellite launch, missile launch and fighter planes navigations need to complete their task within a time frame. Real time system should complete the transaction before elapse of the deadline (Ramamritham, 1993),(Shanker, Misra, & Sarje, 2008). A minor fault can degrade the whole system performance. In the recent few years, mobile distributed real time applications are getting a big attention for the database researchers. Stock trading, online shopping, e- ticketing, E-commerce are some example of real time applications. In a battlefield, a fast processing within a time frame is essential; otherwise, a big loss can occur. In these systems, the transactions should maintain not only the data correctness, but also timely execution. In other words, transaction execution in distributed real time database system depends on

DOI: 10.4018/978-1-7998-2491-6.ch005

various concurrency control schemes (Lindström, 2003),(Lam, Kuo, Tsang, & Law., 2000),(Lee, Lam, Son, & Chan, 2002),(Lee, Lam, & Kuo,2004),(Pandey, & Shanker, 2016,2017a,2017b,2018a,2018b,2018c),(Shanker, Misra, & Sarje, 2006,2008). It also depends on scheduling schemes used in the system. A number of locking and optimistic protocols has been developed to support these systems (Shanker, Misra, & Sarje, 2008). Meanwhile, various pessimistic protocols have also been developed. However, in recent years, researches are focused to develop optimistic concurrency control mechanism (Lindström, 2003). Pessimistic protocols basically support locking schemes. Some of these pessimistic approaches also include the concept of time stamping (Lee, Lam, Son, & Chan, 2002). Optimistic approaches run the transaction unhindered till validation; however, the commit operation is performed only after validation phase. Optimistic CC executes transaction operations in three different phases; first one is read phase, then validation phase and at last writing phase (Lee, Lam, & Kuo, 2004). Every transaction in optimistic CC passes through all these three phases for completion of its task. Here, the validation can follow two types of validation approach, i.e., one is forward and another one is backward validation policy. Both of these approaches have their own importance in the field of mobile database. In optimistic concurrency control backward policy, the transaction data validation is performed against the transactions which are already in committed phase. Further, in the second type of validation policy (forward validation policy), the validation is performed against the active (or read phase) transaction (Lee, Lam, Son, & Chan, 2002). Transaction which passes the validation phase can further proceed for execution. However, most of the researches in mobile environment prefer to perform forward validation in their optimistic approaches (Lee, Lam, & Kuo, 2004). Lee et al. has developed their optimistic approach using forward validation (Lee, Lam, Son, & Chan, 2002).

The Concurrency controls a single supportive part of successful commitment of transaction within a time frame. The other issues should also integrate with it to improve the system performance. Researchers have developed a number of transaction policies to enhance system performance in wireless medium. However, in mobile environment, a number of wireless medium obstacles lies which affect the performance of the system. The asymmetric channel bandwidth, power limitation, multi hop network problem, frequent disconnection etc. are some general intrinsic limitations which should be tackled by the developed policies (Barbará, 1999),(Padmanabhan, Gruenwald, Vallur, & Atiquzzaman, 2008),(Xing, & Gruenwald, 2007), (Madria, Mohania, Bhowmick, & Bhargava,2002),(Mok, Leong, & Si, 1999),(Imielinski, & Badrinath, 1994), (Gruenwald, Banik, & Lau, 2007), (Pitoura, & Samaras, 2012). Apart from these, maintaining the temporal consistency of data item is difficult in mobile environment. To maintain new version of data item timely is a fixed issue in mobile environment. It is a requirement to deal this hot issue in the field of mobile database. In mobile database, maintaining the valid data item timely and execute transaction within its deadline are challenging tasks.

Each real time data storage system needs to fulfil the real time requirements in mobile distributed real time database system (MDRTDBS) which needs to complete the tasks within a deadline (Lam, Kuo, Tsang, & Law., 2000). However, various applications in real life use these concepts. The navigation satellite, e –commerce, bus ticket booking frequently use these ideas. In recent research, the transaction execution is affected from the broadcasting policies. It affects mobile sites in MDRTDBS in a larger scale. Researchers in last three decades have developed a number of broadcasting policies to maintain data consistency (Acharya, Alonso, Franklin, & Zdonik, 1995),(Acharya, Franklin, & Zdonik, 1995),(Acharya,, Franklin, & Zdonik, 1997),(Hameed, & Vaidya, 1999),(Imielinski, Viswanathan, & Badrinath, 1997),(Kim, Lee, & Hwang., 2003),(Lee, Hwang, & Kitsuregawa, 2003),(Lo, & Chen, 2000),(Shigiltchoff, Chrysanthis, & Pitoura, 2004),(Su, Tassiulas, & Tsotras, 1999),(Vaidya, & and Hameed, 1999). In this work, broadcasting heuristic method is discussed which can enhance the system performance. Different characteristic of mobile and wireless medium will impact worst things during broadcasting. These characteristics can lead the failure of commitment of transaction on time.

- **Mobility:** At first, mobility behavior of nodes can cause difficulty in the coordination among themselves and others. Since, mobile distributed real time database system is based on fixed and mobile nodes both; there may be possibility of mobility of various sites and coordinator both in the distributed system. To maintain the updated value and share it with other nodes are difficult in mobile environment. In present situation, it is demand of the time and intelligent peoples to consider this characteristic seriously with smart mobile devices. These movable sites locations should be updated at server site, such that, it can be capable to keep the record of each site. A proper routing management should be maintained because, in some situation, it is very typical to establish connection with them. Replicated data on these mobile sites should be carefully stored or shared. For example, a movable mobile device like a tank in a battlefield can randomly move from one place to other and shares confidential data with other. But, at the server end, it should essentially keep track of the movement of that particular mobile site; otherwise, threats can occur.

- **Long-Lived Mobile Transactions:** In mobile environment, it is a key characteristic during maintaining and executing data. It is observed that mobile environment supports long lived transaction. The main cause behind it is the real time situations in mobile environment. Real time transactions are time constrained transactions and they should complete within a time bound. A short transaction could not be appropriate in a mobile environment. In mobile environment, the wireless medium takes much communication cost due to asymmetric channel bandwidth. The short transaction miss could affect the efficiency of system. The long-lived transactions are not suitable in mobile environment. It could keep various locks. To maintain data consistency within a time frame, long lived transaction should be managed properly in mobile environment. Failures of long-lived transaction at last phase of its execution can lose the communication cost and time both. It is essential to maintain long lived transaction and to care separately during transaction execution.

- **Energy Consumption:** In wireless environment, each and at every step during transaction execution, energy plays a key role. Mobile distributed system needs specially a backup of power to deal energy consumption during transaction execution. In recent years, popularity of portable mobile devices is increasing with the development of new technology. Smart devices, which carry a limited power capacity, need to save energy to execute the transaction in real time system. The completion of transaction happens only when it has enough energy to perform a task. The availability of energy is essential for unhindered transaction execution. A transaction, which has all the locks available and sufficient time to execute, needs one more constraint of the energy availability. Especially, during data broadcasting, it is essential to manage energy requirements. During wireless communication, a site needs a much higher energy requirement than general wired medium. Generally, a broadcast algorithm takes much energy during data broadcast and asymmetric wireless channel needs different level of energy consumption during message exchange between participant and server site. Although, mobile devices manage their power backup, generally fixed site is chosen as coordinator in mobile environment. It is a challenging characteristic in wireless medium. Generally, infrastructure-based architecture is required in mobile environment. Architecture could be infrastructure based as well as mobile ad hoc or combination of both. Infrastructure based system like share stock cannot be executed in mobile ad hoc situation. Coordination among military battle tank is an example of mobile ad hoc network. In some situation, a hybrid infrastructure is needed to perform transaction execution.

- **Channel Bandwidth:** Wireless medium is based on asymmetric bandwidth capacity during message communication. In wireless medium, the channel capacity during uploading and downloading is different, and hence the time consumption is more in case of data transfer. It is entirely different than wired medium. The bandwidth of wireless medium is much lower than wired medium. This is the main reason that the entire communication cost of sending the data from server to client is much lower than uploading same data from client site to server site.

- **Network Partitioning:** In wireless medium, the mobile nodes are free to move from one network to another. During entire transaction execution period, it faces a lot of network challenges like speed, communication failure, different network topology etc. The handoff situation can occur due to mobile participant movement from one network to another network.

- **Data Storage Capacity:** The capacity to store the data in mobile devices is very limited. The portable nature of mobile devices is now bound the limited capacity of data storage. In comparison to fixed nodes, the capacity of mobile site is much lower and needs to manage the data storage in an efficient manner. Gathering and sharing of the data item in broadcast situation is very much dependent on the capacity of data storage at different sites. Data storage depends on the capacity of hardware like memory, cache, hard disk and many others. Data storage capacity of the mobile node is very low due to its portability and power consumption. Due to small size of memory and hard disk, mobile database storage capacity is very low and it makes the transaction execution much more dependable on resource sharing and replicas management techniques.

- **Multi-Hop Networking:** Mobile sites in MDRTDBS may move from one place to another. In some situation, they are in one hop apart from server and in some other situation, they are in multi hop distance from coordinator site. Communication cost increases with the larger value of network hop count. The transaction execution is simple in one hop than multi hop network. The data collection and updating in one hop network is simpler than multi hop network. Broadcasting data in multi hop network needs more energy consumption. In multi hop network, the participant sites communicate with coordinator using another intermediate site which is in range of coordinator. Communication cost in multi hop networking is much more than simple one hop networking. Message latency is much more in multi hop network.

Further, arrangement of the paper is done as follows. At first, relevant related research development in the field of MDRTDBS is discussed briefly in section 2. The proposed broadcasting heuristic scheme is discussed in the section 3. The suggested heuristic scheme favors the data item of the transaction which has less number of conflicts with other transactions. Then in the next section 4, the MDRTDBS model, which is used to develop the broadcasting scheme, is discussed already developed here. The simulation experiment and the system performance are discussed in the section 5. It contains the results which are briefly described in the simulation and performance section. In the last section 6, the conclusion and future scope of the paper is discussed.

RELATED WORK

Mobile distributed real time database is an emerging field of research. In past, various concurrency control and commit protocols have been developed in MDRTDBS. Concurrency control protocols maintain consistency among various transactions executed on coordinator or participant sites. It deals with two major challenges; the first is mobile environment and second one is real time transaction execution. It is not easy to deal both situations. Mobile environment challenges a number obstacles. To deal these obstacles and achieve transaction commitment within a time period is a challenging task. Researchers have done a lot of work in developing commit protocol in the wired medium, but still a commit protocol is needed to develop in MDRTDBS. In recent years, various research works are done to develop broadcasting scheme. In mobile environment, various participants collect and share data with coordinator. Efficiently management of the updated version of data with other is essential to perform system tasks. In last two decades, a number of broadcasting schemes are developed (Lee, Hwang, & Kitsuregawa, 2003),(Lo, & Chen, 2000),(Shigiltchoff, Chrysanthis, & Pitoura, 2004),(Su, Tassiulas, & Tsotras, 1999),(Vaidya, & and Hameed, 1999). Broadcasting schemes are essential to manage the data transfer among coordinator and participant both. A number of broadcasting schemes has been developed. Researchers have categorized these broadcasting schemes in two different types (Acharya, Franklin, & Zdonik, 1997). It is categorized as pull based and push based broadcasting methods.

Pull based and push based broadcasting algorithms have been developed to schedule data item broadcasting (Aksoy, & Franklin, 1998),(Chen, Liu, & Lee, 2009),(Hui, Ng, & Lee, 2005). In push based algorithm in wireless environment, data items are scheduled to broadcast after a certain period. It broadcasts multiple times with or without multi versions of a data item. In push based broadcasting method, the data items are periodically broadcast to the client sites. The basic idea of push based mechanism is to broadcast the popular data at an interval. In this process, the hot data items send at a regular interval. Client site receives the broadcasting information and fetches the individual data as per requirement of transaction executing on that site. The information of current updated version of broadcast method is completely known before the start of that updated version. Apart from this in some broadcasting method, some extra information is also attached with the broadcasting cycle. However, in last few years, the data scheduling mechanism are attached with these broadcasting schemes to feel more realistic in nature and fruitful for real time applications. In modern applications, the real time systems depend on both the transaction and the data time constraint. Researchers are more focused to develop on demand data item broadcasting (Chen, Liu, & Lee, 2009). The push based and pull based schemes have different advantages and disadvantages. In push based scheme, the broadcasting of data items is done without asking the requirement from client side. In on demand approach, each participant client node sends their requirement and server provides the information regarding it on periodic or aperiodic interval. Depend on difference on demand methods, the server provides the data. The issues of the system work with on demand broadcasting schemes are discussed in here. However, in mobile environment, most of the researcher used push based broadcasting schemes. Broadcasting schemes are beneficial in mobile environment to save time and communication cost to fulfill the real time requirement. However, the pull based broadcasting scheme is prone for the wastage of the resources if clients request same data for multiple times. The number of client request decreases the performance of pull based broadcasting. The number of client request increases the load on upload channel which is worst for any broadcasting scheme.

Till now, various scheduling schemes are developed. Xuan et.al. have developed Earliest deadline first (EDF) (Xuan, Sen, Gonzalez, Fernandez, & Ramamritham, 1997). In this scheme, the server broadcasts the data objects based on the deadline and decides priority based on this time constraint. Dykeman et al. have suggested first come first serve scheduling policy (FCFS), which serves based on arriving policy (Dykeman, & Wong, 1986). The first arrived request is broadcasted first and the last arrived will be broadcasted at last. Authors (Wong, 1988) have suggested most request first policies. Sometimes, the clients request for a data item and it is not processed by server. This scheme gives a chance to broadcast a data item which is requested by maximum number of times. In simple words, this scheme broadcast data item, which is demanded by most of the clients. In another word, the hot data items are broadcasted first for this scheme. This broadcasting method is very much appropriate for large scale of distributed system in wireless environment. The priority of much requested data item is broadcasted first. Slack time inverse number of pending request deadline first is another scheduling approach which is suggested in paper (Lee, Wu, & Ng, 2006), (Xu, Tang, & Lee, 2005). Slack time inverse number of pending requests is based on sin value. The sin value is determined using the slack time and the number of waiting requests for the item. It is the ratio of the given slack time and the number of remaining requests for individual data item. It integrates the time constraint and demand of data item both. The most demanded data item with minimum slack time is broadcasted first in this scheme.

Authors have developed on demand broadcasting scheme based on size of data item (Lee, Wu, & Ng, 2006). In this paper, authors discussed the shortest service time first on demand request which is based on size of data item. In shortest service time first approach, the smallest data size data item is broadcasted first. The schedule of broadcast depends on size of data item. But, it has not considered the skewed variable size data item. To consider the variable size data item, authors suggested their developed algorithm which considers the variable size data item. They have developed scheduling approach based on variable size data item. It also integrates the frequency of data items and time constraint of data item. It includes the idea of variable size data item in real time systems. It is a good data dissemination concept to improve real time system which deals with the dynamic access pattern of different data item. Author has shown in their simulation work that it is the better method developed than earlier developed methods. Further, some broadcast schemes are also developed to integrate the data validity concept. Earlier, most of the discussed broadcasting approaches are based on transaction deadline. Real time applications are very much depend on data deadline too. It should be considered during development of broadcasting scheme. Data deadline are defined as the deadline or deadline interval after which the data validity has no meaning. The current data value of each transaction should follow data deadline interval. Lam et al. have developed Absolute validity interval in such a classical policy which is developed in wireless environment (Lam, Chan, & Yuen, 2000). Absolute validity interval is a fixed time interval, for which, the data validity is assumed to be valid. The data should update at each site. After this, validity interval data value should assign updated value. Various semantic approaches are also included in real time system to maintain data consistency.

Temporal and semantic approaches have given the researchers a new dimension of research. Liu et al. have performed simulation experiment to evaluate the impact of concurrency control protocols with using temporal data consistency (Song, & Liu, 1995). Temporal data consistency should maintain at each site to perform transaction execution with correct results. Transaction must read the fresh data during its execution. Data value may expire if it has crossed its age. Temporal consistency is simply understood as the age of the data and difference of ages among different data items. Temporal consistency is maintained if their age value and the difference of ages are small enough to meet the real time application. To commit with correct results, the transaction should complete before assigned deadline and data deadline both. In broadcasting scenario, to achieve data consistency and correct results, the absolute and temporal data validity should integrate with broadcasting techniques. In broadcast situations, it is very difficult to maintain temporal consistency. Mobile environment are very much different than wired medium. The asymmetric channel capacity causes the long wait during data sharing and storage. Further, due to various intrinsic limitations discussed earlier could rise the waiting time of a client to achieve the data items, which could lead to expire of its temporal consistency. In recent time, researchers have found that most of the transactions in mobile transactions are read only transaction (Pitoura, & Samaras, 2012).

Lee et al. has developed forward backward optimistic concurrency control protocol (FBOCC) (Lee, Lam, & Kuo, 2004). It is observed that system using Optimistic method performs better than lock-based approach. FBOCC is developed in wireless environment to enhance the system performance and it is based on optimistic concurrency control method. In FBOCC approach, the initial validation is applied on client site and the second validation phase for update transaction is performed at server site. However, authors have suggested that mobile sites perform backward validation at mobile site. On the other hand, update transactions are further validated at server site. Final validation follows the forward validation at server site. In backward validation approach, the validation is checked against the committed data item in last broadcast cycle. It checks the executing transaction data conflict with committed data item. Read only transaction must commit at the client side if it successfully validated at client site. The update transaction at first performs the backward validation at client site, and finally, forward validation at server end. Forward validation of executing transaction is performed against the executing transaction at server end. In forward validation approach, it is assumed that a transaction in commit phase will definitely commit and hence its abortion can lead the degradation of system performance. Hence, in forward validation scheme the data validity is checked only against the transaction being in execution phase.

Further in another paper (Lee, Lam, Son, & Chan, 2002), Lee et al. have developed partial-validation with time-stamp ordering (PVTO). In this paper, the partial-validation and timestamp ordering are performed at mobile site which follow forward validation. However, the final validation finishes at server end which follows the same forward optimistic validation scheme. PVTO approach is a timestamp-based method, which assigns timestamp for the different transaction. The basic concept of time stamp is to identify the old and young transaction and commits the oldest one first. PVTO improves the system performance with minimizing the miss rate. These two concurrency control methods have also considered the read only transaction (ROT). They discussed various protocols which observed that most of the transactions in wireless environment are basically read only transaction. However, they have not suggested the transaction scheduling schemes in these papers. Even data cycle based broadcasting approach is discussed in (Bowen, Gopal, Herman, Hickey, Lee, Mansfield, Raitz, & Weinrib, 1992), researchers observed and found that much proportion of transaction in mobile environment are read only transaction (ROT) (Garcia-Molina, & Wiederhold, 1982). Authors in the paper (Lam, Chan, & Yuen, 2000) have suggested a time validity interval-based scheme which concluded that the time period of data item is temporally consistent. Transaction scheduling in mobile environment could give better performance results in mobile environment. Some heuristic policies have also been developed in mobile environment (Singh, & Shanker, 2018a,2018b, 2019a). Authors show in their results that the heuristic policies enhance the system performance with concurrency control protocol (Singh, & Shankar, 2017). Different heuristic approaches have been suggested in distributed real time database (Abbott, & Garcia-Molina, 1992),(Lam, Lee, Hung, & Kao, 1997),(Lee, Lam, Kao, Lam, & Hung, 1996),(Shanker, Misra, & Sarje, 2005). However, some of the heuristics have been developed in mobile environment. Singh et al. have developed heuristic approach which depends on number of write data items present in a transaction (Singh, & Shanker, 2017).The higher priority is assigned to the transactions which have lesser number of data item. In the paper, authors developed a heuristic policy with concurrency control mechanism which shows the better performance in wireless environment.

In paper (Singh, & Shanker, 2019a), authors have suggested another heuristic approach which enhances the system performance. Further, all these heuristic approaches have been developed in mobile environment. Authors work on optimistic approach, which is based on different transactions; however, the last validation phase is done on server side. Lee et al. have discussed various broadcasting methods (Lee, Ng, Chong, & Lam, 2004). They have suggested broadcasting method based on age and dispersion of data item. The broadcast concurrency control using time stamp interval (BCC-TI) is a concurrency control method specially designed for wireless medium (Lee, Lam, & Son, 2002). In this approach, the client site is capable to read the consistent updated data off air without any communication with server site. It is not needed to contact a server site for reading of a data item and read it off air. It minimizes the transaction restart rate and improves the overall system performance. In this BCC-TI approach, it is assumed that some of the transaction can dynamically be adjusted. Authors assumed that the ROTs in the serialization order can be dynamically adjusted by using its timestamp value. During transaction execution, the data conflict can be identified using the data interval shut down. ROT has checked the data conflict with the control information attached with each broadcast cycle. In this approach, the position is adjustable using lower and upper bound of time interval. In case of ROT, if it is non serializable with update transaction which is committed already the position of ROT, is decided by adjusting the upper bound of the individual timestamp-interval. Similarly, if the upper bound is greater value than write time stamp value, the upper bound value is again adjusted to write time stamp value.

Based on this protocol, further authors have developed three protocols named as pure BCC-TI, BCC-TI with versioning and BCC-TI with time validity interval (Lee, Ng, Chong, & Lam, 2004). In Pure BCC-TI, the timestamp interval is adjusted, if the read only transaction reads a data value in broadcast cycle. The read only transaction performs restarting when the given time-stamp interval shut down. Upper bound of timestamp interval is adjusted when a read only transaction needs information from control information. In the BCC-TI approach, the data items versions are used to maintain database consistency. On updating a data item, new version of data item is assigned with a version number. In mobile environment, this approach deals with the temporal data items separately than other data items. The assigned version number is used to determine the ages and dispersion ages from control information broadcasted by the server. The read only transaction is restarted whenever its age difference is more than the threshold value. In the BCC-TI with time validity interval, each mobile transaction is associated with a data deadline. In this approach, temporal data items are assigned an expiration time. If this expiration time is less than the current deadline, the data deadline is assigned the current expiration time value. A number of running mobile transaction performs partial-validation at different mobile sites and its final-validation at the system server-site. In this chapter, a new heuristic approach for broadcasting environment has been developed which shows better results in simulation section.

BROADCASTING HEURISTIC APPROACH

A number of broadcasting methods has been developed in mobile environment (Lee, Ng, Chong, & Lam, 2004). Here, a heuristic approach is added with broadcasting. It is biased to consider only the number of locks for assigning priority. It is needed to check the transaction conflict with other transactions before starting its execution. In earlier research work, researchers (Singh, & Shanker, 2017) have focused only on number of required locks in a transaction. It is unfair to consider only number of locks for assigning priority, hence in this work, a new idea is considered. It should check another parameter such as number of transactions it conflicts with other executing transactions. In this section, a novel heuristic approach named as Count Conflict broadcast heuristic (CCBH) is discussed. In this scheme, the broadcasting of data items of the transactions is essential whose priority is higher and entered into commit phase. Consider a situation when number of actual data items requirement is same for the two transactions then how to assign priority. Here, it is unfair to consider only the number of locks. Before starting, it is assumed that a transaction maintains a set of conflict transactions which consists of the transaction's ids conflicting with it. Before executing transactions, transactions with same number of locks may contain different set of transaction. For example, if T_1 and T_2 have same number of data items and same deadline, scheduler should recheck the set of transactions conflicting with it by comparing the read and write set of transactions. Authors (Lee, Lam, & Kuo, 2004) have already discussed this. In real time environment, it is easy to check the read and write pattern of a transaction. Let us take an example to brief our idea.

$T_1 = R(x)w(y)R(z)R(k)$

$T_2 = R(m)W(n)R(x)R(y)$

Here, both the transactions have same number of data items. Let us assume that their deadline is also same. In this case, it should be required to count the number of transactions conflicting with it. A count procedure (CP_i) of transaction Ti, which counts the number of conflict transaction, should perform before each execution. Further, if the number of transactions conflict with transaction T_1 is less than T_2, then obviously, scheduler should assign T1 as higher (Since, $CP_1 < CP_2$). Assume that DS (T_i) is conflict transaction Set for transaction Ti. For example, DS (T_1) and DS (T2) are defined as given below.

DS (T_1) = {T_2, T_7, T_8} and

DS (T_2) = {T_1, T_3, T_4, T_5,....,T_{15}}

Here, it has been easily seen that the $CP_1 = 3$ and $CP_2 = 15$. Although, the number of data items requirement is same in T_1 and T_2, CCBH broadcasts the data items of T_1 than T_2 due to $CP_1 < CP_2$. Thus, system releases the data items of T_1 and broadcasts these data items in next broadcast cycle. This heuristic approach is discussed in our simulation work. The broadcasting disc broadcasts the new versions of data items. It has been discussed the performance of this heuristic approach in mobile environment in section follow.

MOBILE DISTRIBUTED REAL TIME DATABASE SYSTEM (MDRTDBS) MODEL

A mobile distributed real time database model has taken to perform the scheduling task in mobile environment (Singh, & Shanker, 2017) .The MDRTDBS system model is consists of different sites that are either fixed or mobile in nature. It maintains various components which include the fixed database sites, various moving sites, a number of mobile-support-stations (MSS) and limited database server sites. In the MDRTDBS system model, MSS maintains the information and communicates through wired or wireless medium to moving or fixed sites. Each site maintains a transaction generator (TG) which is responsible to generate transactions using poison's distribution method. Transaction manager is attached to each site which manages the transaction execution in the system. System holds central processing unit, waiting queue and storage devices like main memory disk with each site. Transaction generator role is to generate transactions using poison distribution method. Each site holds a sink and broadcast data-receiver at client side.

SIMULATION PERFORMANCE AND HEURISTIC APPROACH

In this part of the chapter, simulation results will be investigated. The simulator is written in c and based on prior related research in the field of MDRTDBS (Singh, & Shanker, 2017,2019a,2019b), (Shanker, Misra, & Sarje, 2005). The system performance has been investigated using transaction miss rate. A comparison graph which is plotted using collected simulation results. A comparison has been performed to investigate the system performance using discussed heuristic approaches. Heuristic approaches are applied with or without proposing priority-assignment policy to check the system performance. As discussed in earlier sections, there are some pros and cons of using optimistic methods which depend upon the resources and environment provided to the database system. In the next sub section, a study has been done on detailed system performance result obtained during experiment. In simulation experiment, miss rate has been taken as the primary metrics to study the effect of proposed heuristic approaches. Basically, localities of transactions are application dependent mechanism which is not our purpose. It is not our simulation objective to develop and perform policies for specific applications. Further, results in simulation are represented in the form of graph. The intensive simulation results are shown in Figure 2.

It shows that the proposed work is better than the broadcasting-based data cycle method (Bowen, Gopal, Herman, Hickey, Lee, Mansfield, Raitz, & Weinrib, 1992) in mobile environment. Simulation has been performed using the simulation parameter used in paper (singh, & Shanker, 2017,2019a), (Lee, Ng, Chong, & Lam, 2004). Miss rate is calculated for developed heuristic approach and scheme discussed. The mobile sites in the simulation are taken as 50. The size of the database is taken as our earlier work in paper (singh, & Shanker, 2017,2019a). The total number of data items are taken in a transaction may vary from 4 to 8. In simulation, the disconnection chance is taken as 0.5%. As discussed in earlier section, most of the transactions in wireless environment are based on read only transactions. The mobile sites are frequently moved from one network to another. There is a chance of handoff during these processes. In the simulation, maximum 2% handoff chance is considered. It is observed that the simulation result for heuristic approach is better than the other approach. In Figure 2, it is clearly seen that the miss rate is

Figure 1. Mobile distributed real time database system (MDRTDBS) model

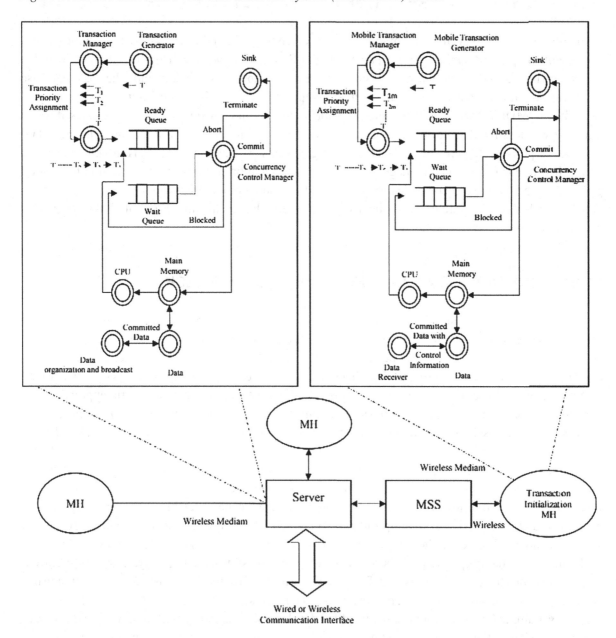

minimum in case of heuristic approach than the data cycle approach. Transaction length consists of the number of data items present in a transaction. It also considers the presence of read only transactions in mobile environment. It is assumed to be 70%. The number of write operation in updated transaction is assumed to be in equal proportion (0.5).

Figure 2. Miss rate (%) vs. transaction length

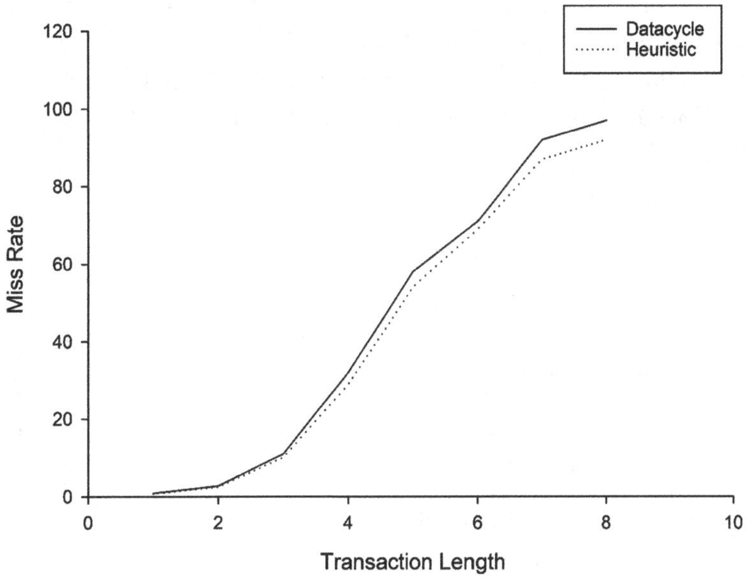

Table 1. Default value settings for simulation

Parameter	Default-Value
Size of database	500
Data size	8 Kb
Uplink channel bandwidth	1.28 Kbps
Downlink channel Bandwidth	2.56Kbps
Disc access	0.02 second
Data updating time	0.004 second
Data items in transaction	4 – 8
Slack time range	2-6
Mobile sites	50
Disconnection chance	0.5 (%)
ROT percentage	70%
Handoff probability	2 (%)

CONCLUSION AND FUTURE SCOPE

Broadcasting schemes have a key role in database transaction execution. Several broadcasting schemes are developed in wireless environment. Mobile environment produces several obstacles in the transaction execution. The flow of data item from server to client should make sure that it will achieve the real time situations. Heuristic approaches make the broadcasting schemes more flexible in wireless environment. In this work, the developed heuristic approach enhances the system performance and speeds up the completion of transaction and minimizes the miss rate. Broadcasting schemes directly affects the database transaction execution in wireless technology. For future work, push based or pull based broadcasting scheme should be improved, so that, mobile sites can be able to commit transaction within the allowed deadline. Concurrency control protocol could be coping with these broadcasting schemes to enhance system performance.

REFERENCES

Abbott, R. K., & Garcia-Molina, H. (1992). Scheduling real-time transactions: A performance evaluation. *ACM Transactions on Database Systems*, *17*(3), 513–560. doi:10.1145/132271.132276

Acharya, S., Alonso, R., Franklin, M., & Zdonik, S. (1995). Broadcast disks: data management for asymmetric communication environments. In *Mobile Computing* (pp. 331–361). Boston, MA: Springer.

Acharya, S., Franklin, M., & Zdonik, S. (1995). Dissemination-based data delivery using broadcast disks. *IEEE Personal Communications*, *2*(6), 50–60. doi:10.1109/98.475988

Acharya, S., Franklin, M., & Zdonik, S. (1997, June). Balancing push and pull for data broadcast. *SIGMOD Record*, *26*(2), 183–194. doi:10.1145/253262.253293

Aksoy, D., & Franklin, M. 1998, March. *Scheduling for large-scale on-demand data broadcasting*. In *Proceedings. IEEE INFOCOM'98, the Conference on Computer Communications. Seventeenth Annual Joint Conference of the IEEE Computer and Communications Societies. Gateway to the 21st Century* (Vol. 2, pp. 651-659). IEEE. 10.1109/INFCOM.1998.665086

Barbará, D. (1999). Mobile computing and databases-a survey. *IEEE Transactions on Knowledge and Data Engineering*, *11*(1), 108–117. doi:10.1109/69.755619

Bowen, T. F., Gopal, G., Herman, G., Hickey, T. M., Lee, K. C., Mansfield, W. H., ... Weinrib, A. (1992). The datacycle architecture. *Communications of the ACM*, *35*(12), 71–82. doi:10.1145/138859.138868

Chen, J., Liu, K., & Lee, V. C. (2009, May). Analysis of data scheduling algorithms in supporting real-time multi-item requests in on-demand broadcast environments. In *2009 IEEE International Symposium on Parallel & Distributed Processing* (pp. 1-8). IEEE

Dykeman, H. D., & Wong, J. W. (1986, January). Scheduling algorithms for videotex systems under broadcast delivery. In *1986 IEEE International Conference on Communications* (pp. 1861-1865). IEEE.

Garcia-Molina, H., & Wiederhold, G. (1982). Read-only transactions in a distributed database. *ACM Transactions on Database Systems*, *7*(2), 209–234. doi:10.1145/319702.319704

Gray, J. N. (1978). Notes on data base operating systems. In *Operating Systems* (pp. 393–481). Berlin: Springer. doi:10.1007/3-540-08755-9_9

Gruenwald, L., Banik, S. M., & Lau, C. N. (2007). Managing real-time database transactions in mobile ad-hoc networks. *Distributed and Parallel Databases*, *22*(1), 27–54. doi:10.100710619-006-7008-2

Hameed, S., & Vaidya, N. H. (1999). Efficient algorithms for scheduling data broadcast. *Wireless Networks*, *5*(3), 183–193. doi:10.1023/A:1019194826654

Hui, C. Y., Ng, J. K. Y., & Lee, V. C. S. (2005, August). On-demand broadcast algorithms with caching on improving response time for real time information dispatch systems. In *11th IEEE International Conference on Embedded and Real-Time Computing Systems and Applications (RTCSA'05)* (pp. 285-288). IEEE.

Imielinski, T., & Badrinath, B. R. (1994). Mobile wireless computing. *Communications of the ACM*, *37*(10), 18–29. doi:10.1145/194313.194317

Imielinski, T., Viswanathan, S., & Badrinath, B. R. (1997). Data on air: Organization and access. *IEEE Transactions on Knowledge and Data Engineering*, *9*(3), 353–372. doi:10.1109/69.599926

Kim, S., Lee, S., & Hwang, C. S. (2003). Using reordering technique for mobile transaction management in broadcast environments. *Data & Knowledge Engineering*, *45*(1), 79–100. doi:10.1016/S0169-023X(02)00155-6

Lam, K. Y., Chan, E., & Yuen, J. C. H. (2000). Approaches for broadcasting temporal data in mobile computing systems. *Journal of Systems and Software*, *51*(3), 175–189. doi:10.1016/S0164-1212(99)00122-3

Lam, K. Y., Kuo, T. W., Tsang, W. H., & Law, G. C. (2000). Concurrency control in mobile distributed real-time database systems. *Information Systems*, *25*(4), 261–286. doi:10.1016/S0306-4379(00)00018-1

Lam, K. Y., Lee, V. C., Hung, S. L., & Kao, B. C. (1997). Priority assignment in distributed real-time databases using optimistic concurrency control. *IEE Proceedings. Computers and Digital Techniques*, *144*(5), 324–330. doi:10.1049/ip-cdt:19971496

Lee, S., Hwang, C. S., & Kitsuregawa, M. (2003). Using predeclaration for efficient read-only transaction processing in wireless data broadcast. *IEEE Transactions on Knowledge and Data Engineering*, *15*(6), 1579–1583. doi:10.1109/TKDE.2003.1245294

Lee, V., Ng, J. K., Chong, J. Y., & Lam, K. W. (2004). Reading temporally consistent data in broadcast disks. *Mobile Computing and Communications Review*, *8*(3), 57–67. doi:10.1145/1031483.1031491

Lee, V. C., Lam, K. W., & Kuo, T. W. (2004). Efficient validation of mobile transactions in wireless environments. *Journal of Systems and Software*, *69*(1-2), 183–193. doi:10.1016/S0164-1212(03)00084-0

Lee, V. C., Lam, K. W., & Son, S. H. (2002). Concurrency control using timestamp ordering in broadcast environments. *The Computer Journal*, *45*(4), 410–422. doi:10.1093/comjnl/45.4.410

Lee, V. C., Lam, K. W., Son, S. H., & Chan, E. Y. (2002). On transaction processing with partial validation and timestamp ordering in mobile broadcast environments. *IEEE Transactions on Computers*, *51*(10), 1196–1211. doi:10.1109/TC.2002.1039845

Lee, V. C., Wu, X., & Ng, J. K. Y. (2006). Scheduling real-time requests in on-demand data broadcast environments. *Real-Time Systems*, *34*(2), 83–99. doi:10.100711241-006-7982-5

Lee, V. C. S., Lam, K., Kao, B. C. M., Lam, K., & Hung, S. (1996). Priority Assignment for Sub-transaction in Distributed Real-Time Databases. *First Int. In Workshop on Real-Time Database Systems*.

Lindström, J. (2003). *Optimistic concurrency control methods for real-time database systems* (Ph.D. Dissertation). Department of Computer Science, University of Helsinki, Finland.

Lo, S. C., & Chen, A. L. P. (2000). An adaptive access method for broadcast data under an error-prone mobile environment. *IEEE Transactions on Knowledge and Data Engineering*, *12*(4), 609–620. doi:10.1109/69.868910

Madria, S. K., Mohania, M., Bhowmick, S. S., & Bhargava, B. (2002). Mobile data and transaction management. *Information Sciences*, *141*(3-4), 279–309. doi:10.1016/S0020-0255(02)00178-0

Mok, E., Leong, H. V., & Si, A. (1999, December). Transaction processing in an asymmetric mobile environment. In *International Conference on Mobile Data Access* (pp. 71-82). Springer. 10.1007/3-540-46669-X_7

Padmanabhan, P., Gruenwald, L., Vallur, A., & Atiquzzaman, M. (2008). A survey of data replication techniques for mobile ad hoc network databases. *The VLDB Journal—The International Journal on Very Large Data Bases, 17*(5), 1143-1164.

Pandey, S., & Shanker, U. (2016). Transaction Execution in Distributed Real-Time Database Systems. *Proceedings of the International Conference on Innovations in information Embedded and Communication Systems*, 96-100.

Pandey, S., & Shanker, U. (2017a). IDRC: A Distributed Real-Time Commit Protocol. *Procedia Computer Science*, *125*, 290–296. doi:10.1016/j.procs.2017.12.039

Pandey, S., & Shanker, U. (2017b). On Using Priority Inheritance Based Distributed Static Two Phase Locking Protocol. *Proceedings of the International Conference on Data and Information System (ICDIS)*, 179-188.

Pandey, S., & Shanker, U. (2018a). A One Phase Priority Inheritance Commit Protocol. *Proceedings of the 14th International Conference on Distributed Computing and Information Technology (ICDCIT)*. 10.1007/978-3-319-72344-0_24

Pandey, S., & Shanker, U. (2018b). Priority Inversion in DRTDBS: Challenges and Resolutions. *Proceedings of the ACM India Joint International Conference on Data Science and Management of Data (CoDS-COMAD '18)*, 305-309. 10.1145/3152494.3167976

Pandey, S., & Shanker, U. (2018c). CART: A Real-Time Concurrency Control Protocol. In *22nd International Database Engineering & Applications Symposium (IDEAS 2018)*. ACM.

Pitoura, E., & Chrysanthis, P. K. (1999, June). Scalable processing of read-only transactions in broadcast push. In *Proceedings. 19th IEEE International Conference on Distributed Computing Systems (Cat. No. 99CB37003)* (pp. 432-439). IEEE.

Pitoura, E., & Samaras, G. (2012). *Data management for mobile computing* (Vol. 10). Springer Science & Business Media.

Ramamritham, K. (1993). Real-time databases. *Distributed and Parallel Databases*, *1*(2), 199–226. doi:10.1007/BF01264051

Shanker, U., Misra, M., & Sarje, A. K. (2005, July). Priority assignment heuristic to cohorts executing in parallel. In *Proceedings of the 9th WSEAS International Conference on Computers* (pp. 1-6). World Scientific and Engineering Academy and Society (WSEAS).

Shanker, U., Misra, M., & Sarje, A. K. (2006). SWIFT—A new real time commit protocol. *Distributed and Parallel Databases, 20*(1), 29–56. doi:10.100710619-006-8594-8

Shanker, U., Misra, M., & Sarje, A. K. (2008). Distributed real time database systems: Background and literature review. *Distributed and Parallel Databases, 23*(2), 127–149. doi:10.100710619-008-7024-5

Shanmugasundaram, J., Nithrakashyap, A., Sivasankaran, R., & Ramamritham, K. (1999, June). Efficient concurrency control for broadcast environments. *SIGMOD Record, 28*(2), 85–96. doi:10.1145/304181.304190

Shigiltchoff, O., Chrysanthis, P. K., & Pitoura, E. (2004, January). Energy efficient access in multiversion broadcast environment. In *IEEE International Conference on Mobile Data Management, 2004. Proceedings. 2004* (p. 168). IEEE. 10.1109/MDM.2004.1263058

Singh, P. K., & Shanker, U. (2017, September). Priority heuristic in mobile distributed real time database using optimistic concurrency control. In *2017 23RD Annual International Conference in Advanced Computing and Communications (ADCOM)* (pp. 44-49). IEEE. 10.1109/ADCOM.2017.00014

Singh, P. K., & Shanker, U. (2018, January). A New Priority Heuristic Suitable in Mobile Distributed Real Time Database System. In *International Conference on Distributed Computing and Internet Technology* (pp. 330-335). Springer. 10.1007/978-3-319-72344-0_29

Singh, P. K., & Shanker, U. (2018). A Priority Heuristic Policy in Mobile Distributed Real-Time Database System. In *Advances in Data and Information Sciences* (pp. 211–221). Singapore: Springer. doi:10.1007/978-981-10-8360-0_20

Singh, P.K., & Shanker, U. (2019). Transaction Scheduling Heuristics in Mobile Distributed Real Time Database System. *Recent Advances in Computer Science and Communications.* doi:10.2174/2213275 912666190809120654

Singh, P. K., & Shanker, U. (2019). *Priority Heuristic in MDRTDBS. International Journal of Sensors, Wireless Communications and Control.* doi:10.2174/2210327909666191119104550

Song, X., & Liu, J. W. S. (1995). Maintaining temporal consistency: Pessimistic vs. optimistic concurrency control. *IEEE Transactions on Knowledge and Data Engineering, 7*(5), 786–796. doi:10.1109/69.469820

Su, C. J., Tassiulas, L., & Tsotras, V. J. (1999). Broadcast scheduling for information distribution. *Wireless Networks, 5*(2), 137–147. doi:10.1023/A:1019134607998

Vaidya, N. H., & Hameed, S. (1999). Scheduling data broadcast in asymmetric communication environments. *Wireless Networks, 5*(3), 171–182. doi:10.1023/A:1019142809816

Wong, J. W. (1988). Broadcast delivery. *Proceedings of the IEEE, 76*(12), 1566–1577. doi:10.1109/5.16350

Xing, Z., & Gruenwald, L. (2007). *Issues in designing concurrency control techniques for mobile ad-hoc network databases. Technical Report.* School of Computer Science.

Xu, J., Tang, X., & Lee, W. C. (2005). Time-critical on-demand data broadcast: Algorithms, analysis, and performance evaluation. *IEEE Transactions on Parallel and Distributed Systems*, *17*(1), 3–14.

Xuan, P., Sen, S., Gonzalez, O., Fernandez, J., & Ramamritham, K. (1997, June). Broadcast on demand: Efficient and timely dissemination of data in mobile environments. In *Proceedings Third IEEE Real-Time Technology and Applications Symposium* (pp. 38-48). IEEE. 10.1109/RTTAS.1997.601342

Chapter 6
Improving Scalability in Replicated DRTDBS

Pratik Shrivastava
Madan Mohan Malaviya University of Technology, India

ABSTRACT

The demand for scalability in replicated distributed real-time database systems (RDRTDBS) is still explorative and, despite an increase in real-time applications, many challenges and issues remain in designing a more scalable system. The objective is to improve the scalability of the system during system scale up with new replica sites. Existing research has been mainly conducted in maintaining replica consistency between different replicas via replication protocol. However, very little research has been conducted towards improving scalability and maintaining mutual consistency and timeliness. Consequently, the ultimate aim of this chapter is to improve scalability in RDRTDBS such that performance of the system does not degrade even though new replica sites are added.

INTRODUCTION

In the current scenario, data is playing a prominent role in many applications and the back-end database system of these application stores such valuable data. This database system requires an efficient and effective management technique (Berrington J., 2007) such that database operation in terms of insertion, deletion, updation, and searching can be processed more easily (Ramakrishnan, R. & Gehrke J., 2000; Ullman, J. D., 1984). Additionally, these database operations can be processed in the centralized manner or distributed manner. The decision to process database operations in the centralized location or distributed location will depend upon the client's requirement (Garcia-Molina H. & Lindsay B., 1990; Bernstein, P. A. et al., 1987). If the application is designed for a small scale, then it is advisable to process database operation in a centralized location. However, if the application is on a large scale, then it is advisable to process database operation in a distributed fashion. Despite this, there are some other factors also that need to be considered such as the number of requests, number of system resources, and so on to quickly decide about the processing location for data operations.

DOI: 10.4018/978-1-7998-2491-6.ch006

Real time database system (RTDBS) in an emerging area of this database system which is specifically designed to work with real time systems (Aldarmi S. A., 1998) such as space shuttle, flight control system and some others. This database system has a stringent requirement to maintain the timeliness and temporal consistency of the admitted real time transaction (RTT) such that the system can be saved from catastrophic failure (Ulusoy Ö., 1995). As this database system continues to evolve, RTDBS is used in a large number of real time applications and is generating massive amounts of data. Distributed real time database system (DRTDBS) is an extension of RTDBS which is specifically designed to work with such a huge amount of data in a timely manner. The primary objective of DRTDBS is to satisfy the timeliness of the admitted RTT and also to maintain the temporal consistency of real time data items. In the past, large number of researches are conducted in different directions of the DRTDBS such that the performance of the system gets increased. These research directions include concurrency control protocol, buffer management, scheduling RTTs, commit protocol, replication technique and so on (Shanker U. et al., 2008).

Replication technique (RT) is the most focused area of research for the researcher in the DRTDBS. In this technique, data replicas are placed in different database sites such that admitted RTT can be processed locally. This extension of DRTDBS with RT is termed as RDRTDBS. Data replicas in DRTDBS is either fully, partially, or virtually fully replicated (Mathiason, G. et al., 2007, August). In Fully RDRTDBS, every admitted RTT is processed locally because, in the fully replicated scheme, all the nodes hold the same data copy. Thus, meeting the RTT deadline in RDRTDBS becomes easy. This replication scheme is suitable for a read intensive environment because read RTT uses a shared lock. This lock allows a greater number of read RTT to work on the same data item concurrently. However, a fully replicated scheme suffers from unnecessary bandwidth utilization, wastage of system resources, and unnecessary replica site updation. Partially replication scheme solves such identified issues more easily because, in partial replication, replicated sites are partially replicated and unnecessary bandwidth utilization gets overcome. The decision of placing the data replica in the partially replicated environment will depend on the number of requests and from the location of requests. This type of replication scheme is suitable for an update intensive environment where the majority of RTTs are of update in nature. Virtual full replication solves the issue of both the replication types more effectively. Thus, this replication type is more suitable for update and read an intensive environment. Apart from the replication type, the replica concurrency control protocol (RCCP)/replication protocol (RP)/replica update technique (RUT) plays a major role in the replication technique. RCCP processes to maintain replica consistency in between replicated sites such that consistent value can be provided to the admitted RTT. Although, majority of researchers have conducted research towards RCCP (Xiong M. et al., 2002; Son S. H. & Kouloumbis S., 1993; Peddi P. & DiPippo L. C., 2002; Haj Said A. et al., 2008; Shrivastava P. & Shanker U., 2018, August; Shrivastava P. & Shanker U., 2018; Syberfeldt S., 2007; Gustavsson S. et al.,2004; Kim Y. K., 1996; Mathiason G. et al., 2007; Son S. H. & Zhang F., 1995, April; Shrivastava P. & Shanker U., 2019, January; Son S. H. et al., 1996; Salem R. et al., 2016; Shrivastava P. & Shanker U., 2018, December; Gustavsson S. et al. 2005, April), research towards scalability, security (Shrivastava P. & Shanker U., 2020), dependency preservation, fault tolerance etc. are still in very infancy stage (Shrivastava P. & Shanker U., 2018 August). Thus, in the current chapter, our objective is to improve the scalability of the RDRTDBS such that more replica sites can be added without degrading the performance of the system.

In recently published article (Shrivastava P. & Shanker U., 2018), the authors have proposed a system model that maintains the replica consistency via the middleware. This system model consists of the master site to process only write and update RTT, slave site to process only read RTT and middleware to maintain the replica consistency and the client. This proposed system model transfers the load of maintaining replica consistency from the database kernel to the middleware. This shifting action makes the master/slave site to process only RTTs. The data replicas of this system model are fully replicated, thus meeting the timeliness demand of RTT becomes easy. Our main objective is to extend such a system model to improve the scalability issue of the RDRTDBS. The ultimate reason behind selecting such system model is because existing system models (Xiong M. et al., 2002; Gustavsson S. et al. 2005, April; Son S. H. et al., 1996; Shrivastava P. & Shanker U., 2018, December; Gustavsson S. et al.,2004; Son S. H. & Zhang F., 1995, April; Haj Said A. et al., 2008; Shrivastava P. & Shanker U., 2019, January; Son S. H. & Kouloumbis S., 1993; Kim Y. K., 1996; Peddi P. & DiPippo L. C., 2002; Salem R. et al., 2016; Shrivastava P. & Shanker U., 2018, August; Mathiason G. et al., 2007; Syberfeldt S., 2007) are kernel-based and my objective is to shift the load of maintaining mutual consistency and scalability solution in the external location such that real time requirement of DRTDBS may easily be satisfied. In order to improve the scalability of the RDRTDBS, it is necessary to reduce the replication effort such that majority of the system resources are invested in the timeliness demand of RTT. Our replication effort is defined as a measure to express the effort of making all the replica sites in a common consistent state.

In order to achieve our intended objective, the developed system identifies the frequent access pattern of the data object. Based on such identification, replica sites are updated with such data items. This frequently access data objects are termed as hot data objects which are most needed by the admitted RTTs. The main reason behind proposing such a solution is in minimizing the transaction miss percentage because the performance of the system is calculated on the number of successfully completed RTTs. Thus, to satisfy the demand of admitted RTTs, frequent data objects are identified and are updated such that admitted RTTs get completed within their deadline. Apart from the hot data objects, cold data objects are updated on demand. Thus, based on the client request, mostly needed data items are identified and are updated. However, in case of any new demand from the client admitted recently, the on-demand approach is used to update the data item.

The rest of the chapter is organized as follows. The existing system models with their pros and cons are presented in the background section. Later, I have briefly discussed the main theme of the work. The solution to the issues discussed in the previous section is presented in the solution and recommendation section. The acceptance of any proposed approach requires proof. Thus, after the solution section, the correctness of our proposed approach has been done in the correctness proof section. Future research direction for the upcoming researchers is also discussed in the future research direction section. Finally, I have presented the conclusion of my chapter.

BACKGROUND

The DRTDBS is a time-constrained system and has a strict requirement to meet the RTT deadline irrespective of logical consistency (Shanker U. et al., 2008). Three types of RTT are processed in the RDRTDBS listed as hard RTT, soft RTT, and firm RTT. Hard RTT has a strict requirement to meet the RTT deadline. Missing the deadline for such type of RTT might cause heavy economical loss or serious damage in the system. Thus, hard RTT is always given high priority in the allocation of resources as compared to other RTTs. Firm RTT leaves no value in the system (Wang F. et al., 2011) on missing its deadline. Thus, these RTTs are always assigned low priority as compared to hard RTTs and are always aborted on missing its deadline. Despite hard RTT and firm RTT, soft RTT leaves some value in the system. Thus, these RTTs are not immediately aborted on missing its deadline. Although, DRTDBS has a stringent requirement to meet RTT deadlines, the presence of a single version of the data object and limitation of system resource causes the majority of RTTs to miss their deadline due to their distributed processing.

Replication technqiue (Shrivastava P. & Shanker U., 2018, August) is used in the DRTDBS to enhance the performance. The necessary condition to achieve such an advantage is to maintain replica consistency between replicated sites. Thus, majority of researchers have conducted the research on designing an efficient and effective kernel-based RCCP (Lokhande D. B., & Dhainje P. B., 2019; Shrivastava P. & Shanker U., 2018; Peddi P. & DiPippo L. C., 2002; Salem R. et al., 2016; Syberfeldt S., 2007; Xiong M. et al., 2002; Son S. H. & Kouloumbis S., 1993; Gustavsson S. et al. 2005, April; Shrivastava P. & Shanker U., 2019, January; Kim Y. K., 1996; Haj Said A. et al., 2008; Mathiason G. et al., 2007; Shrivastava P. & Shanker U., 2018, August; Shrivastava P. & Shanker U., 2018, December; Son S. H. & Zhang F., 1995, April; Son S. H. et al., 1996; Gupta A. K., & Swaroop V., 2018; Gustavsson S. et al.,2004). These kernel-based RCCPs operate from the database kernel to maintain replica consistency. Different researchers have mainly optimized the database kernel such that real time constraint gets easily satisfied. Although these RCCPs are specifically designed to maintain mutual consistency, there exist some more factors that affect the scalability feature of the RCCP. These factors are replica size, replica update frequency, replica distance, and replication type. These all mentioned factors exist in the system model. In order to improve the scalability of the system, these mentioned factors need to be solved. Additionally, the scalability of the RCCP depends on the number of update/write RTTs admitted to the system. As the number of update or write RTTs increases, a greater number of updates are generated and propagated to all the master such that all master sites reach to the common consistent state. Thus, the scalability of the RCCP also depends on the number of update /write RTTs. Our objective is to develop a replication type of system model that plays a major role in improving the scalability of the RDRTDBS.

After exploring the research papers, it has been found that in existing system model data replicas are fully, partially, or virtually fully replicated. Fully replicated system models (Pu C. & Leff A., 1990; Son S. H. & Zhang F., 1995, April; Gustavsson S. et al.,2004; Haj Said A. et al., 2008; Xiong M. et al., 2002) allow every admitted RTTs to get processed locally such that deadline requirement of RTTs gets more easily satisfied. In the fully replicated system model, each replica is holding the same data copy which prevents the distributed processing of admitted RTTs. Although, fully replicated system model shows promising results when the system grows; however, the scalability of the system gets decreased. Additionally, a fully replicated system suffers from the issues of unnecessary bandwidth utilization, unnecessary site updation, and unnecessary system resources utilization. Thus, fully replication type is used for small and medium scale systems. Despite such mentioned issues, Mathiason, G. et al. have proposed an improved version of fully replication type (Mathiason, G. et al., 2007, August) named as virtually fully RDRTDBS (ViFul). In ViFul, all replicated sites fully hold the same data copies such that admitted RTT gets processed locally and only required data items are updated such that unnecessary bandwidth utilization, unnecessary site updation and wastage of resources get prevented. However, when any random RTT gets admitted in the system who have dynamic data requirement causes randomly admitted RTT to miss its deadline. The reason behind missing the deadline is because dynamically required data items exist in the inconsistent state and processing conducted on such stale value causes heavy loss. Thus, for randomly admitted RTTs, ViFul is not fully scalable.

In order to solve such mentioned issues, the system model is partially replicated. In the partially replicated system model, each replica site partially holds the data copies of the real-time and non-real time data items such that admitted RTT gets executed locally. Some researchers have worked in this research direction and designed partially replicated system model ((Ulusoy Ö. 1994; Kim Y. K., 1996; Peddi P. & DiPippo L. C., 2002; Srivastava A. et al.2012; Shrivastava P. & Shanker U., 2018; Shrivastava P. & Shanker U., 2019, January)). The partial replicated system model propagates the replica update message to only those replica sites which are holding the same data copy and prevents the wastage of system resources. Thus, a partially replicated system model offers more scalability than a fully replicated system model. Although, partially replicated system model is better than a fully replicated system model, but in the majority of cases, admitted RTT gets processed in a distributed manner. Distributed processing of the short duration admitted RTT might cause RTT to miss its deadline. Thus, in the partially replicated system model, the prediction of data items for randomly admitted RTT is required that preliminary identifies the data requirement of RTT and stores the data copies of such data items in the local site.

Apart from replication type, existing system models (Lokhande D. B., & Dhainje P. B., 2019; Shrivastava P. & Shanker U., 2018; Peddi P. & DiPippo L. C., 2002; Salem R. et al., 2016; Syberfeldt S., 2007; Xiong M. et al., 2002; Son S. H. & Kouloumbis S., 1993; Gustavsson S. et al. 2005, April; Shrivastava P. & Shanker U., 2019, January; Kim Y. K., 1996; Haj Said A. et al., 2008; Mathiason G. et al., 2007; Shrivastava P. & Shanker U., 2018, August; Shrivastava P. & Shanker U., 2018, December; Son S. H. & Zhang F., 1995, April; Son S. H. et al., 1996; Gupta A. K., & Swaroop V., 2018; Gustavsson S. et al.,2004) is an example of optimized version of database kernel but our argument is that the database kernel can be optimized up to a certain point only because more and more optimization in the database kernel might decrease the performance of the system in place of increasing the performance. Thus, a solution is required that transfers a load of maintaining replica consistency in another location and decreases the database kernel load such that kernel processes the other work of database kernel and system efficiency gets improved. Recently, in the paper (Shrivastava P. & Shanker U., 2018), a solution is proposed that transfers the load of maintaining the mutual consistency from the database kernel to the external location. This proposed solution not only decreases the load of the database kernel but also makes the utilization of the system resources more effectively.

From this discussion, we have identified that both fully replicated, and partially replicated system model have their own pros and cons. Designing a scalable system model for any real time applications needs to consider different factors such as whether the size of the system is static or dynamic ?, whether the system is read intensive or update intensive ?, whether admitted RTT has a dynamic requirement of data items? network structure? and so on. However, the primary factor that needs to be considered for the scalable system model is the replication type and RCCP. Thus, thinking from the future perceptive, it is necessary to design a system model that maintains the real time requirements of RDRTDBS (i.e. timeliness, mutual consistency, and temporal consistency) with improving the scalability of the system during system scale-up.

Overall from this discussion, we can deduce that in RDRTDBS both system model and RCCP have a strong relationship to maintain mutual consistency and improving scalability.

MAIN FOCUS OF THE CHAPTER

From the previous section, I have deduced that the most focused area of research in the RDRTDBS is to maintain the replica consistency between replicated sites. The main reason behind conducting such research is to allow admitted RTT to get processed locally on the consistent value of the real data item and non-real time data item such that consistent result gets returned to the user. Thus, researchers have concentrated on satisfying replica consistency. Satisfying replica consistency becomes more complicated when new replica sites are being added dynamically or existing replica sites are being stopped. Thus, system size plays a major role in maintaining replica consistency. This issue is termed as scalability issue and it is directly linked with the system model of the RDRTDBS.

From the literature survey, we have concluded that existing system model of the work (Pu C. & Leff A., 1990; Son S. H. & Zhang F., 1995, April; Gustavsson S. et al.,2004; Haj Said A. et al., 2008; Xiong M. et al., 2002) holds the full copy of data replica and the system model of the paper (Pu C. & Leff A., 1990; Son S. H. & Zhang F., 1995, April; Gustavsson S. et al.,2004; Haj Said A. et al., 2008; Xiong M. et al., 2002) is acceptable to work for small scale system. However, when the system grows from a small to medium scale, the complexity to maintain the scalability also increases. Thus, it is necessary to propose a solution that improves the scalability of the system during system scale up and allows every admitted RTT to be processed locally. Moreover, I am concentrating to solve the issues of a fully replicated system model because only a fully replicated system allows every admitted RTT to process locally. Although admitted RTT is dynamic or periodic and has random data requirement, RTT processed locally.

Although existing system models are acceptable to satisfy the timeliness demand of RDRTDBS, it suffers from the above-mentioned issues of unnecessary bandwidth utilization, unnecessary replica updation, wastage of system resources and scalability. Resolving such identified issues in the fully RDRTDBS is a complicated task because existing solutions operate in the kernel and optimization of the kernel can be done up to a certain point. Thus, it is necessary to propose a solution that resolves such identified issues more effectively and efficiently. As already mentioned in our introductory section that authors (Shrivastava P. & Shanker U., 2018) have proposed a solution for maintaining mutual consistency via the middleware. This system consists of a master site, slave site, user and middleware. Middleware itself consists of different sub-layers such as data analyzer, conflict detection & correction, and propagation. The data analyzer is the first sub-layer of the middleware that decomposes the RTT into the set of read/write operations. These decomposed operations are then forwarded to the conflict detection & correction sub-layer where the conflict between existing RTTs and admitted RTT is checked. After identification of conflict, a schedule is generated for the RTTs following strict correctness criteria. These scheduled RTTs are then forwarded to the propagation sub-layer to be propagated to the master sites. The master site receives the RTTs from the middleware, identifies the RTT type, and based on its type, process the RTT. If the RTT is read type, then the master site will propagate such RTT into the least loaded slave site. Similarly, if the RTT is write or update RTT, then all master sites processes such RTT on the local site to maintain the consistency of the real time or non-real time data. After processing the RTT in the master/slave site, the result is sent to the client via middleware. Although, this existing solution maintains the mutual consistency easily, when the system grows from small scale to the medium, the complexity of maintaining the mutual consistency between different master/slave sites gets increased ultimately affecting the scalability of the system. Thus, a solution is required in this existing system model that simultaneously maintains the replica consistency and scalability of the system.

In order to achieve the objective, middleware proposed in (Shrivastava P. & Shanker U., 2018) is extended with the inclusion of a sub-layer named as scale sub-layer. This proposed sub-layer counts the frequency of each non-data item and non-real time data item whose frequency is greater than user-defined value. It will be scheduled and forwarded to the master site to be processed. However, non-real time data items of master site, whose frequency value is less than the user-defined value, will not be scheduled and will not be forwarded to the master site for processing. Thus, master sites only have to process those write RTTs whose update value is required by the forthcoming read RTTs. However, if any random new read RTT, whose data requirement is unknown, is admitted in the system, then in such a case on-demand updating of the non-data item is done by the middleware such that randomly admitted RTT gets processed successfully.

Overall, the issue of maintaining scalability and mutual consistency in RDRTDBS is solved via my proposed scalable algorithm embedded in the system model (Shrivastava P. & Shanker U., 2018). The extended system model simultaneously satisfies the real time requirements of the RDRTDBS such as mutual consistency, timeliness, and scalability.

SOLUTIONS AND RECOMMENDATIONS

The normal processing of extended system model (Shrivastava P. & Shanker U., 2018) including communication network, transaction model with the proposed scalability algorithm is shown in figure 1.

Communication Network

Communication between master site, slave site, and middleware is conducted through the network. Thus, the communication network plays a role in improving the scalability of the system. The client submits the request and is primarily forwarded to the middleware via the network. Middleware processes such admitted RTT, and after processing, broadcasted it to the master site via the network. For an update and write RTT, middleware uses total order broadcast. Through total order broadcast, all master sites receive the RTTs in the same order such that simultaneously all master sites consistently reach a consistent state.

Transaction Model

In our extended system model, the user interacts with the system by submitting the request in the form of RTT. RTT is basically a set of operation which operates on the data item value present in the system. Admitted RTTs might conflict with each other if they manipulate the same data item. Conflict occurs when in conflicted RTT, one of the operations is write type. Multiple read RTT does not conflict with each other because read RTT uses shared lock and shared lock allows more than one RTT to operate on the same data item. Additionally, if the processing of the RTTs follows strict consistency criteria, then the consistency of the system will always be satisfied.

Figure 1. Scalable system model of the RDRTDBS

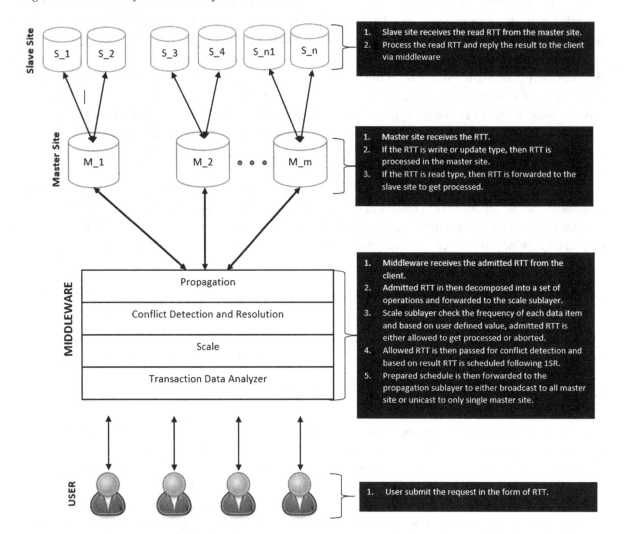

Scale Sub-layer

In this system model, as already mentioned that the main processing of maintaining replica consistency in between replicated sites is conducted by the middleware. The middleware primarily decomposes the admitted RTT into the set of data operations. These identified operations and their data operands are then forwarded to the proposed sub-layer named as scale sub-layer. The proposed scale sub-layer is the main layer that maintains the scalability of the system. This is the necessary step because, in order to maintain the scalability, it is necessary to prevent the processing of unnecessary work such as system resource utilization, bandwidth utilization, and data items updation. This unnecessary work decreases the performance of the system in terms of transaction miss ratio (TMR). In order to conduct such mentioned work, the processing of write RTT, whose updated value is utilized by the read RTT, is only allowed. In the scale sub-layer, no consideration of the update RTT has been done because update RTT is treated as hard RTT and missing the deadline of such RTT will cause serious damage in the system. Thus, these

RTT are always executed in the master site. The decision for the processing of write RTT depends on the frequency of each non-real data item. The frequency of each non-real time data item is compared with the user-defined value. If the frequency of any non-real time data item value crosses the user-defined limit, then such write RTT is forwarded to the conflict detection & resolution sub-layer. After verifying conflict, admitted RTT is then scheduled. Scheduled RTT is then forwarded to the propagation sub-layer to be broadcasted or unicasted to the master/slave sites. The algorithm code for data analyzer, conflict detection & correction, propagation sub-layer is already given in (Shrivastava P. & Shanker U., 2018). The proposed scale sub-layer holds the counter of each data item and based on admitted RTT, such a counter is incremented. The algorithm code of the proposed scale sub-layer is given as follows.

```
Result: RTTs
Requested Write Transaction Tre;
for each DATA_ITEM exist in Tre do
    Increment counter of DATA_ITEM;
end
If counter of Tre crosses the user-defined limit then
Forward Tre to the conflict detection;
Else
Abort the Tre;
```

Let us consider a real time scenario to understand the scalability issue of the system. Assume a system is consisting of N master sites, 2N slave sites, M number of clients and middleware. The client submits the request in the form of write RTT, update RTT or read RTT. Admitted RTT is used to access the updated value of real time data items and non-real time data items. These updated values are manipulated in the master site or slave site to timely return the consistent result to the user. Suppose four read RTTs are admitted in the system, their set of operations is given below.

```
TR1: R (RTD1), R (RTD2), R (NRTD1);
TR2: R (NRTD1), R (NRTD2), R (RTD1), R (RTD2);
TR3: R (NRTD1), R (NRTD2), R (RTD3), R (RTD4);
TR4: R (NRTD2), R (NRTD3), R (RTD3), R (RTD4);
```

Similarly, four write RTTs are admitted in the system to update non-real time data, the set of operations is as follows.

```
TW1: R (NRTD1), W (NRTD1);
TW2: R (NRTD2), W (NRTD2);
TW3: R (NRTD3), W (NRTD3);
TW3: R (NRTD4), W (NRTD4);
```

Despite read and write RTT, four update RTTs are also admitted in the system to update real time data, the set of operations is as follows.

```
TU1: R (RTD1), W (RTD1);
TU2: R (RTD2), W (RTD2);
TU3: R (RTD3), W (RTD3);
TU4: R (RTD4), W (RTD4);
```

After admittance of these RTTs in the middleware, primarily the data analyzer decomposes the RTTs and produces the result. This result is then forwarded to the scale sub-layer to decide which RTT can process and which RTT is prevented to be processed. In order to conduct such step, scale sub-layer checks the frequency of the non-real time data item because non-real time data item is treated as firm RTT and missing its deadline might not cause a heavy loss in the system. Despite non-real time data item, no checking of the frequency of real time data item is done because real time data item is treated as hard RTT and missing its deadline might cause a heavy loss in the system. Thus, these RTTs are auto permitted for processing in the system. Similarly, no checking for read RTTs is done also because read RTTs are processed in the slave site. Thus, in order to decrease the burden of network and site, the model controls the processing of only write RTT. In order to control the processing of write RTT, it basically checks the counter of each non-real time data item against the user-defined limit. if the counter value crosses the user-defined limit, then such admitted write RTT can process in the middleware else admitted write RTT is queued in the local waiting queue already held by the scale sub-layer. The local queue holds the write RTT until an on-demand request is generated by the middleware for the newly admitted read RTT. Moreover, write RTT is prevented to broadcast to the master site until it is required. Thus, an argument can be done that through scale sub-layer one can prevent unnecessary bandwidth utilization. Similarly, if any non-real time data item is not used for a long interval of time, then its counter is again reset to the original value such that unnecessary updation of the non-real time data item can be prevented. Additionally, one can also conclude that only required non-real time data item is processed in the system that will ultimately prevent the wastage of the system resources. Let us suppose that the user-defined limit for each non-real time data item NRTD1, NRTD2, NRTD3, and NRTD4 is 2 and the counter value of each non-real time data item is set to 0. Thus, based on the admittance of the read RTT only 2 write RTT (i.e. TW1 and TW2) can be processed in the middleware and the remaining 2 write RTT (i.e. TW3 and TW4) is kept in the waiting queue. The final counter value of each non-real time is given below.

```
NRTD1 -> COUNTER1=3
NRTD2 -> COUNTER2=3
NRTD3 -> COUNTER1=1
NRTD4 -> COUNTER1=0
```

After processing in the scale sub-layer, TR1, TR2, TR3, TR4, TW1, TW2, TU1, TU2, TU3, and TU4 are forwarded to the conflict detection & resolution layer to identify the conflict and scheduled by following strict correctness criteria (i.e. 1SR). This schedule is then forwarded to the propagation sub-layer for broadcasting or unicasting to the master site.

CORRECTNESS PROOF OF SCALE SUBLAYER

As already mentioned, the scalability of the RDRTDBS depends on the three factors: bandwidth utilization, system resources utilization and the number of update/write operations. Thus, in order to improve the scalability of the system, it is necessary to solve such issues. Through proposing the solution of scalability, dynamically addition and deletion of database sites can be easily handled and a greater number of RTTs get completed within their deadline. In this section, the correctness of proposed scale sub-layer has been done that maintains the scalability of the system more easily.

Lemma 1: Scale sub-layer prevents wastage of system resources.

Proof: In the existing system model, request in the form of RTT is directly admitted from the client to the master/slave site. Master/slave process the task of assigning a deadline, conflict detection & resolution, and scheduling. This whole process uses the CPU cycles. However, if this admitted RTT gets aborted due to preemption from high priority RTT or waiting for the data item, system resources get wasted. Thus, in order to efficiently utilize the system resources, it is necessary to preliminary decide whether admitted RTT can commit or not. The extended system model performs the mentioned task of deadline assignment, priority assignment and so on in the middleware such that master only processes the RTT to update the value of temporal data item or non-temporal data item. This preliminary detection in the middleware allows the master/slave site to process only finalized and scheduled RTT. For instance, let RTT T1 is admitted in an existing system model, where master/slave sites process all the tasks of deadline assignment, priority assignment and so on. Let t1 clock cycles are required to conduct all these mentioned steps. Later, t2 CPU cycles are required to process the T1 in the master site. Thus, the total cycles required to complete the T1 in the master/slave site are t1+t2. However, in our extended system model, t1 CPU cycles are used in the middleware and t2 CPU cycles are used in the master site which makes existing t1 CPU cycles to be utilized for completion of another RTT. Despite saving CPU cycles in the master site, the proposed scale sub-layer also allows the processing of those write RTTs whose updated non-temporal data value is required in the future. Overall, it can be concluded that the proposed scale sub-layer prevents the wastage of system resources and allows the processing of only required RTTs.

Lemma 2 Scale sub-layer prevents unnecessary updation on the master site.

Proof: As already proved in our Lemma 1, scale sub-layer allows the processing of all update RTTs because update RTTs are treated as hard RTT and missing its deadline may cause heavy economic loss. However, scale sub-layer allows the processing of selected write RTTs because non-temporal data items, whose updated value is not required in the future, may cause unnecessary updation. Thus, only selected write RTTs can process in the master sites to update non temporal data items. Overall, we can conclude that our proposed scale sub-layer prevents unnecessary processing in the master site.

Lemma 3 Scale sub-layer prevents the unnecessary utilization of the bandwidth.

Proof: This is the third issue that decreases the scalability of the system. In previous system models, all admitted RTTs are submitted in the master site to be processed. Probably, after admittance, some RTTs get aborted because of low priority value or waiting to access the conflicted data item. Aborted RTTs cause the wastage of network bandwidth because the decision to get commit or abort will depend on the master site status (i.e. the number of processing RTTs, waiting queue to get data access and so on). In the extended system model, read RTT is unicasted to any master site and such site unicast the read RTT to the least loaded slave site. An update RTT is broadcasted and are processed in the master sites because these RTTs are treated as hard deadline RTT. Only selected write RTTs are doing updates requiring non-temporal data items because of these RTTs update those non-temporal data item values whose updated value may be required by the future coming to RTTs. Overall, the proposed scale sub-layer prevents unnecessary bandwidth utilization.

FUTURE RESEARCH DIRECTIONS

Apart from our proposed scale sub-layer, there are still some more research directions that need to be taken care of.

1. To maintain QoS in the system.
2. To enforce security policy in the RDRTDBS to prevent unauthorized access
3. To maintain the minimum availability of the system.
4. To adaptively maintain the desired performance of the system.
5. To enforce the dependency relationship in the middleware.
6. To encode the original message into a smaller set of packets to minimize the communication issue.

CONCLUSION

Replication Technique is usually used in the DRTDBS to increase its performance in terms of availability, reliability, and fault-tolerance. Data replicas in RDRTDBS are either fully, partially, or virtually fully replicated where each replication type has its own pros and cons. In this chapter, a solution for scalability in fully RDRTDBS has been proposed which is an extension of the middleware proposed in (Shrivastava P. & Shanker U., 2018) where middleware maintains the mutual consistency of data replicas. This extended system model calculates the frequency of each data item and based on user-defined value RTT who has crossed such value can proceed to get processed in the master/slave site. However, if randomly any new demand is admitted, then the on-demand technique is used to update required data items such that admitted RTTs get processed with consistent value. It is desirable to implement this extended system model on RDRTDBS and evaluate the performance of the system. This is currently in the development stage.

REFERENCES

Aldarmi, S. A. (1998). *Real-time database systems: concepts and design*. Report-University of York Department of Computer Science YCS.

Bernstein, P. A., Hadzilacos, V., & Goodman, N. (1987). *Concurrency control and recovery in database systems*. Academic Press.

Berrington, J. (2007). Databases. *Anaesthesia and Intensive Care Medicine, 8*(12), 513–515. doi:10.1016/j. mpaic.2007.09.011

Garcia-Molina, H., & Lindsay, B. (1990). Research directions for distributed databases. *SIGMOD Record, 19*(4), 98–103. doi:10.1145/122058.122070

Gupta, A. K., & Swaroop, V. (2018). Overload Handling in Replicated Real Time Distributed Databases. *International Journal of Applied Engineering Research, 13*(18), 13969-13977.

Gustavsson, S., & Andler, S. F. (2004). Real-time conflict management in replicated databases. In *Proceedings of the Fourth Conference for the Promotion of Research in IT at New Universities and University Colleges in Sweden (PROMOTE IT 2004)* (*Vol. 2*, pp. 504-513). Academic Press.

Gustavsson, S., & Andler, S. R. (2005, April). Continuous consistency management in distributed real-time databases with multiple writers of replicated data. In *19th IEEE International Parallel and Distributed Processing Symposium*. IEEE. 10.1109/IPDPS.2005.152

Haj Said, A., Sadeg, B., Amanton, L., & Ayeb, B. (2008). A Protocol to Control Replication in Distributed Real-Time Database Systems. *Proceedings of the Tenth International Conference on Enterprise Information Systems*, 501-504.

Kim, Y. K. (1996). Towards real-time performance in a scalable, continuously available telecom. *DBMS (Redwood City, Calif.).*

Lokhande, D. B., & Dhainje, P. B. (2019). A Novel Approach for Transaction Management in Heterogeneous Distributed Real Time Replicated Database Systems. *International Journal for Scientific Research and Development, 7*(1), 840-844.

Mathiason, G., Andler, S. F., & Son, S. H. (2007, August). Virtual full replication by adaptive segmentation. In *13th IEEE International Conference on Embedded and Real-Time Computing Systems and Applications (RTCSA 2007)* (pp. 327-336). IEEE.

Nie, T., & Zhang, T. (2009, January). A study of DES and Blowfish encryption algorithm. In Tencon 2009-2009 IEEE Region 10 Conference (pp. 1-4). IEEE.

Ouzzani, M., Medjahed, B., & Elmagarmid, A. K. (2009). Correctness criteria beyond serializability. Encyclopedia of database systems, 501-506.

Padmavathi, B., & Kumari, S. R. (2013). *A survey on performance analysis of DES, AES and RSA algorithm along with LSB substitution*. IJSR.

Peddi, P., & DiPippo, L. C. (2002). A replication strategy for distributed real-time object-oriented databases. In *Proceedings Fifth IEEE International Symposium on Object-Oriented Real-Time Distributed Computing. ISIRC 2002* (pp. 129-136). IEEE. 10.1109/ISORC.2002.1003670

Pu, C., & Leff, A. (1990). *Replica control in distributed systems: An asynchronous approach*. Academic Press.

Ramakrishnan, R., & Gehrke, J. (2000). *Database management systems*. McGraw Hill.

Salem, R., Saleh, S. A., & Abdul-kader, H. (2016). Scalable data-oriented replication with flexible consistency in real-time data systems. *Data Science Journal*, 15.

Shanker, U., Misra, M., & Sarje, A. K. (2008). Distributed real time database systems: Background and literature review. *Distributed and Parallel Databases*, *23*(2), 127–149. doi:10.100710619-008-7024-5

Shrivastava, P., Jain, R., & Raghuwanshi, K. S. (2014, January). A Modified Approach of Key Manipulation in Cryptography Using 2D Graphics Image. In *2014 International Conference on Electronic Systems, Signal Processing and Computing Technologies* (pp. 194-197). IEEE. 10.1109/ICESC.2014.40

Shrivastava, P., & Shanker, U. (2018, August). Replica update technique in RDRTDBS: issues & challenges. In *Proceedings of the 24th International Conference on Advanced Computing and Communications (ADCOM-2018), Ph. D. Forum* (pp. 21-23). Academic Press.

Shrivastava, P., & Shanker, U. (2018). Replica control following 1SR in DRTDBS through best case of transaction execution. In *Advances in Data and Information Sciences* (pp. 139–150). Singapore: Springer. doi:10.1007/978-981-10-8360-0_13

Shrivastava, P., & Shanker, U. (2018). Replication protocol based on dynamic versioning of data object for replicated DRTDBS. *International Journal of Computational Intelligence & IoT*, *1*(2).

Shrivastava, P., & Shanker, U. (2019, January). Real time transaction management in replicated DRTDBS. In *Australasian Database Conference* (pp. 91-103). Springer. 10.1007/978-3-030-12079-5_7

Shrivastava, P., & Shanker, U. (2019, January). Supporting transaction predictability in replicated DRTDBS. In *International Conference on Distributed Computing and Internet Technology* (pp. 125-140). Springer. 10.1007/978-3-030-05366-6_10

Shrivastava, P., & Shanker, U. (2020). Secure System Model for Replicated DRTDBS. In *Security and Privacy Issues in Sensor Networks and IoT* (pp. 264–281). IGI Global. doi:10.4018/978-1-7998-0373-7.ch011

Son, S. H., & Kouloumbis, S. (1993). A token-based synchronization scheme for distributed real-time databases. *Information Systems*, *18*(6), 375–389. doi:10.1016/0306-4379(93)90014-R

Son, S. H., & Zhang, F. (1995, April). Real-Time Replication Control for Distributed Database Systems: Algorithms and Their Performance. In DASFAA (Vol. 11, pp. 214-221). Academic Press.

Son, S. H., Zhang, F., & Hwang, B. (1996). Concurrency control for replicated data in distributed real-time systems. *Journal of Database Management*, *7*(2), 12–23. doi:10.4018/jdm.1996040102

Srivastava, A., Shankar, U., & Tiwari, S. K. (2012). A protocol for concurrency control in real-time replicated databases system. *IRACST—International Journal of Computer Networks and Wireless Communications*, *2*(3).

Syberfeldt, S. (2007). *Optimistic replication with forward conflict resolution in distributed real-time databases* (Doctoral dissertation). Institutionen för datavetenskap.

Ullman, J. D. (1984). *Principles of database systems*. Galgotia Publications.

Ulusoy, Ö. (1994). Processing real-time transactions in a replicated database system. *Distributed and Parallel Databases*, *2*(4), 405–436. doi:10.1007/BF01265321

Ulusoy, Ö. (1995). A study of two transaction-processing architectures for distributed real-time database systems. *Journal of Systems and Software*, *31*(2), 97–108. doi:10.1016/0164-1212(94)00090-A

Wang, F., Yao, L. W., & Yang, Y. L. (2011). Efficient verification of distributed real-time systems with broadcasting behaviors. *Real-Time Systems*, *47*(4), 285–318. doi:10.100711241-011-9122-0

Xiong, M., Ramamritham, K., Haritsa, J. R., & Stankovic, J. A. (2002). MIRROR: A state-conscious concurrency control protocol for replicated real-time databases. *Information Systems*, *27*(4), 277–297. doi:10.1016/S0306-4379(01)00053-9

Zhang, H., Zhao, W., Moser, L. E., & Melliar-Smith, P. M. (2011). Design and Implementation of a Byzantine Fault Tolerance Framework for Non-Deterministic Applications. *IET Software*, *5*(3), 342–356. doi:10.1049/iet-sen.2010.0013

Zhao, W. (2014). *Building dependable distributed systems*. John Wiley & Sons; doi:10.1002/9781118912744

Section 2
Databases and Interdisciplinary Expansions

Chapter 7
Feasibility of Providers' Coalition in Reverse Auction-Based Cloud Market

Gaurav Baranwal

Department of Computer Science, Banaras Hindu University, Varanasi, India

Dinesh Kumar

Department of Computer Science and Engineering, Motilal Nehru National Institute of Technology, Allahabad, India

Deo Prakash Vidyarthi

School of Computer and Systems Sciences, Jawaharlal Nehru University, New Delhi, India

ABSTRACT

Cloud computing has revolutionized the IT world by its benefits. Cloud users can take relational and non-relational databases in the form of services or can run their own database on computing resources provided by the cloud. With evolution of cloud, new challenges are emerging, and the responsibility of the professional is to provide solution to these challenges. Dynamic pricing of computing resources in the cloud is now widely acceptable by its users. But in the current market of cloud, reverse auction (a mechanism to implement dynamic pricing) is not getting the attention from professionals that it deserves. This work is an effort to identify the facts in the cloud market that are responsible for current condition of reverse auction. In this work, from the identified limitations of current cloud market and case study on existing model for reverse auction in cloud, one can observe that coalition of small cloud providers with common interoperability standard in reverse auction is a feasible solution to encourage cloud market for adapting reverse auction-based resource allocation.

DOI: 10.4018/978-1-7998-2491-6.ch007

INTRODUCTION

Cloud computing is a business model of computing that delivers computing resources as a service over the internet to users (Sajid and Raza, 2013). Even one can pay using credit card to utilize powerful computing servers in very less time. Among all the services provided by a cloud platform, Database-as-a-service (DBaaS) becomes popular in recent times as many modern business applications and operational systems run using this type of service (Hacigümüş, Iyer and Mehrotra, 2002). Forrester defines DBaaS as *"An on-demand, secure, scalable, and self-service database that automates the database provisioning and administration to support new and existing business applications and operational systems"* (Forrester, 2019).

In this kind of service, a cloud data center has the capability to run database, and access to the cloud service provider (SP) is provided to the cloud users as a service as similar to other type of services e.g. computing, network, storage etc. Using DBaaS, provisioning of relational and Non-relational databases takes only a few minutes without any technical complexity. Moreover, a cloud user can purchase some virtual resources (i.e. virtual machines) and can run its own database on these virtual machines (Hacigümüş, Iyer and Mehrotra, 2002). The report publishes by Forrester (Forrester, 2019) depicts the fact that a large number of SPs are offering Database-as-a-service in cloud market. Some Examples of DBaaS are Amazon's DynamoDB, Google's Cloud FireStore, EnterpriseDB's EDB Postgres Cloud Database Service (CDS), IBM's Db2, MongoDB Atlas etc. (Forrester, 2019).

Dynamic allocation of Virtual Resources is one of the major benefits of cloud. Market of cloud resources are growing very fast and competition is increasing day by day. Even developing countries are encouraging their agencies and professionals to take services of cloud, so that, they would be more focused on effectiveness of their programs (as one knows that cloud computing reduces the overhead related to infrastructure). Recently Government of India announced to provide subsidy for taking services of cloud (Times, 2017). Since number of customer is also increasing, prediction of demand of resource is very tough for SPs. This makes dynamic resource allocation is also an important research problem (Baranwal *et al.*, 2018a). Since it is a business model of computing, price acts as a lever that can help to control this dynamism (Baranwal *et al.*, 2018a).

Though dynamic pricing supports healthy competition and increases the utilization of resource (Mihailescu and Teo, 2010), but dynamism in pricing creates difficulty to customer in budget planning and to SPs in pricing of resource. Auction, which handles dynamism very well, is one of the implementations of dynamic pricing. In auction, there are two important entities; Auctioneer and Bidder. Auction can be of three types on the basis of role of customer and provider: Forward Auction, Reverse Auction, and Double Auction (Baranwal *et al.*, 2018b). In forward auction, SP acts as auctioneer while customers are bidders, which compete to get resources offered by SP in the auction. Highest paying customer is the winner in forward auction. Reverse auction is just opposite of forward auction. In this, customer acts as auctioneer; SPs are bidders who compete to allocate resource and get payment. SP with lowest payment expectation wins in reverse auction. While in double auction, both customers and SPs are bidders i.e. bidding from both sides. Double auction is basically a solution for resource matching problem (Parsons, Rodriguez-Aguilar and Klein, 2011) (Kumar *et al.*, 2017).

CURRENT CLOUD MARKET

From a report of cloud market, there are 17 among top most 20 companies providing cloud services are based on United States and Japan and most of cloud SPs are from non-European countries (Larkin and Rose, 2015). European countries based cloud SPs and small SPs are lacking to attract customer. Reason for this can be identified from the report of Synergy Research Group which is based on released Q2 data about cloud market. According to the report (Reno, 2016), Amazon Web Services (AWS), Microsoft, IBM and Google are four cloud SPs which together control half of the cloud infrastructure available worldwide. In aggregate, these four companies grew their revenues by 68%. Next 20 companies in the Q2 grew their revenues by 41% while all other small cloud SPs grew by 27%. There is very less competition between these four companies and all other companies because their services are available worldwide and they are able to invest huge investments to create new data centers. But strong competition among these four SPs can be understood by the reduction in price by 45 percent by Amazon in March, 2016. This happened just after announcement by Google to reduce price of virtual machines by up to 32 percent.

With special reference to DBaaS, the report published by (Forrester, 2019) states that in cloud market, there are 12 major cloud SPs who are capturing the whole market, especially in the domain of Database-as-a-service. Some names of these SPs are Alibaba, Google, Amazon, Oracle, MongoDB, Microsoft etc. The Report analyzed and scored all these SPs using 27 different criteria. The report finds states that Oracle, Amazon, MongoDB, Google and Microsoft dominate the whole market.

In the nascent age of cloud, SPs used static pricing to sell the computing resources. Important reason for this is simplicity of static pricing. But with the time, cloud market is also evolving. Now-a-days, there is very tough competition among SPs. Amazon launched cloud services known as Elastic Compute Cloud (EC2) in 2006 and revolutionized the IT sector. Since then Amazon has reduced price for their services more than 50 times. Increasing competitive market is one of the reasons for that. Currently, in this competitive market services are using free trial, delivery of resources using various price schemes, tariffs etc. to lure the customers. Customers will prefer those pricing schemes that will be in their favor while ultimate objective of SP is to maximize the revenue. In the dynamic environment of cloud, one pricing scheme cannot be optimal in all scenarios. It is also applicable for static pricing. Static pricing does not follow supply and demand principle of economics that is why it is inflexible and does not form equilibrium price i.e. when demand is more; SP should be able to increase the price while in case of less demand SP should be able to decrease the price. Recently, SPs started offering resource using dynamic pricing.

As discussed in introduction section, auction supports dynamic pricing. Reverse auction, a type of auction, is not getting attention from academicians and professionals. In reverse auction, customer publishes its requirements in the cloud market, and SPs submit bid. Best offer by SPs wins the auction. But in the current market, perhaps giants like Amazon, Google etc. do not bother about this, because they controls most of the cloud market. It may be possible that small SPs are providing better services in comparison to others but they are not able to provide all type of services i.e. to satisfy their customers in terms of offering of various types of services at single place. A major problem for the customer is vendor lock-in i.e. lack of standardization of interface, services, protocols, data formats etc. which make switching cost (cost that customer has to pay if the customer switches from one SP to another SP) for customer high and increase the dependency on a single vendor. Consequence of vendor lock-in is that even better services are available but customer has to choose sub-standard solutions (Williamson, 1975). This type of market is not very effective and is not economically efficient (Ewerhart and Schmitz,

1997). Psychology of customers is to get all type of services at one place that should also satisfy if future requirements change and because of lack of common standard among SPs i.e. interoperability, customer also avoids taking services from various SPs.

COMBINATORIAL REVERSE AUCTION CONSIDERING INTEROPERABILITY ISSUE

In a reverse auction based cloud market, cloud user want to minimize the total procurement cost with higher QoS and a SP want to provide the resources in order to maximize the revenue. Both these objectives can be achieved if there is sufficient competition among the SPs in the market. A market is competitive if there are sufficient number of SPs of all types i.e. giant as well as small SPs who participate, win and able to offer the resources.

In combinatorial auction, whether it is forward, reverse or double, resources have the property of substitutability and complementarity. An example of such type of resources is Virtual machines (VMs). There are some situations where a user requires such type of virtualized resources in the form of bundle (Urgaonkar *et al.*, 2007; Huang, He and Miao, 2014). From the SPs' perspective, a cloud SP allocates a combination of different type of resources in the form of bundle from a resource pool. If the offered resources are insufficient to fulfill the requests, it allocates nothing means partial allocation is not allowed. Combinatorial auctions are more efficient than single-unit and multi-unit recurrent auction (Pal *et al.*, 2007; Xu *et al.*, 2013). These types of auctions have been used in many domain in past such as retail, defense (Klein, 2007), cellular networks (Xu *et al.*, 2013), wireless sensor networks (Pal *et al.*, 2007) etc. Certainly, there are some good works in literature based on combinatorial reverse auction such as works in (Saini and Rao, 2007; Fard, Prodan and Fahringer, 2013; Prasad and Rao, 2014; Baranwal and Vidyarthi, 2016; Baranwal *et al.*, 2018c; Kumar *et al.*, 2019). No work has focused on the coalition among the SPs in a reverse auction based cloud market. In our previous work (Baranwal and Vidyarthi, 2016), Truthful Combinatorial Reverse Auction (TCRA) is formulated with single objective i.e. minimization of procurement cost for customer with no constraint on the number of winning SPs.

We did not consider the above discussed facts about cloud market in the problem formulated in (Baranwal and Vidyarthi, 2016) i.e. customer will hesitate to take services from various SPs in case of lack of interoperability. Considering this, reverse auction is formulated here as given in previous work (Baranwal and Vidyarthi, 2016) but with a new constraint i.e. number of SPs from which a customer is ready to take services. For a particular problem instance, set of winner SPs are observed when acceptable number of SPs by the customer varies. This will help to understand the feasibility of coalition of SPs in the reverse auction.

In reverse auction, customer publishes a Request for Proposal (RFP) in the cloud market which contains specification of various types of computing resources that the customer needs to fulfill its objective. Let l be the number of types of VMs. Let b^c be the required quantity of set of l types of resources by customer c, i.e., $b^c = \left(q_1^c, q_2^c, q_3^c, \ldots, q_l^c \right)$, e.g., q_1^c is quantity of VMs of type 1 required by customer c. Let n^{acc} be the maximum number of SPs from which customer is ready to take services. Let n be the number of SPs, i.e., $\left(p_1, p_2, p_3, \ldots, p_n \right)$, b^i be the available quantity of set of l types of resources, i.e., $b^i = \left(q_1^i, q_2^i, q_3^i, \ldots, q_l^i \right)$ having SP p_i, pp^i be the quoted price by p_i for bundle b^i. Customer c publishes b^c which is RFP in the cloud market and SPs prepare their bids and submit to customer. Here, objective of customer is minimization of procurement cost. Since concern of this work is to understand the feasibility of coalition in reverse auction and allocation is sufficient to find winners of the auction, only allocation is formulated; not pricing. Using integer linear programming, allocation of resource in combinatorial reverse auction i.e. winner determination can be formulated as follows.

$$\text{minimize} \sum_{i=1}^{n} s_i pp_i \tag{1}$$

subject to

$$\sum_{i=1}^{n} s_i q_j^i \geq q_j^c, j = 1, 2, \dots, l \tag{2}$$

$$\sum_{i=1}^{n} s_i \leq n^{acc} \tag{3}$$

where, $s_i \in \{0,1\}$ and $s_i = 1$, if SP p_i wins and otherwise.

Equation (1) is objective function which minimizes the resource procurement cost, equation (2) is the constraint that resource allocated to the customer must be greater than or equal to required resources by user and equation (3) is the constraint of acceptable number of winning SPs.

CASE STUDY

For analysis of above formulation and to understand the effects of current market condition on reverse auction, value of different parameters is taken in such a way that dynamic behavior and effectiveness of this work can be depicted. It is assumed that there are 20 SPs i.e. $(p_1, p_2, p_3, \dots, p_{20})$ and values b^i and pp^i is taken keeping in mind that market is collection of small, medium and giant SPs. SPs p_1 to p_4 are the giant SPs which can provide large quantity of resources at a higher prices. Medium SPs (p_5 to p_{10}) can provide moderate number of resources at a lower prices compared to giant SPs. There are also small SPs (p_{11} to p_{20}) who have very less number of resources as compared to other type of resources. These SPs compete in the market by offering resources at lower prices. Data considered in this case study is $n = 20, l = 3$ and $q^c = (20, 20, 20)$ and b^i and pp^i are shown in Table 1.

To analyze the competition and the effect of interoperability issue, set of winners are observed for different value of n^{acc}. If value of n^{acc} is low, it means customer does not want to take overhead of interoperability issue. While if value is high, either there is an established standard for interoperability so there is no overhead for customer or getting the resource at minimum price is customer's only objective. Value of n^{acc} is taken from 1 to 8 and obtained set of winners are shown in Figure 1.

Table 1. SPs' bids configuration

SP Index (p_i)	b^i			pp^i ($)
	q_1^i	q_2^i	q_3^i	
p_1	20	20	20	1.41
p_2	17	18	20	1.06
p_3	16	18	20	1.32
p_4	17	16	16	1.58
p_5	10	7	7	0.21
p_6	7	10	6	0.24
p_7	10	6	8	0.37
p_8	10	8	10	0.32
p_9	9	7	6	0.34
p_{10}	9	7	7	0.22
p_{11}	2	2	2	0.12
p_{12}	3	2	3	0.9
p_{13}	3	3	3	0.11
p_{14}	2	3	3	0.8
p_{15}	2	3	2	0.7
p_{16}	2	2	3	0.5
p_{17}	2	3	2	0.11
p_{18}	2	3	3	0.11
p_{19}	2	2	2	0.3
p_{20}	2	3	3	0.12

Figure 1. Set of winning SPs

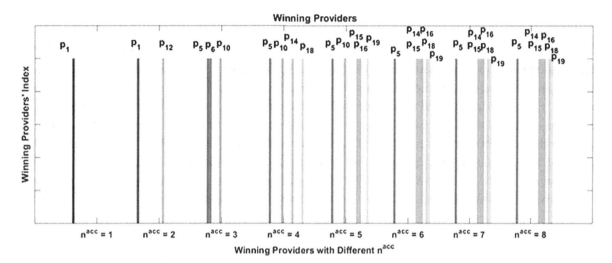

From above figure, it can be observed that as the n^{acc} is increasing, participation from small SPs is also increasing (After the $n^{acc} = 6$, there is no change in coalition structure as small SPs make the whole procurement process optimal with minimum cost). The total procurement cost vector in the above example will be [141 115 67 62 58 55 55 55] when solved with the Matlab *intlinprog*. Discussion on this case study is given in next section along with feasibility of coalition in reverse auction.

FEASIBILITY OF COALITION IN REVERSE AUCTION

From above case study, it can be observed that when value of $n^{acc} = 6$, small SPs p_{14}, p_{15}, p_{16}, p_{18} and p_{19} are winners because they are providing the resources at lower price in compare to giants and they together fulfill the need of customer. But customer will accept this outcome only when there is no interoperability issue or minimization of procurement of price is only objective and overhead of dealing with multiple SPs does not matter. When $n^{acc} = 3$, only medium SPs are winners and when $n^{acc} = 1$, only giant is the winner. Participation from small SPs is decreasing as the n^{acc} is decreasing.

We can observed that high value of n^{acc} means customer is ready to take services from multiple SPs and it will happen only when there is common standard among SPs and no interoperability issues i.e. less overhead and less switching cost at customer side. Other possibility is that minimization of procurement of price is only an objective for customer and overhead of dealing with multiple SPs does not matter. Since giants like Google, Microsoft, Amazon etc. are controlling most of the cloud market, it is logical that they would be not ready for common standard or interoperability. If they support interoperability, customer will have more options to explore. If small SPs will provide better services in the market, it may cause reduction in the participation of giants in the market which in turns will reduce the revenue of giants. For the low value of n^{acc}, participation from small SPs decreases. Explanation for this is quite simple. Customer does not want to take overhead of dealing with multiple SPs, though small providing services are at lower price in compare to giants. We can conclude that interoperability is quite a big issue for small SPs.

Two factors which are responsible for less participation from small SPs i.e. lack of common standards and less services to be offered by small SPs. One possible solution for a small SP for successful participation is collaboration with other SPs to satisfy the customers' need which in turns automatically attract more customers and improve the business. In recent year, it is found that cloud computing is still evolving. For the coalition of SPs, concept of cloud federation has been proposed. Cloud federation is federation of more than one SP who is ready to cooperate among them in order to improve their services to satisfy the needs of customer and to maximize their revenue. (Rochwerger *et al.*, 2011) defines Cloud federation as "...*federations of SPs such that they can collaborate and share their resources. . . . Any federation of Cloud computing SPs should allow virtual applications to be deployed across federated sites. Furthermore, virtual applications need to be completely location free and allowed to migrate in part or as a whole between sites. At the same time, the security, privacy and independence of the federation members must be maintained to allow computing SPs to federate*".

In a multi-agent system, coalition formation is used to implement cooperation. Coalition helps agents to perform tasks jointly in a scenario where without coalition either they are not able to perform or are able to perform poorly (Kraus, Shehory and Taase, 2003). To the best our knowledge, no works support coalition in reverse auction. Small SPs can use the concept of federation and compete with giants in the reverse auction. But now the question is what about interoperability.

Now we need to find, what should be the policies that small SPs should adapt to compete with giants. Though giants might not be ready for interoperability, but small SP belonging to one region or with common interest can define common standards and can form coalition. Small SPs, which are ready to cooperate, need to design common standard. It will make management and administration easy. They also need to design an entity as a representative that acts as a common interface. Whenever a new call for proposal submitted by customer, SP either can bid independently or can bid as a coalition. The Representative entity will submit bid on behalf of coalition and directly deal with customer. Because of common standard among SPs in the coalition, customer will never realize that the customer is dealing with a group of more than one SP.

If small SPs follow above discussed scenario i.e. formation of coalition and development of interoperability standards in reverse auction, they can participate in the market even when they have fewer services and large SPs not ready to design common standards. The European commission is moving ahead in the direction of collaboration of cloud SPs and has funded various projects that support collaboration among SPs. Few of them are TClouds (Tclouds-project, 2016), MODAClouds (ModaClouds, 2015), Cloud4SOA (Cloud4SOA, 2016), REMICS (REMICS, 2016). After initiation from European countries, other countries also started supporting this type of projects. (Grozev and Buyya, 2014) listed various projects that support collaboration. Though interoperability is the main limitation that may affect practical implementation of such projects, but researchers and professionals are working in this direction also. DMTF Cloud Standards Incubator, Cloud Computing Interoperability Forum (CCIF), Open Cloud Manifesto etc. are some organizations that are trying to make some open standards for interoperability.

CONCLUSION

Though reverse auction is an implementation of dynamic pricing and very much beneficial for customers to get resource at minimum price without knowing the market value of that resource, in recent year only a few good works are noticed. One of the possible reasons for this is that most of the market is controlled by few major SPs and because of their large share and long established trust in the cloud market they do not bother about the competition given by small SPs. Unlike small SPs, Giants like Amazon, Google in the field of cloud services are alone to satisfy customers' need. Designing of interoperability standard can improve the competition in the market, but giants might not be ready as they are the controllers of the most of the market. This work analyzes the current market condition and existing model of reverse auction in literature and found that a possible feasible solution to improve the competition by increasing the participation from small SPs in the market is coalition formation of small SPs with common interoperability standard. This work will encourage academicians and professionals to contribute more in this filed. In extension of this work, we will develop models for coalition of small SPs so that they will be able to participate in reverse auction without fear of giants.

REFERENCES

Baranwal, G. (2018a). *Auction based resource provisioning in cloud computing*. Singapore: Springer Singapore (SpringerBriefs in Computer Science). doi:10.1007/978-981-10-8737-0

Baranwal, G. (2018b). Auction theory. SpringerBriefs in Computer Science, 17–31. doi:10.1007/978-981-10-8737-0_2

Baranwal, G. (2018c). Forward auction-based cloud resource provisioning. In *SpringerBriefs in Computer Science* (pp. 33–51). Singapore: Springer; doi:10.1007/978-981-10-8737-0_3

Baranwal, G., & Vidyarthi, D. P. (2016). A Truthful and Fair Multi-Attribute Combinatorial Reverse Auction for Resource Procurement in Cloud Computing. *IEEE Transactions on Services Computing*, 1–1. doi:10.1109/tsc.2016.2632719

Cloud4SOA. (2016). *Cloud4SOA*. Available at: http://www.cloud4soa.com/

Ewerhart, C., & Schmitz, P. W. (1997). Der Lock in Effekt und das Hold up Problem Der Lock-in Effekt und das Hold-up Problem. *MPRA Paper*, *944*, 1–10. Available at: http://mpra.ub.uni-muenchen.de/6944/

Fard, H. M., Prodan, R., & Fahringer, T. (2013). A truthful dynamic workflow scheduling mechanism for commercial multicloud environments. *IEEE Transactions on Parallel and Distributed Systems*, *24*(6), 1203–1212. doi:10.1109/TPDS.2012.257

Forrester. (2019) *The Forrester Wave™: Database-As-A-Service, Q2 2019, The 12 Providers That Matter Most And How They Stack Up*. Available at: https://www.forrester.com/report/The+Forrester+Wave+DatabaseAsAService+Q2+2019/-/E-RES144407

Grozev, N., & Buyya, R. (2014). Inter-Cloud architectures and application brokering: Taxonomy and survey. *Software, Practice & Experience*, *44*(3), 369–390. doi:10.1002pe.2168

Hacigümüş, H., Iyer, B., & Mehrotra, S. (2002). Providing database as a service. *Proceedings - International Conference on Data Engineering*, 29–38. 10.1109/ICDE.2002.994695

Huang, D., He, B., & Miao, C. (2014). A survey of resource management in multi-tier web applications. *IEEE Communications Surveys and Tutorials*, *16*(3), 1574–1590. doi:10.1109/SURV.2014.010814.00060

Klein, S. (2007). Introduction to Electronic Auctions. *Electronic Markets*, *7*(4), 3–6. doi:10.1080/10196789700000041

Kraus, S., Shehory, O., & Taase, G. (2003). Coalition Formation with Uncertain Heterogeneous Information. *Proceedings of the International Conference on Autonomous Agents*, *2*, 1–8. doi: 10.1145/860576.860577

Kumar, D. (2019). Fair mechanisms for combinatorial reverse auction-based cloud market. In *Smart Innovation, Systems and Technologies* (pp. 267–277). Singapore: Springer. doi:10.1007/978-981-13-1747-7_26

Kumar, D., Baranwal, G., Raza, Z., & Vidyarthi, D. P. (2017). A systematic study of double auction mechanisms in cloud computing. *Journal of Systems and Software*, *125*, 234–255. doi:10.1016/j.jss.2016.12.009

Larkin, B., & Rose, M. (2015). *2015 Top Markets Report Cloud Computing*. Available at: http://www.export.gov/industry/infocomm/eg_main_086865.asp

Mihailescu, M., & Teo, Y. M. (2010). Dynamic resource pricing on federated clouds. *CCGrid 2010 - 10th IEEE/ACM International Conference on Cluster, Cloud, and Grid Computing*, 513–517. 10.1109/CCGRID.2010.123

ModaClouds. (2015). *ModaClouds, MOdel-Driven Approach for design and execution of applications on multiple Clouds*. Available at: http://www.modaclouds.eu/

Pal, S., Kundu, S., Chatterjee, M., & Das, S. (2007). Combinatorial reverse auction based scheduling in multirate wireless systems. *IEEE Transactions on Computers*, *56*(10), 1329–1341. doi:10.1109/TC.2007.1082

Parsons, S., Rodriguez-Aguilar, J. A., & Klein, M. (2011). Auctions and bidding: A guide for computer scientists. *ACM Computing Surveys*, *43*(2), 1–59. doi:10.1145/1883612.1883617

Prasad, A. S., & Rao, S. (2014). A mechanism design approach to resource procurement in cloud computing. *IEEE Transactions on Computers*, *63*(1), 17–30. doi:10.1109/TC.2013.106

REMICS. (2016). *REMICS, Reuse and Migration of legacy applications to Interoperable Cloud Services*. Available at: http://www.remics.eu/

Reno. (2016). *Amazon Leads; Microsoft, IBM & Google Chase; Others Trail | Synergy Research Group, Synergy Research Group*. Available at: https://www.srgresearch.com/articles/amazon-leads-microsoft-ibm-google-chase-others-trail

Rochwerger, B. (2011). An Architecture for Federated Cloud Computing. In *Cloud Computing* (pp. 391–411). Principles and Paradigms. doi:10.1002/9780470940105.ch15

Saini, M., & Rao, S. (2007). Fairness in combinatorial auctioning systems. *AAAI Spring Symposium - Technical Report*, 61–67. Available at: http://www.aaai.org/Papers/Symposia/Spring/2007/SS-07-02/SS07-02-009.pdf

Sajid, M., & Raza, Z. (2013). Cloud computing: Issues & challenges. In *International Conference on Cloud* (pp. 34–41). Big Data. Available at https://www.researchgate.net/profile/Mohammad_Sajid4/publication/278117154_Cloud_Computing_Issues_Challenges/links/557c12a908ae26eada8c7097/Cloud-Computing-Issues-Challenges.pdf

Tclouds-project. (2016). *Tclouds-project.* Available at: http://www.tclouds-project.eu/

Times, E. (2017). Subsidy for MSMEs deploying cloud computing. *The Hindu.* Available at: http://economictimes.indiatimes.com/small-biz/sme-sector/government-proposes-subsidy-for-msmes-deploying-cloud-computing/articleshow/57604194.cms

Urgaonkar, B. (2007). Analytic modeling of multitier Internet applications. *ACM Transactions on the Web*, *1*(1). doi:10.1145/1232722.1232724

Williamson, O. E. (1975). *Markets and Hierarchies: Analysis of Antitrust and Implications.* New York: The Free Pres.

Xu, C., Song, L., Han, Z., Zhao, Q., Wang, X., Cheng, X., & Jiao, B. (2013). Efficiency resource allocation for device-to-device underlay communication systems: A reverse iterative combinatorial auction based approach. *IEEE Journal on Selected Areas in Communications*, *31*(9), 348–358. doi:10.1109/JSAC.2013.SUP.0513031

Chapter 8
A Cloud Trusting Mechanism Based on Resource Ranking

Ajai K. Daniel

Madan Mohan Malaviya University of Technology, India

ABSTRACT

The cloud-based computing paradigm helps organizations grow exponentially through means of employing an efficient resource management under the budgetary constraints. As an emerging field, cloud computing has a concept of amalgamation of database techniques, programming, network, and internet. The revolutionary advantages over conventional data computing, storage, and retrieval infrastructures result in an increase in the number of organizational services. Cloud services are feasible in all aspects such as cost, operation, infrastructure (software and hardware) and processing. The efficient resource management with cloud computing has great importance of higher scalability, significant energy saving, and cost reduction. Trustworthiness of the provider significantly influences the possible cloud user in his selection of cloud services. This chapter proposes a cloud service selection model (CSSM) for analyzing any cloud service in detail with multidimensional perspectives.

INTRODUCTION

Cloud computing is one of the emerging fields in modern computing environments like databases. It is an intelligent integration of communication network, programming methodologies, database techniques and the internet. Generally, in a traditional computing environment, if a user wants to access some information resource for short time duration then it is necessary for him/her to buy the resources even if these resources will be of no use after some time period. This unnecessary resource occupying without having no further use was a major concern in past two decades- especially for fast growing organizations. In the present era of computing, cloud computing offers the solutions to such types of problems. The aim of Cloud computing is to deliver the required resources to the end users as per their need and demand. Cloud computing enables the users that they can pay for services based on the duration of resource requirements (Clerk Maxwell et al., 1892).

DOI: 10.4018/978-1-7998-2491-6.ch008

Cloud computing enables anytime and anywhere contact to shared pools of composition system resources and higher-level services that can be quickly provisioned with minimal management effort, often over the Internet. Cloud computing relies on sharing of the resources to achieve coherence and economics of sale similar to a public utility. Cloud computing has emerged as a paradigm to deliver on demand resources (e.g., infrastructure, platform, software, etc.) to customers similar to other utilities (e.g., water, electricity and gas). There are three most popular services provided by Cloud service providers in Cloud computing architecture and these three services are based on the needs of IT customers (G. Eason et.al., 1955). The first and foremost service is Software as a Service (SaaS) and it provides customers to access the complete application like a service. The second one service is called Platform as a Service (PaaS) and it provides customers a platform on which they can create or develop other application on top of it. Third service is called Infrastructure as a Service (IaaS) and it provides customers virtual environment, where they can deploy, run and manage their applications, virtual machines, and data storage. Technically, we can say that IaaS offers to customers and incremental scalability (scale up and down) of on-demand services like computing resources and storage (Maxwell, 1892), (Jacobs and Bean, 1963).

The cloud computing services offer organizations to start out building applications on the cloud infrastructure and creating their businesses agile by versatile and elastic cloud services. However, moving applications and/or information into the Cloud is not simple. The various challenges exist to leverage the complete potential that cloud computing guarantees. These challenging areas are typically associated with the actual fact that existing applications have specific needs and characteristics that require to be met by Cloud service providers.

Other than that, with the expansion of public Cloud offerings, for Cloud customers it is become progressively troublesome to determine that providers will fulfill their QoS needs (Maxwell et al., 1892). Every Cloud supplier offers similar services at totally different costs and performance levels with different sets of options where provided services could be low-cost for storage services; they will be pricy for computation.

Therefore, given the diversity of Cloud service offerings challenge for customers to select the ''right'' Cloud providers that can satisfy their requirements. There may be trade-offs between different functional and non-functional requirements fulfilled by different Cloud providers. So, it makes tough to evaluate the service levels of different Cloud service providers in required quality, reliability and security of an application be ensured. For that reason, it is not enough to simply determine various Cloud services; however, it is important to evaluate and get the best suited Cloud service provider. Third-party clouds enabled organizations are targeted on their base businesses instead of dispensing resources on computer infrastructure and maintenance. Proponents also claim that cloud computing allows enterprises to get their applications up-to-date faster with improved manageability, less maintenance, resources to meet fluctuating and unpredictable demand etc. Cloud providers typically use a "pay-as-you-go" model.

The chapter proposes cloud service trustworthiness selection model which offers customers to evaluate Cloud offered services and rank them based on their ability to satisfy the need of customer's Quality of Service (QoS) of the Cloud. The chapter is organized as follows. Section 2 contains different related works that have been carried out in support of our proposed Cloud service ranking model. Sections 3 explains our proposed work which includes the methodology that has been used to determine a Cloud ranking model using Analytical Hierarchical Process (AHP) based multi-criteria selection discussed in details. Section 4 elaborate analysis and validation of our proposed model where AHP based computation has been performed to get the different parameters (capacity, cost, performance, security and maintenance) values in final matrix form. Section 5 represents simulation results and finally section 6 contains conclusions of our proposed work.

RELATED WORKS

A cloud ranking system generally allocates every user a cloud based on their need. Due to the increasing demand of Cloud computing, several researchers studied the performance of Clouds for various applications like scientific computing, e-commerce, web applications etc. Several performance observance and analysis tools are proposed in the literature. Cloud ranking generally determines the ranking of different Clouds on the basis of their features, services and customer requirements. Cloud ranking indicates priority of different Cloud services (among multiple Cloud services) for the customers based on their cloud service requirements. Ranking of Cloud depends on the features of the services provided by the Cloud. The features of the Cloud are more or less dependent on various attributes of the Cloud. There can be number of attributes and on the basis of those attributes, a Cloud service selection can be done among various Cloud services. Some of the major attributes which can be considered for Cloud ranking are cost, performance, security, capacity and maintenance (Alshehri, 2019).

Cloud service trustworthiness can be defined as degree of confidence of cloud service to meet the set of requirements. It is evaluated in terms of degree of confidence and set of requirements. Trustworthiness value depends on management and technical decisions made by individuals/group evaluating the cloud service and are termed as degree of confidence. Trustworthiness value depends on the selected set of requirements. Trust evaluation is one of the challenging issues in various areas such as software services, mobile ad hoc networks, electronic commerce, etc. Definition of cloud service trustworthiness varies with varying organizational structures and application. The significant research has been carried out for deciding the trustworthiness concept, parameter, definition, and method for enhancing the cloud service trustworthiness. Evaluating the cloud service made by the group or individual trustworthiness value depends on the selected set of requirement (Maxwell et al., 1892).

In (Marsh et al., 1994), trust as a procedure conception in computing has been formalized. Authors argue regarding trust from the purpose of vision of artificial agent. Trustworthiness increases with the rise within the trust value. The trust worth expressed as a real number lies within the range [-1, 1]. In (Zhang et.al, 2012), authors have considered reliability, availability, safety, security and maintainability. Such types of parameters for evaluation of trustworthiness, they have also proposed a model using these parameters for the evaluation of trustworthiness of software services using fuzzy comprehensive evaluation model. In (Ouzzani and Bouguettaya,2004), a model based on query and optimization was proposed that can provide capability to process complex queries to net services. Their model selects and combines virtual and concrete operations respectively on the basis of Quality of Web Services (QoWS), rating matching of degrees, relevancy and feasibleness and also provides optimized query model. In (Hofer and Karagiannis, 2009), a survey has been done and also proposed a taxonomy on numerous existing cloud computing services invented by organizations like Google, Amazon, force.com etc. They additionally used taxonomy and result to spot the area requiring further research. Zhou et al. (Zhou et al., 2010) focused on different cloud computing system provider and focused on issue of privacy and security and found out that these are not adequate and they added more aspects (availability, confidentiality, data integrity, control, audit) in cloud computing service. In (Noor and Sheng,2013), Cloud Armor performs creditability for trust managements for cloud services, provides trust as services. The architecture is

Figure 1. Hierarchical representation of cloud selection parameters

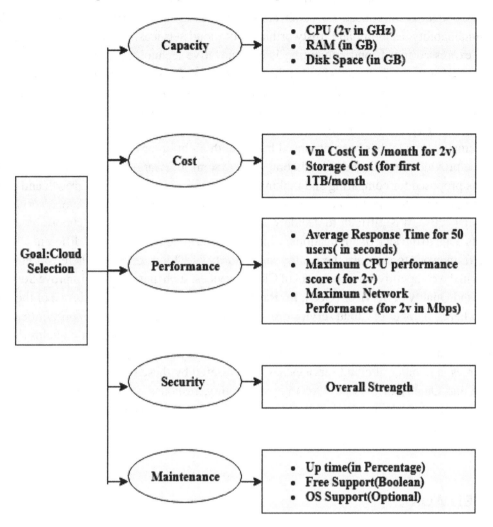

based on decentralization and has components like cloud services, trust, assessment, creditability based on Cloud recommendations.

In (Hu et al., 2010), implemented trustworthiness model using fusion method of service has been done and also description how to acquire and compute trustworthiness has been made. Their model is based on D-S theory and they have shown that fusion trustworthiness enhances the efficiency of service discovery which can be very useful for Cloud service platform. Hu and Liu in (Hu and Liu,2011) proposed a model for trustworthiness using D-S evident theory which is based on fusion technique of computing service trustworthiness in web services. They proposed model to improve the performance and robustness of service discovery. In (Supriya et al.,2014), it has been presented a technique for choosing best cloud service providers based on direct and recommended rating depending on trust for selection of best path. In (Pandey and Daniel, 2016), fuzzy logic-based cloud service trustworthiness model has been introduced to access the trustworthiness services of Cloud. The model takes finance as parameters for improvement in quality of cloud services. Further, the model is used to improve the cost-based quality and service-based selection method based on fuzzy logic. In (Pandey and Daniel, 2017) a model based on multidimensional is introduced for better cloud services using parameters finance, security, reliability, maintainability, usability and trustworthiness of cloud services. In (Rajareshwari et al., 2018), it has been expressed that Cloud computing is an innovative technology in the field of information technology; moreover, the federated cloud is the combination of several cloud service providers. There are many cloud service providers of federated cloud and the user need to choose the best suited cloud according to his need. To choose the best cloud service according to their need from the available and eligible cloud service providers, there is a need of cloud ranking concept. Poincare Plot Method (PPM) based mathematical model has been proposed by the authors in order to find out the rank of different cloud service providers in federated cloud computing system. In (Garg, Versteeg and Buyya, 2011), a framework is proposed for comparing and ranking the cloud services as with the growth and popularity of Cloud computing. More and more companies are currently offering different cloud services. From the user's perspective, it is difficult to decide which Cloud services they should choose based on their requirements. Due to the lack of applications, which can determine the ranking of different Clouds, they proposed a framework to measure the quality and priority of Cloud services. There is a need of such frameworks in the competitive measurement of Cloud services, such that, they can improve Service Level Agreement and Quality of Services (QoS). In (Ray et al.,2017), Cloud federation is one of the emerging paradigms where a number of Cloud service providers group together and made opportunities to deliver their Cloud services with better QoS and interruption free services. Cloud federation helps these Cloud service providers to utilize their idle and less utilized resources and gets earnings. With high demand of cloud resources, a number of cloud services has been offered by these Cloud federations by providing varied price and Quality of Service (QoS) i.e. availability, response time, throughput, reliability and trust. Their proposed model is based on multi-criteria decision analysis and they have applied it in the selection of best federation-based cloud taking the preferences of cloud users on different parameters (price, QoS and trust).

PROPOSED WORK

This work is to create a set of virtual users, for whom, these clouds will be allocated based on user's requirements. User, based on their needs, will give the cloud attribute value and priority of each attribute according to its primary and secondary needs. Multiple challenges are tackled in the determination of a model for getting QoS and evaluation of Cloud's ranking of different Cloud service providers. The first and foremost challenge is in the computation of various SMI attributes of a Cloud service. The value of these attributes varies over time. However, due to the lack of precision in the measurement of each Cloud attribute, it is very difficult to get the comparison of various cloud services. Historical based measurements are considered in Cloud and these historical measurements merges with the committed attributes of Cloud in order to determine the actual value of an attribute. We are also giving a precise metrics for each and every measurable attribute of Cloud that play the role of determining Cloud ranking and different Cloud service providers.

The second major challenge is to give ranking of Cloud services based on these measurable attributes. These measurable attributes are considered for the ranking of Cloud of different Cloud service providers. Generally, there are two types of QoS requirements that a user can have: 1) Functional, 2) Non-functional. Due to nature of Cloud, some of them are complex to measure. User experience and security are also major concerns which are difficult to quantify. Moreover, taking the decision of which cloud service suits best along with various functional and non-functional requirements is a decision-making problem. It is very important to think sincerely before the selection of cloud because it includes multiple-criteria and interdependent relation among them as shown in figure 1. In figure 1, we can see the multi-criteria relationship and this is called the problem of Multi-Criteria Decision Making (MCDM). The service selection process is affected by each individual parameter, and overall ranking is depending on its priority in the selection process.

Analytical Hierarchical Process (AHP) based ranking technique is used in our proposed Cloud ranking model. AHP solves our problem of Cloud ranking by assigning weights to the different parameters and create interdependence between them by providing quantitative basis in the computation of ranking of Cloud services.

After all the data has been captured provided by users, our system will compute remaining unknown data and based on them allocates the best suited cloud to the users so that there need is satisfied. The AHP can be used as a tool to translate qualitative and quantitative pair wise translation by forming a Decision Matrix into a multi-criteria selection model. The working of AHP is simple because it does not require to develop any complex expert system along with its Decision Matrix knowledge which is already embedded in it. Three important concepts in AHP are given below.

1.   AHP is analytic: It converts Decision Matrix's input into numeric values.
2.   The AHP forms the problems into a hierarchy: It performs pair-wise comparison of the hierarchical model of complex decision-making problems.
3.   AHP helps in decision making of multi-criteria problems: It defines a process for decision-making in Decision Matrix.

The Figure 2 shows the attributes and sub-attributes of clouds. The proposed model Architecture basically comprises of all the five basic attributes. The system acts as an interface between user and clouds. To ensure that the system performs well, the user need to know all properties of cloud which are associated to user. The cloud gets remaining attributes of the user requirement from computing the given attributes and sub-attributes of the cloud. The proposed technique is based on multi-criteria decision-making system shown in Figure 1.

The multi-criteria programming made through the use of the analytical hierarchical process (AHP) is a technique used for decision making in complex environments with many variables/criteria for prioritization and selection of alternatives / projects. Various attributes and sub-attributes are selected to rank the Cloud services using analytical hierarchy process (AHP). Different Cloud attributes (Capacity, Cost, Performance, Security and Maintenance) have been taken into consideration and data related to these attributes are collected and represented in tabular format as shown in Table 1.

AHP transforms empirical data into numerical values. The weight is considered for each and every factor that is required in the assessment of each of the elements in the defined hierarchy table. The comparison is made between each other attributes relative weights. The required criteria for numeric probability are calculated for each alternative. These probabilities are used to determine the likelihood that the expected goal has to be fulfilled by the alternative. The higher value of probability represents better chances of alternative to satisfy the required final goal.

Figure 2. Multi-criteria decision

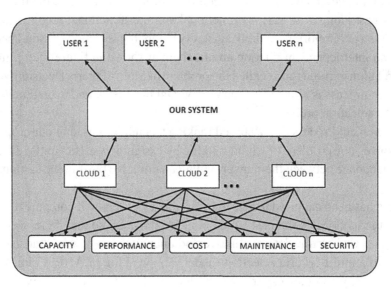

Table 1. Cloud ranking attributes

Attributes	Sub-Attributes	Cloud 1	Cloud 2	Cloud 3	Cloud 4	Cloud 5
Capacity	CPU (2v in GHz)	9.6	12.8	8.8	9.3	10.2
	RAM (in GB)	15	14	15	13	14
	Disk Space (in GB)	1690	2040	630	1250	930
Cost	Storage (first 1TB/month $/GB)	0.024	0.0390	0.03	0.048	0.0312
	Vm Cost ($/month 2v CPU)	162.79	97.10	141.00	110.20	117.12
Performance	Database performance (%)	55	68	65	75	72
	Max. CPU performance Score (2v CPU)	2500	3100	3600	3800	4000
	Max. Network performance (in Mbps) 2v CPU	1000	2100	2200	2700	3000
Security	Average Strength	0.6	0.5	0.8	0.7	0.8
Maintenance	Up time (in %)	99.9079%	99.59%	99.92%	99.45%	99.97%
	Free Support (Boolean)	Yes	Yes	No	No	Yes

The comparisons between two elements using the relative importance scale between two alternatives are the most widely used. Attributing values varies in the range from 1 to 9. The scale determines the relative importance of alternatives when compared with another alternative. The odd numbers are used to make sure that there is a reasonable distinction among the measurement points. The even numbers are adopted for negotiation between the evaluators. When a natural consensus cannot be reached, it raises the need to determine a middle point as the negotiated solution.

PROPOSED MODEL

The proposed model is divided into following sub models for computing the rank of the cloud with respect to user requirements.

1. Priority cloud Model
2. Relative Vector Calculations for Attributes Model
3. Eigen Vectors for sub attributes Model
4. Ranking of Cloud Model

The ranking of the cloud is done on the basis of the user requirement. The user defines the weights to their attributes. To compare the cloud services, user needs to assign weight to each attribute into their relative importance. The weight is assigned into following ways.

1. **User Assigned Weights**: Each cloud is assigned a rank by the users by assigning weights to each of the cloud attributes by having some scale that can indicate the importance of one Quality of Service (QoS) over another. The user expresses his preferences for different attributes according to his requirements.
2. **Random Assigned Weights**: The user puts the weights according to his own scale but on calculating sum of all weights which is not equal to one. So, the weights are to be normalized.
3. **Relative Value Based Weights**: Relative performance is defined by the assigned weights of each Cloud service based on lowest level attribute values. The weights to attributes are not assigned directly since low level attributes can have different types of value attributes.

Defining the relative weights for ranking the Cloud services is based on a strategy proposed by (Zhang et al., 2012).The relative weight metrics designed for the model work on two services Essential and Non-essential service. Let, Wq is the weight assigned by the user for the Cloud attribute q. Let Vi and Vj are the values of attribute q for the taken Cloud service I and j respectively. Let Si and Sj are the Cloud services provided by Clod service provider and Si / Sj represents the relative rank of Cloud service Si over Cloud service Sj. Let V_r is the expected value specified by the Cloud user.

The step for the comparison of the values of each Cloud service is as follows.

1. It is necessary to ensure that the dimensional units of both comparable units should be of same type i.e. if we have to compare two Virtual Machines (VM) instances, then the cost of each CPU, Memory and Hard disk should be same respectively. The cost needs for data communication to be of similar in dimension in the terms of cost per 1 Gigabyte (GB).

2. In the next step, we have to choose the two comparable values based on their types and compare them because the attribute values may be varied from a Boolean value to a Set value. So, it is very important to make sure the type of comparable attributes before comparison. We have also proposed a comparison metric for each type of attribute of Cloud, so that, a proper and systematic comparison approach can be followed.

3. The essential and non-essential attributes can be specified by users. In Cloud framework, specified user's requirement values are optional for non-essential attributes. So, if two services of non-essential attributes are compared then there is a chance that Vr is not taken into consideration and hence not specified by the Cloud's customer.

The proposed ranking model for each type of attribute is defined as given below.
Boolean:

$$S_i / S_j = 1 \text{ if. } V_i \equiv V_j$$

$$= W_q \text{ if. } V_j = 1 \text{ and } V_i = 0.$$

$$= 1 / W_q \text{ if. } V_j = 0 \text{ and } V_i = 1.$$

Numerical:

$$S_i / S_j = V_i / V_j$$

With the help of comparison metrics in above tables for each Cloud service and for every attribute of Cloud service, we have got a one-to-one correspondence comparison. We will get a one-to-one relative ranking matrix having (N x N) size and the matrix will be further used for service ranking computation by calculating 'Eigen Vector' to get the relative ranking for all the cloud computing services for any individual attribute. The computed Vector Matrix is called priority matrix. The computation of relative importance of attributes, computation of priority vector and proposed protocol is defined as per following.

Computing Relative Importance for Each Attribute

In order to compute relative importance Si/Sj for each attribute, the Si/Sj, for any instance is 3. It suggests that cloud Si is of more important than Sj considering the respective attribute. Si/Sj has nothing to do with the absolute value of the cloud for a given attribute; it is purely relative importance value of the cloud Si with respect to the cloud Sj. Hence, it can be described as multi-criteria decision-making system. The cloud attribute values for the given data sets are used for calculation of priority of particular cloud with respect to other cloud for that particular attribute.

Computing Priority Vector of Each Attribute

In order to compute priority index of each cloud attribute, users provide priority values for each pair of attributes. For instance, if we consider cost and performance pair of attribute and user gives 3 as priority value, this implies that user gives more importance to cost than performance. Let us consider if there are n attributes then the user has to provide relative importance value for (n*(n-1))/2 pair of attributes.

Proposed Protocol for Priority Allocation

The priority vector is attained using proposed protocol provided by the overall importance of each attribute among the other attributes to initiate the ranking process. To determine the Comparison Matrix, and Priority Vector, the attribute hierarchy has been maintained and the selection criteria must be pair wise evaluated to determine their relative importance in between them and considered for global goal using their relative weight. The determination of relative weight of Cloud attributes begins with the evaluation process of Cloud.

Steps for allocation of resources considering their priorities:

```
/*Initialize N sampled clouds along with their property attributes. */
/*create some sample users to allot the cloud to assigned user and registered
by name, location, */
/* Set Cloud attribute(s) priority. */
1.        Begin {
2.        Compute the rank of the cloud based on priority attribute value.
} end
Begin {
3.        For each user, provide alternative for the best cloud available ac-
cording to their requirements.
4.        Compute the Relative Matrix and Relative Vector for finding out the
best among all available cloud
} end
Begin {
5.        If Available some best ranked cloud that fails in allotment to the
user because of the dissatisfaction of certain requirements of the user
6.        Then the user may be known about the cloud available.
7.        If Agree, then to be allotted to the user
} end
else
Begin {
8.        User makes certain changes in his requirement according to the
cloud.
9.        Go to step 2
10.        } end
```

Table 2. Priority values of User1

	Capacity	Cost	Performance	Security	Maintenance
Capacity	1	1/3	1/5	1/5	1/3
Cost	3	1	1/3	1	1
Performance	5	1	3	1/9	1/2
Security	5	1	9	1	1/3
Maintenance	3	1	2	3	1
Total	17	6.33	12.53	5.31	3.16

Table 3. Normalized priority value of User 1

	Capacity	Cost	Performance	Security	Maintenance
Capacity	0.0588	0.0521	0.0159	0.0376	0.1053
Cost	0.1764	0.1579	0.0263	0.1883	0.3164
Performance	0.2941	0.4739	0.0798	0.0209	0.1582
Security	0.2941	0.1579	0.7182	0.1883	0.1053
Maintenance	0.1764	0.1579	0.1596	0.5649	0.3164

The comparison matrix for different Resources attributes of clouds according to User 1 on the basis of the priority of Capacity, Cost, Performance, Security and Maintenance are shown in Table 2.

In order to analyze the given relative weights of each attribute criterion, it is important to normalize the computed comparison matrix. The normalization process is simply made by dividing each value by the number of total column value is shown in Table 3.

Total_Capacity = 0.2697

Total_Cost = 0.8653

Total_Performance = 1.1414

Total_Maintenance = 1.3752

Total_Securit= 1.4638

Total sum = 5.1154

The contribution of each criterion to the goal is determined by calculating the priority vector (Eigenvector). The Eigenvector shows the relative weights between each criterion. It is obtained by calculating the mathematical average of all criteria.The Eigen vector attribute is calculated as given below

Table 4. Priority values of User 2

	Capacity	Cost	Performance	Security	Maintenance
Capacity	1	1/5	1/3	1/5	1/3
Cost	5	1	1/3	½	1
Performance	3	3	1	1/3	1/4
Security	5	2	3	1	1/3
Maintenance	3	1	4	3	1
Total	17	7.2	8.66	5.03	2.91

Table 5. Priority values of User 3

	Capacity	Cost	Performance	Security	Maintenance
Capacity	1	2	1/3	1/3	3
Cost	1/2	1	1/5	7	1/4
Performance	3	5	1	¼	1
Security	3	1/7	4	1	1/3
Maintenance	1/3	4	1	3	1
Total	7.71	12.14	6.53	11.58	5.58

Table 6. Priority values of User4

	Capacity	Cost	Performance	Security	Maintenance
Capacity	1	1/4	1/2	1/3	1
Cost	4	1	3	1/5	1/3
Performance	2	1/3	1	9	1/4
Security	3	5	1/9	1	6
Maintenance	1	3	4	1/6	1
Total	11	9.58	8.61	10.7	8.58

Eigen vector Attribute = (Overall sum of attribute) / Total sum

Eigen values for different attributes as Capacity, Cost, Performance, Security and Maintenance of different user are as USER1{0.0527, 0.1691, 0.2231, 0.2861, 0.2688} respectively. The comparison matrix for different Resources attributes of clouds according to User 2 on the basis of the priority of Capacity, Cost, Performance, Security and Maintenance are shown in Table 4.

The Eigen values of different attributes capacity, cost, performance, security and maintenance for User 2 are as {0.0540, 0.1831, 0.1723, 0.246, 0.3440} respectively. The comparison matrix for different Resources attributes of clouds according to User 3 on the basis of the priority of Capacity, Cost, Performance, Security and Maintenance are shown in Table 5.

Table 7. Priority values of User 5

	Capacity	Cost	Performance	Security	Maintenance
Capacity	1	1/2	1	1/7	3
Cost	2	1	1/2	1/5	1/3
Performance	1	2	1	3	1/4
Security	7	5	1/3	1	1/2
Maintenance	1/3	3	4	2	1
Total	11.33	11.5	6.83	6.34	5.08

Figure 3. Cloud service vs Priority

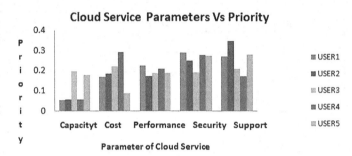

Figure 4. User vs resource priority

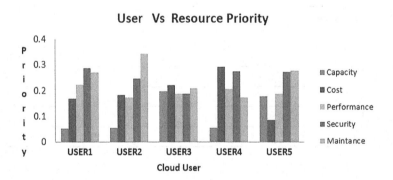

The Eigen values of different attributes capacity, cost, performance, security and maintenance for User 3 are as {0.196, 0.2205, 0.1868, 0.1879, 0.2079} respectively. The comparison matrix for different Resources attributes of clouds according to User 4 on the basis of the priority of Capacity, Cost, Performance, Security and Maintenance are shown in Table 6.

The Eigen values of different attributes capacity, cost, performance, security and maintenance for User 4 are as {0.0553, 0.2902, 0.2070, 0.2753, 0.1720} respectively. The comparison matrix for different Resources attributes of clouds according to User 5 on basis of the priority of Capacity, Cost, Performance, Security and Maintenance are shown in Table 7.

Figure 5. Ranking model

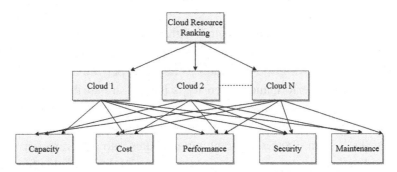

The Eigen values of different attributes capacity, cost, performance, security and maintenance for User 5 are as {0.1781, 0.0867, 0.1861, 0.2713, 0.2775}. The bar chart represented in Figure 3 shows Users priority Vs cloud service parameter requiremets .

The bar chart represented in Figure 4 shows Users vs Resource Priority with respect to different parameters.

From above discussion, following conclusions can be drawn:

For User 1, security is on highest priority. For User 2 and User 5, maintenance is on highest priority. For User 3 and User 4, cost is on highest priority.

CLOUD RESOURCE RANKING MODEL

To produce an efficient ranking methodology, we must adapt good service level agreement to define the terms of QoS guarantee that the cloud user and cloud provider will agree it. Cloud Resource Ranking Model (CRRM) is contracted between a cloud provider and the cloud user that defines the expected level of service that cloud provider should deliver to the user of computing technologies and lot of resources such as CPU, RAM, and Disk storage are required by the cloud users. The cloud architecture gives the opportunity to these users to rent their devices for cloud computing. A Cloud resource ranking model shown in figure 5 is required that can provide the evaluation of different Cloud services based on the need of Cloud users (Srivastava & Daniel, 2019).

The CRRM model provides more expressive and unified way to capture user opinions and preferences of different attributes like capacity, cost, performance, security and maintenance. The proposed CRRM service ranking Model has followed four phases that have been thoroughly discussed in (S.P. Marsh et al., 1994)

1. Expressing ranking attribute into a hierarchical structure
2. Computation of Priority Vector for each user
3. Computation of relative Vector service performances for main Attributes
4. Aggregation of relative service weights.

Expressing Ranking Attributes into a Hierarchical Structure

The hierarchical structure of attributes is represented with their sub attributes as capacity is having sub-attributes CPU, RAM and Disk-space. Similarly, Cost is having sub-attributes as Storage and Virtual Machine Cost. Performance is having sub-attributes as database performance, maximum CPU performance and maximum network performance. Security is having sub-attribute as average strength and finally maintenance is having sub-attributes up-time and free support. Considering all these attributes and sub-attributes shown in Table 8 by different cloud service providers, we are applying these data as a reference to design the system. Expressing ranking attributes into a hierarchical structure provides better understanding of various quality measurements attributes of different cloud services provided by different cloud service providers to measure the quality of services given to users. These attributes and sub-attributes are used in our consideration for the ranking of different Clouds based on the requirements of the Cloud customers and they will be able to choose the best available Cloud to fulfill their requirements; moreover, Cloud service providers can reconsider their Cloud services as per the need of customers based on their Cloud's ranking.

Computation of Relative Vector for Each Main Attribute

The CRRM model provides more expressive and unified way to capture user opinions and preferences of different attributes Capacity, Cost, Performance, Security and Maintenance. This model computes relative vector for main attributes for User1 from Table 1 to Table 7. The computation is performed using Analytical Hierarchical Process (AHP) in which computation is performed by considering the priority vector through Table 1 to Table 7. The priority values of User 1 are represented in Table 2 which is further updated into normalized priority values of User1 in Table 3. Similarly, the same operation is performed for remaining Users. The relative vector is computed in detail for different attributes of Cloud using (AHP) as given below. The first attribute is capacity having sub attribute CPU, RAM, disk storage where CPU speed is in GHz, RAM and disk storage capacity in gigabyte (GB) as in Table 8.

The sub attribute CPU is computed from Table 8

$$\begin{bmatrix} 9.6/9.6 & 9.6/12.8 & 9.6/8.8 & 9.6/9.3 & 9.6/10.2 \\ 12.8/9.6 & 12.8/12.8 & 12.8/8.8 & 12.8/9.3 & 12.8/10.2 \\ 8.8/9.6 & 8.8/12.8 & 8.8/8.8 & 8.8/9.3 & 8.8/10.2 \\ 9.3/9.6 & 9.3/12.8 & 9.3/8.8 & 9.3/9.3 & 9.3/10.2 \\ 10.2/9.6 & 10.2/12.8 & 10.2/8.8 & 10.2/9.3 & 10.2/10.2 \end{bmatrix}$$

$$= \begin{bmatrix} 1 & 0.75 & 1.09 & 1.03 & 0.94 \\ 1.33 & 1 & 1.45 & 1.38 & 1.26 \\ 0.92 & 0.69 & 1 & 0.95 & 0.86 \\ 0.97 & 0.73 & 1.06 & 1 & 0.91 \\ 1.06 & 0.80 & 1.16 & 1.10 & 1 \end{bmatrix}$$

Now S1, S2,…S5 is calculated as follows:

S1 = 1 + 0.75 + 1.09 + 1.03 + 0.94 = 4.81

S2 = 1.33 + 1 + 1.45 + 1.38 + 1.26 = 6.42

S3 = 0.92 + 0.69 + 1 + 0.95 + 0.86 = 4.42

S4 = 0.97 + 0.73 + 1.06 + 1 + 0.91 = 4.67

S5 = 1.06 + 0.8 + 1.16 + 1.1+1.00 = 5.12

S = 25.44

SUM OF S1, S2, S3, S4, S5

S = 25.44

Normalisation of the value

S1 = 0.189
S2 = 0.2524
S3 = 0.1737
S4 = 0.1835
S5 = 0.2012
S = 25.44

The Relative Vector of CPU attributes RV_{CPU} is as follows

RV_{CPU}= [0.1890 0.2524 0.1737 0.1835 0.2012]

We can compute for RV_{RAM}

$$\begin{bmatrix} 15/15 & 15/14 & 15/15 & 15/13 & 15/14 \\ 14/15 & 14/14 & 14/15 & 14/13 & 14/14 \\ 15/15 & 15/14 & 15/15 & 15/13 & 14/14 \\ 13/15 & 13/14 & 13/15 & 13/13 & 13/14 \\ 14/15 & 14/14 & 14/15 & 14/13 & 14/14 \end{bmatrix}$$

$$= \begin{bmatrix} 1 & 1.07 & 1 & 1.15 & 1.07 \\ 0.93 & 1 & 0.93 & 1.08 & 1 \\ 1 & 1.07 & 1 & 1.15 & 1.07 \\ 0.87 & 0.93 & 0.87 & 1 & 0.93 \\ 0.93 & 1 & 0.93 & 1.08 & 1 \end{bmatrix}$$

S1 = 5.29
S2 = 4.94
S3 = 5.29
S4 = 4.6
S5 = 4.94

Sum of S1, S2, S3, S4, S5 = 25.06
Normalizations of values:

S1 = 0.21
S2 = 0.20
S3 = 0.21
S4 = 0.18
S5 = 0.20

$RV_{RAM} = [0.21\ 0.20\ 0.21\ 0.18\ 0.20]$

We can compute for $RV_{disk\text{-}space}$

$$\begin{bmatrix} 1690/1690 & 1690/2040 & 1690/630 & 1690/1250 & 1690/930 \\ 2040/1690 & 2040/2040 & 2040/630 & 2040/1250 & 2040/930 \\ 630/1690 & 630/2040 & 630/630 & 630/1250 & 630/930 \\ 1250/1690 & 1250/2040 & 1250/630 & 1250/1250 & 1250/930 \\ 930/1690 & 930/2040 & 930/630 & 930/1250 & 930/930 \end{bmatrix}$$

$$= \begin{bmatrix} 1 & 0.83 & 2.68 & 1.35 & 1.82 \\ 1.21 & 1 & 3.24 & 1.63 & 2.19 \\ 0.37 & 0.31 & 1 & 0.504 & 0.68 \\ 0.74 & 0.61 & 1.98 & 1 & 1.34 \\ 0.55 & 0.46 & 1.48 & 0.744 & 1 \end{bmatrix}$$

Table 8. Ranking attributes of cloud

Z	Sub-Attributes	Cloud 1	Cloud 2	Cloud 3	Cloud 4	Cloud 5
Capacity	CPU (2v in GHz)	9.6	12.8	8.8	9.3	10.2
	RAM (in GB)	15	14	15	13	14
	Disk Space (in GB)	1690	2040	630	1250	930
Cost	Storage (first 1TB/month $/GB)	0.024	0.0390	0.03	0.048	0.0312
	Vm Cost ($/month 2v CPU)	162.79	97.10	141.00	110.20	117.12
Performance	Database performance (%)	55	68	65	75	72
	Max. CPU performance Score (2v CPU)	2500	3100	3600	3800	4000
	Max. Network performance (in Mbps) 2v CPU	1000	2100	2200	2700	3000
Security	Average Strength	0.6	0.5	0.8	0.7	0.8
Maintenance	Up time (in %)	99.9079%	99.59%	99.92%	99.45%	99.97%
	Free Support (Boolean)	Yes	Yes	No	No	Yes

Table 9. Eigen vector computation

	CPU	RAM	Disk _Space
CPU	1	1/3	1/5
RAM	3	1	1/5
Disk_space	5	5	1
Total	9	6.33	1.4

Table 10. Normalized Eigen values

	Eigen Vector	Priority Vector
CPU	0.1	10%
RAM	0.21	21%
Disk_space	0.69	69%

$S1 = 7.68$
$S2 = 9.27$
$S3 = 2.86$
$S4 = 5.67$
$S5 = 4.23$

Sum of S1, S2, S3, S 4, S5 = 29.71

Table 11. Normalized values

	CPU	RAM	Disk _Space
CPU	0.11	0.05	0.14
RAM	0.33	0.16	0.14
Disk_space	0.55	0.79	0.71

Normalization of values:

S1 = 0.2584
S2 = 0.3120
S3 = 0.0962
S4 = 0.1908
S5 = 0.1423

$RV_{disk-space}$= [0.2584 0.3120 0.0962 0.1908 0.1423]

To calculate the Eigen vector or priority vector of CPU, RAM and Disk space, we follow the steps given below.

We can calculate the Relative Vector of Capacity as follows.

$$RV_{Capacity} = \begin{bmatrix} 0.1890 & 0.21 & 0.2584 \\ 0.2524 & 0.20 & 0.3120 \\ 0.1737 & 0.21 & 0.0962 \\ 0.1835 & 0.18 & 0.1908 \\ 0.2012 & 0.20 & 0.1423 \end{bmatrix} X \begin{bmatrix} 0.10 \\ 0.21 \\ 0.69 \end{bmatrix}$$

$RV_{Capacity}$= [0.2346 0.2716 0.1396 0.1867 0.1671]

Similarly, for second attribute Cost, we have to calculate sub-attribute: Storage, Virtual Machine Cost and for third Attribute Performance. We have to calculate sub-attribute: Database Performance, Maximum Performance Source, and Maximum Network Performance.

We can calculate the respective matrix as given below.

In order to calculate main attribute Cost, we have to calculateSub-attribute:*Storage*

$RV_{Storage}$=[0.1394 0.2268 0.1744 0.2791 0.1802]

So, main attribute: *Cost*

RV_{Cost}= [0.2170 0.1768 0.2056 0.2078 0.1825]

In order to calculate main attribute 'Performance' we have to calculate sub-attributes.

$RV_{DatabaseP}$= [0.1644 0.2033 0.1938 0.2239 0.2144]

RV_{MaxPS}= [0.1445 0.1792 0.2253 0.2196 0.2312]

RV_{MaxNP}= [0.0878 0.1845 0.1933 0.2372 0.2636]

Based on relative vector computation similarly as in relative vector computation from the matrix formed by sub attributes for the attribute capacity, the main attribute: Performance

$RV_{performance}$= [0.1274 0.1831 0.2087 02245 0.2380]

The third attribute is *Security* is computed from Table 5 as

$$\begin{bmatrix} 1 & 1.2 & 0.75 & 0.86 & 0.75 \\ 0.83 & 1 & 0.63 & 0.71 & 0.63 \\ 1.33 & 1.6 & 1 & 1.14 & 1 \\ 1.66 & 1.4 & 0.88 & 1 & 0.88 \\ 1.33 & 1.6 & 1 & 1.14 & 1 \end{bmatrix}$$

S1 = 4.56
S2 = 3.8
S3 = 6.07
S4 = 5.82
S5 = 6.07

Sum of S1, S2, S3, S4, S5=26.38
Normalizations of values:-

S1 = 0.1728 S2 = 0.1440 S3 = 0.23

S4 = 0.2206

S5=0.23

So, $RV_{security}$= [0.1728 0.1440 0.23 0.2206 0.23]

The third attribute is *Maintenance* and to compute this attribute, we have to compute sub-attribues *Up-time* and *Free-support* is computed from table-5 as
Sub-attribute:Up-time

Table 12. Free Support

	Up-time	Free Support
Up-time	1	1/3
Free support	3	1
TOTAL	4	1.33

Table 13. Normalized Eigen, Priority Vector

	Eigen Vector	Priority Vector
Up-time	0.2490	24.90%
Free Support	0.7509	75.09%

Table 14. Boolean representation of Free Support

C1	C2	C3	C4	C5
YES	YES	NO	NO	YES
1	1	0	0	1

$$\begin{bmatrix} 1 & 1.003 & 0.9998 & 1.0046 & 1.0044 \\ 0.9968 & 1 & 0.9967 & 1.0014 & 1.0012 \\ 1.001 & 1.0033 & 1 & 1.0047 & 1.0012 \\ 0.9954 & 0.9985 & 0.9952 & 1 & 0.9998 \\ 0.9956 & 0.9987 & 0.9955 & 1.0002 & 1 \end{bmatrix}$$

S1 = 5.012
S2 = 4.9961
S3 = 5.0126
S4 = 4.9889
S5 = 4.99

Sum of S1, S2, S3, S4, S5 = 24.9996
Normalizations of values:

S1 = 0.2004
S2 = 0.1998
S3 = 0.2005
S4 = 0.1995

S5 = 0.1996

$RV_{\text{Up-time}}$ =[0.20004 0.1998 0.2005 0.1995 0.1996]

Eigen Vector for both sub-attributes of maintenance is shown in table below:
According to Table 8, we can represent the Free Support in tabular form as given below.
Boolean representation:

$S_i / S_j = 1$ if $V_i = V_j$

$= W_q$ if $V_j = 1$ and $V_i = 0$

$= 1 / W_q$ if $V_j = 0$ and $V_i = 1$

According to above method the matrix to represent Free Support looks like:

$$\begin{bmatrix} 1 & 1 & 0.7509 & 0.7509 & 0.7509 \\ 1 & 1 & 0.7509 & 0.7509 & 0.7509 \\ 1.3317 & 1.3317 & 1 & 1 & 1 \\ 1.3317 & 1.3317 & 1 & 1 & 1 \\ 1.3317 & 1.3317 & 1 & 1 & 1 \end{bmatrix}$$

S1 = 4.2527
S2 = 4.9961
S3 = 5.6634
S4 = 5.6634
S5 = 5.6634

Sum of S1, S2, S3, S4, S5 = 25.456
Normalizations of values:

S1 = 0.1668
S2 = 0.1668
S3 = 0.2221
S4 = 0.2221
S5 = 0.2221

$RV_{\text{Free-Support}}$ = [0.1668 0.1668 0.2221 0.2221 0.2221]

Now,

$RV_{Maintenance} = [0.1751\ 0.1750\ 0.2166\ 0.2164\ 0.2165]$

After successfully computation of relative vectors for all the attributes and sub-attributes of Table8, we can get the final relative vector by multiplying Eigen values with all the Relative Vector of main attributes i.e. capacity, cost, performance, security and maintenance.

$$RV = \begin{bmatrix} 0.2346 & 0.2170 & 0.1274 & 0.1728 & 0.1751 \\ 0.2716 & 0.1768 & 0.1831 & 0.1440 & 0.1750 \\ 0.1396 & 0.2056 & 0.2087 & 0.2300 & 0.2166 \\ 0.1867 & 0.2078 & 0.2245 & 0.2206 & 0.2164 \\ 0.1671 & 0.1825 & 0.2380 & 0.2300 & 0.2165 \end{bmatrix} \begin{bmatrix} 0.5270 \\ 0.1691 \\ 0.2231 \\ 0.2861 \\ 0.2688 \end{bmatrix}$$

$RV_{USER1} = [0.1739\ 0.1732\ 0.2127\ 0.2163\ 0.2167]$

Therefore, Relative Vector value of User1 is computed for ranking of Cloud service providerC1, C2, C3, C4 and C5 as follows.

C5 > C4 > C3 > C1 > C2

Therefore, Cloud service provider 'C5' is best suited for User1 requirements.

The Relative Vector value of User 2 is computed for ranking of Clouds service providerC1, C2, C3, C4 and C5 are as follows.

$RV_{USER2} = [0.1772\ 0.1743\ 0.2123\ 0.2156\ 0.2146]$

C4 > C5 > C3 > C1 > C2.

Therefore, Cloud service provider 'C4' is best suited for User2 requirements.

The Relative Vector value of User 3 is computed for ranking of Clouds service providerC1, C2, C3, C4, and C5 are as follows.

$RV_{USER3} = [0.1865\ 0.1898\ 0.1999\ 0.2107\ 0.2056]$

C4 > C5 > C3 > C2 > C1.

Therefore, Cloud service provider 'C4' is best suited for User 3 requirements.

The Relative Vector value of User4 is computed for ranking of Clouds service providerC1, C2, C3, C4, and C5 are as follows.

$RV_{USER4} = [0.1800\ 0.1739\ 0.2111\ 0.2150\ 0.2120]$

Figure 6. Cloud's attribute comparison

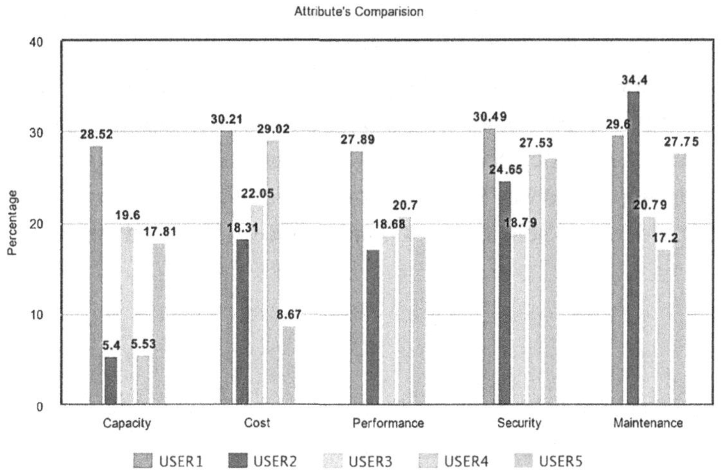

C4 > C5 > C3 > C1 > C2.

Therefore, cloud service provider 'C4' is best suited for User4 requirements.

The Relative Vector value of User5 is computed for ranking of clouds service providerC1, C2, C3, C4, and C5 are as follows.

$$RV_{USER5}=[0.1797\ 0.1854\ 0.2040\ 0.2129\ 0.2123]$$

Based on USER5's requirements, the cloud services are ranked as given below.

C4 > C5 > C3 > C2 > C1.

Therefore, cloud service provider 'C4' is best suited for User5 requirements.

The overall comparison graph of attributes for different clouds is given in Figure 6 below.

The proposed cloud ranking model observed that the attributes which are taken into consideration for various clouds is based on our gathered information in Table 8.It is observed that 'C4' cloud fulfills the requirements of different users on various attributes: capacity, cost, performance, security and maintenance of the users.

CONCLUSION

Cloud computing as an emerging field promises revolutionary advantages over conventional computing infrastructure. Today, cloud providers are offering a huge number of Cloud services with varying number of performance attribute to match the need of customer from the viewpoint of cost involved. The Cloud users are looking for the finest Cloud services that can provide/satisfy their requisites in terms of various parameters i.e. capacity, cost, performance, security and maintenance. The proposed CSSM ranking model uses an Analytical Hierarchical Process and logical model for assessing the Cloud services based on their rankings. The ranking model processes each given attributes for computing the relative ranking of different Cloud services. It also distinctly addresses the different sub-parameters of various parameters for assessing the relative Cloud services rankings for each parameter. The results show the detailed data-oriented cloud service analysis to helps the Cloud users for micromanagement of their needs.

The proposed ranking model presents rank of the Cloud services in much effective way for a given set of parameters as capacity, cost, performance, security, maintenance. It is our belief that our proposed model plays a significant step in the way of determining precise measurement of Cloud services for different Cloud service providers and selection of Cloud services for Cloud customers.

REFERENCES

Alshehri. (2019). *Effective Mechanism for Selection of Cloud Service Provider Using Cosine Maximization Method. Arabian Journal for Science and Engineering.*

Clerk Maxwell, J. (1892). A Treatise on Electricity and Magnetism (vol. 2). Clarendon.

Eason, G., Noble, B., & Sneddon, I. N. (1955). On certain integrals of Lipschitz-Hankel type involving products of Bessel functions. *Philosophical Transactions of the Royal Society of London. Series A, Mathematical and Physical Sciences, 247*(935), 529–551. doi:10.1098/rsta.1955.0005

Garg, S. K., Versteeg, S., & Buyya, R. (2011, December). Smicloud: A framework for comparing and ranking cloud services. In *2011 Fourth IEEE International Conference on Utility and Cloud Computing* (pp. 210-218). IEEE. 10.1109/UCC.2011.36

Hofer, C. N. (2009). Cloud Computing Services: Taxonomy and comparison. *Fifth International Joint Conference on INC, IMS and IDC*, 44-51.

Hu, R., Liu, J., & Liu, X. F. (2011, May). A trustworthiness fusion model for service cloud platform based on DS evidence theory. In *Proceedings of the 2011 11th IEEE/ACM International Symposium on Cluster, Cloud and Grid Computing* (pp. 566-571). IEEE Computer Society. 10.1109/CCGrid.2011.31

Jacobs, I. S. (1963). Fine particles, thin films and exchange anisotropy. *Magnetism*, 271-350.

Marsh, S. P. (1994). Formalising trust as a computational concept. Computing, 184.

Noor, T. H., Sheng, Q. Z., Zeadally, S., & Yu, J. (2013). Trust management of services in cloud environments: Obstacles and solutions. *ACM Computing Surveys, 46*(1), 1–30. doi:10.1145/2522968.2522980

Ouzzani, M., & Bouguettaya, A. (2004). Efficient access to web services. *IEEE Internet Computing, 8*(2), 34–44. doi:10.1109/MIC.2004.1273484

Pandey, S., & Daniel, A. K. (2016, March). Fuzzy logic based cloud service trustworthiness model. In *2016 IEEE International Conference on Engineering and Technology (ICETECH)* (pp. 73-78). IEEE. 10.1109/ICETECH.2016.7569215

Pandey, S., & Daniel, A. K. (2017). QoCS and cost based cloud service selection framework. *Int. J. Eng. Trends Technol., 48*(3), 167–172. doi:10.14445/22315381/IJETT-V48P230

Rajarajeswari, C. S., & Aramudhan, M. (2015). Ranking Of Cloud Service Providers In Cloud. *Journal of Theoretical & Applied Information Technology*, *78*(2).

Ray, B. K., Middya, A. I., Roy, S., & Khatua, S. (2017, January). Multi-criteria based federation selection in cloud. In *2017 9th International Conference on Communication Systems and Networks (COMSNETS)* (pp. 182-189). IEEE. 10.1109/COMSNETS.2017.7945375

Rong, H., & Jian-xun, L. (2010, November). Trustworthiness fusion of web service based on DS evidence theory. In *2010 Sixth International Conference on Semantics, Knowledge and Grids* (pp. 343-346). IEEE. 10.1109/SKG.2010.55

Srivastava, R., & Daniel, A. K. (2019). Efficient Model of Cloud Trustworthiness for Selecting Services Using Fuzzy Logic. In *Emerging Technologies in Data Mining and Information Security* (pp. 249–260). Singapore: Springer. doi:10.1007/978-981-13-1951-8_23

Supriya, M., Sangeeta, K., & Patra, G. K. (2014, October). Estimation of Trust values for Varying Levels of Trustworthiness based on Infrastructure as a Service. In *Proceedings of the 2014 International Conference on Interdisciplinary Advances in Applied Computing* (p. 16). ACM. 10.1145/2660859.2660921

Zhang, Y., Zhang, Y., & Hai, M. (2012, August). An evaluation model of software trustworthiness based on fuzzy comprehensive evaluation method. In *2012 International Conference on Industrial Control and Electronics Engineering* (pp. 616-619). IEEE. 10.1109/ICICEE.2012.167

Zhou, M., Zhang, R., Xie, W., Qian, W., & Zhou, A. (2010, November). Security and privacy in cloud computing: A survey. In *2010 Sixth International Conference on Semantics, Knowledge and Grids* (pp. 105-112). IEEE. 10.1109/SKG.2010.19

Chapter 9
Paradigms of Machine Learning and Data Analytics

Pawan Kumar Chaurasia
https://orcid.org/0000-0001-7213-9157
Mahatma Gandhi Central University, Motihari, India

ABSTRACT

This chapter conducts a critical review on ML and deep learning tools and techniques in the field of heart disease related to heart disease complexity, prediction, and diagnosis. Only specific papers are selected for the study to extract useful information, which stimulated a new hypothesis to understand further investigation of the heart disease patient.

INTRODUCTION

Artificial Intelligence (AI), Machine Learning (ML) and Deep Learning (DL) are emerging fields that can provide businesses with a competitive environment. Machine learning is being developed as one of the most interesting tools for the organizations which are cautious for innovations to help the businesses on a new height. Today, world is investing heavy money to adopt new technology and computational methods developed by researchers, medical practitioners and patients. ML is related with the computing task where designing and programming algorithms are applied. It is sometimes mix with data mining which is more focused on intended data analytics. Machine learning and pattern recognition can be seen as the same field. It is important for organization to realize and make use of relevant advance techniques to preside over development and to be focused on arising changes. It is a systematic approach to look into investigation on advance algorithms and models to continuously train data set and test with other data to put on the most convenient algorithms for the machine learning. Data scientists have already started focusing on using the right algorithm by using the most appropriate data with the best operating models. If all these components come together, it is potential of the model to learn from the data by pattern recognition techniques and performs actions by learning from outputs.

Data is continuously increasing, therefore appropriate models are required to change and predict the future. ML helps and alters a system to acquire knowledge from data rather than programming. It adopts

DOI: 10.4018/978-1-7998-2491-6.ch009

a variety of algorithms that continuously learn from data to improve the existing system and outputs. A ML model generates the output when the algorithms of machine learning train the data. After training of the model, when input is provided to model, the output will be generated. ML and DL provides methodology and technology to extract valuable knowledge for the decision making. Today, healthcare industry generates huge amount of data such as clinical data, e-health data, data generated from health records and prescriptions of medicines. Various machine learning algorithms are used for the structure and study of algorithms that can learn from and prediction on that data. Pattern recognition is one of the fundamental concepts of artificial intelligence. ML and data analytics are the subset of Artificial Intelligence (AI). There are various machine learning techniques and tools available today to extract effective knowledge from databases and to use this knowledge for decision making, fraud detection, email filtering, supermarket analysis etc. AI is being used to make machine intelligent, which can take decision on its own level. The requisite for data analytics has been developed in most of the scientific indoctrination in addition to engineering; economics; business; healthcare and life sciences. Data scientists are using ML techniques to accomplish business objectives. Healthcare deals with the skill, transmission, storage and retrieval of accurate information for the early detection, diagnosis and then for the treatment of the patients. For providing better healthcare facilities, all over world is focusing on providing economic, quality, approachable and seamless healthcare facilities.

There are many grounds to start the machine learning. The modern field of data science (part of supervised learning) has grown in a complex and interesting format to get inputs from various sources, disciplines and fields. It is also a process that involves the use of a machine to make decision based on multiple data inputs. Machine learning is defined as an autonomous process taken out the patterns from data. It restrains an adamant of methods, which give a machine to learn revelatory patterns from data directly with very less human cooperation. The effectiveness of a ML technique relies on human skills. Such skills can make it easier for a machine to learn more accurately through the techniques like effective feature detection, relocation learning and multi-task learning. The most successful kind of ML algorithms is to control a decision making steps by globalizing from known examples. The objective of healthcare is related with diseases, healthcare records and the computational techniques associated with handling of such data. ML algorithms are robotizing the steps of learning a model that is gaining the relationship between the expressive features and the intended features in a dataset.

ROLE OF STATISTIC AND DATA MINING

The purpose of statistics data mining and ML is to understand data by illustrating the specifications of a dataset, interpretations of relationships & patterns in that data to build a model. Data mining and ML algorithms are initiated in traditional statistical analysis. Data scientists and researchers have combined the engineering background with specialization in data mining, ML and statistics to involve in all disciplines. By using statistical model and technology, one can predict outcomes, understand the problem of the business and business objectives. Data mining depends on the fundamental of statistics to course of exploring and analyzing huge amount of data to find unique patterns in that data. Models are used to discover pattern and relationship in that data. It is also helpful to solve a variety of business issues. The purpose of data mining and ML is to explain and realize the data. It is not meant to make predictions or backup hypothesis. The general objective of data mining is to extract data from a large data set

Figure 1. Traditional programming vs machine learning

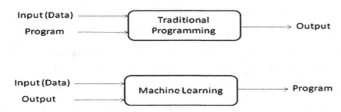

for prediction and classification. The decision making process of human also supports it. Hence, it is proposed to display patterns that can be utilized by human beings.

ML needs to give some context of AI and Deep Learning that are frequently used in progressive technology. AI can be noticeable as the broadest way of describing systems. When we search ML, we concentrate on the capability to learn & comply a model depending on the data rather than rift programming. ML techniques are needed to achieve better accuracy in the models of prediction which depend on the attributes of the business.

TYPES OF MACHINE LEARNING

The idea of ML from technical principles as an ideological tool has had a long history in statistics I. Jordan (Han, Kamber and Pei, 2012). He has also proposed about the data science as ML algorithms to learn from labeled data called supervised learning algorithms. "Teacher" serves guidance in the form of the target outputs to the algorithm.ML is different from traditional programming. Traditional programming required input (data) and program. But in ML, we need input (data) and output (data) which is presented in figure 1 given below. ML is classified into two parts; supervised and unsupervised machine learning techniques.

Supervised Machine Learning (SML)

SML starts with presenting a collection of data and a specific understanding of how that data is separated. The intention of SML is to detect patterns in data that can be used to an analytics progression. For example, millions of images of animals and inclusion of the details of each animal in the form of labels create a machine learning application that distinguishes one animal from another. Therefore, the attributes and the meaning of the data have been detected. It is well explained by the users that train the model data, so that, it can be well-suited to the technicalities of the labels.

In supervised machine learning, every example (or instance) in a dataset is given with known labels used by ML algorithm to train the model (Bekkerman, Bilenko, and Langford., 2011).An algorithm is implemented to learn from the input variable (X) which is the mapping function to the output variable (Y); means Y = f(X). Supervised machine learning has labeled the data and models are trained using this labeled data represented in figure 2. The objective is to estimate the mapping function, so that, the input data (X) can figure out the output variables (Y) for that data. Labeled datasets have both the input and output parameters. It is called supervised learning because it iteratively learns from the training dataset and then uses this learning to predict classes for new observations. Cross-validation is a method

Figure 2. Supervised Learning

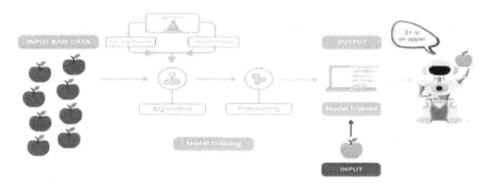

used to calculate predictive models in supervised learning by splitting the original dataset into training set to train the model and a test set to test the accuracy of model. In k-fold cross-validation, the original sample is randomly divided into k equal size subsets from which a single subset is taken as the data for validation purpose as well as testing purpose and the left k-1 subsets are used to train the model. The cross-validation procedure is then repeated k times with each of the k-subsets utilized only once as the validation data. The average accuracy of k-folds is taken as final accuracy(Murphy, 2012). Further, SML is classified into two categories: Classification and Regression.

Classification

It is a type of supervised machine learning technique which is most widely used. The objective of classification is to label the class from the predefined list of possibilities. It is classified into binary classification and multi-class classification. Binary classification is based on exactly two classes while multi-classification is based on more than two classes. The binary classification provides answer either 'Yes' or 'No'. In binary classification, one class is known as the positive class and the other is known as the negative class. It is two stage process; the first one is called learning stage where the model is constructed and trained by a pre-determined dataset with class labels (training set) and second one is classification (testing) stage where the model is used to predict class labels for given data (test data) to estimate the accuracy of classifier model (Bengio, 2009). The class attributes of dataset, used in classification to train and test the model, have categorical (discrete, unordered) values instead of continuous values. Classification is used with the problems where the answer to our question about our business falls under a finite set of possible outcomes such as determining an email as spam or not, analyzing an employee whether he can buy a laptop or not, finding socio-economic status of a person(multi-label) classification (Kotsiantis, 2007) etc. There are various algorithms for the implementation of supervised classification technique namely Support Vector Machine (SVM), Naive Bayes, Decision Trees, Logistic Regression and K-Nearest Neighbour etc. There are basically six types of classification.

Logistic Regression

It is one of the famous machine learning algorithms similar to linear regression. The only differences are in the way of presentation. It is a class of classifier used for classification; whereas, linear regression is used for prediction. Logistic regression is used to predict or classify the probability of dependent variables. These are the binary variables coded as 1 being success or yes and 0 being failure or no. Linear regression is not restricted between 0and 1 but logistic regression predicts the probability strictly between the range of 0 and 1. Logistic regression is applied on the categorical type of dependent variable. For example, logistic regression is used to predict whether an email being spam (1) or not (0),raining outside (1) or not (0) etc. In this type of classification problems, linear regression is not suitable for the example of algorithm predicts value 0.4 and threshold value being 0.5.Then, it will predict no answer which will incorrect and create serious issue. So, logistic regression came in the scenario which strictly bound by 0 and 1 range. Logistic regression is defined by a sigmoid function and it predicts P(Y=1) as a function of X. Logistic regression is of many types as given below.

1. Binary logistic regression- Here, possible outcomes are two such as email being spam or not.
2. Multinomial logistic regression- The possible outcomes are 3 or more such as a person being vegetarian, non-vegetarian or vegan.
3. Ordinal logistic regression- here, categories are in ordersuch as move ratings from 1 to 5.

Naive Bayes Classifier

It is one of the popular algorithms in the machine learning technique. It is based on the rule of Bayesian theorem which describes the probability of events. Below is the theorem of Bayesian from which Naive Bayes are inspired. Let X and Y are events; P (X|Y) is probability of X given with Y; P (Y|X) is the probability of Y given with X; and, P(X) and P(Y) are the independent probabilities of X and Y.

$$P(X \mid Y) = \frac{P(Y \mid X) P(X)}{P(Y)}$$

This is a kind of classification technique which gives result by classifying other events which are related to them. It is very useful algorithm for large datasets and gives better accuracy as compared to other classification techniques. The fundamental principle of Bayesian theorem is Naive Bayes algorithm analysis which is the relationship between attribute values and the classes. This classifiers is used to estimate the probability of having features of continues and discrete feature.

Stochastic Gradient Descent

It is another one of the famous algorithm in machine learning. It is based on the neural network. Gradient means the slope which moves downward to reach the minimum or lowest point. It is one of the optimization algorithms. There are three different type of gradient descent given below.

1. Batch gradient descent- When we sum up all examples for each learning step.
2. Mini batch gradient- When we sum up lower number of example based on the batch size.
3. Stochastic gradient descent- It updates parameters on each example rather than using all examples.

The main difference between three of them is amount of data we used to calculate the gradient of iteration of learning. Stochastic gradient descent selects random point and moves downward to get optimum point. It applies mostly on the deep learning models and on huge training data. The big data is splitted into batch or samples. Stochastic gradient descent algorithm first chooses the sample or batch from training set and then calculates objective function for that one batch.

K-Nearest Neighbor (KNN)

It is one of the basic classification algorithms in machine learning. It belongs to the supervised learning algorithm and is applied mostly for data mining and pattern recognition problems. KNN is a Non-parametric learning algorithm. Non-parametric means there is no assumption. The model structure is defined from dataset. In KNN, K is the number of nearest neighbor which is very important factor in this algorithm. KNN algorithm follows some steps given as (1) calculate distance of neighbors to the objective,(2) find nearest neighbors, and finally, (3) give orders of distance from smallest to largest by the distance. K nearest neighbor algorithm is very simple and easy to apply. This algorithm can be used for classification as well as regression.

Decision Tree

Decision tree algorithm is very important and widely used algorithm in machine learning methods. Most of the time, it is used for classification but sometimes regression problems can also be solved by using decision tree algorithm. Decision tree, as name suggests, takes decision like human brain and solves the problem by making tree like structure. In the tree, each root or internal node represents the attribute and each leaf node represents the class.

Random Forest

It is a class of supervised learning algorithm, which is implemented in both the classification type of problems as well as regret type of problems. As name suggests, the forest means collection of many trees. So, this algorithm is also a collection of many decision trees. It is better to use over decision tree because it reduces the over fitting by averaging the results. Random forest follows steps as given below.

1. Select the random samples from dataset
2. Construct a decision tree for every sample and predicts the result of every tree
3. Give vote to each result, and finally,
4. Select the most voted result.

Figure 3. Linear regression

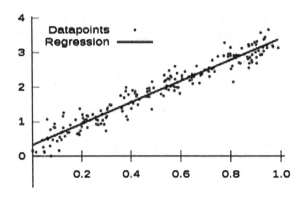

Support Vector Machine (SVM)

It is a type of supervised learning algorithm used for both classification and regression type of problems. In SVM models, examples are represented as the point in space, so that, one category is divided by clear gap. It is defined as the separating hyper plane. In two dimensional spaces, this hyper plane is a line dividing two parts by separating each class.

REGRESSION

Regression is also supervised machine learning technique but used to predict the outputs that have numerical (continuous) values represented in figure 3. It is useful with the problems where we have to represent or predict output by a number rather than being restricted to a set of possible labels (Kotsiantis, 2007). If we want to predict rain in centimeters, price of houses, speed of wind etc., we have to use regression analysis as it develops the models that are used to predict a continuous function (Bengio, 2009). Linear regression supports vector machine. The random forest is one algorithm used to implement regression models.

TYPES OF REGRESSION

There are basically six types of regression model used which are described here.

Linear Regression

Linear regression is very simple and easy algorithm that is used for statistical learning method. It assumes that there is a linear relationship between two variables. Let, a and b predicted the response Y from variable X. Linear regression is implemented by simple and linear equation given below.

$Y = a + bX$,

where, Y is the dependent variable and X is the independent variable; a and b are the constants.

Polynomial Regression

When the data is correlated or linear, it can be implemented with linear regression. But, if the data is not correlated or nonlinear, it is not fitted with a linear line and then linear regression is not suitable. For this type of problems or polynomial equations, polynomial regression is used to fit the equations which are not fitted by the linear regression. For polynomial equations, it is necessary to use polynomial regression to minimize error or minimize the cost function. Polynomial regression method is best to show the relationship between the dependent and independent variables. Polynomial regression is used to implement polynomial equation given below.

$Y = a + bX + cX^2$,

where, a, b and c are the constants.

Quintile Regression

When the prediction is not restricted to one or single estimate but also the likely range which is called prediction interval, the quintile regression method is used. It is different from random forest in the way that in random forest, all the results of decision trees are combined by averaging each tree node. In quintile regression, all the results are stored, so that, quintiles of each leaf can be calculated.

Ridge Regression

Ridge regression is a technique that is used to deal with over fitting type of problems. When the training data is failed to create real relationship instead of using higher order polynomials, then this problem is called as over fitting type of problems. Ridge regression is applied with large dataset and is a kind of regularization type of algorithm. To reduce the error between predicted and actual observation, penalties are introduced. These are called as regularization technique. In ridge regression, L2 penalties are added. When the data is very large and having number of features, parsimonious models are created. The ridge regression is a powerful technique to create so. In ridge regression, penalties are added as equivalent to square of magnitude of co-efficient.

Lasso Regression

It stands for least absolute shrinkage and selection operator. The two terms are highlighted here are absolute and selection. It is used for selection and regularization both to enhance the prediction accuracy and interoperability of the model. Lasso regression is same as ridge regression and deals with over fitting type of problems.

Figure 4. Unsupervised learning

Figure 5. Clustering in ML

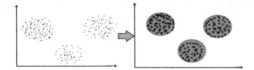

Elastic Net Regression

It is a combination of ridge regression and lasso regression. It is the regularization regression method that combines both L1 and L2 penalties of Lasso and ridge methods. When we have multiple correlated features, elastic net regression is used over ridge and lasso. It is very stable in many cases.

UNSUPERVISED LEARNING (UL)

UL is best suited for the problems requiring enormous quantity of data that is unlabeled. For example, social sites, social media applications, twitter, Instagram, chatting etc. All are generating huge amount of unlabeled data. To understand the meaning of the data, appropriate algorithm is required that can understand the data and classify it according to similar patterns. It is a repetitive process of analyzing the data without human interference. It is applied in email spam detection methodology. There is lot of variables in email spam for an investigator to flag voluntary bulk email. ML classifiers are dependent on association and clustering which are used to identify undesired emails.

Unsupervised machine learning follows a different approach to make models to learn, because patterns are learned from the examples (inputs) without supplying corresponding output (labels) (Alpaydın, 2010). Algorithms are located to discover patterns and inherit structure from the data. It is useful with problems where only unlabeled data is available to build model as shown in Figure 4. Unsupervised learning is further classified into clustering and association.

CLUSTERING

Clustering is basically an unsupervised machine learning technique. It is based on dividing the set of data or population into a number of groups such that records or objects in the same groups are more similar to each other and dissimilar to the records or objects in other groups as represented in figure 5. Clustering helps to understand natural gathering or structure in a dataset and has no predefined classes (She and Chaurasia, 2019). Some of the cluster based algorithms are K-means clustering, Density-Based Spatial Clustering of Applications with Noise (DBSCAN), shift clustering, Density and Agglomerative Hierarchical Clustering.

Types of Clustering

There are basically five types of clustering methods.

Partitioning Method

It is used to create groups of features on the basis of similarities in large dataset. The number of generated clusters is analyzed in the algorithm by different ways. The methods of creating clusters are defined in the section of partitioning algorithm. Partitioning algorithm breaks the clusters in following ways.

1. **K- Means Clustering:** In k-means clustering, dataset is divided into k no. of clusters and each cluster is represented by the cent of the data point. K means clustering is introduced by James Macqueen in 1967.If the dataset is large, k means clustering works faster. Here, in this, clusters are tighter than others. This method is sensitive to outliers.
2. **K-Medoids Clustering or PAM:** It stands for partitioning around medoids. PAM is first introduced by Kaufman and Rousseeuw in 1987. Each cluster is represented as one of the object of the cluster. It works faster and accurately than k means by first selecting k mediods and then swapping those objects with non-mediods. It groups the clusters in the form of objects rather than mean value. It is simple and easy method of clustering. This method is less sensitive to outliers.

CLARA Algorithm

It stands for Clustering Large Applications. It is developed by Kaufman and Rousseeuw in 1988.It is the extension of the PAM used for large datasets than PAM.

CLARANS

It stands for clustering large applications based on randomized search. It is developed by Ng and Han in 1994 to overcome the limitations of K- medoid algorithm. It is more effective and efficient than both PAM and CLARA and very simple and easy to implement.

Hierarchical Clustering

Hierarchical clusters group the data or create clusters of data in the hierarchy of tree. In this grouping, the similar data is represented in the form of dendrogram. The analysts use statistical methods to analyze this structure. Hierarchical clustering is of two types.

1. Agglonerative hierarchical clustering also known as bottom up approach. Here, sub clusters are grouped in the clusters of clusters.
2. Divisive clustering also known as top down approach. Here, clusters are considered as single cluster and spitted into several clusters.

Agglonerative hierarchical clustering and divisive clustering are two important approaches in hierarchical clustering. There are many examples of hierarchical clustering like BRICH (Balance iterative reducing and clustering using hierarchies) and CURE (Cluster using representatives).

Density Based Clustering

Spherical shaped clusters are used in this type of clustering. It is introduced on the basis of density data points. This clustering is very useful to handling noise at some extent by single scan of input data set. The density parameters of data set should be defined properly to reduce noise. It helps the cluster to increase their size as long as density of neighbor exceeds a certain threshold.Example of this clustering is DBSCAN (Density based spatial clustering of applications with noise), DENCLUE (Density based clustering) and OPTICS.

Grid Based Clustering

As the name indicates, grid based clustering method generates clusters in the structure of grid where each cell of the grid has finite number of object space. In this algorithm, the following steps are followed.

1. The data set is first splitted into finite number of cells.
2. The density of cell is calculated.
3. Each cell is arranged according to density of each cell.
4. The centre of the cluster is defined.
5. Finally, calculation of the distance between clusters, that are neighbor to each other, is done.

This algorithm has many advantages as it does not need the distance calculation between data objects and is fast as compared to others. The example of suchalgorithm are STING (statistical information grid approach), Wave Cluster and CLIQOE(clustering in QUEST).

Model Based Clustering Method

It is based on the mathematical and statistical model.It automatically generates clusters according to statistical model. It is based on hypothesizing model for every cluster. STATISTICAL approach and COBWEB are examples of model based algorithm.

Association

Associative rule miming is a technique of data mining which is used to find associative rules or patterns in data. In association rule mining, patterns are identified which depends on a correlation of a specific item to other items in the identical transaction. It finds frequent item sets in data by using predefined support and confidence values (Murphy, 2012). An item set is coming at short interval of item set, if it's calculated value is greater than minimum value experience.

Support

It determines the measure (percentage) of item/item set transactions with respect to all the transactions that are under analysis. For example,

$$\frac{Number\ of\ transactions\ include\ item\ x\ and\ y}{Total\ number\ of\ transactions}$$

Support(X=>Y) = probability(x Union y)

Confidence

It is the ratio of number of items in {X} and items in {Y} from the number of transaction to all items in {X} from the same transaction. Rules are considered as powerful rules that satisfy both minimum confidence threshold (min-conf) and minimum support threshold (min-sup) (Bengio, 2009). Some of the leading algorithms of association are Apriori algorithm and FP-Growth algorithm.

SEMI-SUPERVISED LEARNING

It lies somewhere between unsupervised and supervised learning algorithms and a combination of unlabeled data and labeled data. This learning is used in many applications classification like classification of webpage, speech recognition and genetic sequencing. Semi-supervised learning is broadly classified into two classes, clustering and classification (Castle, 2017).

REINFORCEMENT LEARNING (RL)

Reinforcement learning models are inspired from behavioral learning model. In this, the user can control the best outputs by receiving the feedback from the analyst. RL is different from SL and USL because in the RL, system is not trained with the example data. Therefore, the system learns from hit and trial error method. Hence, a series of successful and unsuccessful outcomes in the procedure is being "reinforced" because it solves the best problem. One of the most famous and popular applications of reinforcement learning is in the game playing and robotics. Robot learns from the outcomes and changes its way of doing approach to solve any problem. Every time when the robot falls, it applies different methods by recalibrating the data and navigates all the previous steps and trains itself by hit and trial error method to know how to climb stairs. In simple words, the robot learns from the successful series of actions. The learning algorithm has to be capable to discover an association between the targets of successfully climbing stairs without failing the series of events to follow the outcome.

In reinforcement learning there is no training labeled set of data. The fundamental concept of reinforcement learning is that a software agent, which interacts with environment, is awarded for best performing actions. As human being learns, the agents do in the same way. For example, a situation is created where a robot has been given a task to find best path from the hurdles of fire to reach to the diamond. The robot starts to try from all the paths and learns by trying all the possible paths and then choosing the path which gives him reward with the least hurdles. Every time a reward is given for every right step and for each wrong step will subtract the reward. When the robot reaches to the diamond for the final reward, total rewards are calculated.

DATA ANALYTICS

Modern organizations collect massive amounts of data. For data to be of valued to an organization, they must be analyzed to extract insights that can be used to make better decisions. To analyze the data, it is found that some of the variation exists in that data. Still, for more clearance about data, it must exist in large amount so that we identify those anomalies that were supposed to be faults. These are actually suggested for the sign of a difference in the patterns of customer purchasing behavior or the satisfaction of customer. As more data is added into a model, trained, and analyzed with the most convenient machine learning algorithms, it becomes clearer that there are changes that will directly impact the future of the business. Data Analytics is the term that explains the processing techniques, extracting information from software and system and allowing the users to figure out conclusions, to support scientific theories, to make best decisions, and to organize assumptions (Han, Kamber and Pei, 2012). Data analytics is one of the demanding jobs nowadays after emergence of the modern scientific disciplines, including engineering, natural, computer and information sciences, commerce, environment, economics, business, healthcare, and life sciences. Efforts to understand the feeling from data is the job of data analytics.

Predictive Analytics

Based on the historical data and current data analysis, predictive analytics makes predictions on future events. For making high profit rates with improved performance and real-time processing, it is necessary for analytics to make better decision that motivates businesses. It uses the understanding of the past to make predictions about the future. Suppose, if anyone visited the e-commerce site and begins to watch products and starts reading reviews, but we're likely presented with other type of similar products that you may find more interesting. These testimonials aren't difficult to be coded by the developers. The suggestions are attended by the site through machine learning model. The model takes browsing history of the customer along with other agents' browsing and purchasing habit related data in order to present other exchangeable products that you may like to purchase. It is applicable in both real-time to affect the operational process "What could happen?".

Descriptive Analytics

It helps the analysts to understand the reality of the business. Therefore, it is needed to understand the circumstances for historical data in order to understand the current status of the business. This methodology supports an organization to get answer and questions such as "Which product styles are performing better in first quarter as compared to last quarter?" or "Which regions are demonstrating the highest growth?". It is simple form of analytics which aggregates the whole data and provides insights. Analytics uses data aggregation and data mining to provide insight into the past and answer "What has happened?". Whether the event has occurred one minute ago or one year ago, it refers to the exact point of time. It allows the machine to learn from past experiences and understand how they might influence the outcomes of future, so that, it is useful.

Prescriptive Analytics

It uses business rules, machine learning and statistical model in order to recommend the best opportunities. Prescriptive analytics employs optimization and simulation algorithms to advice on probable results and answers "What should we do?". By one or more possible courses of action, the analytics goes descriptive and predictive. Basically, they allow companies to assess amount of probable results on the basis of multiple features prediction. It uses several groups of tools and techniques such as machine learning, business rules, algorithms and procedures of computational modeling. These techniques are implemented against input from different data sets including real-time data feeds, historical and transactional data and big data.

Matrices Used in Machine Learning

Square Matrix

Machine learning is inspired by a lot from statistical and mathematical operations. Linear algebra is essential in machine learning. The part of linear algebra which is concerned with machine learning is related with operations on matrices and vectors. There are many different type of matrices defined to minimizes the computational effort. One of them is square matrix. Square matrix is very common among all matrices. The number of rows and the number of columns are equal in square matrix. This is different from rectangular matrix where number of rows and number of columns are not equal. The dimensions of square matrix are denoted as n*n. Square matrix is very simple and used to solve many simple linear transformations. The value from top left to bottom right is called as main diagonal. Below is an example of 3*3 square matrix.

$$M = \begin{bmatrix} 1 & 2 & 3 \\ 1 & 2 & 3 \\ 1 & 3 & 3 \end{bmatrix}$$

Symmetric Matrix

Symmetric matrix is another kind of square matrix. All the properties of symmetric matrix are same as square matrix. The only property, that distinct symmetric matrix from square matrix, is that top right triangle is same as the bottom left triangle. The symmetric matrix is equal to its transpose i.e. $M=M^T$. The matrix is called as symmetric matrix when the axis of symmetry is main diagonal of the matrix from the top left to the bottom left. Below is an example of 3*3 symmetric matrix.

$$M = \begin{bmatrix} 7 & 5 & 1 \\ 5 & 8 & 3 \\ 1 & 3 & 4 \end{bmatrix}$$

Triangular Matrix

It is also a kind of square matrix. The main property of square matrix is that the upper right triangular values or lower left triangular values should be zero. In triangular matrix, the values above the main diagonal in matrix are known as upper triangular matrix. The values below the main diagonal in matrix are known as lower triangular matrix. Below is an example of 3*3 upper triangular matrix.

$$M = \begin{bmatrix} 7 & 5 & 1 \\ 0 & 8 & 3 \\ 0 & 0 & 4 \end{bmatrix}$$

Below is an example of 3*3 upper triangular matrix.

$$M = \begin{bmatrix} 7 & 0 & 0 \\ 5 & 8 & 0 \\ 1 & 3 & 4 \end{bmatrix}$$

Diagonal Matrix

The matrix, where all the values of the matrix are zero except main diagonal values, is called as diagonal matrix. In the case of diagonal matrix, it is not necessary that matrix should be square. In the diagonal matrix, all the elements of main diagonal are either zero or non-zero. Diagonal matrix is denoted as D and it can be represented as full matrix with zero values or can be only with main diagonal elements. Below is an example of 3*3 diagonal matrix.

$$D = \begin{bmatrix} 7 & 0 & 0 \\ 0 & 8 & 0 \\ 0 & 0 & 6 \end{bmatrix}$$

Diagonal matrix is also written as given below.

$$D = \begin{pmatrix} d11 & d22 & d33 \end{pmatrix}$$

$$D = \begin{pmatrix} 7 & 8 & 6 \end{pmatrix}$$

Identity Matrix

Identity matrix is a square matrix in which all elements of main diagonals are defined as value 1 and all other elements of top left or bottom right are defined as zero. The property of identity matrix is that it does not change any vector when it multiplies that vector by that matrix. Identity matrix is denoted as I. Below is an example of 3*3 identity matrix.

$$I = \begin{bmatrix} 1 & 0 & 0 \\ 0 & 1 & 0 \\ 0 & 0 & 1 \end{bmatrix}$$

Orthogonal Matrix

$$\left(Q^{\wedge}T = Q^{\wedge}-T \right)$$

It is a type of square matrix in which dot product is zero and its rows and columns are orthogonal unit vectors. Orthogonal means perpendicular to each other. Orthogonal matrix is denoted as Q. The property of orthogonal matrix is that its transpose is equal to its inverse and its dot product with its transpose is an identity matrix.

$$\left(Q.Q^{\wedge}T = I \right)$$

In the orthogonal matrix, its rows are mutually orthogonal and its columns are mutually orthogonal to one another. Orthogonal matrices are generally indicated as below.

$$\left(Q^\wedge T.Q = Q.Q^\wedge T = I\right)$$

where, Q is the orthogonal matrix; Q^T is the transpose of Q; and, I is the identity matrix.

Orthogonal matrices are simple, easy to calculate its transpose & inverse and stable. Orthogonal matrices have lots of applications such as in linear transformations like reflections and permutations. Below is an example of reflection matrix or co-ordinate matrix.

Q=

Impact of Machine Learning in Daily Life

Machine learning keeps on blooming field with lot of research probabilities. Some of these probabilities can be observed in the current machine-learning approaches in contrast of learning that we observed in naturally occurring systems such as humans and other animals, economies, organizations and biological evolution(Russell and Norvig, 2013) (Lakshmi, and Shivsankar, 2014) etc. Machine learning algorithms are aimed to learn one certain function from one single source of data; whereas, humans need to learn many different types of knowledge and skills from years of diverse training experience, i.e., supervised and unsupervised. In addition to this, ML is also powered with the virtual assistance technology by combining several deep learning models to provide precise context and interpreting natural speech (Divya, Bhargavi and Jyothi, 2018). It is helping the people to take decision in daily life of the work being healthier and more productive. It is more valuable when anyone wants to predict future events when people known what they want but don't know how to take decisions on the basis of input variables.

FUTURE OF MACHINE LEARNING

ML is one of the most emerging areas for the developments of innovative works in software industry. It is one of the important tools to develop value for businesses that need to know the value of their data. Businesses are looking to machine learning techniques to assist them, anticipate and generate competitive environment. More and more ML models are planted into packaged result like customer management solution, factory management systems etc. Here are some of the systems which are fresh and are able to raise the value of the organizations.

Trained Data as a Service

Data scientists have the responsibility for gathering, labeling and training the data. Publicly available data sets or crowd sourcing tools are provided to collect and label the data. To overcome these problems, various promoters are provided for the pre-trained data models.

Continuous Retraining of Models

Presently, most of the ML models are offline. These models are trained using data set and then distributed. After training of the data, a model does not change to influence more data.

Development of NLP

It is the technology that allows machines to understand the structure and meaning of the spoken and written languages. Various researchers have been working from the long time on NLP. The machine language has accelerated and helped the human being to understand and implement NLP. With the help of ML and NLP, systems are able to learn the conditions and meaning of words with sentences.

Automate Selection and Testing Algorithm

It is very difficult for data scientists to understand and develop a particular machine learning algorithms. Various types of data sets are available, but it is not possible to develop models for machine learning. It is not easy to develop and choose the appropriate algorithm to implement as a machine learning model. Data scientists are able to quickly focus on just one or two algorithms instead of manual testing. It also helps to developers and researchers with fewer machines learning experiences working with machine learning algorithms.

CONCLUSION

With the increasing prominence of large-scale data in all areas, human endeavor has a wave of new demands on the underlying ML algorithms. For example, large amount of data sets needs mathematically tractable algorithms. Highly personal data raise the need for algorithms that minimize privacy effects and the availability of huge quantities of unlabeled data raising the challenge of designing learning algorithms to take advantage of it. Despite practical challenges, we are hopeful that informed discussions among policy-makers and the public about data and the capabilities of machine learning will lead to insightful designs of programs and policies that can balance the goals of protecting privacy and ensuring fairness with those of reaping the benefits to scientific research and to individual and public health. It is also helpful to make the ML more declarative, so that, it should become easier for unskilled to specify and interact with different type of data in various fields. It is also helpful in land utilization and land classification applications and explored the benefits of using different classification, clustering and prediction methods.

REFERENCES

Alpaydın. (2010). *Introduction to Machine Learning* (2nd ed.). The MIT Press. Retrieved from http://www.britannica.com/EBchecked/topic/1116194/

Bekkerman, R., Bilenko, M., & Langford, J. (2011). *Scaling Up Machine Learning: Parallel and Distributed Approaches*. Cambridge, UK: Cambridge University Press.

Bengio, Y. (2009). *Foundations and Trends in Machine Learning 2*. Boston: Now Publishers.

Castle. (2017). Retrieved from Https://Www.Datascience.Com/Blog/Supervised-And-Unsupervised-Machine-LearningAlgorithms

Divya, K. S., Bhargavi, P., & Jyothi, S. (2018). Machine Learning Algorithms in Big data Analytics. *International Journal of Computer Sciences and Engineering, 6*(1), 64-70.

Gandomi, A., & Haider, M. (2015, April). Beyond the Hype: Big Data Concepts, Methods, and Analytics. *International Journal of Information Management, 35*(2), 137–144. doi:10.1016/j.ijinfomgt.2014.10.007

Han, J., Kamber, M., & Pei, J. (2012). *Data Mining Concepts and Techniques* (3rd ed.). Morgan Kaufmann Publishers.

Kotsiantis, S. B. (2007). Supervised Machine Learning: A Review of Classification Techniques. *Informatica, 31*, 249–268.

Murphy, K. (2012). *Machine Learning: A Probabilistic Perspective*. Cambridge, MA: MIT Press.

Regression vs. Classification algorithms webpage on Data Science. (n.d.). Available: https://www.datascience.com/blog/regression-and-classification-machine-learning-algorithms

Russell & Norvig. (2003). *Artificial Intelligence A Modern Approach* (2nd ed.). Pearson Education Inc.

Seh & Chaurasia. (2019). A Review on Heart Disease Prediction Using Machine Learning Techniques. *International Journal of Management, IT & Engineering, 9*.

Supervised and Unsupervised Machine Learning Algorithms Webpage on Machine Learning Mastery. (n.d.). Available: https://machinelearningmastery.com/ supervised-and-unsupervised-machine-learning-algorithms/

Venkata Lakshmi & Shivsankar. (2014). Heart Disease Diagnosis Using Predictive Data Mining. *International Journal of Innovative Research in Science, Engineering and Technology, 3*(3).

Chapter 10
A Deep Learning Approach for Detection of Application Layer Attacks in Internet

V. Punitha

National Institute of Technology, Tiruchirappalli, India

C. Mala

National Institute of Technology, Tiruchirappalli, India

ABSTRACT

The recent technological transformation in application deployment, with the enriched availability of applications, induces the attackers to shift the target of the attack to the services provided by the application layer. Application layer DoS or DDoS attacks are launched only after establishing the connection to the server. They are stealthier than network or transport layer attacks. The existing defence mechanisms are unproductive in detecting application layer DoS or DDoS attacks. Hence, this chapter proposes a novel deep learning classification model using an autoencoder to detect application layer DDoS attacks by measuring the deviations in the incoming network traffic. The experimental results show that the proposed deep autoencoder model detects application layer attacks in HTTP traffic more proficiently than existing machine learning models.

INTRODUCTION

The technological advancements bring out new dimensions in application development. The availability of the applications and services are intentionally blocked by Denial of Service/Distributed Denial of Service (DoS/DDoS) attacks. DoS attack is the one of the powerful threats in internet. In this attack, the malicious user makes the server and other network resources unavailable to legitimate users by interrupting the server's regular activities. Malicious user launches this attack by sending overwhelming requests to targeted server continuously, until legitimate access are unable to be processed by the server, and thereby blocking the availability of the server to legitimate users. Malicious user uses single com-

DOI: 10.4018/978-1-7998-2491-6.ch010

puter system to launch this attack over the internet (Douligeris and Mitrokotsa 2004; Peng et al., 2007). DDoS attack is the one of the most vulnerable threats in the internet. Similar to DoS attack, it is also created by sending overwhelming requests to targeted server to block the availability of the server. But, DDoS attacks are launched using multiple compromised computers on the internet (Prasad et al., 2014).

UDP and ICMP flood attacks & TCP SYN flood attack are network and transport layer DDoS attacks. Here, the attacker transmits large number of UDP/ICMP packets to the targeted server. The packets are either transmitted to targeted port or to random ports. In both cases, the sender's identities are spoofed. In TCP SYN attack, the attacker overwhelms the targeted server with huge number of connection requests. This activity forces the server to send connection acknowledgement to each malicious request, and subsequently waiting for connection response indefinitely. Thus, the availability of the server is blocked to legitimate users. These attacks are volumetric attacks. They are detected using arrival statistics and traffic size (Basicevic et al, 2015; Elejla et al., 2018; Perakovic et al., 2017). The recent technological advancements induce the attackers to shift the target of the attack to the application services, and thereby increasing application layer DDoS attacks in internet traffic. The application layer attacks are created to impair specific application or web server. They are not volumetric attacks like network/transport layer attacks. It requires only low or mid bandwidth as it is launched after receiving protocol confirmation, i.e., application layer attacks are launched only after protocol handshakes or connection establishment phase. Therefore, these attacks appear as normal requests. Thus, they are stealthier than network/transport layer attacks. As the botnet apparently transmits legitimate requests to the server, the application layer DDoS attacks are difficult to discriminate (Zhou et al., 2014).

The application layer attacks are low and slow attacks. The attackers use diverse intelligent clients to launch various types of attacks such as HTTP-GET/POST flood, slow rate attack, BGP Hijacking. Unlike the network/transport layer attacks such as SYN flood, ICMP flood & NTP amplification attacks, the application layer attacks cannot be discriminated using traffic rate. It requires deep investigation on requesting behavior of the client and the network packet parameters. Hence, the existing defense mechanisms which are applied to detect network/transport layer attacks are ineffective in detecting application layer DDoS attacks (Mantas et al., 2015).

Hypertext Transfer Protocol (HTTP) is one of the most widely used application layer protocols. Request flooding attack is the most powerful threat in application layer, especially while using HTTP protocol. Here, enormous amount of HTTP requests are generated by botnet and transmitted to intended application server. Initially, the attacker establishes a valid connection to the server, then it transmits huge number of HTTP GET or POST requests through the valid connection. These requests are intentionally transmitted to consume server resources, and thereby blocking their usage to legitimate users (Zhou et al., 2014). In most cases, HTTP-GET or POST flood attacks are launched to crash Apache and OpenBSD servers. Another powerful threat in HTTP traffic is a slow rate attack. Here, the attacker transmits the requests or data very slowly, so that, the server resources are consumed for long time and thereby preventing the legitimate access. Slow read attack is another kind of slow rate attack, where the attacker transmits the valid HTTP request to the server and reading the responses very slow just to continue the session for long duration meaninglessly (Mantas et al., 2015). BGP hijacking is another application layer attack. It impersonates a network and diverts the network traffic to the attacker's destination. Diverse DDoS attacks and avalanche of such threats demand automatic detection techniques to enhance internet security.

RELATED WORK

This section illustrates few significant existing research works on detection of application layer attacks.

Adi et al., (2016) measured CPU response time, memory space, and request for windows size-update to discriminate request flood attacks. Authors detected application layer attacks exclusively in HTTP/2 traffic. But the attacks are detected only after server degradation. Behal et al. (2018) applied traffic rate and generalized entropy value to detect both high and low rate attacks. Generalized entropy value was computed for packet features such as IP addresses, ports and packet arrival rate. But, other packet features are essential for identification of application layer attacks. Wang et al. (2018) constructed hash tables and applied Hellinger distance to differentiate attack traffic from normal. Authors filtered normal traffic by measuring the distribution of the traffic in the hash tables. Sketching technique was proposed to distinguish attack from the remaining traffic. Punitha and Mala (2018) constructed network flows and computed flow features to discriminate application layer attacks. The machine learning model was constructed using Support Vector Machine (SVM).

Sreeram and Vuppala, (2017) and Prasad et al. (2017) detected application layer attacks using bio-inspired methods. Sreeram and Vuppala, (2017) proposed bat algorithm using session features such as session duration, access frequency of each page and inter-arrival time between requests. Prasad et al. (2017) proposed cuckoo search and applied source diversity feature along with the above mentioned session features to detect HTTP attacks. Singh et al. (2018) analyzed the requesting behavior of the botnet. Popularity of a webpage and frequency of requesting replication were computed and applied to discriminate flash event and attacks. Xie et al. (2013) proposed hidden semi-Markov model to detect application layer DDoS attacks. The proposed model captured the traffic towards web proxy and analyzed the behavior of the traffic in terms of temporal-spatial locality. But, the detection accuracy is less when the number of requests from distinct sources are high.

Jazi et al. (2017) proposed a new cumulative sum algorithm for detection of both high and low rate HTTP attacks. Authors used both network and application layer parameters. Authors investigated different sampling methodologies to detect the anomalies in HTTP traffic and proved that selective flow sampling is most suitable for HTTP attack detection. Calvert and Khoshgoftaar, (2019) proposed a novel data sampling technique to improve the detection accuracy of application layer attacks. Authors evaluated their model using real time network traffic and detected five different types of slow rate attacks in HTTP traffic. Authors demonstrated that the random forest learning system is optimal when the attack distribution is 35%.

Huang et al. (2019) proposed a novel honeypot server detection model based on three categories of features. The application layer and network layer parameters were extracted from network traffic and additionally system features were also used for detection of honeypot. Authors applied various learning methodologies such as random forest, SVM, kNN and Naïve-bayes and proved that the prediction accuracy of random forest methodology is higher than other models. Dantas et al. (2014) proposed a new defence system, called 'SeVen' to mitigate network and application layer DDoS attacks. Authors used adaptive selective verification which described the bandwidth consumption to distinguish DDoS attacks. Authors validated their system using statistical checker tool and compared the performance with traffic analysis defence system. But, the proposed defence system does not explore asymmetric attacks and much quantitative measures are not considered.

Figure 1. Schematic diagram illustrating application layer attack

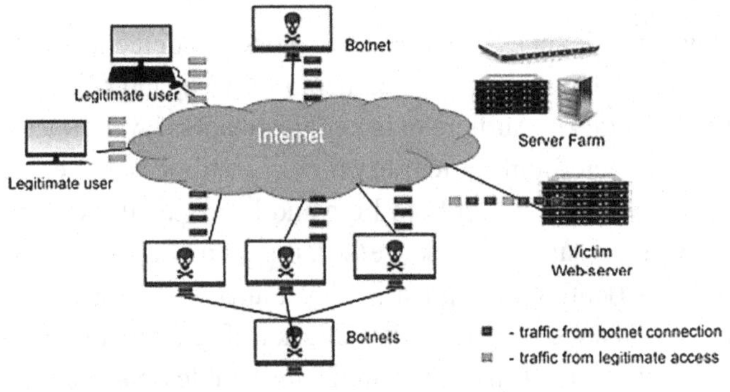

Song et al. (2018) proposed a two layer Xgboost algorithm to classify various attacks in HTTP traffic. Distinct statistic features such as request, behaviour and keyword features are inferred from log information of the web server. At the first phase, for each input traffic, the classification model finds the probability under each category. In second phase, the model functioned as a binary classifier and identified the type of the attack. The detection accuracy of the model is best when all the features are applied in classification. Slow rate attacks in HTTP traffic are launched using different techniques. The attacker transmits partial GET or POST requests in each connection and prolonging the connection for long duration. The slow rate attacks are also launched by transmitting/receiving data to/from the server in long time gap (Mantas et al., 2015; Cambiaso et al., 2017).

It is observed from the survey presented above that the usage of the applications are blocked by the application layer attacks that are intentionally created by botnets. This emphasizes the detection of application layer attacks in real time traffic. Hence, this work proposes a novel Deep Autoencoder Classifier for Detection of HTTP attacks (DACDH).

PROPOSED DEEP LEARNING MODEL

HTTP DDoS Attack and Real-time Scenario

This work detects the application layer attacks exclusively in HTTP traffic. HTTP attacks are also called as request flood attacks. They are launched after establishing the connection with the web server or application server in two different ways. The foremost way is that the botnet transmits enormous number of queries or requests, i.e. either HTTP GET requests or POST requests to the targeted server. Thus, the workload of the server is increased. This attack also exhausts the server resources such as server threads, queue space etc. This activity blocks the availability of the server resources to legitimate users, and thereby increasing the waiting time of the legitimate users. Subsequently, the response time of the server is also increased. Hence, the performance of the server is degraded (Zhou et al., 2014). Another way of launching the HTTP attack is transmitting the HTTP GET or POST requests very slowly to the intended server and maintaining the connection for long duration. It is called slow rate attack. Here, the server resources such as queue space and threads are held for usage for long duration without any purpose, thus preventing legitimate access. The network packet features alone are not enough to detect

Figure 2. Time sequence diagram illustrating HTTP attack

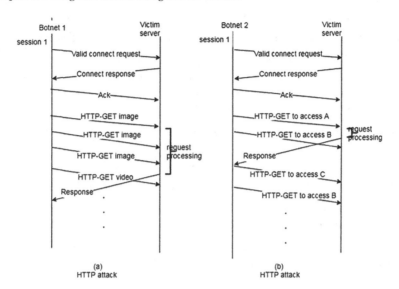

of slow rate application layer attack. Additionally, network flow features are to be computed and applied to detect slow rate attack. Hence, it is planned in the future work.

The schematic diagram presented in Figure 1 illustrates the application layer attack. The figure shows both victim server and normal server farm. The victim server may also be one of the servers in the server farm. For simplicity, a single webserver is chosen as a victim server. Here, DDoS attack is launched with zombies. In the figure, they are represented as botnets. The rate of traffic generated by the legitimate users and the botnets are same. It can be visualized in the figure. The legitimate users transmit valid number of HTTP requests in each session represented as green traffic in the figure. Whereas the botnets transmit abnormal number of requests or queries in each session, represented as red in the figure. The botnet traffic represented in the figure with green bounded rectangle implies that the connection is legitimate. It means that the botnet transmits enormous amount of requests through valid connection.

The botnet applies advanced technologies and uses increased bandwidth to launch HTTP attacks from different hosts over the internet. Sometimes, they are around 10^4 sources per second (Zhou et al., 2014). So, observing the source addresses and blocking them is infeasible. Generally, famous web servers are targeted by the attackers to launch application layer attack, especially, HTTP attack. For an example, when there is an increase in traffic towards an online shopping website, it may be due to flash crowd or DoS or DDoS attacks. If the attack is a network layer attack, it can be detected with the rate of traffic; whereas, HTTP attacks cannot be detected with traffic rate. In Figure 1, it is represented that both botnets and genuine users are establishing same number of sessions to server. But, only the botnet transmits enormous amount of HTTP requests in each session after connection establishment step. So, it is understood that the botnet launches this attack with the application data directly. Thus, the attack pretends to be legitimate access and cannot be identified with network layer data such as rate of traffic. In a real time attack scenario, the HTTP gets request created by the botnet which simply pulls huge number of video or image files from victim server (Punitha and Mala, 2018), thus exhausting the server computing time. In another scenario, botnet transmits large number of queries to the targeted server to exhaust the server resources, thereby denying the availability of the server to legitimate users. These scenarios are presented in Figure 2. The tools like Mirai botnet can be used to generate HTTP attacks. The time sequence diagram illustrating HTTP attack to a web server is depicted in Figure 2. The victim server is a webserver or an application server. Two simple scenarios are described in Figure 2 (a) and 2 (b). In Figure 2 (a), 'botnet 1' initiates a connection request to the server. As the request is genuine and valid, the server accepts the request. Now 'botnet 1' establishes a valid connection with the server. Through this connection, the 'botnet 1' transmits huge number of GET requests to retrieve images and videos from the server. As both the connection and the requests are valid, the server is processing all the requests and responding back to the 'botnet 1' as it is depicted in the figure. Processing image and video requests take much service time than normal text requests. Numerous such image / video requests from 'botnet 1' exhaust the server usage. Hence, the availability of the server is blocked to legitimate users. To create this attack, it is enough to have the information about the image and video files. So, the botnet just launches the attack without much effort. Figure 2 (b) illustrates another scenario. Here also, the server accepts the connection request from 'botnet 2', as it is valid. Then, the 'botnet 2' transmits enormous amount of queries to different applications. For simplicity, only three applications are used and they are named as A, B and C. On receiving these requests, the server identifies the application and processes them accordingly. Finally, the response is sent back to the 'botnet 2'. As illustrated in the figure, the 'botnet 2' transmits the request repeatedly. If the requests are from genuine users, then the requesting pattern will be random. If they are generated by botnets, then there will be some uniformity in the requesting pattern. Moreover, the botnet transmits the requests to prolong the session for long time, so that the usage of the server is blocked. In both scenarios, the connections and the requests are valid, so the attacks pretend to be legitimate access.

Proposed Deep Autoencoder and Classifier for Detection of HTTP Attacks (DACDH)

Generally, the attacks can be detected in two ways, i.e., by measuring the performance depletion of the resources or by observing the deviations in incoming network traffic. In the former way, the attacks are identified only after resource destruction, whereas in the latter case, the attacks are identified before any impairment. So, in this work, the divergence in incoming traffic is recognized and applied for attack detection. They are measured in terms of network packet features. The flow based Intrusion Detection System (IDS) is better than packet based IDS (Elejla et al., 2018). But, for huge amount of input traffic, construction of network flow is complex and flow feature learning is also expensive. Hence, this work applies network packet parameters as features to detect application layer DDoS attacks. Moreover, the proposed deep learning architecture learns more abstract information in the incoming traffic.

Supervised machine learning classification models produce good classification accuracy with multiple features. Multiple features increases the complexity of the algorithm. Moreover, labelling traffic in supervised algorithms is a challenging task. Hence, the work reported here proposes an unsupervised deep learning model to detect stealthier HTTP attacks. As HTTP is extensively used in many applications, the proposed model detects DoS attacks in HTTP traffic. When a client is sending a request to the application server over the internet, a connection is established with the server. Then, the HTTP requests i.e., HTTP GET or POST requests are transmitted over the internet. After processing, the application server transmits HTTP response to the client. Finally, the client request is ended by connection termination. This is called as a session. As HTTP DDoS attacks are launched only after establishing the connection to the server, the incoming traffic during each session is monitored to detect HTTP request

Figure 3. The workflow diagram of the proposed DACDH model

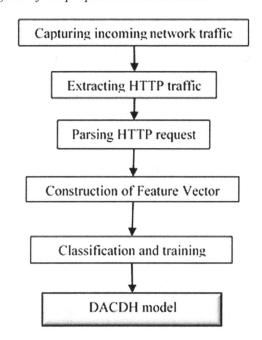

flooding attack. The workflow of the proposed DACDH model is depicted in Figure 3. The proposed model extracts HTTP traffic in real time network traffic. The HTTP requests are parsed and network packet parameters, such as source IP, port, number of GET requests, average inter-arrival time of GET request, average size of the request and GET URL are extracted during each session. Source IP defines the IP address of the client and port defines the port number from which the client transmits the request. A client can transmit multiple requests from various ports. The source IP and port are essential to identify the client. The inter-arrival time of the request defines the time interval between two successive arrivals of GET requests. The inter-arrival time between all successive requests in a session are computed. Then average inter-arrival time is found for this session. Subsequently, the proposed DACDH model computes the average inter-arrival time for each session. Average inter-arrival time and number of GET requests are essential to learn the frequency of GET or POST requests sent to the server in normal and attack situations. During request flooding/HTTP DDoS attack, the frequency of GET or POST requests is high. Sending oversized requests is another attack. So, the size of the request is computed and added as a feature. In each session, the client transmits two or more HTTP get requests to the server. Using the url of these requests, order of accessing the webpages or applications in each session is constructed and it is called access list. The access list discovers the requesting pattern of the attacker or user to ascertain the real requesting behaviour. The proposed model constructs access list for each session using GET URLs. Here, the constructed access list is in string format. The proposed autoencoder model accepts only numeric data. So, the features are transformed into numeric representation. Then, these features are normalized to make the data into uniform representation. The proposed DACDH model learns abstract information in the packet features deep architecture. Finally, with the transformed data, the linear decision boundary discriminates HTTP DDoS attacks from generic traffic.

The proposed deep autoencoder architecture is a multi-layer neural network architecture. It accepts the computed packet features as input. The multi-layer structure transforms the packet features into more conceptual features, i.e., the packet features are compressed and reconstructed by the deeper structure called hidden layers. This technique identifies significant correlation among the features and brings out more accurate information about the network traffic. As the proposed deep autoencoder model learns complex representation in high dimensional data, it is organized to minimize the reconstruction error. Reconstruction error defines the difference between original packet features and the consequent reconstructed packet feature in hidden layers. At the same time, it avoids overfitting. It is achieved using activation function. The regularization parameter in activation function is selected efficiently to avoid overfitting. Thus, the proposed model learns latent information in network packet features instead of memorizing the features. Further, to ensure generalized architecture, the model is constructed with independent number nodes in input layer and in each hidden layer. Using the compressed data, it discriminates HTTP DDoS attacks from generic traffic.

RESULTS AND PERFORMANCE ANALYSIS

The performance of the proposed Deep Autoencoder and Classifier for Detection of HTTP attacks (DACDH) is evaluated in a simulated environment. Wireshark is configured to filter HTTP traffic in real time network traffic (Chappell and G Combs, 2010). It is used to extract packet header information. The proposed DACDH model is evaluated in terms of detection rate and classification metrics such as precision, recall and F-score (Nguyen and Armitage, 2008). It is also compared with the machine learning models such as K-means and DBSCAN. Machine learning models are developed using Matlab. Deep autoencoder is implemented with Tensorflow, Keras and Pytorch.

In the work reported here, precision, recall and F-score are applied to measure the classification performance. Precision defines the ratio of number of network traffic correctly predicted to the total number of predicted traffic of the given class. Recall defines the ratio of number of correctly predicted network traffic to the number of network traffic belong to that class. F-score defines the harmonic average of both classification metrics, i.e., precision and recall (Nguyen and Armitage, 2008). In addition, accuracy is used to evaluate the detection rate of both HTTP DDoS attacks and normal traffic. Accuracy defines the ratio of number of network traffic correctly classified to total number of network traffic (Punitha and Mala, 2018).

$$Precision = \frac{TP}{TP + FP} \qquad (1)$$

$$Recall = \frac{TP}{TP + FN} \qquad (2)$$

Table 1. WIDE dataset

Protocol	Packets	Packets %	Bytes
TCP	818823	81.9	41,44,87,723
UDP	150526	15	29,96,45,349
Others	30651	3.1	93,15,129

Table 2. CTU dataset

Protocol	Packets	Packets %	Bytes
TCP	848047	84.8	84,06,07,510
UDP	121991	12.2	45,19,24,118
Others	29962	3	87,48,123

$$Accuracy = \frac{TP + TN}{N} \tag{3}$$

$$FScore = \frac{2 * Precision * Recall}{Precision + Recall} \tag{4}$$

Here, True Positive (TP) is nothing but number of legitimate traffic that are predicted correctly and True Negative (TN) is the number of HTTP attacks that are predicted correctly.

False Positive (FP) = N–TN;

False Negative (FN) = P-TP;

Here, two benchmark datasets, WIDE and CTU are used to evaluate the proposed DACDH (Garcia et al., 2014; Romain et al., 2010). The traffic traces collected from benchmark datasets are described in Tables 1 and 2.

The deeper structure of the proposed DACDH brings out latent characteristics and correlations in packet features using which it discriminates HTTP DDoS attacks from generic traffic. The machine learning models such as K-means and DBSCAN are developed with the features such as source IP, port, number of GET requests, average inter-arrival time of GET or POST request, average size of the GET or POST request and access list. TP, FP values are measured. Precision, recall, accuracy and F-score values are computed using equation 1 to 4 and plotted in Figure 4. The deep autoencoder architecture is developed with an input layer, three hidden layers and an output layer. The input layer is constructed with 6 nodes to represent network packet features. The output layer produces classification output, say HTTP DDoS attack or normal traffic. Activation functions relu is applied at encoder layer and sigmoid is applied at decoder layer. Additionally, minimization of reconstruction error and loss function improves

Figure 4. Performance metrics Vs Learning models

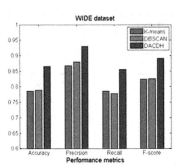 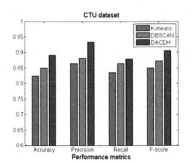

the detection accuracy of the proposed model. Batch size and epoch are fixed as 256 and 50. Batch size defines the number of training data to work through before updating the model output and epoch defines the number of times each data is trained. The classification metrics of the proposed DACDH are computed and plotted in Figure 4.

The models are evaluated in terms of number of attacks predicted. FP defines number of attacks that are wrongly predicted as normal traffic. So, the model that produces low FP predicts the attacks perfectly. As per equation 1, if FP is low, then the precision is high. Thus, precision value is used for evaluating the proposed model with the existing unsupervised machine learning models.

Here, the network packet parameters which are essential to discriminate HTTP attacks are selected and applied as discriminating features. But, the real time network traffic collected from benchmark datasets, WIDE and CTU contain many outliers and noises. Moreover, the shape of the clusters of these network traffic datasets is arbitrary, so that, the K-means model faced difficulties in discriminating HTTP attacks. Hence in Figure 4, precision of K-means model is less than DBSCAN and the proposed DACDH. Whereas K-means model identifies normal traffic perfectly and it is evident in the figure that the recall for K-means model is higher than DBSCAN in WIDE dataset. In DBSCAN model, the cluster configuration can be reorganized using 'Eps' and 'MinPts' parameters. 'Eps' defines the distance between two network traffic data and 'MinPts' defines number of neighbour traffic within the given radius ('Eps'). DBSCAN model groups the traffic data effortlessly even when the size of the dataset is large and the shape of the clusters of the dataset is arbitrary. So, the number of HTTP attacks detected by DBSCAN is high. Hence in Figure 4, the precision of DBSCAN is higher than K-means model.

The proposed DACDH fetches hidden characteristics and correlations in packet features using hidden layer architecture. Three hidden layers and various nodes in each hidden layer and input-output layers recognize the correlation between packet features in both attack and normal traffic. Hence, DACDH proficiently discriminates HTTP DDoS attacks from generic traffic. So, both the precision and recall values in DACDH are significantly higher than DBSCAN. But, the precision of all the three models are above 0.85. So, F-score is computed using equation 4 to evaluate the models. It is observed from Figure 4 that precision and F-score of the proposed DACDH is always higher than existing unsupervised machine learning models. It implies that deep autoencoder architecture in proposed DACDH learns latent characteristics of packet features more perfectly than machine learning models. Hence, the proposed DACDH discriminates HTTP DDoS attacks more effectively than existing unsupervised machine learning models.

The performance of the proposed DACDH model is compared with existing supervised learning model (Punitha and Mala, 2018). Similar to the proposed model, the existing SVM based HTTP Request

Figure 5. Performance metrics Vs Supervised learning model

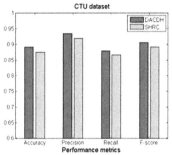

Figure 6. Number of arrivals Vs No. of HTTP attacks predicted

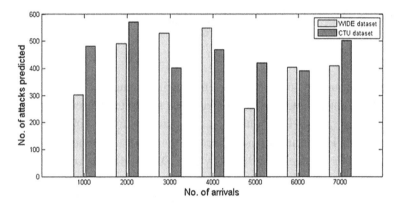

Classification (SHRC) model detects HTTP attacks in real time network traffic (Punitha and Mala, 2018). SHRC applies service time, number of get requests and type of get request as major discriminating features. SHRC is executed with WIDE and CTU datasets. Precision, recall, accuracy and F-score values are computed using equations 1, 2, 3 and 4 and plotted in Figure 5. SHRC model is a supervised learning model. It is trained with predefined labeled dataset. As the attack traffic are well defined in labelled dataset, the F-score value of SHRC model is greater than existing K-means and DBSCAN machine learning models. But the size of real time traffic is huge, so labelling the traffic becomes a complex task. Hence, this work proposes an unsupervised learning technique. The existing SHRC applied network flow features instead of packet features to explore traffic characteristics; whereas, deep autoencoder architecture applies packet features. The packet features are compressed and reconstructed. The proposed DACDH brings out the latent characteristics of input traffic which is applied to discriminate HTTP attacks absolutely. Hence, in Figure 5, the precision and recall of DACDH is higher than SHRC. It implies that deep encoder brings out more conceptual structures in packet features and detects HTTP DDoS attacks more effectively than existing supervised learning model.

More than 1000000 packets are taken from each dataset for evaluation. To make the analysis simple, the number of HTTP attacks predicted for every 1000 packets are computed and plotted in Figure 6. It is observed from Figure 6 that the attacks are existing from the beginning of the arrivals in both the datas-

Figure 7. Number of arrivals vs detection rate of HTTP attacks

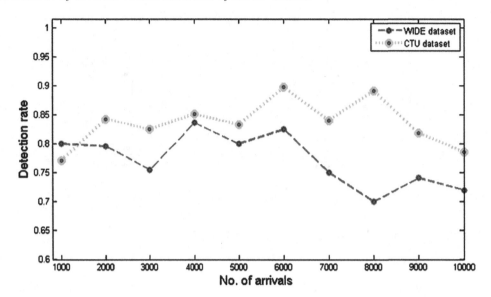

ets. They are present continuously in all arrivals. The maximum number of attacks are predicted during 4000 arrivals for WIDE datasets and during 2000 arrivals for CTU datasets. To evaluate the efficiency of prediction, the detection rate of HTTP attacks is computed for every 1000 arrivals and it is plotted in Figure 7. Detection rate of HTTP attacks is defined as the ratio of number of HTTP attacks predicted correctly to the total number of attacks predicted by DACDH. The false positive rate is low during 8000 arrival period in WIDE dataset. Hence in Figure 7, the detection rate of HTTP attack during this period is minimum for WIDE dataset. As the average false positive rate is high for both datasets, the average detection rate is always above 0.8 for both datasets. Hence, the proposed DACDH model proficiently discriminates HTTP attacks in real time traffic.

CONCLUSION

This chapter proposes a deep learning classification approach to detect stealthier application layer attack in HTTP traffic. The proposed deep autoencoder model observes the deviation in incoming traffic. The deep encoder architecture discovers the latent characteristics and correlation among packet features and detects HTTP attacks competently. The network traffics for analysis are captured and analysed using Wireshark. The proposed deep autoencoder model is developed using Tensorflow, Keras and Pytorch. The performance of the classifier is measured and evaluated in terms of detection accuracy, precision and f-score. It is evidenced from the experimental results that the proposed deep autoencoder model has outperformed existing machine learning models.

The proposed classification model detects application layer attacks exclusively in HTTP traffic. Detection of attacks in other application layers such as attacks in XML based services are considered in the future work. Slow rate attack is the stealthiest application layer DDoS attack. But, network packet parameters alone are not sufficient to detect slow rate attacks in HTTP traffic. Subsequently, the network flow features are to be computed and studied to differentiate the slow rate attack from legitimate access. Detection of different types of slow rate attacks based on network flow features is planned in the future work.

REFERENCES

Adi, Baig, Z. A., Hingston, P., & Lam, C.-P. (2016). Distributed denial-of-service attacks against http/2. *Cluster Computing*, *19*(1), 79–86. doi:10.100710586-015-0528-7

Basicevic, Ocovaj, S., & Popovic, M. (2015). Use of tsallis entropy in detection of syn flood dos attacks. *Security and Communication Networks*, *8*(18), 3634–3640. doi:10.1002ec.1286

Behal, Kumar, K., & Sachdeva, M. (2018). D-face: An anomaly based distributed approach for early detection of ddos attacks and flash events. *Journal of Network and Computer Applications*, *111*, 49–63. doi:10.1016/j.jnca.2018.03.024

Calvert, C. L., & Khoshgoftaar, T. M. (2019). Impact of class distribution on the detection of slow HTTP DoS attacks using Big Data. *Journal of Big Data*, *6*(1), 67. doi:10.118640537-019-0230-3

Cambiaso. (2017). Slowcomm: Design, development and performance evaluation of a new slow dos attack. *Journal of Information Security and Applications*, (35), 23-31.

Chappell & Combs. (2010). *Wireshark network analysis: the official Wireshark certified network analyst study guide*. Protocol Analysis Institute, Chappell University.

Dantas. (2014). A selective defense for application layer ddos attacks. *2014 IEEE Joint Intelligence and Security Informatics Conference*, 75-82. 10.1109/JISIC.2014.21

Douligeris, C., & Mitrokotsa, A. (2004). Ddos attacks and defense mechanisms: Classification and state-of-the-art. *Computer Networks*, *44*(5), 643–666. doi:10.1016/j.comnet.2003.10.003

Elejla. (2018). Flow-based ids for icmpv6-based ddos attacks detection. *Arabian Journal for Science and Engineering*, 1–19.

Garcia. (2014). An empirical comparison of botnet detection methods. *Computers & Security*, (45), 100-123. Retrieved from https://stratosphereips.org/new-dataset-ctu-13-extended-now-includes-pcap-files-of-normal-traffic.html

Huang, Han, J., Zhang, X., & Liu, J. (2019). Automatic Identification of Honeypot Server Using Machine Learning Techniques. *Security and Communication Networks*, *2019*, 1–8. doi:10.1155/2019/2627608

Jazi, Gonzalez, H., Stakhanova, N., & Ghorbani, A. A. (2017). Detecting http-based application layer dos attacks on web servers in the presence of sampling. *Computer Networks*, *121*, 25–36. doi:10.1016/j.comnet.2017.03.018

Mantas, Stakhanova, N., Gonzalez, H., Jazi, H. H., & Ghorbani, A. A. (2015). Application-layer denial of service attacks: Taxonomy and survey. *International Journal of Information and Computer Security*, *7*(2-4), 216–239. doi:10.1504/IJICS.2015.073028

Nguyen, T. T. T., & Armitage, G. (2008). A survey of techniques for internet traffic classification using machine learning. *IEEE Communications Surveys and Tutorials*, *10*(4), 56–76. doi:10.1109/SURV.2008.080406

Peng, Leckie, C., & Ramamohanarao, K. (2007). Survey of network-based defense mechanisms countering the dos and ddos problems. *ACM Computing Surveys*, *39*(1), 3, es. doi:10.1145/1216370.1216373

Perakovic, Perisa, M., Cvitic, I., & Husnjak, S. (2017). Model for detection and classification of ddos traffic based on artificial neural network. *Telfor Journal*, *9*(1), 26–31. doi:10.5937/telfor1701026P

Prasad. (2014). *Dos and ddos attacks: defense, detection and traceback mechanisms-a survey. Global Journal of Computer Science and Technology.*

Prasad. (2017). Bifad: Bio-inspired anomaly based http-flood attack detection. *Wireless Personal Communications*, *97*(1), 281–308. doi:10.100711277-017-4505-8

Punitha & Mala. (2018). Svm based traffic classification for mitigating http attack. In *Mobile Internet Security (MobiSec 18), 2018 The 3rd International Symposium*. KIISC Research Group on 5G Security, University of San Carlos.

Romain. (2010). MAWILab: Combining Diverse Anomaly Detectors for Automated Anomaly Labeling and Performance Benchmarking. *ACM CoNEXT '10*. Retrieved from http://mawi.wide.ad.jp/mawi/samplepoint-F/2017/

Singh, Singh, P., & Kumar, K. (2018). User behavior analytics-based classification of application layer http-get flood attacks. *Journal of Network and Computer Applications*, *112*, 97–114. doi:10.1016/j.jnca.2018.03.030

Song, Wang, X., Jin, L., & You, J. (2018). Malicious behaviour classification in web logs based on an improved Xgboost algorithm. *International Journal of Web Engineering and Technology*, *13*(4), 334–362. doi:10.1504/IJWET.2018.097560

Sreeram & Vuppala. (2017). *Http flood attack detection in application layer using machine learning metrics and bio inspired bat algorithm.* Applied Computing and Informatics.

Wang, Miu, T. T. N., Luo, X., & Wang, J. (2018). Skyshield: A sketch-based defense system against application layer ddos attacks. *IEEE Transactions on Information Forensics and Security*, *13*(3), 559–573. doi:10.1109/TIFS.2017.2758754

Xie, Tang, S., Xiang, Y., & Hu, J. (2013). Resisting web proxy-based http attacks by temporal and spatial locality behaviour. *IEEE Transactions on Parallel and Distributed Systems*, *24*(7), 1401–1410. doi:10.1109/TPDS.2012.232

Zhou, Jia, W., Wen, S., Xiang, Y., & Zhou, W. (2014). Detection and defense of application-layer ddos attacks in backbone web traffic. *Future Generation Computer Systems*, *38*, 36–46. doi:10.1016/j.future.2013.08.002

Chapter 11
Self–Managed System for Distributed Wireless Sensor Networks:
A Review

Sneh Garg

Chandigarh College of Engineering and Technology, India

Ram Bahadur Patel

Chandigarh College of Engineering and Technology, India

ABSTRACT

With the advancements in technology, wireless sensor networks (WSNs) are used almost in all applications. These sensor network systems are sometimes used to monitor hostile environments where human intervention is not possible. When sensing is required to be done in areas that are hostile, there is need for autonomous/self-managing systems as it is very difficult for the human to intervene within such hostile environmental conditions. Therefore, in such systems, each node is required to do all functionalities and act like autonomous decision taking node that performs both data forwarding and network control. Therefore, introducing a self-management for large-scale distributed wireless system is a highly tedious task due to resource constrained nature of these nodes. It is very difficult to achieve required quality of service by large systems as a huge amount of energy is dissipated by systems in radio communication. Owing to resource constraint as well as vulnerable nature, developing a self-managing system for distributed WSN is a very challenging and demanding task.

DOI: 10.4018/978-1-7998-2491-6.ch011

Figure 1. Wireless sensor network

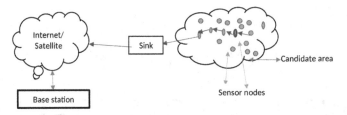

Figure 2. Architecture of sensor node

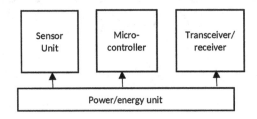

INTRODUCTION

Extensive work and research is going on in wireless sensor networks (WSNs). These are the networks that are composed of sensor nodes which are distributed in a candidate area either densely or sparsely depending upon the requirement of application, sensing range of nodes, kind of territory and other environmental factors.

In sensor networks, active entity sensor nodes (SNs) are deployed in an area whose physical parameters need to be monitored and these areas may be open or closed. Sometimes SNs need to be deployed in hostile environments, where it is not possible for a human to intervene in a system. Monitoring and management of systems in such hostile environments e.g. under water battlefields, volcano prone area, flood or land slide areas need to be self-manageable, so that, little or no intervention of human is required. In such systems, nodes communicate with one another via wireless means; do their sensing work and other tasks autonomously and smartly. These nodes are smart enough to take decisions by their own according to the changing demands of the environment. These systems are used in large number of applications now-a-days but still sometimes they fail to give throughput up to their full potential as these nodes, which are main constituent of the WSNs, are the resource constrained nodes and possess very less memory, processing capability and energy. These nodes are battery operated devices and these batteries get depleted with time and therefore, battery life decides the life of node (Song, Kim and Sung, 2005). When a node gets scarce from battery, it becomes dead and is unable to communicate with other nodes and base station (BS). The dead nodes greatly affect the working of the overall system. Energy management, energy harvesting, power management are the challenging areas of WSN in which many researches are still going on so as to provide energy externally from some mobile charging sources or by harvesting energy from natural resources or managing internal energy of nodes. All these efforts are

Figure 3. Applications of WSN

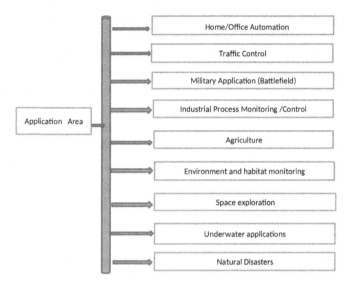

Figure 4. Objectives of wireless sensor network

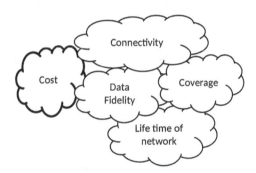

done so as to properly utilize the energy that is provided with internal batteries in node and to increase the overall life of system (Ma, Chen, Huang and Lee, 2010).

The WSNs are highly application specific. Their size also depends upon the type of application for which they are used. Therefore, size of networks varies from small sized network to very large sized networks. Owing to dependency on applications, there is need of a different architectures, communication technologies and sensing technologies for different applications. Wireless sensor networks are used in many different applications such as Home/Office automation (Sharma and Reddy, 2012), Military (Winkler, Hughes and Barclay, 2008), Traffic Control (Castillo-Effer and Westhoff, 2004), Irrigation, Marine Environment Monitoring, Industrial Process Monitoring, Environmental monitoring and natural disaster.

With the growth in the size of wireless sensor network, the management of sensors becomes a tedious task. It is difficult to achieve required quality of service (QoS) by a large system as a fact of energy dissipation in radio communications. Another factor for deterioration of system performance is fault occurrences. The challenges faced by sensor networks are coverage, data fidelity, and cost of network,

network life time and connectivity. Therefore, main objectives for wireless sensor networks are maximization of coverage, secured transmission of data among nodes, good connectivity among nodes and economic to establish, use and maintain.

These networks are implemented either in centralized or in distributed ways. The way is chosen depends upon the size of area, number of nodes and their sensing range. As nodes communicate with each other as well as with base stations (BS), their massive amount of energy gets consumed while they communicate.

In distributed wireless sensor network, nodes are not assigned only task of monitoring or processing of data but also assigned a task of taking decision in accordance with the changing conditions of the network or environment. These systems are smart enough to manage whole system by own without human intervention.

Distributed systems are preferred over centralized system (Zhao, Huangfu, Liu and Sun, 2011) due to the following reasons.

- Sensors nodes are very much prone to failures as they get easily depleted from energy.
- No risk of failure of central node
- Distributed systems are reliable as network remains working even after failure of few nodes.
- Collection and aggregation of data at microscopic level saves lots of communication overload.

Self-Management System for Large Distributed WSN

Self-management system is a system that manages all its functionalities without human or with little interference of the user. The autonomy of self- management of system depends upon the degree to which auto feature is inculcated in it. In self–managed systems, nodes can be assigned different tasks by reprogramming or reconfiguring them again. This auto feature makes them independent of their application specific nature. Self- management system adjusts itself and changes its parameters based on the conditions. E.g. system automatically reduces service quality when energy resources become scarce (Mills, 2007). Therefore, owing to critical requirements, developing a self-managing system for distributed wireless sensor network is extremely challenging and demanding task. In such systems, each node does all functionalities independently and acts like autonomous decision taking node.

Basic Principle for Self-Management Systems

Some mechanisms are required to incorporate in a system to introduce autonomy/self-managing feature. These mechanisms are as follows.

- Self-monitoring
- Self-maintainability
- Self-healing
- Self-configuring

Figure 5. Basic feedback control in self-managing system

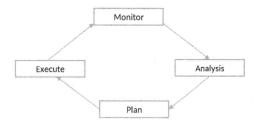

Management of wireless sensor network should permit for declaration of functions' set which enhance integrity and production in a disciplined way of configuration, operation, maintenance and services of the wireless sensor network. Self–management system (Macías-Escrivá, Haber and Hernandez, 2013) follows four steps listed below.

- Monitoring of data collection
- System requirements
- Analysis by the use of Data mining, Pattern analysis, Inferences etc.
- Planning by Stochastic methods, Simulation, Optimization methods etc.
- Execution for the Effectors management, Reporting, System re-configuration etc.

To manage the functionality in distributed sensor network, various managing methods have been proposed (Van Roy,Haridi, Reinefeld, Stefani,Yap and Coupaye, 2007). All these management methods considers following metrics.

- Consumption of Energy
- System Life or Duration
- Latency/Delay
- System tolerance to faults
- Accuracy in acquiring data or the Quality of Service
- Security

Self- management is composite of sub-management systems with each having its own functionalities. Such management system allows adaptation, re-configuration of topologies, adjustment of topology as new nodes can be injected etc. These self-management systems should be simple and adaptive to network dynamic behavior as well as efficient in the utilization of the resources of the system.

- **Configuration Management:** All tasks/issues that are associated with the management of the configuration of the system/network listed here. It includes the following.
    ◦ Implementation of protocols
    ◦ Programming, testing and deployment of nodes
    ◦ Configuration of acquired data
    ◦ Servicing of network
    ◦ Programming Issues at Network level.

- **Topology Management:** This category handles issues related to the layout/connections of nodes in the sensor networks. Under this, tasks are listed below.
  - Distribution of sensor nodes as well as their location management
  - Distribution of network activity among nodes.
  - Communication among nodes as well as with gateways
- **QoS Management:** The issues/jobs considered and taken care under this division are to ensure an optimum quality of service of the network. These are listed below.
  - Delay/latency of data
  - Performance of system
  - System tolerance to failures
  - Accuracy of system in acquiring the data
- **Energy Management:** All parameters that are related to consumption of energy in a system are taken care under this management. This takes care of the following.
  - Sources of energy in sensor networks
  - Minimization in consumption of energy in a whole system
  - Enhancing the system life/duration by considering all available energy resources
  - Harvesting energy from natural resources
  - Management of overall available power of the system
- **Security Management:** It is necessary to protect network from malicious attacks as sensitive/critical information is being transmitted over networks. This management component handles all activities in network security that is listed below.
  - Encryption of data by using different key distribution techniques
  - Detection of security threats and preventive actions to avoid breaching of security
  - Recovery of system from attacks
- **Maintenance Management:** Wireless sensor networks issues related to maintenance of the operation of the system are considered under this management category.
  - Observation /monitoring of network performance
  - Detection of energy level
  - Detection of faults and correction

Design Criteria for Self-Management System

Management systems can be tailored according to available management techniques given below to achieve some design criteria.

- **Energy Efficiency**: This criterion considers the efficiency of a system in conserving energy and permitting operations on limited power for long durations so as to improve network lifetime.
  - Conserve Energy
  - Limited power utilization
  - Longevity of the system
- **Robustness**: It ensures that a system performs according to the expectations regardless of the changes or dynamic behavior of an environment. A robust system is considered as a system that should generate expected outcome in spite of network variations like failure of nodes, power un-

availability and instabilities due to the motion of nodes. Network reconfiguration is the one of the important characteristics of robust system.

- **Scalability**: Wireless sensor networks are expected to grow up/shrink down according to requirement of application. Therefore, a management system should take care of this fact, so that, overall system may work efficiently at any scale level.
- **Adaptability:** It is the ability of a system to adapt itself with the variations in the network and work efficiently to meet expectations. Adaptive systems should work effectively and accurately in dynamic environment conditions such as fluctuations of energy, changes in topology and variation of tasks. The capability of a system to reconfigure itself and re-assigning of tasks play an important role in achieving this design criterion

SELF-MANAGED SYSTEMS

Wireless management system can be classified in main three categories in accordance with their network architecture.

- Central Management Systems
- Distributed management Systems
- Hierarchical Management Systems

Many authors proposed /designed various different systems in above mentioned network architectures with different functionalities and design criteria that are explained below.

Central Management Systems

In central management system, central manager gathers all data and information from all the nodes and then controls the entire WSN. In this kind of system, manager can do complicated task and provides management decision by getting full knowledge of the entire network. This scheme has few limitations, i.e., central server is single manager and its failure may cause overall system down. There is high communication overhead on manager as well as security risk is also high in such management systems.

H. Songet et al. (2005) proposed a management framework that is required to control and configure sensors. It is based on the service discovery protocol, UPnP (Universal plug and play). It is not economical to embed UPnP protocol in each tiny resource constrained node. To solve this issue, framework includes an agent that is called BOSS (bridge of the sensorS) which is implemented on the base station and that lies between non UPnP tiny sensor nodes and UPnP devices. The basic idea of this architecture is to use non-UPnP tiny devices to use UPnP with the help of a bridge. Boss assists in interpretation and transmission of messages between sensor network and control point. It also helps in other network services such as node localization, context awareness, etc. A software framework called MOTE-VIEW was proposed by M. Turon et al. (2005) that is scalable and is used for managing, monitoring and visualization of sensor network deployment. This framework is used to identify the health of individual nodes as well as the health of whole network. It is used to review comprehensively the issues that come during the deployment of nodes or during administrative tasks. By monitoring above issues, it uses extensible set of user interface components that are used for the improvement in management and deployment of wireless sensor network. An application co-operative system called SNMS (sensor network management system) developed by G. Tolle et al. (2005) basically provides three core services viz. query system, record keeping system and light weight network layer. Query system is used to fire query to enquire for health of network and acquisition of data. Record keeping system is used to record the events generated in the system and light weight network layer deals with applications network layer. It is quite simple, open and flexible. It provides query based health monitoring and event logging. A WSN VIEW designed by Y.W. Ma et al. (2010) shows the connections and relationships among nodes. Its primary task is monitoring, collecting and analyzing of the information that is obtained from sensor network. It performs performance analysis which helps in the management of sensors in the network. This system manages all the abilities of sensor, communication control, configuration and backup support. This system sends command with user interface through TOSSIM (an event WSN simulator). Its user interface shows different functions listed at the top to perform different functions such as location map of nodes. The wireless sensor network manager obtains information by performing different tasks with help of different tabs provided in graphical user interface (GUI). It gives information about the coverage of sensors and faulty sensor nodes.

The debugging architecture developed by Ramanathan et al. (2005) continues its monitoring process even when application is running. It enhances overall vision of system by collecting and identifying micro-level metrics and events. These metrics are used to inspect system health and also identify unexpected correlation among these events and help in detecting and debugging of failures in the system. It logs metrics as they get changed. This defines a minimal set of metrics that are enough to infer the health of the system. The metrics are directly collected from the application and then analyzed. Sympathy system has two types of nodes according to the task assigned to them. On detection of event, sympathy sink updates its data structure and notifies it to the client.

Distributed Management Systems

In distributed management systems, there are many managers and each manager is dedicated to control and manage their sub networks. These managers can communicate among themselves and perform managerial functions. In these kinds of systems, local processing reduces network bandwidth and therefore reduces communication cost. These systems provide better reliability and energy efficiency but it also has few limitations. These are complex and difficult to manage and computationally very expensive for resource constrained nodes.

C. Hsin et al. (2006) proposed a distributed two phase (TP) alarm system that is used for surveillance and monitoring the health of the network. It has less probability of sending false alarm as compared with one alarm system. TP uses local coordination and active probing. Two metrics are used viz. false alarm probability and response delay. First metric is used to detect dead node and second one depicts the time between sensor dying time and when this event is detected. This system does active neighbor monitoring in distributed fashion. Nodes detect actively its neighbors and dead nodes with the help of timer associated with them. It uses neighbor coordinating scheme in which nodes consults with its neighbor nodes before sending alarm to center system. Nodes use two phase timer system. In first phase, sensor nodes wait for update message from neighbor and in the second phase it consults with other neighbors to take correct and accurate decision.

A. Boulis et al. (2003) has proposed differently a management of finite energy of sensor network with a set of different distributed applications having different user reward points. This energy management is done at micro level (node) by taking system level hints from different applications. It is the requirement of identification of the energy consumed by different applications. Real time measurement of energy consumption by different applications is estimated by considering extra energy consumption that is due to the execution of the new application with the set of the current executing applications. Energy management is done at node level by using admission control and policing approach and maximizes user rewards. The whole mechanism is divided in two tasks. First task is the estimation of the cost due to energy which is calculated based on the provided parameters of the applications currently running in the node. Second task is the calculation of the energy cost of the new application which is based on the behavior of new admitted application and behavior of other applications running on same node. The system of M. Perillo et al. (2003) provides enough data to get the reliable description of the environment with consideration of energy and other constraints like bandwidth .These goals are contradicting and they should be balanced at the some optimization point. The maximization of network is achieved by scheduling active sets of sensors and finding different paths for routing. The overall life of the network gets increased with the optimization of the scheduling and data routing. The routes are chosen in such a way that nodes, which are very important for use as sensors, are routed around more often. Whereas when the duration period for sensor set is determined then it is critical to consider that the affected sensors are taken from active sets as well as from the chosen paths to the data sink. It is effective to couple the sensor scheduling with selection of routes. C. Fok et al. (2005) proposed a system called Agilla which has used mobile agent middleware which aids in the rapid deployment in sensor networks. Mobile agents are special programs written by user on nodes and these programs coordinate with each other through local tuples. They can migrate across sensor network as to perform specific tasks. This migration feature makes network shared and computing platform which is capable of running several independent applications simultaneously and uses full potential of network system. Agilla is used to deploy complex applications in networks where number of applications can share a network at a time. Tuple space-based communication enhances network flexibility.

The scheme developed by A. Erdogan et al. (2003) uses a direction antenna to activate or deactivate a specific region at any time. In this scheme, central node is having a directional antenna that is used to broadcast tasks. These broadcasted tasks are assigned with unique Id's for each region. Nodes which receives task start sensing and disseminating reports. This scheme reduces the requirement of additional hardware or software for location or management of nodes. This scheme is called Sectoral Sweeper (SS). This sweeps sensor area in sectoral manner and it saves lot of energy consumption. It immediately disseminates tasks to particular sector. This scheme activates only those sensors which are present in a desired region. So, this scheme reduces the number of sensors that are operating at the same time and hence it saves energy and it works very effectively. In this scheme, response to queries is quick as task is broadcasted to sensors at a single hop. The task dissemination is done effectively and therefore more control over the sensor network. Sensor nodes can be easily located. Since, this scheme reduces the number of active sensors at a time, energy is saved. Data routing and its aggregation become easier. A management architecture in (Z. Ying et al., 2005) uses the concept of mobile agents with policy technologies. Mobile agents are distributed and artificial intelligent agents that can transfer its data and its state to other node. There is no need for the collection of data on a single node. This fact saves bandwidth of the system, degree of parallel processing and real time performance of the system. A policy in this system implies some pre-determined action list that is executed when certain condition is met.

The architectural components of the Policy Framework include a Policy Decision Point (PDP), Policy Enforcement Points (PEP) and a policy repository. The PDP uses rules stored in the policy repository. It defines processes and results of different policy rules. It interprets data and translates it into device-dependent format. It configures the relevant PEPs which enforces the logical entities. These abilities of system can provide configuration and control functions and also it can reconfigure or re-task system with the changing network conditions. These policy based agents provide scalability and autonomy in the system. It is suitable for geographically distributed network environment. R. Tynan et al. (2005) proposed intelligent power management system by using agents. As nodes are resource constrained devices, their battery gets depleted with time. So, intelligent power management is required to increase the overall life of a system. Intelligent power agents do such power management activities in distributed environment. Agents have to take potential decisions for the power management of the system. Intelligent agent based system provides autonomy and adaptability in a system. There is always a trade-off for cost to decision taken for power management not to exceed the benefits received from this decision.

L.B. Ruiz et al. (2003) has also proposed management architecture called MANNA that considers three management dimensions viz. management levels, functional areas and functionalities. The management architecture of MANNA for wireless sensor network is based on the principles of sensor network models, their functionalities and their management levels. It provides great flexibility in defining functional, information, and physical architectures. Three planes are coordinated with each other by using policy-based management. The functional architecture deals with configurations that are possible for the management entities. The information architecture deals with classes, objects, information of syntax and semantics exchanged among the entities. The physical architecture of the system considers the flexibility of the functional architecture. An energy- efficient system suitable for wireless sensor networks called EMWSN (Furthmuller et al., 2009) allows micro-level control over the latency tolerance for the requests by management so as to reduce energy consumption. It studies whether sending the sensing data along with management of data in spite of sending separately can reduce the energy consumption or not. It uses the idea of cooperative requests, that allows the clustering of data sent by the sensor network and the management agent and hence the number of packets sent can be reduced. It shows when the more latency is tolerated in the fulfillment of management requests, then this reduces more the number of packets that needs to be sent, and hence decreases the traffic which results in the energy savings . A lightweight and component based service platform (P. Javier et al., 2009) for wireless sensor network manages network software resources based upon the specifications of service level agreements (SLA) and also optimizes the behavior of the component in accordance with the collected environment information. The distrinet adaptive resource management architecture (DARMA) is capable of optimizing the components that are used by multiple services. It separates application logic from resource management and this feature helps it in easy deployments.

Hierarchical Management Systems

Hierarchical management systems are hybrid of centralized and distributed management systems. In these systems, multiple managers exist and these managers are classified as intermediate and manager stations. The main function of an intermediate manager is to distribute the management functions. These intermediate managers do not directly communicate among themselves. Each manager manages its sub-network's nodes. It provides information to its higher-level manager. It also distributes management functions that it receives from the higher manager to its sub-network.

B. Deb et al. (2001) proposed an algorithm to construct a topology of network by finding a set of distinguished nodes and using its neighborhood information. This algorithm reduces communication overhead as only few nodes reply back to discovery probes. The algorithm TopDisc (topology discovery) forms a tree of clusters with monitoring of the node as root of the tree. This helps in easy dissemination /aggregation of data, duty cycle assignments and network state retrieval. This is fully distributed mechanism and is well suitable for sensor network as it uses only local information and only one packet per node. An algorithm called STREAM (sensor topology retrieval at multiple resolutions) (B. Deb et al., 2004) used to retrieve topology for sensor having number of resolutions. It traded-off between the details of topology and resources expended. It is a parameterized distributed algorithm that extracts topology at multiple resolutions. Node discovery process finds suitable minimal virtual dominating set (MVDs) and its selection depends upon the characteristics of the information sought. The number of neighbors, about which a reporting node responds, is provided by the resolution-factor. With the help of eavesdropping, nodes can gather information about its nodes that are present in its neighborhood. By filtering with the query-type parameter, few neighbor scan be chosen. A hybrid distribution framework RRP (region based routing protocol) proposed in (W. Liu et al., 2004) for sensor network conceptually partitions the whole sensor network into many functional areas in accordance of supply chain methodology. It uses distinct routing schemes for different areas for better reliability and efficient energy usage. It has used zone/region flooding method that is the combination of both geometric and flood technique. It provides good reliability, scalability, flexibility, and energy efficiency.

W. Louis Lee et al. (2006) proposed a self-management system WinMS(WSN-management system). It provides self-management features and maintains the overall performance of the network. It also achieves effective nodes operations without human interference. This system is adaptive to dynamic conditions and it reconfigures itself in accordance with the current conditions. WinMS uses resource transfer function that systematically allows time slots (resources) to be transferred from one to another part. It provides non-uniform and reactive sensing by using resource transfer function. It provides auto-stabilization and auto-configuration both locally and globally. The transfer function is run either centrally or locally based on the neighborhood state. This provides efficient monitoring, control, and management of sensor networks.The policy based feedback management architecture (PFMA) available in (L. Zhigang et al., 2009) focuses on the performance improvement of perception. The perception management system gives the feedback that is obtained from the result of information which can enhance the overall quality of data collecting process. By using management policies, system management and network management are integrated. Here, system makes policies in accordance with the requirements of an application that is very much different from traditional policy based network management systems. Network management system executes policies and manages performance, configuration, faults and states of the network and also it submits the state of network to system management as feedback. Zhao et al. (2011) proposed a management system for a very large sensor networks (WSNMS) with the characteristics of WSNs. WSNMS includes four management functionalities viz. configuration, performance, fault and accounting management. It is capable of undertaking the very high-level management functions and provides a very accurate and good performance. Presently, it has many shortcomings like there is very high communication overhead because of data polling done by a single manager. Grichi et al. (2017) has also proposed a wireless sensor networks RWSNs (reconfiguring wireless sensor networks) that are reconfigurable and adaptable to their external environments in such a way that all communication operations among nodes consume minimum energy, and hence, try to enhance the lifetime of the whole system. A reconfigurable wireless sensor network is considered to be of a set of nodes that are located in different distributed zones. Each node in a zone executes reconfigurable software tasks and controls its zone's local sensors. In this scheme, all reconfiguration forms are used in the network so as to make it adaptable to its environment under energy constraints. In this, new power oriented method is used that handles the zones and the mobility of nodes so as to control the total consumption of energy. Two dynamic methods are used viz. the resizing of zones and the mobility of nodes. It has been concluded that more amount of energy can be conserved during the communication among stations, nodes and agents.

Junaid Ahmed et al. (2015) reported and devised in his paper about different energy harvesting resources. Energy management in sensor networks is a supreme issue especially in case of nodes that are deployed remotely and energy constrained. These energy constrained nodes are charged or given power by attaching rechargeable batteries. A lot of battery-driven energy conservation methods are researched to provide efficiency in energy consumption during network operations. Limited battery constraints shifted the researcher's attention towards harvesting energy from natural resources. Mills et al. (2007) presented a review paper on self-organizing wireless sensor network. It has revised various self-organizing systems and research areas that need attention of researcher .Author suggested a need to design self-organizing systems that can simultaneously address multiple dimensions of performance, security, and robustness. It has suggested that a framework is needed that encompass and satisfy all design objectives of self –managed system. Paradis et al. (2007) reviewed fault tolerance issues in WSN. As wireless sensor networks are energy constrained and often deployed in hostile environments to collect data and events of outside world, event of interest delivery with reliability is one of the main concerns of the most sensor networks. But, the nature of communication in sensor networks is very much prone to failures, so it is required to provide fault tolerant techniques for large scale distributed sensor networks. Macías-Escrivá et al. (2013) have also reviewed self-adaptive systems in his work. These systems are capable to adapt their own i.e. they change their behavior whenever the evaluation of output shows that the system is not accomplishing what it was intended to do. The main aim is to review latest progress on auto-adaptation from different aspects. It has analyzed that feedback control techniques and artificial intelligent techniques are the most promising disciplines that will enhance the development of self-adaptive systems. Van Roy et al. (2007) proposed a project "The SELFMAN (self-managing)" that builds a management system for WSN, tackles the frequent occurred problems viz. updating of software, failures of nodes, malicious attacks, and hotspots. It has combined two technologies to add the self-managing feature in the system. These techniques are advanced component models and structured overlay networks. Structured overlay networks (SONs) provides scalability, robustness, guaranteed communication and efficiency. Component models extends the self-managing features of Structured overlay networks over the whole system. Interacting feedback loops are used for building self-managing systems.

Yan et al. (2010) proposed an idea about Complex Adaptive System (CAS) having characteristics of self –organization, adaptation, routing energy consumption and elongation of whole system life. It would change the communication between human being and nature. So, many sensors, when connected wirelessly with one another, communicate with the real world and interrogate the events of interest. Pignaton de Freitas et al. (2008) has reviewed about adaptable middleware for sensor network and analyzed their behavior in changing environment. The main common problem in adaptive middleware is lack of quality of service (QoS) support. The concentration in system is given only on one feature. Therefore, a need for a solution that would manage to address more than one of the features at same time, and not only one of them, so that system become less application dependent. A hierarchical framework developed by Mengjie et al. (2008) uses lightweight middleware system which helps wireless sensor networks' in handling network management in a real time. The main objective of using middleware is to provide management services to different sensor applications so as to maintain service quality without or very less human intervention. The middleware of these sensor nodes is capable of reconfiguring itself to its functionality so as to reflect the changes in external network environment or resources of nodes. It has also proposed a solution to achieve energy efficiency in sensor networks by using power management. It controls the performance management of sensor nodes. It reduces node energy consumption by considering the fact of not reconfiguring management structure frequently. Ndiaye et al. (2017) reviewed the main highlights of the latest work on traditional wireless sensor networks (WSN) management. It has also reviewed software defined network (SDN) based management techniques used in wireless sensor networks. It investigates challenges for wireless configuration and management to make it more flexible and easier with SDN. In this paper, author has reviewed numerous works and schemes that are used to for traditional wireless sensor networks management and also for SDN-based management of WSNs. Dhage et al. (2014) has also reviewed about the scalability of wireless sensor network. Scalable system means that it is able to modify itself to fulfill the demands of changing load on the system. Scalability of a system depends upon so many factors and these factors decide whether the system is able to scale up or not. Therefore, it is required to consider all the factors and their solutions to provide scalable systems. Scalability is one of the main design criteria that is required to design and implement large scale distributed wireless sensor networks. Breza et al. (2007) proposed a protocol called BioANS (bio-inspired automatic network services) for wireless sensor networks that is based and inspired from nature processes. BioANS uses the concepts of emergence engineering so as to fulfill the requirements of wireless sensor networks. It includes randomization and light weight messages. In this, delayed-bid scheme is also included. To give responses to the requests done by sensor node, this uses a component called random timing. A stop-bid message is generated and sent to other nodes when an accurate response is received. A self-configuration and self-healing concept presented in (Narayan et al., 2014) is based on modulation parameter scaling and on error correction respectively. The elongation of life and throughput of network can be increased using these methods. Simulation has been carried out using MATLAB software. The overall impact of above schemes is to provide transactional security and to enhance network lifetime by applying autonomic characteristics to WSN. In a self-organized system (Chunawale et al., 2017), whole behavior is controlled by the local interactions among nodes of the system. It is self-organized wireless sensor network in which local nodes take decision without the involvement of any central entity. Its working is based upon the residual energy of the nodes. Node clustering is done in this scheme that saves energy and also cluster head (CH) selection is done through local communication and mutual decision of the nodes. It proposes new scheme of node clustering. Cluster formation depends upon the residual energy of nodes and nearest distance parameter. Node having highest residual energy becomes cluster head (CH) and other nodes join the nearest CH. When CH residual energy gets down than the threshold energy then current cluster gets broken down and new cluster is formed. This scheme is focused to solve the energy hole problem caused due to higher energy consumption by CHs near Sink Node or Base Station (BS). An ant colony optimization (ACO) algorithm (Kellner et al., 2017) is inspired from nature and is suitable for distributed and self-organizing nature of WSN. The original parent ant colony optimization based algorithm and its derived children algorithm consider only one objective, i.e., these algorithms concentrate on only achieving one parameter whereas in multi-objective (MOACO), multiple (conflicting) objectives are considered altogether simultaneously . Fei et al. (2017) provided a research survey on multi-objective optimizations (MOO) in wireless sensor network. As we know, it's a very challenging task to trade-offs amongst various optimization criteria, such as coverage, lifetime, energy dissipation and data loss rate which conflicts with each other. It gives a review on optimization objectives that are used in WSNs and also studied various approaches that are used for MOO, such as scalarization methods with mathematical programming, heuristics optimization algorithms and other advanced techniques. Multiple objectives algorithms give a set of Pareto-optimal solutions instead of giving a single optimal solution. Another Quantum Ant Colony Evolutionary Algorithm (QACEA) (Wang et al., 2017) solved a coverage problem in self-organizing WSN. This method introduces new concept of quantum state vector into the existing ant colony algorithm and it realizes the dynamic adjustment of ant colony through quantum rotation port. It shows that the quantum ant colony evolutionary algorithm effectively improves the coverage of sensor networks. Kim et al. (2017) proposed a self-organized underwater wireless sensor network called SOUNET. Here, sensor nodes form a tree like topological network for data gathering in a self-organized way. Packet flooding is used for the discovery of network topology. The sensor nodes inform their parent nodes so as to ensure connectivity by using the time-varying neighbor tables. It is self-adaptive technique that gives high network connectivity without any centralized control.

Giuntini et al. (2017) proposed the self-organizing as well as fault-tolerating model for wireless sensor network for the detection of fire in particular area. Self-organization as well as tolerance for faults is achieved in distributed manner by local conversations among neighboring nodes. Supervisor node, which is encompassed with a framework used for the development of applications, co-ordinates the tasks of nodes monitoring same area. A reconfiguration system proposed by (Grichi et al., 2014) is adaptable in environment changes and considers energy constraints. Here, the set of nodes communicate with each other and executes reconfiguration system. Author considers three types of reconfiguration in WSN viz. software reconfiguration, hardware reconfiguration and protocol reconfiguration. It is a zone –based multi-agent architecture. The complexity of whole work is handled by modeling each agent with nested state machine. A coordination protocol is defined for agents for their coordination and communication. Jurenoks et al. (2016) has also proposed modified Bellman-Ford and Dijkstra's algorithms for enhancing the planning for flow monitoring and also provided the required components for the network which increases the overall life duration of the sensor network. It maintains an optimal data flow route and increases the life. The residual energy is used to choose the path within network during iterative stage. Sneh et al. (2017) has reviewed deployment schemes of sensors deployed randomly in environment. Sensor nodes self-manage their deployment after being randomly placed in environment. These types of networks contain both types of nodes, i.e., static and mobile nodes. Mobile nodes relocate themselves so as to achieve maximum coverage. As nodes are energy constrained so their mobility is controlled in a way to maximize the longevity of network by controlling energy consumption during their mobility.

Comprehensive Knowledge for Required Areas and Simulation Tools

WSN management systems are application specific. Their architecture and management functions depend upon the type of application for which they are used. The example are architecture and characteristics of system used in marine detection system different from the requirements of management system used for habitat monitoring etc. As wireless sensor networks are application specific so there is need of different architectures; however, communication technologies and sensing technologies are entirely for different applications. The main application area of sensor networks are home/office automation, Military, Traffic Control, Irrigation, Marine Environment Monitoring, Industrial Process Monitoring, Environmental monitoring, monitoring natural disaster etc.

Table 1. Self-Managing systems evaluation for functionalities

Management Schemes	Functionalities
MANNA	Policy Inclusion, Fault Measurement
BOSS	Detecting Network state, Power management
Agilla	Detection of events
Sectoral Sweepers	On/OFF(nodes switching)
Power management with agent Intelligently	Lowering of power management
Power management based on mobile agents	Management dependent on policy
RRP	Data collection/aggregation
SNMS	Events and health detection
SNMP	Monitoring and definition of network function
WSN Management	Error /fault/Performance management
WinMS	Synchronization, retrieval of states and repairs
Management of energy levels	Managing of power
Mote-View	visualization and N/W state

SIMULATION TOOLS

Nayyar et al. (2015) has reviewed simulation tools used for WSN which help researchers in selecting most appropriate tool for their research work. Here, author has reviewed 31 simulating tools along with their respective features. On considering various parameters and comparing performance of WSN simulators, it is considered that NS-2, NS-3 and QualNet are best simulators to do any kind of research in the area of Wireless Sensor Networks. It is suggested that researchers should design their own simulator using existing development tools/languages (viz. Matlab, Python, Java etc.)

Comparison of Wireless Sensor Network Management Systems

The evaluation of functionalities and designing criteria for self –managing systems are summarized in Table 1 and Table 2 respectively.

SCOPE FOR FUTURE RESEARCH

After intensive study of literature, following points are inferred for the future research works.

- There is lack of designing of effective sensing model considering environmental factors and dynamic environmental issues.
- There is also lack of detection and measurement of the presence or degree of self-feature of state-of-art management systems of WSN.

Table 2. Self-Managing systems evaluation for design criteria

Management Schemes	Energy-Efficient	Robust	Adaptable	Scalable
MANNA	N	N	N	N
BOSS	Y	Y	N	Y
Agilla	Y	N	N	Y
Sectoral Sweepers	Y	N	N	N
Power management with agent Intelligently	Y	N	N	Y
Power management based on mobile agents	Y	Y	N	Y
RRP	Y	N	N	N
SNMS	Y	Y	N	N
SNMP	N	Y	N	Y
WSN Management	N	Y	N	Y
WinMS	Y	Y	Y	Y
Management of energy levels	Y	Y	N	N
Mote-View	Y	N	Y	N

Y—yes (feature is present) and N-(Not Present)

- Routing in Self-Management is challenging task due to unpredictable change in the behavior of an environment or system which results in the change of topology of network. So, research on efficient adaptive routing is required that changes itself with the change of topology.
- Minimization in the mobility of sensor during reconfiguration of nodes in the presence of obstacles in path during their motion phase is needed to be considered.
- Quick recovery from failures and quick reconfiguration of the system is challenging task in dynamic environments. Extensive research is required for quick reconfiguration and recovery of network.
- Due to IoT applications in the future, there is a need of consideration of security issues in management systems of WSN.
- There is lack of algorithms that provide solutions for a problem of deciding or selecting a number of self-decisive nodes needed for efficient working of whole system.
- There is also lack of bio-inspired models for overall management of the whole large scale distributed WSN.
- Designing a Self-Management system for large-scale distributed wireless sensor network bears many issues. These issues/troubles are due to restricted number of resources available viz. computational capacity, battery life, and memory of the sensor nodes.
- Efficient Mobility algorithms are required for mobile nodes in heterogeneous wireless sensor networks. Efficiency in mobility of nodes is required during self –management processes.
- Network design for futuristic applications must consider many factors to achieve optimal performance by trading-offs multiple different objectives. Therefore, MOAs i.e. Multi-objective Algorithms are basically very important, which must trade-off between the different performance metrics. There is a lack of multi-objective algorithms for self-management systems in WSN.

- There are few algorithms that are independent of the area in which sensors are deployed. There is a need to give attention to the development of the terrain independent algorithms. Algorithms should be capable of handling uneven or irregular shaped terrains for the deployment of sensor and self-deploy themselves in an uneven terrain.
- From literature, it has been observed that effective sensing model need to be introduced which considers the environmental factors and their dynamic nature so as to be usable in real life applications. System should adapt itself according to its environmental change.
- Obstacles are handled during self-deployment but the total movement of nodes for handling this problem is not considered. So, work is needed to introduce self-mobility algorithms that give attention to the fact of minimizing the movement of sensors for energy efficient networks.
- Some critical applications need very quick recovery systems. But systems take time to recover themselves from failures. Systems need reconfiguration on change in parameters to achieve its objective. So very quick and efficient self –recovery and reconfiguration feature is required.
- It is highly required that less number of sensor nodes should be used in area to cut the overall cost of the whole system. There is a requirement of algorithms that give prior information about the number of self-decisive nodes required in the field for efficient monitoring and working of whole system.
- Routing in Self-Management is a challenging task due to unpredictable change in the behavior of an environment or system which results in the change of topology of network. So, research on efficient adaptive routing is required that change itself with the change of topology.
- Designing a Self-Management system for large-scale distributed wireless sensor network faces many challenges. These challenges are mainly caused by the limited resources available in WSNs including battery lifetime, computing capacity, and memory space at the sensor nodes, and also due to the dynamic topology especially in adhoc sensor networks.
- Multi-objective self- management algorithms are required for WSN. There is need of self-management system for large scale distributed sensor network that inculcate all self-features viz. self-deployment, self-configuration, self-healing and scalability. Therefore, multi-objective optimization algorithms, which must trade-off between the different performance metrics, are required as there is a lack of multi-objective algorithms for self-management systems in WSN.

CONCLUSION

With literature, we came to know that most of the management system's concentration is on the achievement of one or two design criteria of wireless sensor network. E.g. Agilla management is energy efficient but it does not give attention to robustness, scalability and adaptability. So, there is need of self-management system for large scale distributed sensor network that inculcates all self-features viz. self-deployment, self-configuration, self-healing and scalability. There is also lack of multi-objective algorithms for self-management systems in wireless sensor networks. WSN management should meet four design criteria viz. energy efficiency, robustness, scalability and adaptability. To conclude, requirements of systems that after deployment manage themselves, i.e., automatically adapt itself in the dynamic conditions of environment. These systems should be capable of reconfiguring themselves in changing conditions without any human help in accordance with the management policies having operations like inclusion/removal of sensor nodes, performance tuning, failure detection and recovery. We are in the process of designing a self- management system using the above suggested design parameters (attributes). The proposed / designed systems will be used in applications given in figure 3. Besides this, the said system will also be used to control in time flood, earth quakes, tsunami and other natural disasters.

REFERENCES

Boulis, A., & Srivastava, M. (2004). Node-level energy management for sensor networks in the presence of multiple applications. *Wireless Networks, 10*(6), 737–746. doi:10.1023/B:WINE.0000044032.41234.d7

Breza, M., Anthony, R., & McCann, J. (2007). Scalable and efficient sensor network self-configuration in bioans. In *First International Conference on Self-Adaptive and Self-Organizing Systems (SASO 2007)*, (pp. 351-354). IEEE. 10.1109/SASO.2007.47

Castillo-Effer, M. (2004). Wireless sensor networks for flash-flood alerting. In *Proceedings of the Fifth IEEE International Caracas Conference on Devices, Circuits and Systems* (pp. 142-146). IEEE. 10.1109/ICCDCS.2004.1393370

Chen, D., Liu, Z., Wang, L., Dou, M., Chen, J., & Li, H. (2013). Natural disaster monitoring with wireless sensor networks: A case study of data-intensive applications upon low-cost scalable systems. *Mobile Networks and Applications, 18*(5), 651–663. doi:10.100711036-013-0456-9

Chunawale, A., & Sirsikar, S. (2017, March). RED: Residual Energy and Distance Based Clustering to Avoid Energy Hole Problem in Self-organized Wireless Sensor Networks. In *International Conference on Information and Communication Technology for Intelligent Systems*, (pp. 155-163). Springer.

Deb, B., Bhatnagar, S., & Nath, B. (2002). *A topology discovery algorithm for sensor networks with applications to network management*. Academic Press.

Deb, B., Bhatnagar, S., & Nath, B. (2004). STREAM: Sensor topology retrieval at multiple resolutions. *Telecommunication Systems, 26*(2-4), 285–320. doi:10.1023/B:TELS.0000029043.27689.3f

Del Cid, P. J., Hughes, D., Ueyama, J., Michiels, S., & Joosen, W. (2009, December). DARMA: adaptable service and resource management for wireless sensor networks. In *Proceedings of the 4th International Workshop on Middleware Tools, Services and Run-Time Support for Sensor Networks*, (pp. 1-6). ACM. 10.1145/1658192.1658193

Dhage, M. S. V., Thakre, A. N., & Mohod, S. W. (2014). A review on scalability issue in wireless sensor networks. *International Journal of Innovative Research in Advanced Engineering, 1*, 463–466.

Erdogan, A., Cayirci, E., & Coskun, V. (2003, October). Sectoral sweepers for sensor node management and location estimation in adhoc sensor networks. In *IEEE Military Communications Conference, 2003. MILCOM 2003* (Vol. 1, pp. 555-560). IEEE.

Fei, Z., Li, B., Yang, S., Xing, C., Chen, H., & Hanzo, L. (2016). A survey of multi-objective optimization in wireless sensor networks: Metrics, algorithms, and open problems. *IEEE Communications Surveys and Tutorials, 19*(1), 550–586. doi:10.1109/COMST.2016.2610578

Fok, C. L., Roman, G. C., & Lu, C. (2005, April). Mobile agent middleware for sensor networks: An application case study. In *IPSN 2005. Fourth International Symposium on Information Processing in Sensor Networks*, (pp. 382-387). IEEE.

Furthmüller, J., Kessler, S., & Waldhorst, O. P. (2010, February). Energy-efficient management of wireless sensor networks. In *2010 Seventh International Conference on Wireless On-demand Network Systems and Services (WONS)*, (pp. 129-136). IEEE. 10.1109/WONS.2010.5437120

Garg, S., & Patel, R. B. (2017, February). Review of different deployment schemes in wireless sensor networks. In *2017 3rd International Conference on Computational Intelligence & Communication Technology (CICT)*, (pp. 1-8). IEEE. 10.1109/CIACT.2017.7977367

Giuntini, F. T., Beder, D. M., & Ueyama, J. (2017). Exploiting self-organization and fault tolerance in wireless sensor networks: A case study on wildfire detection application. *International Journal of Distributed Sensor Networks*, *13*(4), 1550147717704120. doi:10.1177/1550147717704120

Grichi, H., Mosbahi, O., & Khalgui, M. (2014, August). Reconfigurable Wireless Sensor Networks new adaptive dynamic solutions for flexible architectures. In *2014 9th International Conference on Software Engineering and Applications (ICSOFT-EA)*, (pp. 254-265). IEEE. 10.5220/0005005602540265

Grichi, H., Mosbahi, O., Khalgui, M., & Li, Z. (2017). New power-oriented methodology for dynamic resizing and mobility of reconfigurable wireless sensor networks. *IEEE Transactions on Systems, Man, and Cybernetics. Systems*, *48*(7), 1120–1130. doi:10.1109/TSMC.2016.2645401

Gutiérrez, J., Villa-Medina, J. F., Nieto-Garibay, A., & Porta-Gándara, M. Á. (2013). Automated irrigation system using a wireless sensor network and GPRS module. *IEEE Transactions on Instrumentation and Measurement*, *63*(1), 166–176. doi:10.1109/TIM.2013.2276487

Hsin, C., & Liu, M. (2006). Self-monitoring of wireless sensor networks. *Computer Communications*, *29*(4), 462-476.

Jurenoks, A. (2016). Developing the Reconfiguration Method to Increase Life Expectancy of Dynamic Wireless Sensor Network in Container Terminal. *Applied Computer Systems*, *20*(1), 15–20. doi:10.1515/acss-2016-0010

Kellner, A. (2017). Multi-objective Ant Colony Optimisation in Wireless Sensor Networks. In *Nature-Inspired Computing and Optimization* (pp. 51–78). Cham: Springer. doi:10.1007/978-3-319-50920-4_3

Khan, J. A., Qureshi, H. K., & Iqbal, A. (2015). Energy management in wireless sensor networks: A survey. *Computers & Electrical Engineering*, *41*, 159–176. doi:10.1016/j.compeleceng.2014.06.009

Kim, H. W., & Cho, H. S. (2017). SOUNET: Self-organized underwater wireless sensor network. *Sensors (Basel)*, *17*(2), 283. doi:10.339017020283 PMID:28157164

Lee, W.L., Datta, A., & Cardell-Oliver, R. (2006). *Winms: Wireless sensor network-management system, an adaptive policy-based management for wireless sensor networks*. Academic Press.

Li, Z., Li, S., & Zhou, X. (2009, September). PFMA: Policy-based feedback management architecture for wireless sensor Networks. In *2009 5th International Conference on Wireless Communications, Networking and Mobile Computing* (pp. 1-4). IEEE.

Liu, W., Zhang, Y., Lou, W., & Fang, Y. (2004, October). Managing wireless sensor networks with supply chain strategy. In *First International Conference on Quality of Service in Heterogeneous Wired/Wireless Networks*, (pp. 59-66). IEEE. 10.1109/QSHINE.2004.29

Ma, Y. W., Chen, J. L., Huang, Y. M., & Lee, M. Y. (2010). An efficient management system for wireless sensor networks. *Sensors (Basel)*, *10*(12), 11400–11413. doi:10.3390101211400 PMID:22163534

Macías-Escrivá, F. D., Haber, R., Del Toro, R., & Hernandez, V. (2013). Self-adaptive systems: A survey of current approaches, research challenges and applications. *Expert Systems with Applications*, *40*(18), 7267–7279. doi:10.1016/j.eswa.2013.07.033

Mills, K. L. (2007). A brief survey of self-organization in wireless sensor networks. *Wireless Communications and Mobile Computing*, *7*(7), 823–834. doi:10.1002/wcm.499

Muñoz-Gea, J. P., Manzanares-Lopez, P., Malgosa-Sanahuja, J., & Garcia-Haro, J. (2013). Design and implementation of a P2P communication infrastructure for WSN-based vehicular traffic control applications. *Journal of Systems Architecture*, *59*(10), 923–930. doi:10.1016/j.sysarc.2013.08.002

Narayan, R., Mallikarjunaswamy, B.P., & Supriya, M.C. (2014). *Self-optimization and Self-Protection (Transactional Security) in AODV Based Wireless Sensor Network*. Academic Press.

Nayyar, A., & Singh, R. (2015). A comprehensive review of simulation tools for wireless sensor networks (WSNs). *Journal of Wireless Networking and Communications*, *5*(1), 19–47.

Ndiaye, M., Hancke, G. P., & Abu-Mahfouz, A. M. (2017). Software defined networking for improved wireless sensor network management: A survey. *Sensors (Basel)*, *17*(5), 1031. doi:10.339017051031 PMID:28471390

O'hare, G. M. P., Marsh, D., Ruzzelli, A., & Tynan, R. (2005, May). Agents for wireless sensor network power management. In *Proceedings of International Workshop on Wireless and Sensor Networks (WSNET-05)*. IEEE Press.

Othman, M. F., & Shazali, K. (2012). Wireless sensor network applications: A study in environment monitoring system. *Procedia Engineering*, *41*, 1204–1210. doi:10.1016/j.proeng.2012.07.302

Paradis, L., & Han, Q. (2007). A survey of fault management in wireless sensor networks. *Journal of Network and Systems Management*, *15*(2), 171–190. doi:10.100710922-007-9062-0

Perillo, M., & Heinzelman, W. B. (2003, May). Providing application QoS through intelligent sensor management. In *Proceedings of the First IEEE International Workshop on Sensor Network Protocols and Applications*, (pp. 93-101). IEEE. 10.1109/SNPA.2003.1203360

Pignaton de Freitas, E. (2008). *A survey on adaptable middleware for wireless sensor networks*. Academic Press.

Ramanathan, N., Kohler, E., & Estrin, D. (2005). Towards a debugging system for sensor networks. *International Journal of Network Management*, *15*(4), 223–234. doi:10.1002/nem.570

Ruiz, L. B., Nogueira, J. M., & Loureiro, A. A. (2003). Manna: A management architecture for wireless sensor networks. *IEEE Communications Magazine*, *41*(2), 116–125. doi:10.1109/MCOM.2003.1179560

Sharma, U., & Reddy, S. R. N. (2012). Design of home/office automation using wireless sensor network. *International Journal of Computers and Applications*, *43*(22), 46–52. doi:10.5120/8428-2195

Song, H., Kim, D., Lee, K., & Sung, J. (2005, April). UPnP-based sensor network management architecture. *Proc. International Conference on Mobile Computing and Ubiquitous Networking*.

Tolle, G., & Culler, D. (2005, February). Design of an application-cooperative management system for wireless sensor networks. In *Proceedings of the Second European Workshop on Wireless Sensor Networks*, (pp. 121-132). IEEE. 10.1109/EWSN.2005.1462004

Turon, M. (2005, May). Mote-view: A sensor network monitoring and management tool. In *The Second IEEE Workshop on Embedded Networked Sensors, 2005. EmNetS-II* (pp. 11-17). IEEE. 10.1109/EMNETS.2005.1469094

Van Roy, P., Haridi, S., Reinefeld, A., Stefani, J. B., Yap, R., & Coupaye, T. (2007, October). Self-management for large-scale distributed systems: An overview of the selfman project. In *International Symposium on Formal Methods for Components and Objects*, (pp. 153-178). Springer.

Wang, L. L., & Wang, C. (2017). A self-organizing wireless sensor networks based on quantum ant Colony evolutionary algorithm. *International Journal of Online Engineering*, *13*(07), 69–80. doi:10.3991/ijoe.v13i07.7284

Winkler, M., Tuchs, K.D., Hughes, K., & Barclay, G. (2008). Theoretical and practical aspects of military wireless sensor networks. *Journal of Telecommunications and Information Technology*, 37-45.

Xu, G., Shen, W., & Wang, X. (2014). Applications of wireless sensor networks in marine environment monitoring: A survey. *Sensors (Basel)*, *14*(9), 16932–16954. doi:10.3390140916932 PMID:25215942

Yan, C., & Ji-Hong, Q. (2010, October). Application analysis of complex adaptive systems for WSN. In *2010 International Conference on Computer Application and System Modeling (ICCASM 2010)*, (Vol. 7, pp. V7-328). IEEE.

Ying, Z., & Debao, X. (2005, September). Mobile agent-based policy management for wireless sensor networks. In *Proceedings. 2005 International Conference on Wireless Communications, Networking and Mobile Computing*, (Vol. 2, pp. 1207-1210). IEEE. 10.1109/WCNM.2005.1544270

Zhao, Z., Huangfu, W., Liu, Y., & Sun, L. (2011, December). Design and Implementation of Network Management System for Large-Scale Wireless Sensor Networks. In *Seventh International Conference on Mobile Ad-hoc and Sensor Networks*, (pp. 130-137). IEEE. 10.1109/MSN.2011.33

ADDITIONAL READING

Agre, J. R., Clare, L. P., Pottie, G. J., & Romanov, N. P. (1999, July). Development platform for self-organizing wireless sensor networks. In *Unattended Ground Sensor Technologies and Applications* (Vol. 3713, pp. 257–268). International Society for Optics and Photonics. doi:10.1117/12.357141

Clare, L. P., Pottie, G. J., & Agre, J. R. (1999, July). Self-organizing distributed sensor networks. In *Unattended Ground Sensor Technologies and Applications* (Vol. 3713, pp. 229–237). International Society for Optics and Photonics. doi:10.1117/12.357138

Dong, Z., Meyland, S., & Karaomeroglu, M. (2018). A case study of an autonomous wireless sensor network system for environmental data collection. *Environmental Progress & Sustainable Energy, 37*(1), 180–188. doi:10.1002/ep.12716

Durresi, A., & Paruchuri, V. 2005, March. Adaptive clustering protocol for sensor networks. In *IEEE Aerospace Conference*, pp. 1-8, IEEE.

Pathan, A. S. K. (Ed.). (2016). *Security of self-organizing networks: MANET, WSN, WMN, VANET.* CRC press. doi:10.1201/EBK1439819197

Sohrabi, K., Gao, J., Ailawadhi, V. and Pottie, G.J., 2000. Protocols for self-organization of a wireless sensor network. IEEE personal communications, 7(5), pp.16-27.

Sohraby, K., Minoli, D., & Znati, T. (2007). *Wireless sensor networks: technology, protocols, and applications.* John Wiley & Sons. doi:10.1002/047011276X

Yang, G. Z. (Ed.). (2006). *Body sensor networks* (Vol. 1). London: Springer. doi:10.1007/1-84628-484-8

Yu, M., Mokhtar, H., & Merabti, M. (2008). A self-organised middleware architecture for Wireless Sensor Network management. *International Journal of Ad Hoc and Ubiquitous Computing, 3*(3), 135–145. doi:10.1504/IJAHUC.2008.018400

KEY TERMS AND DEFINITIONS

Candidate Area: The area is said to be candidate area whose parameters need to be monitored.

Data Fidelity: This term is used to define when data is transmitted from one sensor node to another, retains its actual meaning and granularity.

Deployment: Placement of nodes in candidate area is called deployment of nodes.

Network Lifetime: It is the time period in which network is capable of performing intended work/functions up to acceptable level.

Quality of Service: It is defined as the measurement of the overall performance/throughput of network system.

Scalability: It means network grows/shrinks with increasing/decreasing network load.

Sensor Nodes: The wireless sensor networks are composite of sensor nodes that are used monitor, measure and gathering the information of candidate area.

Chapter 12
A Backbone Formation Protocol Using Minimum Spanning Tree in Cognitive Radio Networks

Santosh Kumar

ⓘD https://orcid.org/0000-0002-4121-4123

National Institute of Technology, Kurukshetra, India

Awadhesh Kumar Singh

National Institute of Technology, Kurukshetra, India

ABSTRACT

Numerous research articles exist for backbone formation in wireless networks; however, they cannot be applied straightforward in cognitive radio networks (CRN) due to its peculiar characteristics. Since virtual backbone has many advantages such as reduced routing overhead, dynamic maintenance, and fast convergence speed, the authors propose a backbone formation protocol in CRN. In this chapter, a backbone formation protocol is proposed using the concept of minimum spanning tree. The protocol is based on non-iterative approach, thus leading towards limited message overhead. The proposed algorithm first forms the minimum spanning tree, and second, the nodes having more than one neighbor are connected together to form the backbone.

INTRODUCTION

Recently, due to advent of new application areas and tremendous popularity of social networks, the number of network devices has proliferated creating huge demand for wireless spectrum. Thus, the spectrum scarcity has become problem of central interest to industry as well as research community. Moreover, the unlicensed spectrum band, ISM band (2.4GHz range) have been exhausted due to escalated use by the ad hoc networks, e.g. Wi-fi hotspots, wireless mesh networks, and mobile ad hoc networks in various applications, such as environmental monitoring, battlefields surveillance, and commercial usage. Furthermore, the ISM band is affected by the interference created by household appliances and electro-

DOI: 10.4018/978-1-7998-2491-6.ch012

mechanical infrastructure. On the other hand, it has also been observed that licensed (reserved) spectrum such as TV white spaces are not being used effectively. As per Federal Communications Commission (FCC) estimate, the licensed spectrum utilization varies between 15% to 85% (Akyildiz, Lee, Vuran, & Mohanty, 2006). Note that the utilization of licensed spectrum is low also due to current spectrum allocation policies (Li, Liu, Li, Liu, & Li, 2013). The huge demand for the spectrum and inefficient spectrum usage has motivated FCC to approve the opportunistic use of licensed spectrum such as TV white spaces (Nekovee, 2009). Consequently, a new network paradigm has emerged, called cognitive radio network.

The CRN is a promising technique to boost spectrum utilization in wireless networks. The spectrum holder node is called primary user (PU). However, PU may not constantly occupy the entire owned (licensed) spectrum. Thus, the nodes that do not own any spectrum get opportunity to use the part of spectrum (channels) unused by PU. Such opportunistic user node is called secondary user (SU). However, SU node must vacate the channel on detecting PU appearance in that channel. In fact, CRN is the network of SU nodes only. The concept of CRN was first introduced by J. Mitola (Mitola & Maguire, 1999) in 1999 to utilize the radio spectrum in opportunistic manner. In article (Akyildiz et al., 2006), two architecture of CRN is discussed: 1) cognitive radio ad hoc network (CRAHN), and 2) infrastructure based CRN. In infrastructure based CRN, a base station exists which controls SU communication and manages the spectrums. Further, CRAHN has two types of network: 1) cognitive radio sensor network, and 2) cognitive radio mobile ad hoc networks. In CRAHN, SU node senses the available channel without interfering to PUs; however, it switches to another channel in case PU appears. Thus, CRAHN is quite challenging environment as compared to mobile ad hoc networks.

RELATED WORKS

The virtual backbone is a powerful technique for routing in wireless networks. Therefore, numerous research articles have been published towards backbone construction; however, we mentioned here only the techniques that are adaptable in cognitive radio networks (Alzoubi, Wan, & Frieder, 2003; Basagni, 1999; Wu & Li, 1999). These techniques are based on connected dominating set formation, which do not address the node mobility. There are some other research articles (Bandyopadhyay & Coyle, 2003; Youssef, Youssef, & Younis, 2009). These techniques are cluster based backbone formation which can't be applied straightforward due to their limitations related to spectrum management and mobility. Also, in mobile ad hoc networks (MANETs), many research articles (Akyildiz, Lee, & Chowdhury, 2009; Amis, Prakash, Vuong, & Huynh, 2000; Baker & Ephremides, 1981; Bao & Garcia-Luna-Aceves, 2003; Chatterjee, Das, & Turgut, 2002; Chiang, Wu, Liu, & Gerla, 1997; Kawadia & Kumar, 2003; Lin & Gerla, 1997; Srivastava & Ghosh, 2002; Yeh, Hsieh, & Li, 2012) exist for backbone formation. However, these techniques do not address challenges such as spectrum management, and link failure due to PU appearance. Some protocols (Celik & Kamal, 2016; Jiang, Cui, & Chen, 2009; Shirke, Patil, Kulkarni, & Markande, 2014; Yilmaz & Tugcu, 2015) have been proposed for clustering in CRN, which focus on energy consumption based parameters such as energy consumption minimization, throughput maximization, reducing communication overhead, and delay. In CRN, a limited number of articles (Dai, Wu, & Xin, 2013; Kumar & Singh, 2018a, 2018b; Wen-Jiang, Di, Wei-Heng, & Nian-Long, 2011) have been proposed towards backbone formation. These techniques follow the iterative approach to form clusters first, and next, cluster heads are connected to construct backbone. Since, these techniques are based on iterative approach; they suffer high message overhead. We can also design non-iterative algorithm

Table 1. Notations/data structures

Notations/Data Structures	Description	Initial Value
$COCH_i[j]$	Set of common channels between node i and j	ϕ
chn	Communication channel	-
NBL_i	List of immediate neighbors on node i	ϕ
w_{ij}	Weight of link between nodes i and j	-
$PriL_i$	List of neighbors of node i, based on link priority in descending order.	ϕ
$CONC_i$	List of nodes connected to node i either directly or indirectly	ϕ
$CONC_{i[j]}$	List of nodes connected to node i through node j	ϕ
BND_i	List of immediate backbone nodes maintained by node i	ϕ

Note: the function send(m, j, ch) shows that node i send message m to node j on channel ch.

to construct backbone in the form of graphical structures, like tree, ring etc. Therefore, we propose a minimum spanning tree based backbone formation protocol in CRN.

SYSTEM MODEL AND PRELIMINARY ASSUMPTIONS

A CRN is a collection of SUs, where SU node periodically senses the availability of channels. Once, it detects the available channel, it starts its communication. Also, it switches to another channel in case PU appears on the channel occupied by SU. Further, a node is equipped with multiple interfaces to support multi channel communication. We also assume that each node has neighborhood information after running the neighbor discovery algorithm proposed in (Kumar & Singh, 2018a). In addition, the data structures and types of messages are detailed below in table 1 and 2 respectively.

ALGORITHM CONCEPT

In this chapter, we propose an algorithm to form virtual backbone in CRN, which is based on two phases. First, we construct the minimum spanning tree and second the 'eligible' nodes in tree are connected together to form the backbone. Initially, all nodes in the network send "hello" messages on each chan-

Table 2. Messages

Message Type	Notation	Description
Connect me	$CONNECT_{me}$	Sent by initiator/intermediate nodes
Acknowledgment	ACK	Sent by intermediate node
I am backbone node	IM_BN	Sent by backbone node to its neighbors
Negative acknowledgment	$NACK$	Sent by intermediate node
To delete a node k	$DELETE_k$	Sent by intermediate node

Table 3. Algorithm description

A1. Initialization
1. **If** $\left(PriL_i \, ! \right)$ **then**
2. select $j : j PriL_i$
3. select *chn* $: chn COCH_i \left[j \right]$
4. send $\left(CONNECT_{me} \left\langle CONC_i \right\rangle, j, chn \right)$
5. $PriL_i \leftarrow PriL_i \setminus \left\{ j \right\}$
6. **End If**

A2. On receiving CONNECT_ME message from node j, action taken by node i
1. **If** $\left(CONC_i CONC_j == \right)$ **then**
2. select $chn : chn COCH_i \left[j \right]$
3. send $\left(ACK, j, chn \right)$
4. $PriL_i \leftarrow PriL_i \setminus \left\{ j \right\}$
5. $CONC_i \leftarrow CONC_i j$
6. $CONC_{i[j]} \leftarrow CONC_{i[j]} j$
7. **If** $\left(PriL_i \, ! \right)$ **then**
8. select $k : k PriL_i$
9. select $chn : chn COCH_i \left[k \right]$
10. send $\left(CONNECT_{me} \left\langle CONC_i \right\rangle, k, h \right)$
11. $PriL_i \leftarrow PriL_i \setminus \left\{ k \right\}$
12. **End If**
13. **Else For** $k : k CONC_i$
14. **If** ($CONC_{i[k]} CONC_j \, ! = \, \& \& \, P_j P_k$) **then**
15. $flag \leftarrow$ true;
16. **Break;**
17. **End If**
18. **End For**
19. **If** (flag==true)
20. select $chn : chn COCH_i \left[j \right]$
21. send $\left(ACK \left\langle CONC_i \right\rangle, j, chn \right)$
22. $CONC_{i[k]} \leftarrow CONC_{i[k]} \setminus \left\{ j \right\}$
23. $CONC_{i[j]} \leftarrow CONC_{i[j]} j$
24. select $chn : chn COCH_i \left[k \right]$
25. send $\left(DELETE \left\langle j \right\rangle, k, chn \right)$
26. **Else** select $chn : chn COCH_i \left[j \right]$
27. send $\left(NACK, j, chn \right)$
28. **End If**
29. **End If**

continued on following page

Table 3. Continued

A3. On receiving ACK from node j, node i takes following actions
1. $CONC_i \leftarrow CONC_i \ j$
2. $CONC_{i[j]} \leftarrow CONC_{i[j]} \ j$
Execute Action A1
A4. On receiving NACK from node j, node i takes following actions
1. **If** $\left(j CONC_i \right)$ **then**
2. $CONC_i \leftarrow CONC_i \setminus \{j\}$
3. $CONC_{i[j]} \leftarrow$
4. **End If**
5. Execute Action A1.
A5. On receiving DELETE$_k$ message from node j, node i takes following actions
1. **If** $\left(k NBL_i \right)$ **then**
2. $CONC_i \leftarrow CONC_i \setminus \{k\}$
3. $CONC_{i[k]} \leftarrow$
4. **Else For** $m : m CONC_i$
5. **If** $\left(k CONC_{i[m]} \right)$ **then**
6. select $chn : chn COCH_i[m]$
7. send $\left(DELETE\langle k\rangle, m, chn \right)$
8. **Break;**
9. **End if**
10. **End For**
11. **End If**
A6. Backbone formation by eligible node i
1. **If** $\left(Eligible_i == true \right)$ **then**
2. **For** $j : j CONC_i$
3. select $chn : chn COCH_i[j]$
4. send $\left(IM\_BN, j, chn \right)$
5. **End For**
6. **End If**
A7. Action taken by i on receiving IMBN message:
$BND_i \leftarrow BND_i \{j\}$

nel from their channel lists to immediate neighbors. Consequently, a node becomes able to compute the weight of each link connecting to its neighbors. A node prioritizes its neighbors based on the computed weight of links. The weight of a link is computed by following formula:

Figure 1. A network graph

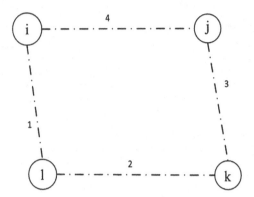

$$w_{ij} = Nch_{ij} + \sum_{k=C_1}^{C_n} T_k,$$

where α and β are scaling factors; Nch_{ij} denotes the number of common channels between nodes i and j; $C_1, C_2 \ldots C_n$ are common channels between nodes i and j; T_k represents the propagation time of "hello" message on channel k.

Once a node, say i computes the weight of each links, it sends *CONNECTme* message one by one to the nodes from its *PriLi* list. The receiver node sends *ACK* to sender, if it is not already connected to sender either directly or indirectly (through other nodes). Secondly, if the receiver is already connected with sender and the weight of new link is bigger than the previous link, it replies with *ACK*; otherwise, it sends *NACK*. Finally, a node, having more than one connected nodes, declares itself as a backbone node and informs the same to its neighbours to whom it is connected to. The detailed of the algorithm is given in Table 3 in event driven style.

Initialization

Initially, a node i selects j from $PriL_i$. It sends $CONNECT_{me}$ to j on corresponding common channel and removes it from $PriL_i$.

Action Taken by a Node on Receiving CONNECT_me

On receiving $CONNECT_{me}$ from node j, node i sends *ACK* to node j on corresponding common channel, if it is not connected to j at all. Secondly, assume node i is connected to node j through a node k; and if w_{ik} is bigger than w_{ij} then i sends *NACK* to j; otherwise, it sends *ACK* to j and subsequently sends *DELETE* message to k. Further, if $PriL_i$ is not empty, node i selects another node m from the list and sends $CONNECT_{me}$ message to m on corresponding channel; it removes m from $PriL_i$ list.

Action Taken by a Node on Receiving ACK Message

On receiving *ACK* message from node j, node i inserts j into the list $CONC_i$. If the list $PriL_i$ is not empty, node i executes the algorithm as mentioned in initialization phase.

Action Taken by a Node on Receiving NACK Message

On receiving *NACK* from node j, node i removes j from $CONC_i$; and execute the algorithm mentioned in initialization phase.

Action Taken by a Node on Receiving DELETE Message

On receiving *DELETE<k>* message from node j, node i looks for node k in its neighbour list. If k exists in the list then i removes k from the list $CONC_i$. In another case, when node k does not belong to the neighbor list of node i, node i finds the node m such that i is connected with k through m; and forwards the *DELETE<k>* message to m on corresponding channel.

Virtual Backbone Formation

An eligible node i sends *IM_BN* message to all nodes from $CONC_i$ one by one on corresponding common channel. Further, the receiver nodes update their list (*BND*) by inserting the sender id into the list.

PERFORMANCE STUDY

To compute the time complexity and message overhead of our protocol, we use following notations.

n: number of nodes in the network
d: average degree of a node
t: time consumed in one message flow
b: average number of backbone nodes, where bn

Time Complexity

According to our protocol, for construction of minimum spanning tree, each node may send and receive d number of messages; consequently, $2dt$ time is consumed by each node. Thus, time taken to construct minimum spanning tree is $2ndt$. In the next phase, for backbone formation, a backbone node sends d number of *IM_BN* messages leading towards bdt time consumption. Thus, time complexity of the proposed protocol is computed as $2ndt + bdt$; which is $O(n)$.

Figure 2. Minimum spanning tree formation

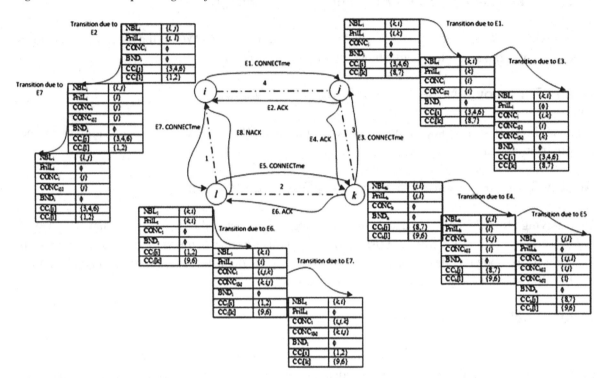

Figure 3. Backbone formation

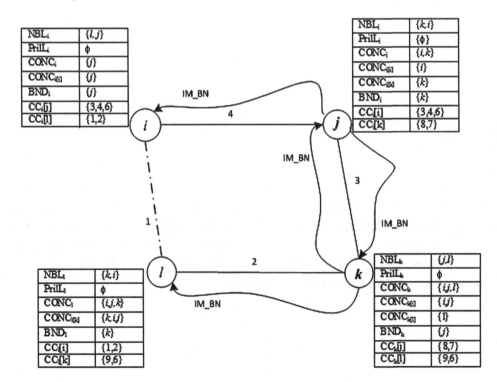

Message Overhead

For construction of minimum spanning tree, each node may send d number of $CONNECT_{me}$ messages and may receive d number of $ACK/NACK$ messages; thus $2dn$ number of messages exchanged. In addition, during the backbone construction phase, a backbone node sends d number of IM_BN message; thus bd number of messages is exchanged. Therefore, the message overhead of our protocol is $d(2n + b)$.

Correctness Proof

Theorem 1: The constructed minimum spanning tree is loop-free.

Proof: It can be proved by contradiction. Assume that there exists a cycle in the constructed tree. In a tree, to create a loop atleast three nodes are required, say nodes i, j, & k are parts of the loop. It means, the intersection of any two lists among $CONC_i$, $CONC_j$, and $CONC_k$, is not empty. According to our hypothesis, node i sends ACK message to node j despite of having $CONC_i \cap CONC_j = \{k\}$ which is contradiction of the proposed heuristic. Thus, the theorem holds.

Theorem 2: The backbone formation algorithm will terminate eventually.

Proof: Each node sends d number of $CONNECT_{me}$ messages sequentially to its neighbors. In response to $CONNECT_{me}$ message, a receiver node sends ACK/NACK to sender. As we know that d is a finite number, thus the number of message flow will be finite. Therefore, the algorithm will terminate eventually.

ILLUSTRATION OF THE PROTOCOL

Consider a network graph shown in Fig. 1 where a node is represented by a circle along with unique identifier mentioned within the circle. There are four nodes in the network named i, j, k, and l, where node i has j, and l as neighbors; node j has i, and k as neighbors; node k has j, and l as neighbors; similarly node l has i, and k as neighbors. Each link is assigned a unique weight; the higher the weight is the higher the link priority is. Figure 2 shows the working of our protocol. Initially each node sends the $CONNECT_{me}$ message to the neighbor that has the highest priority. Thus, node i sends the $CONNECT_{me}$ message to node j first and waits for response from node j; node j sends ACK to node i as response. Node k sends the $CONNECT_{me}$ to node j and receives ACK in response. Similarly, node l sends $CONNECT_{me}$ to k and receives ACK in response. Thus, nodes j, and k terminates their process as they have explored all its neighbors available in priority list. Further, we observe that node i sends $CONNECT_{me}$ message to node l; node l response with $NACK$ because it is already connected to node i through node k; which has higher priority. Finally, node j, and k declare themselves as backbone nodes and inform their status to immediate neighbors. Figure 3 shows the constructed backbone. During the backbone formation many events take place. These events are represented by E1, E2…En. The events are detailed below along with their effects on data structures/variables.

Events Occurred on Node i

1. Sends $CONNECT_{me}$ to j on channel 4: it removes node j from $PriL_i$.
2. Receives ACK from node j on channel 4: it makes entry of j into list $CONC_i$.
3. Sends $CONNECT_{me}$ to l on channel 1: it removes node l from $PriL_i$.
4. Receives $NACK$ from node l on channel 1: it terminates its process as $PriL_i$ gets empty.
5. Receives IM_BN message from node j on channel 6: it updates its list BND_i by inserting node j into list.

Events Occurred on Node j

1. Receives $CONNECT_{me}$ from i on channel 4: it removes i from $PriL_j$, and it updates $CONC_j$ by adding node i.
2. Sends ACK to node i on channel 4: it sends ACK in response to $E1$.
3. Receives $CONNECT_{me}$ from k on channel 7: it removes k from $PriL_j$, and it updates $CONC_j$ by adding k.
4. Sends ACK to node k on channel 7: it sends ACK in response to event $E3$.
5. Declares itself as backbone node and sends IM_BN to node i, and k on channel 6 and 7 respectively.
6. Receives IM_BN from node k: it updates BND_j by adding node k into the list.

Events Occurred on Node k

1. Sends $CONNECT_{me}$ to node j on channel 7: after sending this message, it deletes the entry of node j from list $PriL_k$.
2. Receives ACK from node j on channel 7: it inserts the node j into list $CONC_k$.
3. Receives $CONNECT_{me}$ from node l on channel 9: node l is added into list $CONC_k$; also, removes l from list $PriL_k$.
4. Sends ACK to node l on channel 9: it sends ACK in response to event $E5$.
5. Declare itself as backbone node and sends IM_BN message to node j, and l on channel 7 and 9 respectively.
6. Receives IM_BN from node j: it updates BND_k by adding node j into the list.

Events Occurred on Node l

1. Sends $CONNECT_{me}$ message to node k on channel 9: it removes node k from list $PriL_l$.
2. Receives ACK from k on channel 9: it updates the list $CONC_l$.
3. Receives $CONNECT_{me}$ message from node i on channel 1: it removes node i from list $PriL_l$.
4. Sends $NACK$ to node i on channel 1: it sends this message in response to event $E7$.
5. Receives IM_BN message from node k on channel 9: it updates the list BND_l by inserting node k into the list.

CONCLUSION

In this chapter, we used the concept of minimum spanning tree to construct the backbone in CRN. The theoratical analysis shows that time complexity of our protocol is $O(n)$. Thus, we can say that the convergence time of our protocol is fast. Furthermore, we also observed that message overhead is $d(2n + b)$; which is approximately three times of the number of nodes. This analysis shows that the number of messages exchanged is quite less which results in a good feature of our protocol. Also, the constructed backbone is robust because it might handle more number of link failures due to PU appearance as the weight of link is based on channel quality and its number.

REFERENCES

Akyildiz, I. F., Lee, W.-Y., & Chowdhury, K. R. (2009). CRAHNs: Cognitive radio ad hoc networks. *Ad Hoc Networks*, *7*(5), 810–836. doi:10.1016/j.adhoc.2009.01.001

Akyildiz, I. F., Lee, W.-Y., Vuran, M. C., & Mohanty, S. (2006). NeXt generation/dynamic spectrum access/cognitive radio wireless networks: A survey. *Computer Networks*, *50*(13), 2127–2159. doi:10.1016/j.comnet.2006.05.001

Alzoubi, K. M., Wan, P.-J., & Frieder, O. (2003). Maximal independent set, weakly-connected dominating set, and induced spanners in wireless ad hoc networks. *International Journal of Foundations of Computer Science*, *14*(02), 287–303. doi:10.1142/S012905410300173X

Amis, A. D., Prakash, R., Vuong, T. H., & Huynh, D. T. (2000). Max-min d-cluster formation in wireless ad hoc networks. *Proceedings IEEE INFOCOM 2000. Conference on Computer Communications. Nineteenth Annual Joint Conference of the IEEE Computer and Communications Societies.* 10.1109/INFCOM.2000.832171

Baker, D., & Ephremides, A. (1981). The architectural organization of a mobile radio network via a distributed algorithm. *IEEE Transactions on Communications*, *29*(11), 1694–1701. doi:10.1109/TCOM.1981.1094909

Bandyopadhyay, S., & Coyle, E. J. (2003). *An energy efficient hierarchical clustering algorithm for wireless sensor networks.* Paper presented at the INFOCOM 2003. Twenty-Second Annual Joint Conference of the IEEE Computer and Communications. IEEE Societies. 10.1109/INFCOM.2003.1209194

Bao, L., & Garcia-Luna-Aceves, J. J. (2003). Topology management in ad hoc networks. *Proceedings of the 4th ACM international symposium on Mobile ad hoc networking & computing.* 10.1145/778415.778432

Basagni, S. (1999). Distributed clustering for ad hoc networks. *Parallel Architectures, Algorithms, and Networks, 1999. (I-SPAN'99) Proceedings.* 10.1109/ISPAN.1999.778957

Celik, A., & Kamal, A. E. (2016). Multi-objective clustering optimization for multi-channel cooperative spectrum sensing in heterogeneous green crns. *IEEE Transactions on Cognitive Communications and Networking, 2*(2), 150-161.

Chatterjee, M., Das, S. K., & Turgut, D. (2002). WCA: A weighted clustering algorithm for mobile ad hoc networks. *Cluster Computing, 5*(2), 193–204. doi:10.1023/A:1013941929408

Chiang, C.-C., Wu, H.-K., Liu, W., & Gerla, M. (1997). Routing in clustered multihop, mobile wireless networks with fading channel. *Proceedings of IEEE SICON.*

Dai, Y., Wu, J., & Xin, C. (2013). Virtual backbone construction for cognitive radio networks without common control channel. *INFOCOM, 2013 Proceedings IEEE.* 10.1109/INFCOM.2013.6566940

Jiang, W., Cui, H., & Chen, J. (2009). *Spectrum-aware cluster-based routing protocol for multiple-hop cognitive wireless network.* Paper presented at the Communications Technology and Applications, 2009. ICCTA'09. IEEE International Conference on.

Kawadia, V., & Kumar, P. (2003). *Power control and clustering in ad hoc networks.* Paper presented at the INFOCOM 2003. Twenty-Second Annual Joint Conference of the IEEE Computer and Communications. IEEE Societies.

Kumar, S., & Singh, A. K. (2018a). Fault tolerant backbone construction in cognitive radio networks. *AEÜ. International Journal of Electronics and Communications, 87,* 76–86. doi:10.1016/j.aeue.2018.02.010

Kumar, S., & Singh, A. K. (2018b). A localized algorithm for clustering in cognitive radio networks. *Journal of King Saud University-Computer and Information Sciences.*

Li, C., Liu, W., Li, J., Liu, Q., & Li, C. (2013). *Aggregation based spectrum allocation in cognitive radio networks.* Paper presented at the Communications in China-Workshops (CIC/ICCC), 2013 IEEE/CIC International Conference on. 10.1109/ICCChinaW.2013.6670566

Lin, C. R., & Gerla, M. (1997). Adaptive clustering for mobile wireless networks. *IEEE Journal on Selected Areas in Communications, 15*(7), 1265–1275. doi:10.1109/49.622910

Mitola, J., & Maguire, G. Q. (1999). Cognitive radio: making software radios more personal. *IEEE Personal Communications, 6*(4), 13-18.

Nekovee, M. (2009). *Quantifying the availability of TV white spaces for cognitive radio operation in the UK.* Paper presented at the Communications Workshops, 2009. ICC Workshops 2009. IEEE International Conference on. 10.1109/ICCW.2009.5208035

Shirke, N., Patil, K., Kulkarni, S., & Markande, S. (2014). *Energy efficient cluster based routing protocol for distributed Cognitive Radio Network.* Paper presented at the Networks & Soft Computing (ICNSC), 2014 First International Conference on. 10.1109/CNSC.2014.6906712

Srivastava, S., & Ghosh, R. (2002). Cluster based routing using a k-tree core backbone for mobile ad hoc networks. *Proceedings of the 6th international workshop on Discrete algorithms and methods for mobile computing and communications.* 10.1145/570810.570813

Wen-Jiang, F., Di, W., Wei-Heng, J., & Nian-Long, J. (2011). *The Formation of Virtual Backbone Network in MANETs Based on Cognitive Radio. In Advanced Electrical and Electronics Engineering* (pp. 451–458). Springer.

Wu, J., & Li, H. (1999). On calculating connected dominating set for efficient routing in ad hoc wireless networks. *Proceedings of the 3rd international workshop on Discrete algorithms and methods for mobile computing and communications*. 10.1145/313239.313261

Yeh, C.-H., Hsieh, M.-Y., & Li, K.-C. (2012). *An Efficient Clustering Authentication Mechanism for Mobile Ad Hoc Networks*. Paper presented at the Ubiquitous Intelligence & Computing and 9th International Conference on Autonomic & Trusted Computing (UIC/ATC), 2012 9th International Conference on. 10.1109/UIC-ATC.2012.134

Yilmaz, H. B., & Tugcu, T. (2015). *Energy efficient MAC protocol for cluster formation in mobile cooperative spectrum sensing*. Paper presented at the Wireless Communications and Networking Conference Workshops (WCNCW).

Youssef, M., Youssef, A., & Younis, M. (2009). Overlapping multihop clustering for wireless sensor networks. *IEEE Transactions on Parallel and Distributed Systems*, *20*(12), 1844–1856. doi:10.1109/TPDS.2009.32

Chapter 13
Vehicular Ad Hoc Networks (VANETs):
Architecture, Challenges, and Applications

Pavan Kumar Pandey

Dr. A. P. J. Abdul Kalam Technical University, Lucknow, India

Vineet Kansal

Institute of Engineering and Technology, Lucknow, India

Abhishek Swaroop

Bhagwan Parshuram Institute of Technology, Delhi, India

ABSTRACT

Over the past few years, there has been significant research interest in field of vehicular ad hoc networks (VANETs). Wireless communication over VANETs supports vehicle-to-vehicle (V2V), vehicle-to-infrastructure (V2I) communication. Such innovation in wireless communication has improved our daily lives through road safety, comfort driving, traffic efficiency. As special version of MANETs, VANETs bring several new challenges including routing and security challenges in data communication due to characteristics of high mobility, dynamic topology. Therefore, academia and the auto mobile industry are taking interest in several ongoing research projects to establish VANETs. The work presented here focuses on communication in VANETs with their routing and security challenges along with major application of VANETs in several areas.

INTRODUCTION

In recent years, mobile computing has enjoyed a tremendous rise in popularity. The continued minimization of the cost of mobile computing devices and the extraordinary rise of processing power in mobile, laptop, and computers are the main reasons behind this growth. This leads to providing better mobile-

DOI: 10.4018/978-1-7998-2491-6.ch013

Figure 1. Vehicular ad-hoc network (VANET)

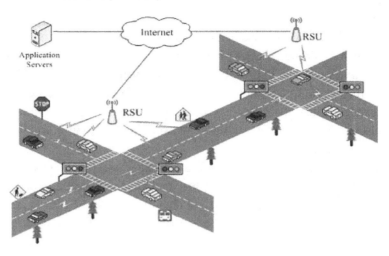

based applications into the hands of a growing segment of the population. Therefore, wireless mobile computers or mobile ad hoc networks (MANETs) have become very popular in recent years.

A mobile ad hoc network is a collection of autonomous nodes or terminals that communicate with each other by forming a multi-hop radio network. Nodes in MANETs maintain connectivity in a decentralized manner (Sarkar et al., 2016). Since, the nodes communicate over wireless links, they must contend with the effects of radio communication such as noise, fading, and interference. Additionally, the links are typically having less bandwidth than in a wired network. MANETs are characterized by mobility of nodes, and dynamic topology that makes routing more challenging. The decentralized nature of MANETs makes them suitable for a variety of applications. MANETs are more useful for environment where nodes are frequently changing their positions with reduced bandwidth.

Vehicular ad hoc networks (VANETs) are one of the prominent sub-classes of MANETs. Vehicular Ad Hoc Networks (VANETs) are wireless networks, where vehicles are connected to each other's and can be connected to the internet also (Basagni et al., 2013). VANETs are a special subclass of Mobile Ad Hoc Networks (MANETs), where nodes can move freely without any movement constraint. Each node will have to be connected by following changes in its locations. Consequently, VANETs have highly dynamic topology. The nodes can communicate with each other either in single-hop or multi-hop channel, and nodes in VANETs can be any vehicle or Road Side Unit (RSU). However, VANETs also come with several challenging characteristics, such as potentially large scale and high mobility.

The nodes in the vehicular environment are much more dynamic because most cars usually move at a very high speed and change their positions constantly. However, there is a pattern in the mobility of nodes and randomness is less as compared to other mobile networks. As per Figure-1, VANETs form a communication network by using vehicles and RSUs, where vehicles have participated as mobile nodes connected in an ad-hoc manner. Every participating vehicle behaves like a wireless router or node to communicate with each other. The fixed roadside units like traffic light towers establish in VANETs as the backbone of a network to provide connectivity for exchanging safety-related information reliably.

The VANETs architecture can be further divided into three layers. First one is the sensor layer which uses On-Board Units (OBUs) installed in vehicle and other devices sense the vehicles around and collect traffic data. Second is the communication layer that includes cellular networks and the internet to communicate among vehicles. The last one is the data process layer providing a framework to collect data and analysis of data.

In VANETs, vehicles are supposed to exchange the traffic-related information with each other on time to avoid accidents as well as for the efficient distribution of the contents such as data, audio, and video. VANETs are kind of networks which are used to establish vehicle to vehicle (V2V) communication and vehicle to infrastructure (V2I) communication. This kind of network supports several applications related to vehicles management, traffic data, driver's convenience, and several infotainment applications. VANETs are the start of next-generation intelligent and smart transportation and will play an important role to enhance the transportation system.

In order to increase co-operation between vehicles, messages need to be passed between them. Due to the special characteristics of VANETs, routing mechanisms from source to destination is an important research challenge. Additionally, the security of data to maintain privacy is also an important and challenging task in VANETs. Efficient routing and sufficient security will enhance the applicability of VANETs in their applications.

Across the world, millions of people die in road accidents every year. Moreover, on a long expressways, there may be stretches where internet and mobile network rarely exists. In such areas, VANETs are helpful to handle emergency cases. VANETs are targeted to support vehicular safety, traffic efficiency, traffic monitoring, and other infotainment services. There is consensus among authorities, industry, and academia on the need for secure and efficient vehicular communication (VC) system. We must provide some secure solution and privacy-enhancing VC schemes having reliability in communication, reduced processing overhead, and impact on transportation safety applications. The study of related literature indicates that secure and efficient VC can be in practice. Therefore, the work presented here captures most of the challenges in VANETs with few already proposed solutions that can provide detailed information to researchers and developers to understand the several challenges in VANETs.

VANET BACKGROUND

In the literature, several articles have attempted to summarize the issues in vehicular networks. Hartenstein-Laberteaux (Hartenstein & Laberteaux, 2008) presented an overview of the communication and networking aspects of VANETs and summarizes the current state of the art at that time. They investigated the communication and networking aspects of this technology and addressed the security and privacy issues. Raya-Hubaux (Raya & Hubaux, 2007) addressed the security of VANETs comprehensively and provides a set of security protocols as well. While, Li and Wang (Li & Wang, 2007) focus on the routing protocols of VANETs and their requirements to achieve better communication time with less consumption of network bandwidth. The authors propose a taxonomy of a large range of mobility models available for vehicular ad hoc networks. These articles did review specific research areas in VANETs. Besides, other papers provide a comprehensive overview of applications, architectures, protocols, and challenges in VANETs and especially introduce VANETs projects and standardization efforts in different regions (i.e., USA, Japan, and Europe). The several routing and safety-related challenges in VANETs have been comprehensively covered in the work presented here.

Routing Challenges

Over the years, the researchers have proposed numerous routing protocols for transmitting data among vehicles in VANETs. These protocols can be classified based upon various criteria such as protocol characteristics, information routing technique, quality of service and network architecture. Recently, Taleb (Taleb, 2018) presented a comprehensive survey of routing protocols for vehicular ad-hoc networks (VANETs). In the present exposition, VANETs routing protocols are divided into the following categories based on the characteristics and techniques used by the routing protocol.

Position-Based Routing

The Protocols under this category use vehicle positions and location information obtained from different sources such as Global Positioning Systems (GPS) and maps. Therefore, the source and destination rely on information of node's positions to transmit messages. Few traditional representatives of position-based routing protocols are Distance Routing Effect Algorithm for Mobility (DREAM) and Greedy Perimeter Stateless Routing (GPSR). In DREAM (Basagni &Stefano, 1998), the location received from GPS is exchanged and stored in a location table. Frequent updates in the location table indicate changes in topology due to nodes mobility. DREAM is based on two algorithms. First algorithm is based on flooding packets to distribute location packets, and the second one is used to disseminate data packets. GPSR (Karp & Kung, 2000) uses greedy routing. GPSR uses the position of other neighbor nodes, own position and destination node information to route packets to the destination. In GPSR, a source node sends a data packet to several intermediate nodes until the packet arrives to the destination. This algorithm uses a stateless routing algorithm to obtain information about the first hop neighbors of a node. GPSR is based on a greedy approach using only information of immediate neighbor in the network topology.

Besides these protocols, recently few routing approaches Mobility Prediction Based Routing Protocol (MPBRP) and SDN based Geographical Routing Protocols (SDGR) are also proposed in this category. MPBRP (Ye et. al., 2019) uses geographical data of vehicles to define a driver's intention and behavior. By following the driver's intention, MPBRP proposes an algorithm to detect neighborhoods, packet transmission, and path recovery in VANETs. This approach uses predictive forwarding strategies instead of static model. Therefore, MPBRP can easily deal with dynamic changeable topology and varies vehicle speeds. SDGR (Ji et. al., 2016) is based on software-defined networking (SDN), where the central controller collects geographical information of vehicles and provides a global view to find an optimized route from source to destination. In this approach, SDN is integrated with VANETs to enhance routing efficiency by decoupling the control planes and data planes. The Major advantage of position-based routing is to know geographical knowledge of neighbor's nodes that determines the next node toward the destination node. The recovery mechanism is not very well defined for position-based routing mechanism.

Topology Based Routing

Topology based protocols find the shortest path between nodes by using the routing table to have all updated routing-related information. According to the way of updating routing tables, this category can be further divided into three subcategories: Proactive routing, Reactive routing, and Hybrid routing protocols.

In the **Proactive routing protocol**, routing table must be up to date always. Proactive routing has a major advantage for exchanging network information timely such as bandwidth, delay, topology, etc. Whenever any node joins or leaves the network, this protocol keeps the routing table updated. This mechanism adds network overhead to protocol and degrade network throughput. Destination Sequenced Distance Vector (DSDV), Optimized Link State Routing (OLSR), and Fisheye State Routing (FSR) are few protocols under this category. DSDV (Dhankhar & Agarwal, 2014) enables each node in the network to maintain the routing table by capturing routing information of every other node. In OLSR (Clausen & Jacquet, 2003), every node maintains routing table with set of neighbors reachable with 1-hop or 2-hop that should be updated periodically. In FSR (Fishy State Routing) protocol (Pei et al., 2000), every node maintains topology that is supposed to be updated based on information received from neighbor nodes and the same update shall be broadcasted to different other nodes in network.

In **Reactive routing**, each node finds route only whenever it is required. Ad hoc On Demand Distance Vector (AODV) and Dynamic Source Routing (DSR) are mainly examples of this category. In AODV (Perkins et al, 2013) routing mechanism, the routing table is expected to be maintained by each node having information regarding active routes with next hop. Route discovery mechanism should be initiated to determine the updated route to the destination node. Route discovery uses route request messages to broadcast in the network until messages reached to the destination node. DSR (Johnson &Maltz, 1996) contains two processes route discovery and route maintenance.

Hybrid routing combines both proactive and reactive routing approach to find a route from source to destination. This approach intent is to decrease the route discovery delay of reactive routing protocol and reduces the control overhead of a proactive routing approach. Zone Routing Protocol (ZRP) is one of the hybrid routing protocols. ZRP (Haas, 1997) follows proactive mechanism while communication within the neighborhood and uses reactive approach while communicating between neighborhoods.

Apart from these traditional protocols, several further enhancements are also proposed in these protocols by researchers. GreeAODV is one of the recent routing enhancement in a reactive routing protocol. GreeAODV (Baker et. al., 2018) proposes a greedy technique with AODV routing protocol to select the most efficient route in terms of total energy consumption between two nodes. Total energy consumption between nodes includes consumption on intermediate nodes also. In AODV, route gets selected based on the number of hops between nodes but it is modified in this approach by considering power consumption in place of hops.

Cluster-Based Routing

This category of protocols allows the network to be divided into different groups known as clusters and one vehicle from each cluster to act as cluster head. There could be several criteria to form clusters such as the position of vehicles, the direction of movement, etc. Cluster head shall be responsible for communication between clusters. One of the popular cluster-based protocols is a location-based routing algorithm with cluster-based Flooding (LORA-CBF). LORA-CBF (Gayathri & Kumar, 2015) allows the cluster head to send beaconing message periodically to update routing parameters and to collect information of other clusters as well. Clustering for Open IVC Network (COIN) (Blum, 2003) another example of cluster-based routing. The author proposed that cluster head shall be picked based on some factors like dynamics of vehicles, inter-vehicle distance and driver intentions, etc.

Recently, researchers have proposed several new clustering approaches to make routing more efficient. Reliable Multi-level Routing Protocols with Tabu Search (RMRPTS) and Cluster-based Dynamic Routing Approach (CDRA) are a few of them. RMRPTS (Moridi& Barati, 2017) is designed for the cases when topological changes are frequent. Multi-level routing enables the possibility of self-organizing and route maintaining. Improved AODV with fuzzy logic used to find reliable routing between cluster members and tabu search has been used at higher-level between cluster head and destination node. CDRA (Poonia et. al., 2015) is a combination of the clustering approach with AODV routing protocol to make AODV more efficient. CDRA has optimized the AODV routing approach by minimizing the number of routes between nodes and healing the routing paths in order to minimize the number of hops. The main advantage of cluster-based routing is scalability. However, it increases network overhead by dividing it into several clusters.

Broadcast Routing Protocol

Protocols under this category use flood technique to get routing information in VANETs. These protocols are very useful when destination vehicle is out of range from a source node, like an exchange of information in an emergency or exchange of road condition. The broadcast scheme delivers packets through several different nodes. Therefore, it provides reliable communication with the consumption of high network bandwidth because many replicas of packets reached to each node. This approach ensures reliable packet transmission. However, it leads to large bandwidth consumption. By using flood technique, packets are sent from one node to all other nodes in the network.

Distribute Vehicular Broadcast (DV-CAST) and Hybrid Data Dissemination (HYDI) protocols are examples of a broadcast routing protocols. DV-CAST (Tonguz et al., 2007) protocol is based on local topology information to handle flooded messages in network. HYDI (Tonguz et al., 2007) protocol is more suitable in spreading information on highways. It works in well-connected networks by using some broadcast suppression techniques to avoid packet collision. In intermittently connected network, HYDI follows a store-carry-forward technique to deliver messages even without end to end path.

Geocast Routing Protocol

Geocast routing protocol followsthe mechanism to spread and forward information towards particular area related to that information. Objective of this routing approach is to deliver packets from a source node to some set of multiple nodes placed in the zone of relevance (ZOR). ZOR is supposed to be defined with some set of vehicles that will receive that geo cast message. No routing table required for this approach. Geocast approaches provide high reliability in data transmission. Even in a very dynamic topology network, it reduces network overhead and congestion as well. However, due to frequent disconnections, packet transmission delay may be increased.

RObust VEhicular Routing (ROVER) and Distributed Robust Geocast (DRG) are few examples of geo cast routing protocols. ROVER (Kihl, 2007) uses flooding to send control data and sends one to one message for communication data in the network. DRG (Joshi et al., 2007) reduces network load by forwarding data packets quickly in the best possible manner. However, this is not suitable for applications where the destination is far away from the source.

Comparative Study of Routing Strategies

Although several researchers are working in VANETs routing, still routing mechanism is one of major design challenges because of the high speed of vehicles in the network. In this work, we have reviewed most of the well-known routing protocols proposed in VANETs and presented the strategy of routing protocols. Each routing mechanism has its advantages and disadvantages. Therefore, we summarize the main advantages and limitations of each routing strategies presented in this section.

Position-based routing depends on the geographical location of vehicles. This mechanism enforces all vehicles to be equipped with GPS devices and deadlock may also occur at the server. But, this protocol follows beaconless techniques and supports highly dynamic topology. Topology-based routing is also a beaconless technique and suitable for several communication types. However, topology-based routing never gets complete path, and have high overhead because different kinds of messages are used to establish routes and maintain routes. Cluster-based routing approaches having huge clustering overhead, however, the packet delivery rate is significantly high in comparison to position-based and topology-based routing mechanisms.

Broadcast-based routing protocols also provide very reliable communication with high packet delivery ratio, however, it consumes high bandwidth to broadcast packets to all other vehicles. In geocast-based routing, network congestion is acceptable due to the zone of relevance selected and targeted for a destination instead of the complete network and it supports scalability as well as highly dynamic topologies. Geocast-based routing uses greedy forwarding. Therefore, node outside of the zone of relevance cannot be altered and this kind of mechanism needs position determination services.

Security Challenges

Besides routing challenges, security is another most important issue in VANETs. VANETs are vulnerable to several attacks because of their nature of open access medium. A review of various security issues and techniques to handle those issues in VANETs have been presented by Singh-Kad (Singh & Kad, 2016). Safeand secure VANETs must be provided by introducing some security features like authentication, information consistency, availability, and non-repudiation, etc. There can be several types of attacks also. Some of them are malware, DoS (Denial of Service) attack, spamming, black-hole attack, message tempering/suppression/alteration, certificate replication, eavesdropping and identity revealing. A few important and more critical attacks are presented below to illustrate security concerns completely.

- **Availability Attacks**: Availability guarantees that VANETs are properly functional and information on that network is reliable enough. This security section makes sure the liveliness of users in network and attackers try to breach the user's liveness. This section includes attacks such as Denial of Services (DoS), Jamming attack, Blackhole attack, Grayhole attack, Sinkhole attack, Wormhole attack, Broadcast tempering attack and Greedy behavior attack, etc.
- **Confidentiality Attacks**: Confidentiality is a very important security feature, which makes sure that data is to be accessed by authorized users only. In absence of confidentiality in the network, messages are exchanged between vehicles vulnerable to attacks by unauthorized personals. In such attacks, several confidential data can be accessed like the location of vehicles and routes history etc. These kinds of attacks include eavesdropping attack and traffic analysis attacks etc.

- **Non-Repudiation:** This security feature ensures that parties are correctly identified in the communication. Sender and receiver of any message should be verified whosesoever claimed to send and receive that message respectively. Otherwise, false alarms can be raised that message sent by someone or in same way. Message can be falsely claimed to be received by someone. Non-repudiation section contains a loss of events traceability attack.
- **Attacks on Integrity**: Data integrity shows that exchanged messages are not altered while transmission. This section ensures protection for information against any unauthorized addition, deletions and modification. Integrity attacks mainly target V2V communication compared to V2I communication. Integrity attacks include masquerading attack, replay attack, message tampering, message alteration/suppression and illusion attacks etc.
- **Attacks on Identification and Authenticity**: Authenticity is one of the major security challenges in VANETs. It provides a framework to authenticate every entity in the network before accessing available services in VANETs. Any violation of authenticity and identification mechanism may expose a complete network to face serious consequences. To provide identification and authentication in VANETs, some mechanism should be forced for every vehicle joining VANETs. These attacks include GPS spoofing, position faking attack, Sybil attack, Node impersonation attack, key and/or certificate replicating attack and tunneling attack etc.

Hence, by following different security concerns and a variety of attacks, several security mechanisms have been proposed. Some of them are discussed below.

- **Mutual Key Management**: This mechanism allows sharing common key among several vehicles without any centralized authorities. Therefore, group authentication is also not required for exchanging data because the mutual key is already shared.
- **Efficient Conditional Privacy Preservation**: This mechanism described by producing few unknown keys between On-Board Units (OBUs) and Road Side Units (RSUs) which can be used for quick authentication and privacy tracking.
- **Reputation and Plausibility Checks**: This technique ensures secure communication against data alteration and incorrect information collection. Under this mechanism, defective hubs are supposed to be removed from the system after identifying them.
- **Protected Architecture**: Communication framework should be restricted with maximum size of a message that the vehicle can send. Therefore, the system will be prevented by hostile nodes to telecast false bulk messages in the system. If any node attempts to send a higher number of messages or larger size messages than the defined standards then that node would be blocked for further message exchanges.
- **Real-Time Path Planning**: This approach uses a hybrid method to update run time traffic data. By following real-time path planning, traveling time is supposed to be reduced by decreasing the probability of vehicles getting stuck.
- **Advance Security Scheme**: This security scheme is based on grouping of networks and key distribution among vehicles and group heads in the network. This approach is majorly useful in security requirements of verification, integrity, privacy, and unforgeability.

It is evident from the VANET background section that efficient routing and security is one of the most important challenges in VANETs. The speed, processing power, communication capabilities and other characteristics of vehicles are rapidly changed now-a-days. Therefore, the routing protocols are also needed to be adopted or modified to enhance their efficiency by following new requirements. Moreover, the new type of attacks and security challenges are emerging day by day which makes the security issue of VANETs even more important than previous years.

Recent Communication Technologies in VANETs

Several high-speed wireless technologies are already proposed and most of them are recommended and considered for VANETs connectivity. Some of the technologies are presented below being capable to provide high-speed communication in vehicular networks.

Several **Cellular Technologies** such as 2G, 3G, and 4G etc. having their features, like 2G and 2.5G provide reliable security and a wide range of communication. However, 3G and 4G are taking over in terms of offering high improved communication capacity and data bandwidth. In different countries, like USA, Europe, and Japan, telematics projects use different generation of cellular technologies. However, limited bandwidth, higher cost and high latency rate reduce possibilities to use these technologies in VANETs.

Several variations in **IEEE 802.11,** family support wireless communication in a vehicular network. The protocol based on air interface is still under developing state by IEEE and is supposed to provide inter-vehicle communication at vehicular speed ranging from 200 km/h to 300 km/h with coverage of 1000 m of communication range. Medium Access Control (MAC) and Physical Access Control (PHY) are based on IEEE 802.11a. Many vehicle manufacturing industries heavily prompted IEEE 802.11p technologies across the world. The estimated deployment cost of **IEEE 802.11p** is predicted relatively low by comparing with cellular technologies because of substantial production volume. Hence, this technology seems more suitable for VANETs over cellular technologies.

The international standard Organization-Technical committee (ISO-TC) has performed unification efforts of the various wireless access technologies. The result of the unification process is a vehicular communication standard called the **Continuous Air interface for Long and Medium range (CALM M5)**. This protocol has combined several related air interface protocols and parameters on top of IEEE 802.11p architecture with the support of cellular technologies. These standards combined into single, unified and standard are expected to provide improved vehicular network performance through flexibility, increased capacity and redundancy in packet transmission and reception.

Message Broadcasting

Several applications in VANETs require exchange, gathering and processing of large volumes of data in term of electronic messages and packets. In such cases, message broadcasting mechanisms and techniques are suggested as better alternative approaches by researchers because of low-cost implementation and support of a huge volume of data in broadcasting. These techniques contain the restricted and unrestricted digital solution apart from these solutions. It includes satellite broadcasting solutions as well. Broadcasting techniques have a problem with huge data transmission overhead. This problem could be handled by reducing or eliminating broadcast range specifically on a particular area based on interest that will help to remove unnecessary network overhead. This mechanism is known as location-aware broadcasting.

Another approach may be clustering and network can be divided into multiple clusters. Each cluster is having neighbor nodes then broadcasting will be manageable within the cluster. Several cluster-based broadcasting (Yang et al., 2013) schemes have already been proposed earlier. In order to solve broadcast storm problem which occurs due to simultaneously forwarding warning messages in VANETs, several researchers have already been proposed many ways to approach this problem.

Power Management

In terms of energy efficiency, power management is not a big issue for VANETs due to batteries installed in vehicles. However, power management in terms of transmission power is challenging issue that must be addressed in near future to achieve effective vehicular communication. In urban areas, high transmission power may lead to disruption of an ongoing transmission with other transmissions at the distant vehicles because of interference of transmission. Therefore, reduced transmission power should be the solution of transmission in dense areas to provide reliable and efficient transmission. Additionally, routing could also be more efficient by reducing transmission power. Adjustment of transmission power increases the overall throughput and reduces interferences. So far, no much work has been done in this area. Hence, power management is one of the important challenges to be addressed further by the researchers.

VANETs APPLICATIONS

In India, millions of people die due to road accidents every year. Moreover, on a long expressway, there may be stretches where the internet and mobile network may be nonexistent or week. In such scenarios, VANETs may be helpful in the case of an emergency. Due to their characteristics, VANETs application hasa major role in daily lifestyle on road. Some of the major applications of VANETs (Karagiannis et al., 2011) have been described below.

Transportation Safety

One of the main driving forces of the development of vehicular communication (VC) systems is transportation safety which relies on high-rate safety messaging (beaconing). The main objective of any transportation safety application is to reduce the probability of accidents and loss of life. This can be achieved by sharing information among vehicles and roadside units. Typical transportation safety applications include lane change assistance, overtaking vehicle warning, head-on collision warning, rear-end collision warning, cooperative forward collision warning, emergency vehicle warning, pre-crash sensing, wrong-way driving warning, traffic condition warning, etc. Another safety application can be sending emergency messages to the call center that transfer notification to other responders accordingly. Sometimes, for a better response from emergency services, live video may be required to transmit using vehicle cameras etc.

Traffic Efficiency and Management Applications

These applications focus on improving the vehicle traffic flow, traffic assistance, and the traffic flow. The speed management applications allow the driver to handle the speed of the vehicle for comfort driving to avoid unnecessary braking. The co-operative navigation is used to increase traffic efficiency by controlling the navigation of vehicles by increasing cooperation among vehicles. To improve traffic efficiency, a driver needs to analyze traffic and emergency alerts while driving only. Traffic management takes care of certain other situations like crossroads, and intersections etc. To communicate cross points and intersections points to vehicles avoid unexpected collisions and help the driver to make their driving more efficient. In addition of all these applications, road congestion management is one area where VANET plays an important role and makes traffic more efficient. The road congestion management derives best route dynamically towards destination by following current traffic situations.

Comfort Driving

It includes information that can be exchanged among vehicles or between vehicles to the roadside unit to make driving more convenient. In this section, the information can be broadcasted to vehicles through vehicular communication like weather information, fuel stations, parking lots, restaurants, road charging points, and route navigations. As part of this section, several announcements and advertisements can also be broadcasted to all or some selected vehicles.

Infotainment Applications

Interactive entertainment targets to exchange entertainment related information to other drivers and passengers. The infotainment applications can be either local services based or internet services based. The local services typically include local e-commerce, point of interest of notification, local media downloading, etc. The internet-based services are fleet management, parking zone management, insurance, and other financial services management. Several other applications in a distributed environment can also be part of infotainment applications like distributed game, chat and file-sharing applications, etc.

Urban Sensing

Urban sensing includes traffic monitoring in the urban area and sharing data on common interests. A vehicular network can be used as urban sensing (cuff & Kang, 2008) where all vehicles are equipped with onboard sensors and other GPS devices. Environmental conditions and several social activities in urban areas can be recorded using a vehicular network that plays an important role in urban sensing. Urban sensing can play an important role when smartphone devices get integrated with OBUs deployed with vehicles in VANETs. Virtual Sensor Network (VSN) introduces new challenges that are different from traditional wireless sensor network. Therefore, this seems to be a promising research area in the recent future, if vehicles can be equipped with powerful processing units, different wireless communication devices, navigation devices, and other sensor devices. The combination of the sensor network and vehicular networks creates tremendous opportunities for large scale application in VANETs.

CHALLENGES AND FUTURE PERSPECTIVES

As mobile wireless equipment and networks become increasingly important, the demand for Vehicle-to-Vehicle (V2V) and Vehicles-to-Roadside (V2R) or Vehicle-to-Infrastructure (V2I) Communication will continue to grow. VANETs have some dissimilar properties than MANETs (Basagni et al. 2013) like road pattern restrictions, no restriction on network size, dynamic topology, mobility models, and infinite energy supply, etc. All these characteristics made VANETs environment challenging for developing **Efficient Routing** protocols.

With a sharp increase of vehicles on the road, new technology is intended to provide premium facilities to the passengers including safety applications, assistance to the drivers, emergency warnings, etc. At the same time, there is a consensus among authorities, industry, and academia on the need to **Secure Vehicular Communication** (VC) systems.

With specific proposals in the literature, a critical question must be answered. Can secure VC systems to be practical and satisfy the requirements of safety applications, inspite of the significant communication, processing overhead and other restrictions like security and privacy-enhancing mechanisms imposed? To answer this question, we must provide some secure solution and privacy-enhancing VC schemes having the reliability of communication, reduced processing overhead at each node, and the impact on a safety application.

The study of related literature indicates that with the appropriate system design including sufficiently high processing power and applications enabled by secure VC can be in practice as effective as those enabled by unsecured VC. With several challenges and characteristics of VANETs, some future perspective should be mentioned to design a better communication framework. In the last few years, we can see significant development in the mobile computing environment and an increase in new technologies in the area on wireless communication.

Diverse Wireless Technologies

As consequences of such rapid technologies changes, several non-interoperable wireless technologies get involved in communication framework. In such a heterogeneous environment, it is very complex to maintain seamless connectivity among various wireless communication technologies in terms of Quality of Service (QoS), routing protocols, and security efficiency. Therefore, next generation of intelligent transport system tends more comprehensive and integrated approach to network solutions.

Data Management and Storage

Handling data is also one of the areas for future work. In the coming times, vehicular networks are expected on a large scale as vehicles are getting increased day by day. That will generate huge amounts of distributed data that will be required to be stored in some well-defined manner. This massive network in terms of the number of vehicles will produce such huge data causing unique challenges to manage and store the data. In recent days, big data boosts the way to manipulate data and produces concrete information from raw data.

Design of Common Protocol

It tends to use the same protocols for different kind of vehicles in the communication framework. VANETs include several kinds of vehicles such as bicycles, cars, buses, trucks, taxis, and motorbikes etc. Therefore, it is important to have a single protocol that can be used in communication among all kinds of vehicles. It is possible, if academia, government and other researchers get involved in standardizing protocol in vehicular communication. Any protocol should support communication between different types of vehicles.

Network Fragmentation

Network fragmentation is also a key challenge for network designers in vehicular ad hoc networks. Due to network fragmentation, some of the nodes in the network become unreachable. Generally, network fragmentation occurs in rural areas or light traffic zone. Additionally, a small number of vehicles are equipped with onboard units (OBUs) also cause frequent network fragmentation in VANETs. Therefore, routing protocols based on network topology are not appropriate for VANETs.

Network Varieties

In VANETs, it is very much possible that drivers and passengers of vehicle communicate with someone in the other vehicles traveling in other networks. Therefore, the maintenance of the communication frameworks among different networks is also very challenging. This kind of communication is possible by making coordination of each network with other networks with the use of sensors, internet and other communication services. Apart from different networks, the network topology may also vary in term of density and the number of nodes in networks can be different. There is a difference in vehicles communicating in urban areas and highways. Therefore, the same protocol will not suit both cases because highways will have intermittent connectivity and urban network will have very dense connectivity. It's a big challenge to design some common approaches to work in both environments.

Geographical Changes of Vehicles

The geographical position of vehicles is one of the necessary factors to perform proper data communication. Therefore, geographical addressing families proposed by (Navas & Imielinski, 1997), have three different addressing mechanisms, application-layer solutions, GPS multicast solutions, and unicast IP routing. Therefore, the driver's behavior and the vehicle's movement pattern needs to be tracked to predict the position of vehicles shortly. The geographical position of nodes also plays an important role to locate destination in the network. Tracking of destination vehicle requires a mechanism to establish a path from source to destination that is also known as a routing mechanism.

CONCLUSION

Vehicular ad hoc network is a key area of research because of its popularity in recent times. The wireless vehicular communication framework provides an intelligent transport system for smart vehicles and smart infrastructure. VANETs contains several vehicles equipped with onboard units with the ability to communicate with each other through the wireless channel. Self-organized networks in a collaborative environment have huge applications to improve the safety and efficiency of traffic. Particularly high mobility of nodes, frequently link breakage, multi-hop path and several other characteristics of VANETs leads to many network challenges like efficient routing, secure communication and design of framework in a fully distributed environment.

Many researchers have already contributed in areas on VANETs communication. However, there are many more research challenges in VANETs which have been identified and mentioned in this survey. Apart from researchers, several automotive companies, research institutions, and government organizations are also investing their effort and money in evaluating and creating future engineering systems. This effort brought details of VANETs communication framework including architecture details, challenges, major applications and their future research scope in the same area.

REFERENCES

Baker, T., & Jose, M. (2018). Greeaodv: an energy-efficient routing protocol for vehicular ad hoc networks. *Proceedings of international Conference on Intelligent Computing*, 670-681. 10.1007/978-3-319-95957-3_69

Basagni, S., Conti, M., & Giordano, S. (2013). *Mobile Ad hoc Networking: cutting edge directions* (2nd ed.). Willey IEEE Press Publisher. doi:10.1002/9781118511305

Basagni & Stefano. (1998). A distance routing effect algorithm for mobility (DREAM). *Proceedings of the 4th annual ACM/IEEE international conference on Mobile computing and networking*.

Blum, J. (2003). *Mobility management in IVC networks*. Academic Press.

Clausen, T., &Jacquet, P. (2003). *Optimized Link State Routing Protocol (OLSR)*. RFC-3626.

Cuff, D., Hansen, M., & Kang, J., (2008). *Urban sensing: out of the woods*. ACM.

Dhankhar, S., & Agrawal, S. (2014). VANETs: A survey on routing protocols and issues, *Int. J. Innovative Res. Sci. Eng. Technol.*, (3), 13427-13435.

Gayathri, N., & Kumar, S. R. (2015). Critical analysis of various routing protocols in VANET, *Int. J. Adv. Res. Computer Science. Software Engineering*, 5, 619–623.

Haas, Z. J. (1997, Nov). *The Zone Routing Protocol*. Academic Press.

Hartenstein, H., & Laberteaux, K. P. (2008). A tutorial survey on vehicular ad hoc networks. *Communications Magazine, IEEE*, 46(6), 164–171. doi:10.1109/MCOM.2008.4539481

Ji, X., Yu, H., Fan, G., & Fu, W. (2016). SDGR: an SDN-based geographic routing protocol for vanet. *Proceedings of IEEE International Conference on Internet of Things (iThings) and IEEE Green Computing and Communications (GreenCom) and IEEE Cyber, Physical and Social Computing (CPSCom) and IEEE Smart Data (SmartData). IEEE,* 276–281. 10.1109/iThings-GreenCom-CPSCom-SmartData.2016.70

Johnson, D. B., & Maltz, D. A. (1996). *Dynamic Source Routing in Ad Hoc Wireless Networks. In* T. Imielinski & H. Korth (Eds.), *Mobile Computing* (pp. 153–181). Kluwer.

Joshi, H. P., Sichitiu, M., & Kihl, M. (2007, May). *Distributed Robust Geocast Multicast Routing for Inter-Vehicle Communication.* Academic Press.

Karagiannis, G., Altintas, O., Ekici, E., Heijenk, G., Jarupan, B., Lin, K., & Weil, T. (2011). Vehicular networking: A survey and tutorial on requirements, architectures, challenges, standards and solutions. *IEEE Communications Surveys and Tutorials, 13*(4), 584–616. doi:10.1109/SURV.2011.061411.00019

Karp, B., & Kung, H. T. (2000). GPSR: Greedy perimeter stateless routing for wireless networks. *Proceedings of the 6th annual international conference on Mobile computing and networking,* 243-254.

Kihl, M. (2007). *Reliable Geographical Multicast Routing in Vehicular Ad-hoc Networks.* Academic Press.

Li, F., & Wang, Y. (2007). Routing in vehicular ad hoc networks: A survey. *IEEE Vehicular Technology Magazine, 2*(2), 12–22. doi:10.1109/MVT.2007.912927

Moridi, E., & Barati, H. (2017). RMRPTS: A reliable multi-level routing protocol with tabu search in VANET. *Telecommunication Systems, 65*(1), 127–137. doi:10.100711235-016-0219-6

Navas, J. C., & Imielinski, T. (1997). Geocast - geographic addressing and routing, 1096. *Proceedings of the 3rd annual ACM/IEEE international conference 1097 on Mobile computing and networking, in: MobiCom '97, ACM,* 66–76.

Pei, G., Gerla, M., & Chen, T. W. (2000, June). Fisheye State Routing: A Routing Scheme for Ad Hoc Wireless Networks. *Proc. ICC 2000.*

Perkins, C., Belding-Royer, E., & Das, S. (2013). *Ad hoc On-Demand Distance Vector (AODV) Routing.* RFC-3561.

Poonia, R. C., Bhargava, D., & Kumar, B. S. (2015). CDRA: Cluster-based dynamic routing approach as a development of the AODV in vehicular ad-hoc networks. *Proceedings of International Conference on Signal Processing and Communication Engineering Systems (SPACES),* 397-401. 10.1109/SPACES.2015.7058293

Raya, M., & Hubaux, J. P. (2007). Securing vehicular ad hoc networks. *Journal of Computer Security, 15*(1), 39–68. doi:10.3233/JCS-2007-15103

Sarkar, S. K., Basavaraju, T. G., & Puttamadappa, C. (2016). *Ad Hoc Mobile Wireless Networks: Principles, Protocols and Application* (2nd ed.). CRC Press. doi:10.1201/b13094

Singh, A., & Kad, S. (2016). A Review on the various security techniques for VANETs. *Procedia Computer Science, 78,* 284–290. doi:10.1016/j.procs.2016.02.055

Taleb, A. A. (2018). VANET Routing Protocols and Architecture: An Overview. *Journal of Computational Science*, *14*(3), 423–434. doi:10.3844/jcssp.2018.423.434

Tonguz, O. K., Wisitpongphan, N., Bai, F., Mudalige, P., & Sadekar, V. (2007, May), Broadcasting in VANET. *Proc. IEEE INFOCOM MOVE Workshop.*

Yang, F., Tang, Y. L., & Huang, L. F. (2013). A novel cooperative MAC for broadcasting in clustering VANETs. *Proceedings of International Conference on Connected Vehicles and Expo*, 893–897. 10.1109/ICCVE.2013.6799922

Ye, M., Guan, L., & Quddus, M. (2019). MPBRP- Mobility Prediction Based Routing Protocol in VANETs. *2019 International Conference on Advanced Communication Technologies and Networking (CommNet)*. 10.1109/COMMNET.2019.8742389

Chapter 14

Performance Enhancement of Outlier Removal Using Extreme Value Analysis– Based Mahalonobis Distance

Joy Christy A

School of Computing, SASTRA University (Deemed), India

Umamakeswari A

School of Computing, SASTRA University (Deemed), India

ABSTRACT

Outlier detection is a part of data analytics that helps users to find discrepancies in working machines by applying outlier detection algorithm on the captured data for every fixed interval. An outlier is a data point that exhibits different properties from other points due to some external or internal forces. These outliers can be detected by clustering the data points. To detect outliers, optimal clustering of data points is important. The problem that arises quite frequently in statistics is identification of groups or clusters of data within a population or sample. The most widely used procedure to identify clusters in a set of observations is k-means using Euclidean distance. Euclidean distance is not so efficient for finding anomaly in multivariate space. This chapter uses k-means algorithm with Mahalanobis distance metric to capture the variance structure of the clusters followed by the application of extreme value analysis (EVA) algorithm to detect the outliers for detecting rare items, events, or observations that raise suspicions from the majority of the data.

INTRODUCTION

Outlier detection is a part of data analytics that helps user to find discrepancies in working machine by applying outlier detection algorithm on the captured data for every fixed interval. An outlier is a data point that exhibits different properties from other points that are due to some external or internal forces.

DOI: 10.4018/978-1-7998-2491-6.ch014

These outliers can be detected by clustering the data points. To detect outliers, optimal clustering of data points is important. Problem, which arises quite frequently in statistics, is identification of groups or clusters of data within a population or sample. The most widely used procedure to identify clusters in a set of observations is K-Means using Euclidean distance. However, Euclidean distance is not so efficient for finding anomaly in multivariate space. To remedy this shortfall in the K-Means algorithm, Mahalanobis distance metric is used to capture the variance structure of the clusters that is followed by the application of Extreme Value Analysis (EVA) algorithm to detect the outliers. This method serves as a significant improvement over its competitors and will provide a useful tool for detecting rare items, events or observations which raise suspicions by differing significantly from the majority of the data.

In this Information era, it is believed that information leads to power and success (Alberts, 2003). Future of many companies and government organizations relies on the information what they have with them. With the improvement in the storage techniques, now it is possible to collect and store a tremendous volume of information. Organizations have been collecting an immeasurable data from simple text documents to more complex information such as Medical data, Satellite data, spatial data and multimedia data. Mining of these data, using sophisticated mathematical algorithms, provides much useful information regarding the probability of future events, unusual events that might be interesting or data errors that require further investigation. Data mining is the process of uncovering patterns and finding anomalies and relationships in large datasets that can be used to make predictions about future trends. The main purpose of data mining is extracting valuable information from available data. It is also popularly known as Knowledge Discovery in Databases (KDD) (Tembhurne, 2019) (Krochmal, 2018). Data Mining comprises of few steps starting from preliminary raw data collections to some form of identifying new knowledge It is an iterative process and uses the following steps such as Data cleaning, Data integration, Data selection, Data transformation, Data mining, Pattern evaluation and Knowledge Representation. Once the extracted information is offered to the user, the assessment measures can be improved and further refined to get more fitting results.

One of the important applications of data mining is outlier detection. Outlier detection is the process of detecting and subsequently excluding inappropriate data from the given set of data. An outlier is a piece of data that deviates drastically from the standard norm or average of the data set. Outlier detection has two-steps viz., Clustering and detecting deviated data among the clustered sets. Therefore, the process of grouping observations into cluster is a foremost problem in analyzing data sets. So far, the most widely used algorithm to identify clusters in a set of observations is K-Means. But, the main constraint of this algorithm is that it uses Euclidean distance metric, which is prone to noisy data and outliers, which in turn give a non-spherical cluster. Also, this distance suites well only for univariate datasets. Hence, this book chapter introduces the technique of Mahalanobis distance (MD) to detect an observation having an unusual pattern. The MD measures the relative distance between two variables with respect to the mean of the multivariate data. These calculated distance values are used by Extreme Value Analysis (EVA) algorithm to find outliers, and thereby, eliminating the need of deciding threshold value manually.

For detecting outliers in a set of observations, it is important to cluster the points accurately. Clusters are characterized by groups of data points which are in "close" proximity to one another. While it is much easier to visually detect clusters in univariate or bivariate data, the task becomes increasingly difficult as the dimensionality of the data increases. One of the largest used clustering algorithms is K-Means using Euclidean distance. Euclidean distance suffers from a scaling effect that describes a situation where the variability of one parameter masks the variability of another parameter and it happens when the measurement ranges or scales of two parameters are different; thus, makes it difficult to find the true outliers. Hence, to overcome this shortfall, the idea of using K-Means with Mahalanobis distance (MD) is put forth. The MD methodology distinguishes multivariable data groups by a univariate distance measure, which is calculated from the correlated values of all the parameters that the dataset is dependent on. Thus, MD value is calculated using the normalized value of observations and their correlation coefficients thus makes MD more efficient. After obtaining univariate distance, an EVA algorithm is used to detect the outliers.

REVIEW OF LITERATURE

This section reviews different methods present in the existing literature on outlier detection methods. In (Kadam and Pund, 2013), several approaches were reviewed to detect outliers, including the cluster-based approach. The authors have identified the outlier objects by partitioning the data into chunks. The clustering method is invariably applied to every chunk of data to find out the candidate outlier objects using distance measures. In (Gan, 2011), the CHB-K-Means algorithm is proposed which uses a weighted attribute matrix to detect outliers. The authors have extended K-Means algorithm by simultaneously introducing an additional cluster for holding outliers. In (Jiang et al., 2004), a data filter-cleaner has been proposed that resists outliers. The authors have used an online outlier resistant estimator that combines a priori process model and Kalman filter. In this section, the authors have focused on clustering methods with the built-in mechanism of outlier detection and give a review of those methods. In (Jiang et al., 2001), a two-phase clustering algorithm for outlier detection is proposed. In the first phase, the k-means algorithm is modified to partition the data in such a way that a data point is assigned to be a new cluster centre if the data point is far away from all clusters. In the second phase, a minimum spanning tree is constructed based on the cluster centers obtained from the first phase. Clusters in small sub trees are considered as outliers. Later, the concept of cluster-based local outlier is introduced that elucidates the importance of local data behavior (Liu et al., 2004). The authors have used a measure that evaluates the physical significance of outlier called cluster based local outlier factor (CBLOF) and Find CBLOF algorithm to identify outliers.

The Outlier Removal Clustering (ORC) algorithm (Hautamäki et al., 2003) is proposed to identify clusters and outliers from a dataset simultaneously. The ORC algorithm consists of two consecutive stages: the first stage is a purely k-means algorithm and the second stage iteratively removes the data points that are far away from their cluster centroids. In (Zhou et al., 2009), a three-stage k- means algorithm is proposed to cluster data and detect outliers. In the first stage, the fuzzy c-means algorithm is applied to cluster the data. In the second stage, local outliers are identified and the cluster centers are recalculated. In the third stage, certain clusters are merged and global outliers are identified. The Outlier Detection and Clustering (ODC) algorithm (Ahmed and Naser, 2013) is proposed to detect outliers. The ODC algorithm is a modified version of the k-means algorithm. In the ODC algorithm, a data point that is at least p times the average distance away from its centroid is considered as an outlier. The Non-exhaustive Overlapping k-means (NEO- k-means) algorithm is proposed which is also able to identify outliers during the clustering process (Whang et al., 2015). In (Guojun Gan and K.Michael, 2017), a K-Means Outlier Removal (KMOR) algorithm is proposed that extends k-means algorithm to provide data clustering and outlier detection simultaneously by introducing an additional "cluster" to the algorithm to hold all outliers. Unlike most existing clustering algorithms with outlier detection, the KMOR algorithm assigns all outliers into a group naturally during the clustering process. An approach

Figure 1. K-Means algorithm with Mahalanobis distance

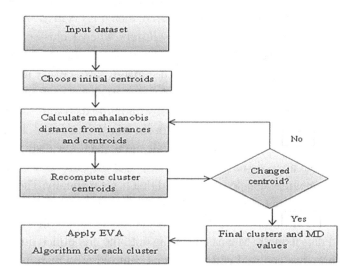

to detect outliers based on the Mahalanobis distance is proposed in (Jayakumar and Thomas, 2013). In (Sachin Kumar et al., 2009), a probabilistic approach has been employed for defining warning and fault threshold MD values to improve upon the traditional approaches where threshold MD values are decided by experts and demonstrates that the approach to define threshold MD value is a major improvement. A new algorithm to extend K-Means algorithm with Mahalanobis distance is proposed to take into account of variance structure of the clusters (Igor and Melnykov, 2014).

Most of the algorithms presented in the review do not differentiate strong and mild outliers through multivariate analysis. Hence, this work presents a Mahalanobis distance with extreme value analysis based outlier detection algorithm which is proposed to effectively identify the mild and strong outliers present in a dataset.

METHODOLOGY

The objective of the proposed model is to find the outliers in the dataset more accurately by using k-means algorithm with Mahalanobis distance and extreme value analysis. The proposed algorithm is then compared with k-means algorithm with Euclidean distance and extreme value analysis for measuring the performance of the proposed work. The methodology first employs K-means clustering algorithm with Mahalanobis distance. The steps to be followed to implement k-means clustering with mahalnobis distance are shown in the Figure 1.

Final MD values are given as input for calculating threshold using Extreme value analysis algorithm, EVA, to detect the outliers. Thus, this algorithm has three steps.

- K-Means clustering
- Distance calculation using Mahalanobis Distance metric
- EVA -Extreme value analysis to set threshold.

K-Means algorithm takes 'n' points as input and clusters these 'n' points into each of the 'k' clusters as much as possible. If any of the point cannot be clustered, then it is taken as an outlier. As an extension of K-Means algorithm, this algorithm maintains (k+1) clusters, where k clusters are to hold the clustered points while (k+1)th cluster holds the outlier points. After, choosing the cluster centres at random, MD values and mean for each cluster is recalculated at each step as a part of every iteration until the optimal cluster is obtained. The Mahalanobis distance accounts for the variance of each variable and the covariance between variables. Geometrically, it does this by transforming the data into standardized uncorrelated data and computing the ordinary Euclidean distance for the transformed data. In this way, it provides a way to measure distances that takes into account the scale of the data. The distance obtained is analyzed using EVA, an extreme value analysis based algorithm, to get the outliers with the help of algorithm itself instead of finding them with the help of threshold that is set manually. The Mahalanobis Distance measures the relative distance between two variables with respect to the mean of the multivariate data. Thus, the univariate distance of multivariate dataset is obtained with the Mahalanobis distance that can be used to cluster the test data using K-Means clustering until the predefined number of iterations or till the difference between previous centroid and the current centroid is so marginal. Formula to calculate Mahalanobis distance is:

$$D = [(X_i - M)^T C^{-1}(X_i - M)]^{0.5} \tag{1}$$

where

D = Mahalanobis distance
X_i = an object vector
M = arithmetic mean vector
C^{-1} = Inverse Covariance matrix of independent variables
T = Indicates vector should be transposed

After clustering the points using K-Means with Mahalanobis distance algorithm, final step of methodology is to find the outliers based on the extreme value Analysis algorithm that takes the threshold for deciding outlier as a part of algorithm rather than fixing it manually. From the MD values that are obtained, Extreme SR value analysis with single representation of data objects is implemented to identify the outliers. The EVA method is used to find the threshold for the normal data and to detect the outliers. Normally, the threshold value is decided by the user manually which is a big shortfall since he/she cannot predict the threshold value always and that may in turn gives false outliers as output. This research work employs EVA based threshold for determining the outliers. The process of EVA is shown in Figure 2.

The pseudo code of the proposed work is given below.

Figure 2. EVA algorithm

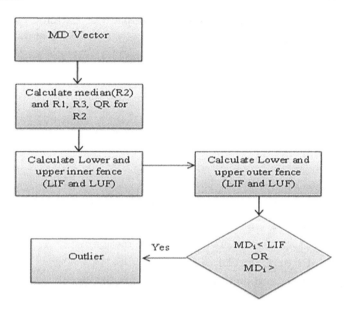

Algorithm 1

```
Input:
S, k where S is a dataset, k is set of initial centroids
 Output:
k clusters
Algorithm:
1.         initialize k random centroids
2.         repeat
3.         for all instance i in s do
4.         shortest<-0
5.         membership<-null
6.         for all centroid c do
7.         dist<-[(I - c) T C⁻¹(I - c)] 0.5
8.         if dist<shortest then
9.         shortest<-dist
10.         membership<-c
11.         end if
12.         end for
13.         end for
14.         recalculatecentroids(c)
15.         until convergence
16.         end
```

Use Extreme Value Analysis algorithm EVA **[Algorithm 2]** to find the outliers in each clusters. Final cluster's MD values are given as input to EVA algorithm that uses Extreme value Analysis to find the deviated data objects in the dataset.

Algorithm 2

```
Input:
        => MD values
Output:
=> outliers
Algorithm:
1.         for all clusters in the k clusters do
a.         compute median of dis from cluster members
b.         calculate interquartile
c.          compute lower and upper fencing of outliers
2.         end for
3.         end
```

EXPERIMENTATION AND RESULT DISCUSSIONS

The algorithm is implemented using python to get better results. Python has built-in packages for data analytics application and thereby making it easy to learn and code. Moreover, it has built-in packages for illustrating results in much clearer formats like graphs, charts, scatter-plots. Thus, python is considered for implementing this concept. Packages that are used here are Numpy, Sklearn, Matplotlib, mpl_toolkits. Numpy is used to handle very large datasets. Sklearn package contains cluster function that can be used to cluster the data. Matplotlib is used for graphical representation of datasets and how they are clustered using graphs, scatter-plots and others. Thus, these packages should be pre-installed before implementing.

Main hardware requirement of the paper is the type of Processor, Memory, RAM. 32-bit or 64-bit Operating System, having x32 or x64-based processor. Processor used is Intel(R) Core™ i3-6100U CPU @2.30GHz 2.30GHz. Implementation of outlier detection using Mahalanobis distance produces much more accurate results, than K-Means Outlier Removal algorithm proposed in (Gan and Michael, 2017). This work compares KMOR and Modified K-Means Clustering using Mahalanobis distance outlier detection algorithm to prove the efficiency of Mahalanobis distance based clustering outlier detection over other algorithms by implementing these algorithms on the real time shuttle dataset that contains 43,000 instances and Gas sensor array temperature modulation data set. The description of the shuttle dataset is shown in Table 1.

Gas sensor array temperature modulation dataset is a chemical detection platform consisting of 14 temperature-modulated metal oxide gas sensors exposed during three weeks to the mixtures of carbon monoxide and humid synthetic air in a gas chamber. The dataset contains 20 attributes with 409500 instances. The description of the shuttle dataset is shown in Table 2.

Table 1. Shuttle Dataset Description

S. No	Attribute Name
1	Rad.Flow
2	Fpv.Close
3	Fpv.Open
4	High
5	Bypass
6	Bpv.Close
7	Bpv.Open

Table 2. Gas Sensor Dataset Description

S. No	Attribute Name
1	Time
2	Concentration (ppm)
3	Humidity (%r.h.)
4	Temperature (A°C)
5	Flow Rate (mL/min)
6	Heater Voltage(V)
7	Resistance of Gas Sensor 1
8	Resistance of Gas Sensor 2
9	Resistance of Gas Sensor 3
10	Resistance of Gas Sensor 4
11	Resistance of Gas Sensor 5
12	Resistance of Gas Sensor 6
13	Resistance of Gas Sensor 7
14	Resistance of Gas Sensor 8
15	Resistance of Gas Sensor 9
16	Resistance of Gas Sensor 10
17	Resistance of Gas Sensor 11
18	Resistance of Gas Sensor 12
19	Resistance of Gas Sensor 13
20	Resistance of Gas Sensor14

The cluster plots of outliers from all clusters with shuttle dataset in shown in Figure 3. From the results, it has been observed that the proposed extreme value analysis based Mahalanobis algorithm clearly elucidates the number of outliers present in the shuttle dataset than the traditional KMOR algorithm.

Figure 3. Cluster Plots of Shuttle Dataset

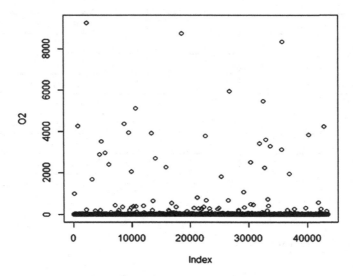

Figure 4. Cluster Plots of Gas Sensor Dataset

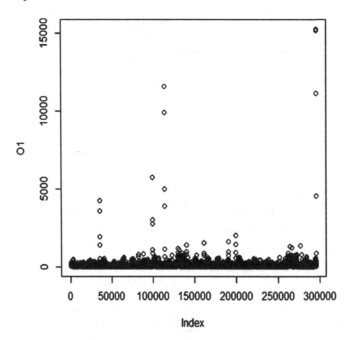

The cluster plots of outliers from all clusters with gas sensor dataset in shown in Figure 4. The results clearly depict the proposed extreme value analysis based Mahalanobis algorithm correctly identifying the number of outliers present in the gas sensor dataset than the traditional KMOR algorithm.

Table 3 denotes the outlier analysis of the proposed algorithm with KMOR method. The number of outliers obtained was 54. While in this case, the algorithm has encountered 124 outliers. Likewise, in

Table 3. Outlier Analysis

Algorithm	Outliers	
	Shuttle	Gas Sensor
K-Means Outlier Removal Algorithm	54	5283
Modified K-Means Using Mahalanobis Distance Outlier Detection Algorithm	124	12678

Figure 5. Outlier Analysis

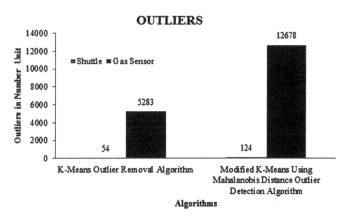

Table 4. Silhouette distance measure analysis

Algorithm	Silhouette Distance	
	Shuttle	Gas Sensor
K-Means Outlier Removal Algorithm	6.8	6.3
Modified K-Means Using Mahalanobis Distance Outlier Detection Algorithm	7.1	7.4

gas sensor dataset, it extensively identifies strong outliers and mild outliers with 12678, while in this case the KMOR algorithm identifies 5283 instances. This proves that the proposed algorithm performs better than the all other existing algorithms. The pictorial representation of the performance of outlier analysis is shown in Figure 5.

Silhouette distance measures the relatedness of an object with its own cluster with other clusters. Table 4 denotes the silhouette distance measure of the proposed algorithm with KMOR method. Removal of outliers helps to create compact cluster with K-means algorithm thus, improves the silhouette measure of the proposed algorithm. For, shuttle dataset the silhouette distance of KMOR algorithm is 6.8 and extreme value analysis based Mahalanobis algorithm is 7.1. Likewise, the silhouette distance measure of KMOR algorithm is 6.3 and 7.4 for the proposed algorithm. This proves that the proposed algorithm performs better than the existing algorithm. The pictorial representation of the performance of outlier analysis is shown in Figure6.

Figure 6. Silhouette Distance Measure

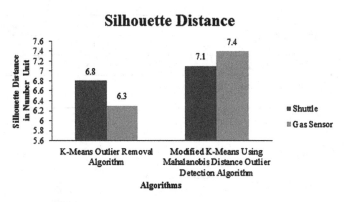

Table 5. Accuracy analysis

Algorithm	Accuracy	
	Shuttle	Gas Sensor
K-Means Outlier Removal Algorithm	0.763	0.797
Modified K-Means Using Mahalanobis Distance Outlier Detection Algorithm	0.831	0.862

Figure 7. Accuracy Analysis

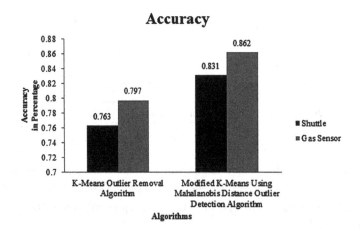

With respect to descriptive analysis, prediction accuracy refers to the fraction of correctly clustered instances with total number of instances. Table 5 denotes the prediction accuracy of the proposed extreme value analysis based Mahalanobis distance algorithm with KMOR method. Removal of outliers helps to create compact cluster with K-means algorithm which in turn enhances the accuracy in grouping instances in the right clusters. For, shuttle dataset the prediction accuracy of KMOR algorithm is 76% and extreme value analysis based Mahalanobis algorithm is 83%. Likewise, the prediction accuracy of KMOR algorithm for the gas sensor data set is 79% and 86% for the proposed algorithm. Since, the proposed algorithm identifies both strong and mild outliers of the results obtained from Mahalanobis distance, it improves the accuracy of clusters built by K-Means algorithm. This proves that the proposed algorithm performs better than the existing algorithm. The pictorial representation of the performance of outlier analysis is shown in Figure7.

The proposed algorithm is seemed to be effective in terms of identifying the outliers that in turn reflects the silhouette distance and accuracy. Silhouette distance is the intra clustered relatedness of data objects. The distance of a data object with its own cluster must be minimum than other clusters. The silhouette distance of the proposed algorithm is 7.4 which means, the algorithm poses a strong structure pattern for descriptive analysis and is greater than the KMOR. The accuracy of the proposed algorithm is also comparatively high than KMOR algorithm, which means, the number of data objects correctly clustered by the proposed algorithm is higher than KMOR. Thus, the proposed algorithm can perfectly be replaced with the traditional KMOR algorithm.

CONCLUSION

Modified K-Means Clustering using Mahalanobis distance outlier detection algorithm is used to cluster and detect outliers using Mahalanobis distance. Mahalanobis distance could be used as an alternative for Euclidean distance as it employs multivariate approach. One of the major advantages is EVA algorithm to find the outlier points. This is because threshold is set by the user manually in most of the cases that may not be optimal all the time. Hence, this algorithm decides the threshold using extreme value analysis automatically relieving the user from the burden of setting the threshold. Hence, this work proves that Modified K-Means clustering using Mahalanobis distance outlier detection algorithm is much efficient in case of accuracy. It provides clusters of spherical shape and find true outliers that KMOR algorithm has failed to provide. One of the issues with using Mahalanobis distances is that accuracy of the distance is sensitive to initialization. Thus, for further enhancements, initialization procedure should be altered to the selected points closer to cluster centres. Research has been going to identify points that will help finding the point close to clusters which have more neighbours to be favoured in the initialization step.

REFERENCES

Ahmed, M., & Mahmood, A. N. (2013, June). A novel approach for outlier detection and clustering improvement. In *2013 IEEE 8th Conference on Industrial Electronics and Applications (ICIEA)* (pp. 577-582). IEEE. 10.1109/ICIEA.2013.6566435

Alberts, D. S., & Hayes, R. E. (2003). *Power to the edge: Command... control... in the information age. Office of the Assistant Secretary of Defense Washington DC Command and Control Research Program.* CCRP.

Aparna, K., & Nair, M. K. (2016). Effect of outlier detection on clustering accuracy and computation time of CHB K-means algorithm. In *Computational Intelligence in Data Mining—Volume 2* (pp. 25–35). New Delhi: Springer. doi:10.1007/978-81-322-2731-1_3

Gan, G. (2011). *Data Clustering in C++: an object-oriented approach.* Chapman and Hall/CRC. doi:10.1201/b10814

Gan, G., & Ng, M. K. P. (2017). K-means clustering with outlier removal. *Pattern Recognition Letters,* *90*, 8–14. doi:10.1016/j.patrec.2017.03.008

Hautamäki, V., Cherednichenko, S., Kärkkäinen, I., Kinnunen, T., & Fränti, P. (2005, June). Improving k-means by outlier removal. In *Scandinavian Conference on Image Analysis* (pp. 978-987). Springer. 10.1007/11499145_99

He, Z., Xu, X., & Deng, S. (2003). Discovering cluster-based local outliers. *Pattern Recognition Letters,* *24*(9-10), 1641–1650. doi:10.1016/S0167-8655(03)00003-5

Jayakumar, G. D. S., & Thomas, B. J. (2013). A new procedure of clustering based on multivariate outlier detection. *Journal of Data Science: JDS,* *11*(1), 69–84.

Jiang, M. F., Tseng, S. S., & Su, C. M. (2001). Two-phase clustering process for outliers detection. *Pattern Recognition Letters,* *22*(6-7), 691–700. doi:10.1016/S0167-8655(00)00131-8

Jiang, S. Y., & An, Q. B. (2008, October). Clustering-based outlier detection method. In *2008 Fifth International Conference on Fuzzy Systems and Knowledge Discovery* (Vol. 2, pp. 429-433). IEEE. 10.1109/FSKD.2008.244

Kadam, N. V., & Pund, M. A. (2013). Joint approach for outlier detection. *International Journal of Computer Science Applications,* *6*(2), 45–4.

Krochmal, M., & Husi, H. (2018). Knowledge discovery and data mining. Integration of Omics Approaches and Systems Biology for Clinical Applications, 233-247.

Kumar, S., Chow, T. W., & Pecht, M. (2009). Approach to fault identification for electronic products using Mahalanobis distance. *IEEE Transactions on Instrumentation and Measurement,* *59*(8), 2055–2064. doi:10.1109/TIM.2009.2032884

Liu, H., Shah, S., & Jiang, W. (2004). On-line outlier detection and data cleaning. *Computers & Chemical Engineering,* *28*(9), 1635–1647. doi:10.1016/j.compchemeng.2004.01.009

Melnykov, I., & Melnykov, V. (2014). On K-means algorithm with the use of Mahalanobis distances. *Statistics & Probability Letters,* *84*, 88–95. doi:10.1016/j.spl.2013.09.026

Tembhurne, D.S., Adhikari, J., & Babu, R. (2019). *A Review study on Application of Data Mining Techniques in CRM of Pharmaceutical Industry.* Academic Press.

Whang, J. J., Dhillon, I. S., & Gleich, D. F. (2015, June). Non-exhaustive, overlapping k-means. In *Proceedings of the 2015 SIAM International Conference on Data Mining* (pp. 936-944). Society for Industrial and Applied Mathematics. 10.1137/1.9781611974010.105

Zhou, Y., Yu, H., & Cai, X. (2009, December). A novel k-means algorithm for clustering and outlier detection. In *2009 Second International Conference on Future Information Technology and Management Engineering* (pp. 476-480). IEEE. 10.1109/FITME.2009.125

Chapter 15
Spam Mail Filtering Using Data Mining Approach:
A Comparative Performance Analysis

Ajay Kumar Gupta
 https://orcid.org/0000-0001-9666-5047
Madan Mohan Malaviya University of Technology, India

ABSTRACT

This chapter presents an overview of spam email as a serious problem in our internet world and creates a spam filter that reduces the previous weaknesses and provides better identification accuracy with less complexity. Since J48 decision tree is a widely used classification technique due to its simple structure, higher classification accuracy, and lower time complexity, it is used as a spam mail classifier here. Now, with lower complexity, it becomes difficult to get higher accuracy in the case of large number of records. In order to overcome this problem, particle swarm optimization is used here to optimize the spam base dataset, thus optimizing the decision tree model as well as reducing the time complexity. Once the records have been standardized, the decision tree is again used to check the accuracy of the classification. The chapter presents a study on various spam-related issues, various filters used, related work, and potential spam-filtering scope.

INTRODUCTION

SPAM (Attri, 2012) is one of the electronic messaging systems which includes most broadcast media through which it sends or receives the unsolicited messages on the computer, mobile or PDA etc. indiscriminately. Junk e-mail (E-mail spam), is a subset of spams that involves approximately same e-mail messages transmitted to no. of recipients. Spam (Attri, 2012) is use of electronic messaging system to send unsolicited bulk messages indiscriminately. When the number of messages in your inbox started to increase, it became annoying for us to remove the unwanted e-mail. IE- mail spam is also known as unsolicited bulk e-mail (or junk e-mail). The current survey shows an increasing trend for amount of incoming spam and scammer attacks are becoming targeted, and consequently more of a threat. When

DOI: 10.4018/978-1-7998-2491-6.ch015

targeted attacks first emerged five years ago, Symantec message labs intelligence tracked between one or two attacks per week. Subsequently, attacks have increased to 10 per day to 60 per day in 2010. The number of spam sent by the countries of Europe will increase to 40 percent to 45 percent of all spam. These facts state that the spam is a big problem for today and also for tomorrow and it actually makes sense to investigate new effective methods against spam. The purpose of this work is to discover the techniques to filter the spam from incoming emails. Filtering spam is a technique to categorize all the incoming emails in network into spam and ham messages. Here, important issues related to spam filtering, the applicable steps for classification, methods and the evaluation measures in the spam filtering are discussed in detail. A lot of works have been done before in this spam filtering domain. These include Bayesian Networks, Decision Tree, K-Nearest Neighbor etc. (Ma, 2009), (Razmara, 2012) with some extra features or with some additional methods in it. With advancement, Spammers frequently change their email's external sign to misguide spam filtering systems, so, there arises a need for adaptive filtering systems, which have the power of quick reaction to the changes and provides fast and qualitative self-tuning with a new set of features. The study so far concludes that there are many of the filtering techniques which are based on text categorization methods but none of them can claim to provide an ideal solution i.e. zero percent false positive and zero percent false negative. Still, there are lots of scopes for research in classifying text messages as well as multimedia messages. This is not possible to maintain 100% accuracy and efficiency of filtering spam. But, one should try to make sure that the model is more efficient, reliable and accurate as possible. Classifier should avoid the following two cases to be more accurate.

- **Ham Misclassification:** The genuine mail should not be classified as a spam mail. Due to this misclassification, the receiver may get unaware of important mails which may be very damaging sometimes by causing serious risks.
- **Spam Misclassification:** The spam should not be classified as important mails as it causes many more financial and behavioral damage.

Process of Spam Filtering

A spam may be of different forms as image spam, blank spam, sms spam, email spam etc. The spam mail usually contains advertisement contents. As per common aspect, the filter focuses on the modules of emails to primarily classify the spam and hams. On that basis the spam, filters are of 3 types on the strategy of focusing on emails to classify spam.

1. Subject of message
2. Body content of message (content based filter)
3. Senders status (sender's reputation based on past history as spammer or not)

A general machine learning based spam filter (Zhong, 2010) consists of at least the following sequences.

1. **Collection of Emails:** First of all, all the network emails are collected from individual users which are considered as both spam and legitimate email.
2. **Pre-Processing:** The next is the transformation process. In this phase, the task of pre-processing is usually defined by the author what strategies she/he is using. Generally, it consists of removal of conjunctions, stop words etc. It also has tokenization process in it.

3. **Feature Selection:** The attributes are selected in this phase from several words of email. Attributes are selected from words which contribute major participation in filtering spam. Feature selection occurs according to the authors' choice which methodology he/she is using.

4. **Machine Learning Application:** Now, among all the different machine learning/data mining algorithms (supervised learning & unsupervised learning), one can use either a single or a hybrid of algorithms for rule generation.

5. **Rule Extraction:** According to the algorithms used, some rules are extracted for the given email that play an important role to classify the email as ham/spam.

6. **Classification:** Finally, the network email is classified as spam or ham and decided about whether to send this email to user or not.

The pre-processing is performed after the collection of all network emails. At the last, the machine learning techniques are used to provide training and testing to the mails whether to decide the decision as ham/spam.

Aim as to Discover Better Spam Filter by Removing Previous Flaws

The simple spam filters are no more effective in this spam era due to the smarter spammers. Some of the categorized filters with their flaws are listed below.

1. **Blacklists:** This model was slow and inefficient. Also, this was having high false positive hence punishes the innocents.

2. **Rule-Based:** This model was slow and labor intensive. Also, it was having a less classification accuracy; it fails in case of smarter spammers.

3. **Content Inspection:** It consumes much memory, relies on end users reporting and has security and privacy restrictions.

4. **Grey-Listing:** Easy for breaking the barriers for smarter spammers. Unacceptable delay.

5. **Decoys and Honeypots:** This relies on humans to write rules, which is a slow process. Problem in differentiating similar messages.

6. **Collaborating Checksum:** Vulnerable sometimes for complex spam.

These show the anti-spam techniques which get failed due to their given limitations. Now, to overcome the limitations, much more effective and accurate filters have been made and also in process to make more efficient spam filter. In day to day life as the numbers of effective filters are in process, the spammers have become smarter as they also are able to search the method to crack the spam filter. The problem is increasing day by day at the rate of spam mails and the harm causes by the spam. The aim is to construct a more efficient spam filter having high accuracy in filtering spam and also having low complexity. A hybrid model of J48 decision tree (cho, 2011) and Particle Swarm Optimization (Talukder, 2010) as model 1 and J48 decision tree and Adaptive Particle Swarm Optimization (Zhan, 2009) as model 2 is being proposed to improve the classification accuracy by optimizing the data set.

Rest of this chapter is organized as follows. Section II presents literature survey on various existing methods for classification. Section III presents Overview of classifiers and optimizers. Section IV presents proposed model for improvement in classifier. Section V elaborates the well-known datasets used in machine learning process given by different repository. Section VI concludes the paper and elaborates some future works.

LITERATURE SURVEY

The previous year shows the interest and applications for spam filtering in increasing trends. Several techniques have been tried to deal with this unwanted tasks. We recall some of them in this section. Cohen has proposed RIPPER rule learning algorithms for the aim to classify incoming emails into pre-define categories by using Keyboard-spotting rules which are automatically learned from corpus. Cohen showed that RIPPER algorithm can achieve comparable performance to a traditional TF-IDF weighting method on a multi-class categorization tasks with greater comprehensibility. Spam does not need an introduction. Anyone with an e-mail account knows the frustration of receiving unwanted offer, financial proposition that does not exist. Wallace, a professional e-mail marketer from New Hampshire who also likes to be called Stamford, used ill-gotten password to surreptitiously log into user account for the purpose of sending advertisements to combat it. The spam will cost firms an estimated $130 billion worldwide in 2009 in loss of productivity and technical costs according to Ferris research. The first unsolicited messages came over the wires as early as 1864, when telegraph line was used to send dubious investment offer. In late 1994, use-net, a newsgroup precursor to the internet was inundated by an advertisement for the immigration law services. Now, spam comprises the vast majority of e-mail messages sent- 78 percent of the 210 billion of e-mails sent each day and 93 billion of these manage to get past the technical defenses like spam filter and blacklists. The growth of sites like MySpace and Facebook has opened up a whole new sub-industry for spammers, who trick users into surrendering their password and then uses their account to send advertisement everywhere. Spam filtering tool makers Akismet estimates that 93 percent of comments on all blogs are spam; their software has caught more than 13 billion so far. With so many different technologies available for spamming, the best solution might be a legal one. In 2003, the U.S. passed the CAN-SPAM act, which gives the federal trade commission some regulatory power to curb spammers. CAN-SPAM regulation required that commercial messages provide a means for recipients to opt out, prevent the modification of e-mail header to hide the identity of the sender and stop the use of e-mail addresses harvested from the internet without the permission. Still, there is a very clear loop hole; nowhere in the CAN-SPAM regulations does it say that spammers need your permission to send you an e-mail. Now, our survey gives a brief view of spam mail filtering tasks and techniques which provides a systematic study of its previous and present work. This literature survey has not covered all the past and present work performed with the existing algorithm but it tries to cover some of the related work from algorithm of data mining as example of spam filtering.

Bayesian Algorithm based Adaptive Spam Filtering

This subsection has covered the Bayes theorem approach. The paper (Firte, 2010) includes a two-step filtering method as shown in figure 1 (Islam, 2010).

In (JH, 2006), the classification stage is termed as the testing stage. In this 2 stage process, the first one is the dynamic training (due to the frequent and regular training and processing of words from the initial stage it is called dynamic) provided to the emails where the word probability (using Bayes theorem) is calculated and the second one is to classify emails as ham/spam. Now, the paper (Gulys, 2006)

Figure 1. Step spam filter

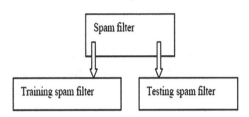

shows the weakness of the simple Bayesian algorithm that model discussed above is the lack in its self-learning, self-adaptability unlike the decision trees.

A Comparative Analysis of Different Data Mining Approaches for Spam Mail Filtering

Yanhui Guo Proposed the Origin-based filtering method in which the filter is used before a message is received by the receiver. The two well-known Origin based spam filtering method are given below.

- Blacklists: The Blacklists are used to decline IP or TCP connections from spam originators, but also to decline mail if the domain name specified at the MAIL EROM Command. Blacklists Filter extracts the load of bulk E-mail automatically by using public blacklists. Third-party blacklists service providers check the IP.
- White-Lists: White Lists are used to arrange the users email addresses legally. Emails addresses are saved within the address book which are considered to be a "White-listed". White lists can be used in blocking those unwanted messages and allowing only the legally proved emails, but it is not to be considered always as a correct email.

Traffic Based Filtering

Liu et al. described about the Traffic-based spam filtering method to check and control the email traffic by watching the flows of several host's traffic in a network and its aim is to save it from the large volume of spam attack. It uses the record files of the SMTP server to represent anomalies in the standard traffic flow.

Content Based Filtering

Content based spam filter depends on the assumption and it goes through the text in order to detect the distinctive feature that is used for purpose of describing a message. This text is used to separate the header, subject and body of an email message using feature matching or statistical method to determine whether it is spam/ legal email.

Bayesian analysis

Bayesian Analysis is a new attempt of spam e-mail filtering. In Bayesian classifier, a mathematical formula is used to analyze the content of a message and learning from the user for valid and spam message identification. A Bayesian spam filter concentrates on two things to work more effectively.

1. How good the Bayesian classifier formula has been implemented?
2. How good a sample of data it has to work?

The Bayes theorem is used to calculate the probability of words being a spam. It is estimated to decide the spam probability of mail as a whole.

As per Bayes theorem: The conditional probability of item X belongs to class C i.e. P (C | X) for the known attribute description of X

$$P (C | X) = P (C) * P (X | C) / P(X)$$

Decision Tree

Decision Tree is the most popular classification technique for spam filtering. The aim is to train the model which provides a target output for several given inputs. Now, the question is this. Since, a simple decision tree is capable enough for classification then why we use additional functions to it? The answer might be that in simple decision tree, the leaf nodes provide a class label which is better for the given data set but it becomes complex for large data sets. Now, when we add the extra functions to the child nodes, it gives a function as its leaf node such that we can adjust result according to the data sets availability. Next is to introduce 3 decision trees as naive bayes classifier, C 4.5 / J48 decision tree and Logistic Model Tree for the purpose of spam filtering discussed in (Attri, 2012). As per figure 2, it provides an experimental result of the comparative study of the 3 decision trees as logistic model, C4.5/ J48 and Naive Bayes decision tree.

Naive Bayes Tree Classifier

This classification approach (Gulys, 2006) combines the advantages of Naive Bayes classifier with Decision Tree. In this, at each node of decision tree, the Bayes rule is applied. Naïve Bayes classifier is suitable when database is of arbitrary size and attributes need not to be necessarily independent.

C4.5 Decision Tree

C4.5 is a well-known classification technique (Attri, 2012). This algorithm chooses some attributes at every node to further classify samples into subsets where each leaf denotes a class or a decision. If all the samples belong to the same class then the tree only gives a leaf node of a single class. J48 is an open source implementation of C4.5. At each node, the information gain is calculated and on the basis of more informative attribute, the sample on a node further splits into its subsets.

Figure 2. Comparative study of the 3 decision trees

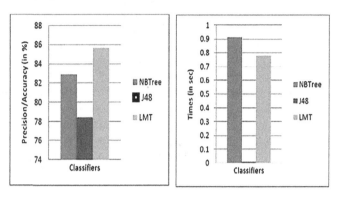

Spam features are used at the time of feature selection when the more informative words having high information gain is selected for the purpose of node splitting.

Logistic Model Tree Induction

This model in (Attri, 2012) has the advantages of decision tree with Logistic Regression as regression is about making predictions and is a model of correlation between two or more variables. Now, logistic regression, which deals with the binary classification, maps a point x in d-dimensional feature space (features can be continuous or categorical) to a value in range of 0 to 1. This logistic regression is performed to the tree at each of its leaves. The tree generated by logistic regression model is more accurate and smaller but it takes more time. Logistic regression and decision tree are special case of logistic model tree. As logistic regression is the linear regression function with categorical data sets, the logistic tree model gives in general the 90% of accuracy level to classify the mails.

As per figure 2, it provides an experimental result of the comparative study of the 3 decision trees as logistic model, C4.5/ J48 and Naive Bayes decision tree. Now, moving towards the experimental results, LMT provides the accuracy of 86% and the false positive rate is much more lower than other. NB requires highest training time. Here, the authors have used the cross validation to predict the accuracy. J48 is considered to be the best whenever training time is being considered as a critical parameter because it takes minimum training time than other Decision Tree algorithms discussed here. LMT has higher accuracy but it takes more working time. The same happens with NB tree. Now, in case of C4.5/J48, it takes less time to perform but fails in accuracy level in comparison to LMT.

SPAM MAIL FILTERING PROCEDURE

The following steps are generally followed in data mining based spam filter.

1. Collection of emails
2. Pre-processing
3. Feature selection
4. Machine learning application

Figure 3. Spam filtering process

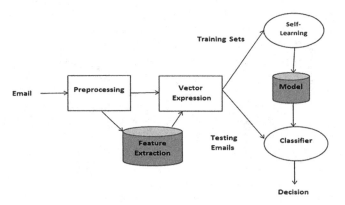

5.   Rule extraction
6.   Classification

The pre-processing is performed after the collection of all network emails. Feature selection is important in text categorization of different text document which has large no. of terms. It removes a smaller amount of informative and noisy terms which minimizes the computational rate and improves the classification performance. There is several popular feature selection Methods. Some of them are given below.

- Document Frequency (DF): DF is a set of documents having collection of features. We compute the document frequency for each specialized terms in a training examples and terms are rejected from the feature space whose document frequency was less than some predetermined threshold. DF threshold is applicable for unsupervised data. Koller et al. presented a theoretically justified model which evolves measuring entropy of the given set of attributes for the aim of optimal feature selection. It characterizes the impurity of collection.
- Term Frequency Variance (TFV): TFV method chooses informative terms having high variance. The terms presented in the training examples are included into the informative measures and it can be retained or removed based on the legal class or spam class.
- Information Gain (IG): IG is the Statistical Filtering Technique to find the purity of the text to use the training sample. It measures the distance between two probability of distributions class, spam class, and legal email class.

Lastly, the machine learning techniques are used to provide training and testing to the mails whether to decide the decision as ham/spam. Table 1 represents an email classification confusion matrix.

Table 1. Confusion matrix in email classification

		Actual	
		Legitimate	**Spam**
Predicted by the Classifier	Legitimate	A	B
	Spam	C	D

OVERVIEW OF CLASSIFIERS AND OPTIMIZERS

Decision Tree as J48: Why Decision Tree? Why J48?

The advantage of using decision tree is that it breaks down the complex structure into simpler rules. C4.5/J48:J48, is an open source Java implementation of the C4.5 decision tree algorithm. C4.5 is the successor to ID3. It avoids the limitation of handling only categorical attributes of the ID3 algorithm and works better with both categorical and discrete variables. It has the ability to generate the rule sets as by making the 'if-then' rule for the tree model generated by ID3. If the accuracy of the rule improves without any of its rule then by removing a rules precondition pruning is done. The advantages of J48 decision tree are listed below.

1. The train model is easy to understand and interpret.
2. It has ability of handling both continuous and discrete attributes.
3. Ability to handle training data with missing attribute values as it marks the missing values and these values are simply not used in gain and entropy calculations.
4. Generates if-then rules sets.
5. It is possible to validate a train model using statistical tests. Tree pruning can be done easily.
6. Time taken by it to create decision tree is minimum.

BASIC IDEA OF ID3/C4.5 ALGORITHM

Entropy

Entropy measures the impurity (uncertainty) of an arbitrary collection of examples. For a collection S, entropy is given as given below.

$$E(S) = \sum_{i=1}^{N} -pi \log 2 (pi)$$

where, S is the collection of instances, E(S) is the entropy of S. N is the number of classes in the entire dataset and pi is the probability that a particular instance belongs to class i. In most of the cases, the datasets have only two classes that are ham and spam. But, there arises some situation, where it has three classes in which second class is further divided into spam and phishing. By the use of entropy, we can test the effect of each feature to reduce this entropy. The entropy is measured by the use of information gain metric.

For a collection S having positive and negative examples

$$Entropy(S) = -p_+ \log_2 p_+ - p_- \log_2 p_-$$

where, p_+ is the proportion of positive examples and p_- is the proportion of negative examples. In general, Entropy(S) = 0 if all the members of S belong to the same class. Entropy(S) = 1 (maximum) when all members are split equally.

Information Gain

Information Gain (IG) measures the expected reduction in entropy. The higher the IG, more is the expected reduction in entropy. The information gain of attribute A over the dataset S is given by the following Equation.

$$G(S,A) = E(S) - \sum_{v \in values(A)} \frac{Sv}{S} E(Sv)$$

PROPOSED ALGORITHM

A hybrid model is proposed which is composed of PSO based approach and J48 decision tree algorithm. The PSO based approach in proposed Algorithm 1 has been used to optimize the dataset in first phase. Then, in the next phase, J48 algorithm has been used to construct the classification model using the optimized dataset obtained from the first phase. The model consists of 2 algorithms; proposed PSO based algorithm (Algorithm 1) and J48 decision tree algorithm.

Proposed algorithm is consisting of 2 phases.

Phase 1: Where proposed Algorithm 1 is being used.
Phase 2: Where decision tree construction / classification model construction is being done. Here, the standard J48 decision tree algorithm has been used for classification.

```
Algorithm 1: Proposed Algorithm
D is the input dataset
1: for each instance do          i = 1 to ins
2:   Position xᵗ ← 0
3:        velocity vᵗ ← 0
4: end for
5: Set c1 = c2 = 0, ω = 0.729, rand1 = 0.4 and rand2 = 0.6
6: for each iteration t=1 to total number of iterations do
```

```
7:          Let no of instances for dataset D, |D| = ins
8:          No of features in D=n
9:      for each feature f_j do          j=1 to n
10:             Calculate Information Gain of f_j and store it in set IG.
11:        end for
12:        for each instance i=1 to ins do
13:        sub_i = 0
14:        end for
15:        for each instance do          where i=1 to ins
16:        for each feature f_j do          where j=1 to n
17:        Calculate subset info of f_j[i]          where f_j[i] is
Value of feature j for instance i
18:        SI_j^i ← subset info of f_j[i] /IG_j          IG_j is gain of feature j
20:        sub_i = sub_i  + SIji
20:        end for
21:        fit_i = sub_i          fit_i is fitness of instance i calculated
22:        Fitness_t ← fit_i          Insert fit_i into set Fitness_t
23         If fit > x^t_I then
24:        update x_i^t ← fit_i
25:        else
26:        x^t will remain same.
27:        end if
28:        end for
29:        for Each instance i =1 to ins do
30:        pbest^t ← max(i Fitness_1[i], Fitness_2[i].....Fitness_t[i] [i])
where
31:        end for
Fitness_j[i] is the fitness of instance i in J^th iteration
32:        Set gbest_t = instance_i having fit_i = max(Fitness_t)
33:        D← D-gbest_t
34:        Remove instance_i from dataset D, instance_i = gbest_t
35:        for each instance i do
36:        Update the velocity v_i^{t+1}, position x_i^{t+1} for next iteration t+1
t=1
37:        v_i^{t+1} = w * v_i^t + c_1 * rand_1 *  (pbest_i^t - x_i^t) + c_2 *  rand_2 * (gbest^t -
x_i^t)
38:        x_i^{t+1} = x_i^t + v_i^{t+1}
39:        end for
40: end for
41: Exit
```

Proposed Fitness Function for Algorithm 1

Using the concept of Information Gain, a fitness function being a function of Information Gain is used to calculate the fitness of each record. Here, the higher the fitness function value of a record, the higher will be the fitness of that record and the best will be the instance among the records. Now, the proposed fitness function f for instance i is expressed as given below.

$$f = \sum_{A=1}^{m} \frac{SI_A^i}{gain_A}$$

where, SI_A^i is the subset of 'infoA(D)' or weight of the instance i corresponding to Ath attribute/variable.

$gain_A$ is the information gain of feature A. Again the expression for calculating the subset info SI_A^i is given below. Let, instance i has value k for attribute A. Then,

$$Info(D) = \sum_{i=1}^{m} - p_i \left(\log_2 p_i \right) \tag{1}$$

$$Info_A(D) = \sum_{j=1}^{v} \frac{|D_j|}{|D|} \times Info(D_j) \tag{2}$$

$$gain_A = Info(D) - Info_A(D) \tag{3}$$

where, Info(D) is termed as the entropy of D. Pi is the probability of the arbitrary tuple in D belonging to class Ci. M is the number of classes. Here, m=2 (Spam and Ham class). The term $|D_j|$ is the weight of the jth partition. InfoA(D) is required information (expected) to classify a tuple from D based on the partitioning by attribute A. V is number of bins in categorical data. Here v=10. $Gain_A$ is the information gain of feature A.

Simulation of the Proposed Algorithm 1 in Model 1 with Example Dataset

The Algorithm 1 (based on PSO) is being illustrated with an example (subset of) spam base dataset (numeric) retrieved from UCI Repository having 4601 instances and 58 attributes given in figure 4.

Here, a subset of whole dataset including feature selection in preprocessing (to reduce number of attributes) is used to have ease in manual calculations. The manual calculation is performed here on the subset of dataset which contains 40 instances and 7 attributes.

Figure 4. Flow chart for proposed model

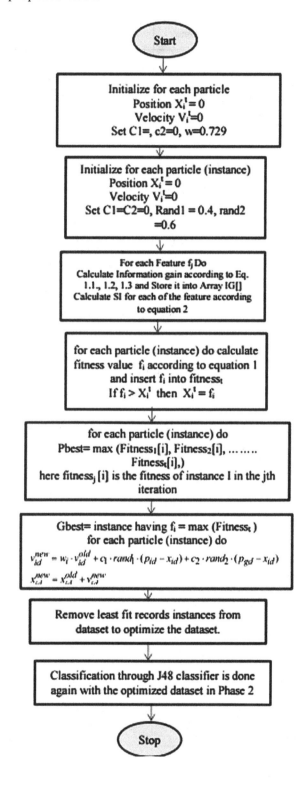

Table 2. Categorizing Dataset into intervals part 1

Attribute \ Context	'Our'	'Your'	'Money'	'!'	'$'	'#'
Min	0.0	0.0	0.0	0.0	0.0	0.0
Max	2.04	3.22	0.93	3.588	0.429	1.41
Size of Each Interval	(0.0+2.04)/10 =0.204	(0.0+3.22)/10 =0.322	(0.0+0.93)/10 =0.093	(0.0+3.588)/10 =0.3588	(0.0+0.429)/10 =0.0429	(0.0+1.41)/10 =0.141

$$X\_Word\_Frequency\_Numeric = \frac{Total\ Number\ of\ X\_Words\ in\ given\ instance}{Total\ Number\ of\ Words\ in\ given\ instance} \times 100$$

The finding of equal interval and categorizing of different dataset into intervals is given in table 2 and Table 3 respectively. The original spam base taining dataset and test datasest are given in following figure 5 and figure 6.

The fitness function and PSO parameters are being updated manually. Also, the classification accuracy is checked over WEKA. The calculations made on a subset of spam base dataset having 40 records with 7 variables (included class variable) to implement the optimization using PSO are given below.

Phase 1: Apply PSO over the dataset given in above figure to optimize it.

Initialize v=0,x=0 for all 40 records.
Calculate the fitness of each instance by the proposed fitness function.
As by using equation 1.1, 1.2 and 1.3 the GainA(D) is calculated for each variable.
p_i is the probability of arbitrary tuple in D belongs to class C_i

$$p_1 = \frac{Total\ Number\ of\ instances\ belongs\ to\ class\ 1\left(Spam\right)}{Total\ Number\ of\ instances}$$

$$p_0 = \frac{Total\ Number\ of\ instances\ belongs\ to\ class\ 0\left(Ham\right)}{Total\ Number\ of\ instances}$$

$p_1 = 18/40 = 0.45$

$p_2 = 22/40 = 0.55$

$$Info\left(D\right) = \sum_{i=1}^{m} - p_i\left(\log_2 p_i\right)$$

Info (D) = $- 0.45 \log_2 (0.45) - 0.55 \log_2 (0.55) = 0.99247$

Table 3. Categorizing Dataset into intervals part 2

S.N.	'Our'		'Your'		'Money'		'!'		'$'		'#'	
	Label	Count $\mid D_j \mid$	Label	Count $\mid D_j \mid$	Label	Count $\mid D_j \mid$	Label	Count $\mid D_j \mid$	Label	Count $\mid D_j \mid$	Label	Count $\mid D_j \mid$
1.	-∞ to 0.204	27	-∞ to 0.322	22	-∞ to 0.093	31	-∞ to 0.3588	26	-∞ to 0.0429	27	-∞ to 0.141	39
2.	0.204 to 0.408	2	0.322 to 0.644	3	0.093 to	2	0.3588 to	8	0.0429 to	1	0.141 to	0
3.	0.408 to 0612	2	0.644 to 0.966	2	0.186 to	0	0.7176 to	2	0.0858 to	2	0.282 to	0
4.	0.612 to 0.816	2	0.966 to 1.288	3	0.279 to	0	1.0764 to	2	0.1287 to	4	0.423 to	0
5.	0.816 to 1.02	2	1.288 to 1.61	2	0.372 to	3	1.4352 to	0	0.1716 to	3	0.564 to	0
6.	1.02 to 1.224	1	1.61 to 1.932	4	0.465 to	1	1.794 to	0	0.2145 to	2	0.705 to	0
7.	1.224 to 1.428	1	1.932 to 2.254	0	0.558 to	0	2.1528 to	1	0.2574 to	0	0.846 to	0
8.	1.428 to 1.632	1	2.254 to 2.576	1	0.651 to	1	2.5116 to	0	0.3003 to	0	0.987 to	0
9.	1.632 to 1.836	0	2.576 to 2.898	1	0.744 to	1	2.8704 to	0	0.3432 to	0	1.128 to	0
10.	1.836 to ∞	2	2.898 to 3.22	2	0.837 to 0.93	1	3.2292 to 3.588	1	0.3861 to 0.429	1	1.269 to 1.41	1

** |D$_j$| is weight of jth partition. Data Is discretize in to 10 partition (bins).

$$Info_A\left(D\right) = \sum_{j=1}^{v} \frac{\left| D_j \right|}{\left| D \right|} \times Info\left(D_j\right)$$

Here v=10 as the dataset is discretized using 10 bins to change format from numeric to categorical data.

$Info_{word\_freq\_our}(D)$

$$= \frac{\left| D_1 \right|}{\left| D \right|} \times Info\left(D_j\right) + \frac{\left| D_2 \right|}{\left| D \right|} \times Info\left(D_j\right) + \ldots\ldots\ldots + \frac{\left| D_{10} \right|}{\left| D \right|} \times Info\left(D_j\right)$$

=27/40[-(18/27)log(18/27)-(9/27)log(9/27)] + 2/40[-(0/2)log(0/2)- (2/2)log(2/2)]

Figure 5. Original Spam-base Dataset

No.	word_freq_our Numeric	word_freq_your Numeric	word_freq_money Numeric	char_freq_! Numeric	char_freq_$ Numeric	char_freq_# Numeric	class Nominal
1	0.93	1.86	0.93	2.306	0.164	0.0	1
2	0.68	1.13	0.45	1.103	0.133	0.033	1
3	0.54	2.44	0.54	0.329	0.141	1.41	1
4	0.12	2.92	0.38	0.661	0.088	0.0	1
5	0.0	0.0	0.0	0.207	0.207	0.0	1
6	0.0	0.64	0.0	1.16	0.116	0.0	1
7	0.0	0.0	0.0	0.207	0.207	0.0	1
8	0.0	0.0	0.0	3.588	0.0	0.0	1
9	1.03	1.55	0.0	0.6	0.429	0.0	1
10	0.0	0.59	0.0	0.0	0.049	0.0	1
11	0.0	1.36	0.68	0.238	0.238	0.0	1
12	0.8	0.7	0.1	0.488	0.157	0.015	1
13	0.33	1.0	0.0	0.057	0.23	0.0	1
14	0.0	0.69	0.0	0.0	0.0	0.038	1
15	0.0	2.76	0.79	0.64	0.192	0.0	1
16	0.38	1.15	0.38	0.51	0.0	0.0	1
17	0.53	3.22	0.0	0.082	0.0	0.0	1
18	0.0	1.69	0.1	0.887	0.032	0.049	1
19	0.0	0.0	0.0	0.022	0.022	0.022	0
20	0.0	1.7	0.0	0.149	0.0	0.0	0
21	0.0	0.0	0.0	0.0	0.0	0.0	0
22	0.0	0.0	0.0	0.262	0.0	0.0	0
23	0.0	0.0	0.0	0.0	0.0	0.011	0
24	2.04	0.0	0.0	0.0	0.0	0.0	0
25	0.0	0.0	0.0	0.0	0.0	0.136	0
26	0.0	0.0	0.0	0.0	0.0	0.0	0
27	0.0	0.0	0.0	0.393	0.0	0.0	0
28	0.0	0.0	0.0	0.729	0.0	0.0	0
29	0.0	0.0	0.0	0.149	0.0	0.0	0
30	0.9	1.8	0.0	0.0	0.0	0.0	0
31	0.0	0.0	0.0	0.0	0.0	0.0	0
32	0.0	0.0	0.0	0.0	0.032	0.0	0
33	1.85	0.0	0.0	0.0	0.0	0.0	0
34	0.0	0.0	0.0	0.0	0.0	0.0	0
35	0.0	0.0	0.0	0.546	0.0	0.0	0
36	0.0	0.0	0.0	0.115	0.0	0.0	0
37	1.51	0.0	0.0	0.0	0.0	0.0	0
38	0.0	0.0	0.0	0.375	0.0	0.0	0
39	1.27	0.63	0.0	0.0	0.0	0.0	0
40	0.0	0.0	0.0	0.282	0.0	0.0	0

Relation: spambase-weka.filters.unsupervised.attribute.Remove-R1-4,6-20,22-23,25-51,55-57

Figure 6. Test set in original
** |D$_j$| is weight of jth partition. Data is discretized into 10 partition (bins).

No.	word_freq_our Numeric	word_freq_your Numeric	word_freq_money Numeric	char_freq_! Numeric	char_freq_$ Numeric	char_freq_# Numeric	class Nominal
41	1.27	1.27	0.42	0.572	0.063	0.0	1
42	0.94	2.83	0.0	0.428	0.0	0.0	1
43	0.0	2.11	0.0	1.975	0.37	0.0	1
44	1.11	0.92	0.0	0.455	0.0	0.0	1
45	1.59	1.91	0.63	0.055	0.496	0.0	1
46	0.0	0.0	0.0	0.729	0.0	0.0	1
47	0.76	1.57	0.0	0.25	0.046	0.059	1
48	2.94	0.0	0.0	0.809	0.0	0.0	1
49	1.16	1.75	0.0	0.667	0.0	0.0	1
50	0.0	0.0	0.0	0.392	0.196	0.0	1
51	0.0	0.0	0.0	1.458	0.0	0.0	0
52	0.08	0.08	0.0	0.0	0.0	0.007	0
53	0.0	0.19	0.0	0.0	0.026	0.0	0
54	0.09	0.0	0.09	0.0	0.1	0.0	0
55	0.05	0.15	0.0	0.0	0.015	0.0	0
56	0.24	0.0	0.0	0.0	0.163	0.0	0
57	0.59	0.59	0.0	0.078	0.0	0.235	0
58	0.0	0.46	0.0	0.0	0.0	0.0	0
59	0.45	1.35	0.0	0.072	0.072	0.036	0
60	1.15	2.31	0.0	0.076	0.076	0.025	0

Relation: spambase-weka.filters.unsupervised.attribute.Remove-R1-4,6-20,22-23,25-51,55-57

$+ 2/40[-(0/2)\log(0/2)-(2/2)\log(2/2)] + 2/40[-(0/2)\log(0/2) - (2/2)\log(2/2)]$

$+2/40[-(1/2)\log(1/2)-(1/2)\log(1/2)] + 1/40[-(0/1)\log(0/1) -(1/1)\log(1/1)]$

$+ 1/40[-(1/1)\log(1/1)-(0/1)\log(0/1)] +1/40[- (1/1)\log(1/1) -(0/1)\log(0/1)]$

$+ 0/40(-0/0\log0/0 - 0/0\log0/0) + 2/40[-(2/2)\log(2/2) -(0/2)\log(0/2)]$

$= 0.91829 + 0 + 0 + 0 + 0.025 + 0 + 0 + 0 + 0 + 0 = 0.94329$

$$gain_{word\_freq\_our} = Info\left(D\right) - Info_{word\_freq\_our}\left(D\right)$$

$gain_{word\_freq\_our} = 0.99247 - 0.94329 = 0.04918$

$Info_{word\_freq\_your}(D) = 0.4348$

Figure 7. Original training dataset after discretization
1: Blue - Ham
0: Red - Spam

Relation: spambase-weka.filters.unsupervised.attribute.Remove-R1-4,6-20,22-23,25-51,55-57-weka.filters.unsupervis...

No.	word_freq_our Nominal	word_freq_your Nominal	word_freq_money Nominal	char_freq_! Nominal	char_freq_$ Nominal	char_freq_# Nominal	class Nominal
1	'(0.816-1.02]'	'(1.61-1.932]'	'(0.837-inf)'	'(2.1528-2...	'(0.1287-0....	'(-inf-0.141]'	1
2	'(0.612-0.816]'	'(0.966-1.288]'	'(0.372-0.465]'	'(1.0764-1...	'(0.1287-0...	'(-inf-0.141]'	1
3	'(0.408-0.612]'	'(2.254-2.576]'	'(0.465-0.558]'	'(-inf-0.35...	'(0.1287-0...	'(1.269-inf)'	1
4	'(-inf-0.204]'	'(2.898-inf)'	'(0.372-0.465]'	'(0.3588-0...	'(0.0858-0...	'(-inf-0.141]'	1
5	'(-inf-0.204]'	'(-inf-0.322]'	'(-inf-0.093]'	'(-inf-0.35...	'(0.1716-0....	'(-inf-0.141]'	1
6	'(-inf-0.204]'	'(0.322-0.644]'	'(-inf-0.093]'	'(1.0764-1...	'(0.0858-0...	'(-inf-0.141]'	1
7	'(-inf-0.204]'	'(-inf-0.322]'	'(-inf-0.093]'	'(-inf-0.35...	'(0.1716-0....	'(-inf-0.141]'	1
8	'(-inf-0.204]'	'(-inf-0.322]'	'(-inf-0.093]'	'(3.2292-inf)'	'(-inf-0.0429]'	'(-inf-0.141]'	1
9	'(1.02-1.224]'	'(1.288-1.61]'	'(-inf-0.093]'	'(0.3588-0...	'(0.3861-inf)'	'(-inf-0.141]'	1
10	'(-inf-0.204]'	'(0.322-0.644]'	'(-inf-0.093]'	'(-inf-0.35...	'(0.0429-0....	'(-inf-0.141]'	1
11	'(-inf-0.204]'	'(1.288-1.61]'	'(0.651-0.744]'	'(-inf-0.35...	'(0.2145-0....	'(-inf-0.141]'	1
12	'(0.612-0.816]'	'(0.644-0.966]'	'(0.093-0.186]'	'(0.3588-0...	'(0.1287-0...	'(-inf-0.141]'	1
13	'(0.204-0.408]'	'(0.966-1.288]'	'(-inf-0.093]'	'(-inf-0.35...	'(0.2145-0....	'(-inf-0.141]'	1
14	'(-inf-0.204]'	'(0.644-0.966]'	'(-inf-0.093]'	'(-inf-0.35...	'(-inf-0.0429]'	'(-inf-0.141]'	1
15	'(-inf-0.204]'	'(2.576-2.898]'	'(0.744-0.837]'	'(0.3588-0...	'(0.1716-0....	'(-inf-0.141]'	1
16	'(0.204-0.408]'	'(0.966-1.288]'	'(0.372-0.465]'	'(0.3588-0...	'(-inf-0.0429]'	'(-inf-0.141]'	1
17	'(0.408-0.612]'	'(2.898-inf)'	'(-inf-0.093]'	'(-inf-0.35...	'(-inf-0.0429]'	'(-inf-0.141]'	1
18	'(-inf-0.204]'	'(1.61-1.932]'	'(0.093-0.186]'	'(0.7176-1...	'(-inf-0.0429]'	'(-inf-0.141]'	1
19	'(-inf-0.204]'	'(-inf-0.322]'	'(-inf-0.093]'	'(-inf-0.35...	'(-inf-0.0429]'	'(-inf-0.141]'	0
20	'(-inf-0.204]'	'(1.61-1.932]'	'(-inf-0.093]'	'(-inf-0.35...	'(-inf-0.0429]'	'(-inf-0.141]'	0
21	'(-inf-0.204]'	'(-inf-0.322]'	'(-inf-0.093]'	'(-inf-0.35...	'(-inf-0.0429]'	'(-inf-0.141]'	0
22	'(-inf-0.204]'	'(-inf-0.322]'	'(-inf-0.093]'	'(-inf-0.35...	'(-inf-0.0429]'	'(-inf-0.141]'	0
23	'(-inf-0.204]'	'(-inf-0.322]'	'(-inf-0.093]'	'(-inf-0.35...	'(-inf-0.0429]'	'(-inf-0.141]'	0
24	'(1.836-inf)'	'(-inf-0.322]'	'(-inf-0.093]'	'(-inf-0.35...	'(-inf-0.0429]'	'(-inf-0.141]'	0
25	'(-inf-0.204]'	'(-inf-0.322]'	'(-inf-0.093]'	'(-inf-0.35...	'(-inf-0.0429]'	'(-inf-0.141]'	0
26	'(-inf-0.204]'	'(-inf-0.322]'	'(-inf-0.093]'	'(-inf-0.35...	'(-inf-0.0429]'	'(-inf-0.141]'	0
27	'(-inf-0.204]'	'(-inf-0.322]'	'(-inf-0.093]'	'(0.3588-0...	'(-inf-0.0429]'	'(-inf-0.141]'	0
28	'(-inf-0.204]'	'(-inf-0.322]'	'(-inf-0.093]'	'(0.7176-1...	'(-inf-0.0429]'	'(-inf-0.141]'	0
29	'(-inf-0.204]'	'(-inf-0.322]'	'(-inf-0.093]'	'(-inf-0.35...	'(-inf-0.0429]'	'(-inf-0.141]'	0
30	'(0.816-1.02]'	'(1.61-1.932]'	'(-inf-0.093]'	'(-inf-0.35...	'(-inf-0.0429]'	'(-inf-0.141]'	0
31	'(-inf-0.204]'	'(-inf-0.322]'	'(-inf-0.093]'	'(-inf-0.35...	'(-inf-0.0429]'	'(-inf-0.141]'	0
32	'(-inf-0.204]'	'(-inf-0.322]'	'(-inf-0.093]'	'(-inf-0.35...	'(-inf-0.0429]'	'(-inf-0.141]'	0
33	'(1.836-inf)'	'(-inf-0.322]'	'(-inf-0.093]'	'(-inf-0.35...	'(-inf-0.0429]'	'(-inf-0.141]'	0
34	'(-inf-0.204]'	'(-inf-0.322]'	'(-inf-0.093]'	'(-inf-0.35...	'(-inf-0.0429]'	'(-inf-0.141]'	0
35	'(-inf-0.204]'	'(-inf-0.322]'	'(-inf-0.093]'	'(0.3588-0...	'(-inf-0.0429]'	'(-inf-0.141]'	0
36	'(-inf-0.204]'	'(-inf-0.322]'	'(-inf-0.093]'	'(-inf-0.35...	'(-inf-0.0429]'	'(-inf-0.141]'	0
37	'(1.428-1.632]'	'(-inf-0.322]'	'(-inf-0.093]'	'(-inf-0.35...	'(-inf-0.0429]'	'(-inf-0.141]'	0
38	'(-inf-0.204]'	'(-inf-0.322]'	'(-inf-0.093]'	'(0.3588-0...	'(-inf-0.0429]'	'(-inf-0.141]'	0
39	'(1.224-1.428]'	'(0.322-0.644]'	'(-inf-0.093]'	'(-inf-0.35...	'(-inf-0.0429]'	'(-inf-0.141]'	0
40	'(-inf-0.204]'	'(-inf-0.322]'	'(-inf-0.093]'	'(-inf-0.35...	'(-inf-0.0429]'	'(-inf-0.141]'	0

Figure 8. Visualization of BAR graph for original training dataset after discretization

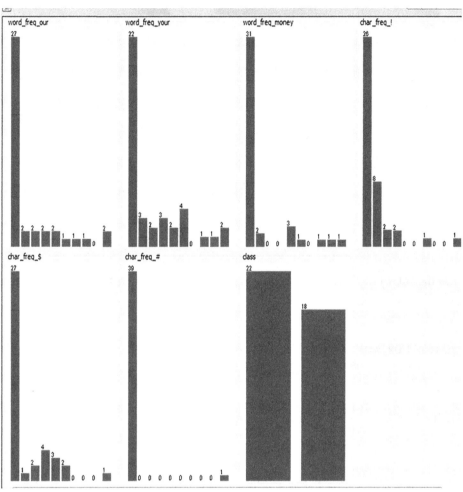

$$\text{gain}_{word\_freq\_your} = 0.99247 - 0.4348 = 0.55767$$

$$\text{Info}_{word\_freq\_money}(D) = 0.7462$$

$$\text{gain}_{word\_freq\_money} = 0.99247 - 0.74623 = 0.24634$$

$$\text{Info}_{word\_freq\_!}(D) = 0.7621$$

$$\text{gain}_{word\_freq\_!} = 0.99247 - 0.7621 = 0.23035$$

$$\text{Info}_{word\_freq\_\$}(D) = 0.76419$$

$$\text{gain}_{word\_freq\_\$} = 0.99247 - 0.76419 = 0.22827$$

$$\text{Info}_{word\_freq\_\#}(D) = 0.9634$$

$$\text{gain}_{word\_freq\_\#} = 0.99247 - 0.9634 = 0.0206$$

PSO

Position $x_i^t = 0$ $w = 0.729$

Velocity $v_i^t = 0$ $rand_1 = 0.4$

$C_1 = C_2 = 0$ $rand_2 = 0.6$

Fitness Function:-

$$f = \sum_{A=1}^{m} \frac{SI_A^i}{gain_A}$$

Where, SI_A^i is the subset of 'info$_A$ (D)' or weight of the instance i corresponding to Ath attribute/variable.

$$SI_{word_{freq_{our}}}\left(0.816 - 1.02\right) = \frac{2}{40}\left(-\frac{1}{2}\log_2\frac{1}{2} - \frac{1}{2}\log_2\frac{1}{2}\right) = 0.025$$

$$SI_{word_{freq_{your}}}\left(1.61 - 1.932\right) = \frac{4}{40}\left(-\frac{2}{4}\log_2\frac{2}{4} - \frac{2}{4}\log_2\frac{2}{4}\right) = 0.05$$

$$SI_{word_{freq_{money}}}\left(0.837 - \infty\right) = \frac{1}{40}\left(-\frac{1}{1}\log_2\frac{1}{1} - \frac{0}{1}\log_2\frac{0}{1}\right) = 0.00$$

$$SI_{word_{freq_!}}\left(2.1528 - 2.5116\right) = \frac{1}{40}\left(-\frac{1}{1}\log_2\frac{1}{1} - \frac{0}{1}\log_2\frac{0}{1}\right) = 0.00$$

$$SI_{word_{freq_\$}}\left(0.1287 - 0.1716\right) = \frac{4}{40}\left(-\frac{4}{4}\log_2\frac{4}{4} - \frac{0}{4}\log_2\frac{0}{4}\right) = 0.00$$

$$SI_{word_{freq_\#}}\left(-\infty - 0.141\right) = \frac{39}{40}\left(-\frac{17}{39}\log_2\frac{17}{39} - \frac{22}{39}\log_2\frac{22}{39}\right) = 0.9634$$

Fitness Function f_1 (=x_1) value for 1st instance (record) of dataset is given as:-

$$f_1 = x_1 =$$

Table 4. Fitness Value of training instances

X1=2.195991	X2=1.000008	X3=2.371318	X4=13.432376	X5=19.571095
X6=16.756535	X7=19.571095	X8=17.874786	X9=4.858023	X10=19.127859
X11=15.975018	X12=1.828681	X13=6.400659	X14=19.679371	X15=14.432382
X16=1.828681	X17=7.075672	X18=14.675091	X19=20.246103	X20=19.858688
x21=20.246103	x22=20.246103	x23=20.246103	x24=7.642405	x25=20.246103
x26=20.246103	X27=18.703468	x28=18.091846	x29=20.246103	X30=8.271662
X31=20.246103	X32=20.246103	X33=7.642405	X34=20.246103	X35=18.703468
X36=20.246103	X37=7.642405	X38=18.703468	X39=7.199172	X40=20.246103

$$\frac{SI_{word_{freq_{our}}}\left(0.816-1.02\right)}{gain_{word\_freq\_our}} + \frac{SI_{word_{freq_{your}}}\left(1.61-1.932\right)}{gain_{word\_freq\_your}} + \frac{SI_{word_{freq_{money}}}\left(0.837-\infty\right)}{gain_{word\_freq\_money}}$$

$$+\frac{SI_{word_{freq_!}}\left(2.1528-2.5116\right)}{gain_{word\_freq\_!}} + \frac{SI_{word_{freq_\$}}\left(0.1287-0.1716\right)}{gain_{word\_freq\_\$}} + \frac{SI_{word_{freq_\#}}\left(-\infty-0.141\right)}{gain_{word\_freq\_\#}}$$

$$X1=\frac{0.025}{0.04918} + \frac{0.05}{0.55767} + \frac{0.00}{0.24634} + \frac{0.00}{0.23035} + \frac{0.00}{0.76419} + \frac{0.9634}{0.9634} = 1.59799$$

Similarly, other fitness values are calculated for rest of the instances. The values after calculations are given in table 4.

Set the fitness value of an instance as its pBest because it is better than previous position. This was zero. Set current fitness value as the new pBest. Choose the particle with the best fitness value of all as gBest. Here, records (19,21,22,25,26,29,31,32,34,36,40) are the best record which are most fit among all records having highest (same) value. For this iteration gbestvalue = *20.246103*

For each instance(record) set

Pbest = current fitness value

Gbest= best (highest) fitness value among all the particle (instance)

Update position and velocity of each particle (instance) by below equation:-

$$Particle\,(instance)\,velocity = v_{id}^{new} = w_i \cdot v_{id}^{old} + c_1 \cdot rand_1 \cdot \left(p_{id} - x_{id}\right) + c_2 \cdot rand_2 \cdot \left(p_{gd} - x_{id}\right)$$

$$Particle\,(instance)\,position = x_{id}^{new} = x_{id}^{old} + v_{id}^{new}$$

Pid=particle best local value till now.

Pgd=particle's global value.

Figure 9. Optimized training spam-base dataset

No.	word_freq_our Numeric	word_freq_your Numeric	word_freq_money Numeric	char_freq_! Numeric	char_freq_$ Numeric	char_freq_# Numeric	class Nominal
1	0.93	1.86	0.93	2.306	0.164	0.0	1
2	0.68	1.13	0.45	1.103	0.133	0.033	1
3	0.54	2.44	0.54	0.329	0.141	1.41	1
4	0.12	2.92	0.38	0.661	0.088	0.0	1
5	0.0	0.0	0.0	0.207	0.207	0.0	1
6	0.0	0.64	0.0	1.16	0.116	0.0	1
7	0.0	0.0	0.0	0.207	0.207	0.0	1
8	0.0	0.0	0.0	3.588	0.0	0.0	1
9	1.03	1.55	0.0	0.6	0.429	0.0	1
10	0.0	1.36	0.68	0.238	0.238	0.0	1
11	0.8	0.7	0.1	0.488	0.157	0.015	1
12	0.33	1.0	0.0	0.057	0.23	0.0	1
13	0.0	0.69	0.0	0.0	0.0	0.038	1
14	0.0	2.76	0.79	0.64	0.192	0.0	1
15	0.38	1.15	0.38	0.51	0.0	0.0	1
16	0.53	3.22	0.0	0.082	0.0	0.0	1
17	0.0	1.69	0.1	0.887	0.032	0.049	1
18	0.0	0.0	0.0	0.022	0.022	0.022	0
19	0.0	1.7	0.0	0.149	0.0	0.0	0
20	0.0	0.0	0.0	0.0	0.0	0.0	0
21	0.0	0.0	0.0	0.0	0.0	0.011	0
22	2.04	0.0	0.0	0.0	0.0	0.0	0
23	0.0	0.0	0.0	0.0	0.0	0.136	0
24	0.0	0.0	0.0	0.0	0.0	0.0	0
25	0.0	0.0	0.0	0.729	0.0	0.0	0
26	0.0	0.0	0.0	0.149	0.0	0.0	0
27	0.0	0.0	0.0	0.0	0.0	0.0	0
28	1.85	0.0	0.0	0.0	0.0	0.0	0
29	0.0	0.0	0.0	0.546	0.0	0.0	0
30	0.0	0.0	0.0	0.115	0.0	0.0	0
31	1.51	0.0	0.0	0.0	0.0	0.0	0
32	0.0	0.0	0.0	0.375	0.0	0.0	0
33	1.27	0.63	0.0	0.0	0.0	0.0	0
34	0.0	0.0	0.0	0.282	0.0	0.0	0

Relation: spambase-weka.filters.unsupervised.attribute.Remove-R1-4,6-20,22-23,25-51,55-57

Particle (instance) position = pbest = fitness value till current = x_{id}^{new}

Here c1 = c2 = 2 w = 0.729, rand1 = 0.4 and rand2 = 0.6

The values of velocity and position of record 1 is calculated below:

$$v_2^{t+1} = 0.729 \times 0 + 2 \times 0.4(2.195991 - 2.195991) + 2 \times 0.6(20.246103 - 2.195991) = 21.6601344$$

$$x_2^{t+1} = 2.195991 + 21.660134 = 23.856125$$

Similarly, the velocity and position for each (rest from removing previous gbest) is calculated. The values after calculation are further checked for the gbest. In this (second) iteration, record x7 is best among all other having a highest value that is gbest value of 28.18633047. At last, after 15 iterations, records 10, 22, 27, 30, 32 and 34 are found to be the least fit records, so remove these instances from dataset to optimize the dataset.

Figure 10. Same test set used after optimization

No.	word_freq_our Numeric	word_freq_your Numeric	word_freq_money Numeric	char_freq_! Numeric	char_freq_$ Numeric	char_freq_# Numeric	class Nominal
35	1.27	1.27	0.42	0.572	0.063	0.0	1
36	0.94	2.83	0.0	0.428	0.0	0.0	1
37	0.0	2.11	0.0	1.975	0.37	0.0	1
38	1.11	0.92	0.0	0.455	0.0	0.0	1
39	1.59	1.91	0.63	0.055	0.496	0.0	1
40	0.0	0.0	0.0	0.729	0.0	0.0	1
41	0.76	1.57	0.0	0.25	0.046	0.059	1
42	2.94	0.0	0.0	0.809	0.0	0.0	1
43	1.16	1.75	0.0	0.667	0.0	0.0	1
44	0.0	0.0	0.0	0.392	0.196	0.0	1
45	0.0	0.0	0.0	1.458	0.0	0.0	0
46	0.08	0.08	0.0	0.0	0.0	0.007	0
47	0.0	0.19	0.0	0.0	0.026	0.0	0
48	0.09	0.0	0.09	0.0	0.1	0.0	0
49	0.05	0.15	0.0	0.0	0.015	0.0	0
50	0.24	0.0	0.0	0.0	0.163	0.0	0
51	0.59	0.59	0.0	0.078	0.0	0.235	0
52	0.0	0.46	0.0	0.0	0.0	0.0	0
53	0.45	1.35	0.0	0.072	0.072	0.036	0
54	1.15	2.31	0.0	0.076	0.076	0.025	0

Figure 11. Classification using original training dataset via standard J48 over WEKA

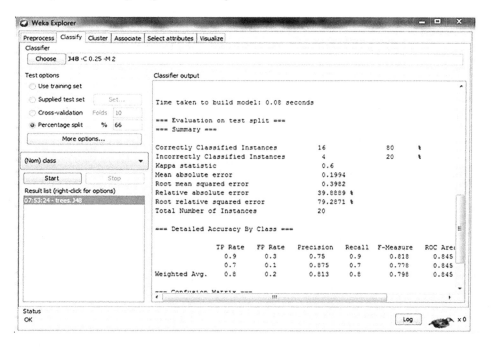

Figure 12. J48 tree structure using original training dataset over WEKA

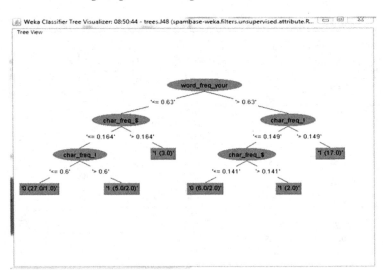

Figure 13. Classification using optimized training dataset via standard J48 over WEKA

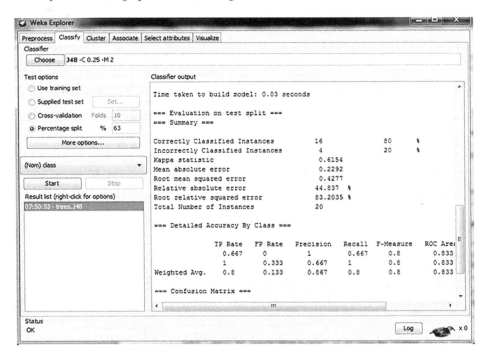

Figure 14. J48 tree structure using optimized training dataset over WEKA

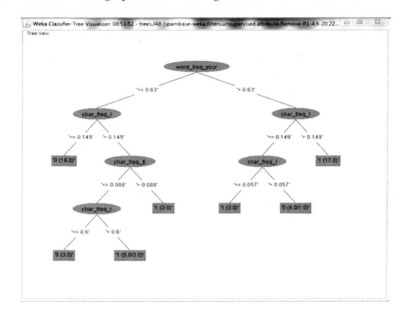

Table 5. Comparison of results between proposed model and standard J48 (without optimization)

Method	Total No of Instances	No of Train Instances	No of Test Instances	Accuracy	Time Taken to Build Model (seconds)
J48 (without optimization of dataset)	60	40 (66%)	20 (34%)	16 80%	0.08
Proposed Model	54	34 (63%)	20 (37%)	16 80%	0.03

The classification using J48 is done through WEKA given in followings figure 11. This will be used to compare the classification accuracy results before optimization and after optimization.

Figure 11 shows the application of simple J48 algorithm to create the decision tree. Also, the figure 12 shows the graphical representation i.e. tree structure of 11. It consists of the 40 records as train set and 20 records as test set among the 60 instances with an accuracy of 80%. Phase 2 Constructs decision tree using J48 from the dataset optimized by PSO. So, after removing the least fit values from dataset i.e. optimizing dataset, the classification accuracy using j48 is given in figure 13

Again, figure 13 shows the application of PSO algorithm towards the same dataset to optimize it. At last, figure 14 shows the creation of decision tree by J48 by using the optimized dataset generated by PSO. Now, this re-creation of decision tree provides a better training time complexity with the optimized dataset as train set and having the same accuracy.

Table 5 shows the classification accuracy of J48 using the example dataset before optimization and after optimization using PSO. Figure 15 and 16 shows the comparative view of CART and J48 decision trees. As from the table 6, it is clear that the J48 decision is better than the CART for the spam-base dataset.

Figure 15. CART classification in weka

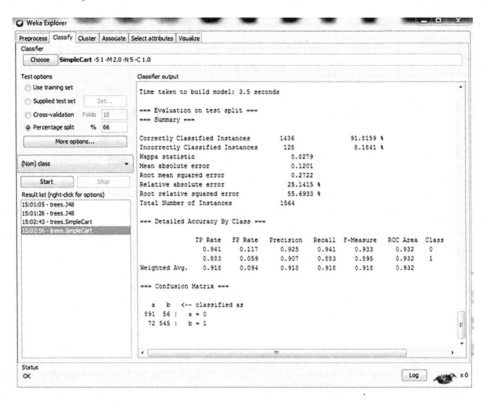

CONCLUSION

This paper discussed the important issues related to spam filtering, the applicable steps for classification, methods and the evaluation measures in the spam filtering. The optimization of the spam base dataset is done through the PSO to reduce the time complexity without compromising to its classification accuracy by removing the outliers from the dataset. The proposed fitness function has been manually validated for the phase of proposed model 1 to optimize the dataset. The idea is to store the best records and removal of outliers as to make the training model which helps in classifying the email with lower complexity and good accuracy. The future work is to implement the different fitness functions in the PSO phase. As this model consists of J48 classifier, the next aim is to replace it by other more enhanced hybrid classifier than J48 to improve accuracy and time taken by it to build model.

Figure 16. J48 classification in weka

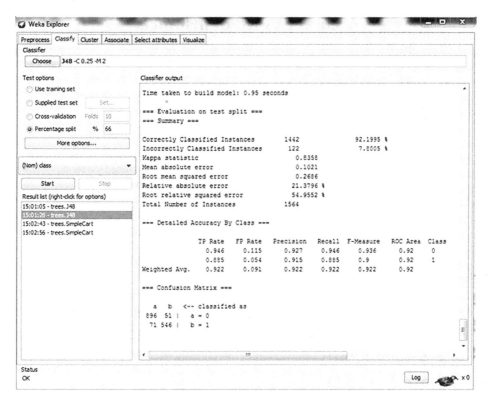

Table 6. Comparison between CART and J48

Decision Tree	Dataset	Accuracy	Time Taken to Build Model
CART	Spambase	91.8159%	3.5 seconds
J48	Spambese	92.1995%	0.95 seconds

Figure 17. Training time comparison graph

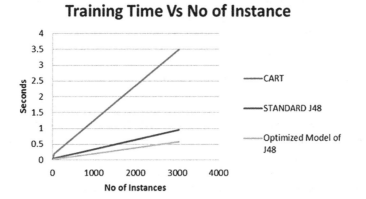

Figure 18. Accuracy comparison graph

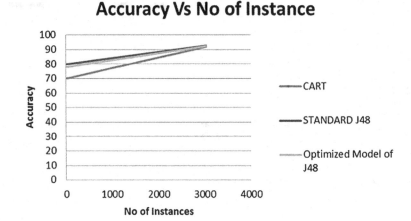

REFERENCES

Attri, U., & Pal, S. (2012). A survey of Performance Evaluation Criteria for Spam E-mail Classifiers. International Journal of IT. *Engineering and Applied Sciences Research*, *1*, 65–68.

Cho, Y. J., Lee, H., & Jun, C. H. (2011). Optimization of Decision Tree for Classification Using a Particle Swarm. *IEMS*, *10*(4), 272–278. doi:10.7232/iems.2011.10.4.272

Clark & Poon. (2003). A Neural Network Based Approach to Automated E-mail Classification. *Proc. of IEEE International Conference on Web Intelligence*, 702-705. 10.1109/WI.2003.1241300

Firte, L., Lemnaru, C., & Potolea, R. (2010). Spam Detection Filter using KNN Algo-rithm and Resampling. *IEEE International on Conference Intelligent Computer Communication and Processing*, 27-33.

Goli, B., & Govindan, G. (2011). Weka A Powerful Free Software for Implementing Bio-Inspired Algorithms. *CSI Communications*, 9–12.

Huang, H., Guo, W., & Zhang, Y. (2008). A Novel Method for Image Spam Filtering. *9th International Conference for Young Computer Scientists*. 10.1109/ICYCS.2008.440

Islam, M. R., & Xiang, Y. (2010). Email Classification Using Data Reduction Method. *5th International ICST Conference on Communications and Networking*, 1-5.

JH, MK, & JP. (2006). Data Mining: Concepts and Techniques (2nd ed.). Morgan Kaufmann Publication.

Ma, W., Tran, D., & Sharma, D. (2009) A Novel Spam Email Detection System Based on Negative Selection. *4th International Conference on Computer Sciences and Convergence Information Technology*, 987-992. 10.1109/ICCIT.2009.58

Razmara, Asadi, Narouei, & Ahmadi. (2012). A Novel Approach Toward Spam Detection Based on Iterative Patterns. *2nd International eConference on Computer and Knowledge Engineering*, 318-323.

Talukder, S. (2010). *Mathematical Modelling and Applications of Particle Swarm Optimization*. Masters Thesis on Mathematical Modelling and Simulation, Thesis no: 2010:8.

Zhan, Z. H., Zhang, J., Li, Y., & Chung, H. S. H. (2009). Adaptive Particle Swarm Opti-mization. *IEEE Transactions on Systems, Man, and Cybernetics. Part B, Cybernetics*, *39*(6), 1362–1380. doi:10.1109/TSMCB.2009.2015956 PMID:19362911

Zhong, S., Huang, H., & Pan, L. (2010). An Effective Spam Filtering Technique Based on Active Feedback and Maximum Entropy. *7th International Conference on Fuzzy Systems and Knowledge Discovery*, *5*, 2437-2440. 10.1109/FSKD.2010.5569301

ADDITIONAL READING

Chakraborty, S., & Mondal, B. (2012). Spam Mail Filtering Technique using Different Decision Tree Classifiers through Data Mining Approach - A Comparative Performance Analysis. *International Journal of Computers and Applications*, *47*(16), 26–31. doi:10.5120/7274-0435

Delany, S. J., Buckley, M., & Greene, D. (2012). SMS spam filtering: Methods and data. *Expert Systems with Applications*, *39*(10), 9899–9908. doi:10.1016/j.eswa.2012.02.053

Saad, O., Darwish, A., & Faraj, R. (2012). A survey of machine learning techniques for Spam filtering. *International Journal of Computer Science and Network Security*, *12*, 66–73.

Wang, Y., Wu, Z., & Wu, R. (2008) Spam Filtering System Based on Rough Set and Bayesian Classifier. *IEEE International Conference on Granular Computing*, 624-627.

Yeh, C. C., & Chiang, S. J. (2008) Revisit Bayesian Approaches For Spam Detection. 9th international conference for young computer scientists, 659-664.

APPENDIX

WEKA

Weka is an open source machine learning library in Java, released under the General Public License and developed by Waikato University, New Zealand. Weka is very versatile and allows users to check and compare the different algorithms easily. This consists of a series of algorithms for machine learning used in data mining and data preprocessing tasks for data exploration (Goli, 2011). It provides easy access to its apps.

The 4 applications of WEKA are:

1. **Explorer:** Environment for exploring data.
2. **Experimenter:** Performs tests by using machine learning experiments which evaluates classification and regression methods.
3. **Knowledge Flow:** It is the drag and drop interface. Also a Java Beans application which allows the same kind of data exploration, processing and visualization as the Explorer.
4. **Simple CLI:** It as a command line interface for executing the Weka commands.

The main panels in Explorer are:

- **Preprocess:** Transforms data through filters
- **Classify:** Provides access to all the classification algorithms. Cluster: Helps to learn the different clustering schemes.
- **Associate:** Helps to learn the different association rules.
- **Select Attributes:** Helps in selecting the relevant attributes of data. Visualize: Provides the plot view of data.

Chapter 16
Term Ordering–Based Query Expansion Technique for Hindi–English CLIR System

Ganesh Chandra
(iD) https://orcid.org/0000-0002-7046-7613
Babasaheb Bhimrao Ambedkar University, Lucknow, India

Sanjay K. Dwivedi
Babasaheb Bhimrao Ambedkar University, Lucknow, India

ABSTRACT

The quality of retrieval documents in CLIR is often poor compared to IR system due to (1) query mismatching, (2) multiple representations of query terms, and (3) un-translated query terms. The inappropriate translation may lead to poor quality of results. Hence, automated query translation is performed using the back-translation approach for improvement of query translation. This chapter mainly focuses on query expansion (Q.E) and proposes an algorithm to address the drift query issue for Hindi-English CLIR. The system uses FIRE datasets and a set of 50 queries of Hindi language for evaluation. The purpose of a term ordering-based algorithm is to resolve the drift query issue in Q.E. The result shows that the relevancy of Hindi-English CLIR is improved by performing Q.E. using a term ordering-based algorithm. The outcome achieved 60.18% accuracy of results where Q.E has been performed using a term ordering based algorithm, whereas the result of Q.E without a term ordering-based algorithm stands at 57.46%.

INTRODUCTION

Information access refers to the process of making information accessible and usable to the user. With the development of social websites, every Web user not only plays a role of Web information consumer but also an information creator. As a result, communication in different languages on the Web becomes critical. Due to globalisation a Web user is more aware of the things like education, research, business,

DOI: 10.4018/978-1-7998-2491-6.ch016

multimedia, medical etc. This increases the searching of documents other than user language (Salton 1973; Varshney and Bajpai 2013; Duque, Araujo and Martinez-Romo 2015; Mala and Lobiyal 2016).

Information on Web (Kern, Mutschke and Mayr 2014) is available in various languages such as English, Hindi, Chinese and Spanish etc. and in different formats (like text, audio, & video). This increases the demand for searching information in cross -lingual and multilingual environment instead of monolingual (Rahimi, Shakery and King 2015). One of the greatest challenges of Cross-Lingual Information Retrieval (CLIR) & Multilingual Information Retrieval (MLIR) is to develop the relationship between the query and document language (Grefenstette 2012; Salton 1973).

CLIR (Gaillard, Bouraoui, de Neef and Boualem 2010; Flores, Barron-Cedenio, Moreno, Rosso 2015; Ujjwal, Rastogi and Siddhartha 2016; Dwivedi and Chandra 2016) provides a convenient way that can solve the problem of language boundaries, where users can submit query in their own language to retrieve the documents of another language (Pigur 1979). In CLIR (Banchs and Costa-Jussa 2013), translation plays an important role in searching of documents against query of different languages and may be achieved by: (a) query translation, (b) document translation (Sanchez-Martinez and Carrasco 2011) and (c) dual translation. The query translation is performed by translating the query into document language whereas, for document translation, the documents are translated into query language instead of a query. In dual translation, the translation of both query and document are required.

On the basis of resources, translation in CLIR can also be classified into three classes (Aljlayl and Frieder 2001): (a) dictionary-based translation, (b) machine translation (MT) and (c) corpora (parallel or comparable corpora) based translation. The dictionary-based approach (Davis 1996; Kwok 1997; Levow, Oard and Resnik 2005) is one of the traditional approach of CLIR where problem occur when query contains words or phrases that do not appear in the dictionary. The machine translation is used to automatically translate query/documents of one language into another language using a context. MT suffers various issues such as ambiguity and un-translated words.

The third translation approach of CLIR is corpus-based approach which uses a multilingual term for query translation in CLIR (Oard 2003). This approach can be classified into two types: (a) parallel corpora based and (b) comparable corpora based approach (Sheridan and Ballerini 1996; Savoy 2012). A parallel corpus contains a pair or set of documents that are identical but in different languages (i.e. original text and their translation). The comparable corpora are made up of similar documents in different languages. Comparable corpora for a specific domain on the Web can be obtained from electronic copies of newspaper and articles.

A huge amount of information on various domains available over the Web are in English language (Joshi, Bhatt and Patel 2013), but in India, a large amount of population uses Hindi language for communication. Hence, Internet environment increases the demand of Hindi-English CLIR (Ponte and Croft 1998). The searching of documents in CLIR suffers from various problems such as multiple representations of query terms and poor translations. Q.E (Zhou, Lawless, Liu and Zhang 2015) is one of the effective techniques used for solving these problems and are discussed in other section.

The objective of this chapter is to explain how CLIR systems can be improved by Q.E techniques. The chapter discusses the process of Q.E applied to Hindi-English CLIR system. It also proposes a term ordering based techniques to further improve the quality of results in the system.

The remainder of the chapter is organised as follows: "Background" section describes previous work & defines the problem to be solved and "Query Expansion Based on Pseudo Relevance Feedback" describes the process of query expansion. "Addition of Most Suitable Term(S) Using Proposed Algorithm in a Query" section discusses addition of most suitable term(s) using proposed algorithm in a query and next section contains experimental result respectively. Finally, last two sections present a final discussion and finish with conclusions & lines for future research.

BACKGROUND

The aim of this section is to analyze the existing techniques, approaches, ideas, and standards from the field of CLIR. It provides a high-level overview of the relevant state of the art in this area, the achievements in search, limitations and problems. This tries to address the relevant subject areas by analyzing the current problems and remaining problems with the current solutions. For convenience, the entire review of literature has been grouped into two categories: (i) Previous Work & (ii) Problem Definition.

Previous Work

Related work analyses the performance of a query, which is a significant challenge due to the various issues involved, for instance, the size of a query that decreases the retrieval performance. The (short) query alone is not very reliable for retrieving relevant documents (Hauff, Hiemstra and de Jong 2008).

The Q.E (Jothilakshmi, Shanthi and Babisaraswathi 2013) is an effective technique that helps in improving the efficiency of query. However, sometimes the drift query issue decreases the quality of Q.E. Researchers hence motivated to deal with these issues. Some of the significant works have been mentioned in this section.

Macdonald C. and Iadh O. (Macdonald and Ounis 2007) used Q.E in an expert system using relevance feedback method on TREC dataset of 2005 and 2006. In this work, top-ranked documents were considered relevant and used to expand the initial query to fetch the highly relevant documents. This work shows that the quality of Q.E decreases due to drift query. For this different experiments were performed by them on TREC dataset using various methods such as: (a) counting the number of documents associated with each candidate terms, (b) Cosine measure and (c) Kullback-Leibler (KL) divergence.

In another work, Zighelnic and Oren (Zighelnic and Kurland 2008), worked on the prevention of drift query issue in Q.E. They used queries from TREC corpora for the experiment by using a fusion based method where original queries were fused with expanded queries. In this, cluster-based approach was also incorporated and documents were re-ranked. The outcomes of result have achieved an improvement in retrieved results.

In the same year, Liu and Nicholas (Liu and Belkin 2008) conducted an experiment using TREC dataset for query reformulation in Question- Answering tasks. Capturing context within query during query reformulation helped users in searching highly relevant documents. Query reformulation was performed using relevance feedback (RF) and local context analysis (LCA) method. This study proved that the proper query reformulation can't change the meaning of the original query and increased the relevancy of retrieved documents.

In 2010, Xuhang Xu (Xu and Hu 2010) and their team conducted an experiment on TREC ad-hoc retrieval task and proposed a cluster-based Q.E technique using language modeling. In this work, clusters were created on the basis of whole document collection or the initial list of retrieved documents against original query. This helped to improve the overall efficiency and performance of IR in the biomedical domain.

In the next year, Bashar Al-Shboul (Al-Shboul and Myaeng 2011a) stated that the Q.E using relevance feedback method generally suffered from the drift query issue. In order to minimize the impact of this issue, they proposed a novel Q.E approach that utilized the Wikipedia semantic annotations. This approach also utilizes WordNet to handle the synonyms and ambiguities. This analysis achieved an improvement in legal IR.

Yet another work was performed by Anna Shtok (Shotk, Kurland, Carmel, Raiber and Markovits 2012), who proposed an approach for predicting the performance of the query by computing the score of retrieved documents using standard deviation method. They argued that the retrieval methods that are based on document-query surface-level similarities and standard deviation are capable of reducing the impact of drift query.

In 2013, Anastasiu, David C. et al., (Anastasiu, Gao, Jiang, and karypis 2013), worked on ambiguity issues that decreases the relevancy of precision-oriented search results. They proposed two-box technique in the context of Web search for query disambiguation and drift query. They implemented a system called Bobo where contextual terms were used to capture the domain knowledge from users and helped in increasing the relevancy of search results.

In 2014, Bashar Al-Shboul (Al-Shboul and Myaeng 2014 b) again performed an experimental analysis on NTCIR dataset to predict and resolve the issue of drift query in Q.E. They proposed a new framework where queries after expansion could be analyzed. This framework helped to identify the negative role of drifting queries that occurred after Q.E for exploration of documents. The outcome of this work stated topic pairwise similarity and attributes were used to achieve better results.

Some of the most prominent researchers on Q.E after year 2000 in Hindi-English CLIR are described in table1.

Problem Definition

In recent years, the amount of online information from the government, scientific, business, and private sectors has risen dramatically. Most of the Web pages are written in English languages. However, English is not the native language of nearly half of all Internet users and the number of non-English speaking users is growing. In India, people prefer Hindi language for communication and other purposes. This creates a demand for research that can develop the relationship between Hindi and English languages.

Ambiguity in CLIR offers the retrieval of irrelevant documents. A number of research works has been reported in literature to deal with the ambiguity in CLIR with some degree of success, the area is still wide open and has scope for further improvement to achieve better retrieval effectiveness.

QUERY EXPANSION BASED ON PSEUDO RELEVANCE FEEDBACK

Users usually feel that effective retrieval through query modification is a very hard process, especially if they don't have complete knowledge about the document collection. So, to improve the effectiveness, the users query must be modified such that it can express the needed documents more accurately. Relevance feedback is one such technique for automatic query modification that came into existence in mid 1960s. The relevance feedback method can be differentiated into three types on the basis of user involvement such as: Implicit feedback, Explicit feedback and Pseudo feedback (Salton and Buckley 1990; Singhal 2001). The implicit feedback requires the least amount of effort from the user to improve the effective-

Table 1. Some prominent researches of Hindi- English CLIR

Author	Title	Year
G. Chandra & S. Dwivedi (Chandra and Dwivedi 2017a)	Query Expansion Based on Term Selection for Hindi–English Cross Lingual IR	2017
Dasu Ujjwal et al. (Ujjwal et al., 2016)	Analysis of retrieval models for cross language information retrieval	2016
Eva Kattaet al. (Katta and Arora 2015)	An improved approach to English-Hindi based Cross Language Information Retrieval system	2015
Shukla, S. & Sinha, U. (Shukla and Sinha 2015)	Categorizing sentence structures for phrase level morphological analyzer for English to Hindi RBMT	2015
Varshney, Saurabh & Jyoti Bajpai (Varshney et al.2013)	Improving Retrieval performance of English-Hindi based Cross-Language Information Retrieval.	2013
S.K Dwivedi (Dwivedi 2012)	HSC based method for disambiguation of web queries in Hindi language	2012
Danish Contractor, Govind Kothari, et al. (Contractor, Kothari, Faruquie, Subramaniam and Negi 2010)	Handling noisy queries in cross language FAQ retrieval.	2010
Das, Sujoy, Anurag Seetha, M. Kumar, and J. L. Rana (Das, Seetha, Kumar and Rana 2010)	Post Translation Query Expansion Using Hindi Word-Net for English-Hindi CLIR System	2010
Anurag Seetha, Sujoy Das and M.Kumar (Seetha, Das and Kumar 2009a)	Improving performance of English-Hindi CLIR system using linguistic tools and techniques	2009
Mandal, Debasis, et al. (Mandal, Dandapat, Gupta, Banerjee and Sarkar 2008)	Bengali and Hindi to English CLIR Evaluation	2008
Bandyopadhyay, Shivaji, et al. (Bandyopadhyay, Mondal and Naskar 2008)	Bengali, Hindi and Telugu to English Ad-Hoc Bilingual Task	2008
Prasad Pingali, Kula Kekeba Tune and Vasudeva Varma (Pingali, Tune and Verma 2007)	Improving Recall for Hindi, Telugu, Oromo to English CLIR	2007
Chinnakotla, Manoj Kumar et al. (Manoj, Sagar, Pushpak and Om 2007)	Hindi to English and Marathi to English Cross Language Information Retrieval at CLEF	2007
Mandal, Debasis, et al. (Mandal et al. 2007)	Hindi to English Cross-language Text Retrieval under Limited Resources.	2007
Anurag Seetha, Sujoy Das, M. Kumar (Seetha, Das, Kumar 2007b)	Evaluation of the English-Hindi Cross Language Information Retrieval System Based on Dictionary Based Query Translation	2007
Sekine, Santoshi & Ralph Grishman (Sekine and Grishman 2003)	Hindi-English cross-lingual question-answering system	2003

ness of retrieved documents. The commonly used behaviours involved in this process are reading time, scrolling and interaction. In explicit feedback, the user's opinion is considered to decide whether the document is relevant or not. The pseudo feedback (or blind feedback) method, fully eliminates the user interaction by considering the assumption that the top K documents of the initial search are relevant.

In this chapter for experiment, query expansion (Q.E.) is performed using pseudo feedback method for the modification of query. The purpose of Q.E (Lin, Li, Hsu and Wu 2010) is to improve the quality and relevancy of retrieved results (Xu and Croft 2000; Billerbeck 2005 a; Maxwell and Schafer 2010). The most common factors behind the poor performance of CLIR is the lack of availability of resources and multiple senses of query words (Ballesteros and Croft 1998 a; Lee, K.S., Kageura, K. and Choi, K.S. 2002; Chandra and Dwivedi 2014 b). To overcome the second issue, query expansion (Ballesteros and

Croft 1997 b) may be used to enhance the translated query with related terms extracted from various resources with the help of initially retrieved document collection. In Hindi-English CLIR model, steps that play an important role in document searching using Q.E. are: (a) translation of queries, (b) ranking of retrieved documents and (c) selection of candidate term(s) and addition of suitable term(s) at an appropriate location in query (Chandra et al.,2017 a).

Translation of Queries

Fifty queries (as shown in table 4) of Hindi language have been taken from FIRE 2012 dataset for experimental analysis. In order to translate these queries into the English language, Google translator is used. The translation accuracy of queries is assessed automatically using Back-Translation approach (Miyabe and Yoshino 2015; Chandra and Dwivedi 2017c).

The certain queries which have been identified as incorrect translation by Back-Translation, were corrected manually with the help of linguists because incorrect query translation may affect the Q.E. process (Billerbeck, Scholer and Williams 2003 b; Raju, Raju and Satyanarayana 2014; Miyabe et al., 2015; Rapp, Sharoff and Zweigenbaum 2016). The research work of Chandra et al. (Chandra and Dwivedi 2017 c) shows that, only 12% of the total queries were found incorrect or partially incorrect as reported by back-translation approach. Hence, it is found that back-translation approach is very effective in eliminating the need of human intervention to manually check each query for the translation accuracy.

Back-translation is very useful in global market because it creates the bridge between cultures and distances. Many areas such as medical, academic, business etc used back-translation as an effective way of transferring information. For example, WHO (World Health Organization) controls many medical organizations that used back-translation as a quality control process in various health studies at international level (Ozolins 2008). The interesting part of back-translation process is that it does not require the prior knowledge of target language.

Ranking of Retrieved Documents

In this chapter, for ranking of retrieved dcouments OkapiBM25 is used (Billerbeck et al. 2003 b; Gupta, Saini and Saxena 2014; Miyabe et al. 2015; Ermakova and Mothe 2016). The OkapiBM25 measure is an effective method which can be used in Q.E to increase the relevancy of retrieved documents. The purpose of documents ranking (Chandra et al. 2017 a) is to identify the most suitable documents against each query which could be used as corpus for Q.E., as the appropriate document collection would help to match the best candidate term (from among the candidate terms available in the narration and description of FIRE for each query). In OkapiBM25 (Whissell and Clark 2011; Daoud and Huang 2013, Chandra and Dwivedi 2019 d), 'BM' is the abbreviation of "Best Match", and in this case 25, is a combination of BM11 and BM15 (Harman 1993). The value of OkapiBM25 is computed by using equation 1.

$$bm25(q,d) = \sum_{t \in q} \log\left(\frac{N - f_t + 0.5}{f_t + 0.5}\right) \times \frac{(K_1 + 1)f_{d,t}}{k + f_{d,t}} \qquad (1)$$

where: 'q' is a query containing terms 't'; 'd' is a document; 'N' is the number of documents in the collection; 'f_t' is the number of documents containing term 't' and '$f_{(d, t)}$' is the number of occurrences of 't' in d; and the value of 'k' is obtained by equation 2.

$$k = k_1((1-b) + b \times L_d / A_L))$$
(2)

where the values of 'k_1' and 'b' depend on the nature of query and document collection, a default set to 1.2 and 0.75, respectively. Here, 'L_d' and 'A_L' are document length and average document length respectively. The document length (L_d) and average document length (A_L) for the analysis of OkapiBM25 are computed using UAM corpus tool. UAM Corpus Tool (UAM Corpus 2012) developed at Autonomous University of Madrid by the computational linguist Mick O` Donnell. This tool is used to compute the frequencies of terms occurring in retrieved documents and also the length of each retrieved documents have been computed using this tool.

Selection of Candidate Terms

Once the top-ranked (most suitable) document for each query has been identified, these documents are used as a corpus to select the appropriate term from the collection of candidate terms (extracted from description and narration of queries of FIRE dataset). This has been done by computation of Term Selection Value (TSV) for each candidate terms using e.q. (3) (Rijsbergen 1979; Harman 1993; Buckley, Salton, Allan and Singhal 1995; Aljlayl et al. 2001; Bertoldi and Federico 2004; Chandra et al. 2017 a; Lin et al. 2010; Sari and Adriani 2014). In this work, the lowest TSV has been used to select the expansion term(s) from among the available candidate terms for each query.

$$TSV_t = \left(\frac{f_t}{N}\right)^{r_t} \left(\frac{R}{r_t}\right)$$
(3)

where 'R' is the number of top-ranked (most relevant) documents examined, 'r_t' is the number of documents that contain a candidate term 't', 'N' is the number of documents in the collection, and 'f_t' is the number of occurrences of term (except query) in the document collection.

For example, for Query No.4 (as shown in table 4) i.e. *"Australian Embassy Bombing"*, for computation of TSV, three candidate terms (*i.e. 'Front', 'Jakarta', 'Investigations)* have been taken from description and narration for this query as available in the FIRE. The frequency of occurrence of these terms (in the top-ranked doc @ 5) is computed using UAM corpus tool (UAM Corpus 2012). For the first candidate term *"Front"* value of r_t is 4 (table 2) and $f_t = 7$ (total no. of occurrences of term *"Front"* in top 5 documents). TSV of this term is computed as follows:

TSV of keyword i.e. *"Front"* is 1.2005. Similarly, TSV for rest of the keywords of this query has been obtained (i.e. table 2).

Here, the keyword *"Jakarta" has* minimum TSV, so this will be inserted into the original query to form a new query. Term *"Jakarta"* could have been placed anywhere in the query, however, based on the pattern (narration) available in the FIRE for this query it has been placed at the end. Similarly, Q.E for other queries has been performed, as shown in column 4 of table 4.

Table 2. Term selection (using raking) for query "Australian embassy bombing"

Keywords	Rank1	Rank2	Rank3	Rank4	Rank5	f_t	r_t	TSV
Front	2	1	1	3		7	4	1.2005
Jakarta	2	3		1	6	12	4	0.010368
Investigations	1	3	2	1	3	9	5	0.6561

ADDITION OF MOST SUITABLE TERM(S) USING PROPOSED ALGORITHM IN A QUERY

As discussed in the previous section, a simple pattern matching approach of FIRE narration is used to place an expansion term in the original query. However, it's not always possible to do so, as these narrations are very limited and may not be available for each query. Therefore a more generalized approach would be required to identify the suitable location of terms in each query as; an inappropriate location may lead to an expanded query for which the retrieved results are poor.

This chapter proposes a term ordering based algorithm and its purpose is to enhance the capability of the query to retrieve highly relevant documents during Q.E. The term ordering based algorithm also helps to resolve the drift query issue (Macdonald et al. 2007). It is one of the issues that can occur during Q.E., which can change the meaning of required user's information if the new term(s) added to the query at an inappropriate location. For this, an algorithm has been derived. Assuming that first ranked document to be the most relevant among the collection of documents for each query, it is considered only for computation of frequency of occurrence of expansion term(s) on either side (left or right) of each query word. The proposed term ordering based algorithm is shown in figure 1.

In order to understand the working of this algorithm, let us take the same query *"Australian Embassy Bombing"* the expansion term obtained after computation of TSV is *"Jakarta"* and the term ordering based algorithms computed the left and right location frequency for this term i.e. *"Jakarta"* with respect to each query words in a top-ranked document. It is shown in table 3.

Here, the left frequency means the occurrence of a term to the left side of corresponding query word whereas right frequency means the occurrence of a term to the right side of corresponding query word in the first ranked document.

From table 3, the left location frequency with respect to query word *"Australian"* for expansion term i.e. *"Jakarta"* is 3 whereas right location frequency is NIL which indicates that the term i.e. *"Jakarta"* never occurs to the right side of query word *"Australian"* in a first ranked document. Similarly, the frequency of left and right location for all the query words can be visualized. Out of 6 frequencies (i.e. 3 left sides and 3 right sides) of all query words, one can easily find that right location frequency against query word *"Bombing"* is the highest among all. So, the expanded query after addition of term using proposed algorithm become *"Australian Embassy Bombing **Jakarta**"*. Similarly, the algorithm provides the term ordering of expansion term(s) in each of the 50 test queries of FIRE during Q.E. process.

Table 4, shows the expanded queries. The column 4 shows the expanded queries without using term ordering based algorithm, where the term(s) obtained after TSV analysis is added in a query using narration pattern of queries as available in FIRE dataset for all queries. The column 5 shows the expanded queries where term(s) are added using proposed term ordering based algorithm.

Figure 1. Proposed term ordering based algorithm for Q.E

Where, Q_j indicates the number of queries, T_k represents expansion terms (i.e. candidate terms) obtained from FIRE test collection, $L_{Q_{ji}}$ represents a left location of expansion term with respect to query words and $R_{Q_{ji}}$ represents right location of expansion term with respect to query words.

Algorithm: Proposed Term Ordering Based Query Expansion
Input: Queries Q_j , expansion term(s) T_k

Output: Location of Term(s) in Query Q_j
1:   for (int j = 1; j ≤ m; j++) | where m = no. of queries
2:    {
3:     for (int k =1; k ≤ n; k++) | where n = no. of expansion term(s)
4:     {
5:     for (int i =1; i ≤ w; i++) | where w = no. of query words
6:     {
7:      $L_{Q_{ji}}$ = find immediate left frequency of expansion term(s) T_k with respect to each query words in document (D_1);
8:      $R_{Q_{ji}}$ = find immediate right frequency of expansion term(s) T_k with respect to each query words in document (D_1);
9:     }
10:    Find max frequency from the collection of left and right frequencies ($L_{Q_{ji}}$ & $R_{Q_{ji}}$)
13:     If max frequency = single value
15:     {
16:      Add T_k in query Q_{ji} at location of maximum frequency
17:     }
18:     else
19:     {
20:      if (max frequency (($L_{Q_{ji}} = R_{Q_{ji}}$))
23:      {
24:       Add T_k in query Q_j at left side of Q_{ji} on moving from left to right in query
     }
26:      else
27:      {
28:       $F_{Q_{ji}}$ = find frquency of query words in D_1
29:       find max of $F_{Q_{ji}}$
30:       Add term(s) T_k at respective location of Q_{ji} having maximum frequency
     }
32:     }
33:    }
34:    Run expanded query Q_j
35: }

By analyzing table 4, it is found that in both (with & without term ordering based algorithm) the cases, that Q.E is not performed for two queries due to unavailability of expansion terms in FIRE narration.

Table 3. Frequency of location for expansion term "appointment" with respect to query words

S. No.	Query Words	Left Frequency	Right Frequency
1	Australian	3	NIL
2	Embassy	4	2
3	Bombing	5	6

EXPERIMENTAL RESULT

The expanded queries are fire on Google search engine to retrieve the documents and perform the evaluation of results. The purpose of evaluation is to compare the relevant documents before and after query expansion.

For the evaluation of relevancy in CLIR, three measures are considered such as: Precision, Average Precision and Mean Average Precision. For calculating these, a number of relevant documents are selected manually from the top @10 retrieved documents.

Precision is the proportion of a number of relevant retrieved documents to the number of retrieved documents. Precision for each query is computed as follows:

$$Precision = \frac{Relevant\ Retrieved\ Documents}{Retrieved\ Documents} \tag{4}$$

Average Precision (AP) is the average of precision values obtained for the set of top 'K' documents existing after each relevant document is retrieved, and this value is then averaged over information needs. Mean Average Precision (MAP) for a set of queries is the mean of the average precision scores for each query. The data in table 5 shows the results in term of precision, AP and MAP obtained after Q.E with and without location-based algorithm for all the queries.

Figure 2 describes the change in MAP values before and after Q.E. Similarly, figure 3 shows the effective change in precision values in some queries after applying term ordering based algorithm. Out of 50 sample queries, we observed considerable change in term of precision for query no. 6, 8,13,25,27 and 36 (as shown in figure3). Due to this the MAP has also improved from 0.5746 to 0.6018 (as shown in table5). The effect could be more visible with extended number of queries (as shown in figure3).

DISCUSSION

The collection of queries in the Hindi Language from FIRE dataset consists of three parts: a title of the query, descriptions of query and narration of query that provides a collection of candidate terms for Q.E. The narration and description part of these queries provide valuable information regarding what kinds of documents should be considered relevant or irrelevant. The precision computation for each query is based on this information.

Table 4. Original, translated and expanded queries (using q.e. with & without term ordering based algorithm)

Query	Hindi Queries	Translated Queries	Without Term Ordering Algorithm (After OkapiBM25 Ranking)	With Term Ordering Algorithm
1.	वाई एस आर रेड्डी की मौत	YSR Reddy's Death	**Chief Minister** YSR Reddy's Death	*Chief Minister* YSR Reddy's Death
2.	संगीतकारों को भारत रत्न	Bharat Ratna Musicians	Bharat Ratna **Awarded** Musicians	Bharat Ratna *Awarded* Musicians
3.	नरेगा योजना	NREGA Scheme	**Mahatma Gandhi** NREGA Scheme	*Mahatma Gandhi* NREGA Scheme
4.	ऑस्ट्रेलियाई दूतावास बम विस्फोट	Australian Embassy Bombing	Australian Embassy Bombing **Jakarta**	Australian Embassy Bombing *Jakarta*
5.	यूरो अपनाने वाले देश	Countries Adopting Euro	Countries Adopting Euro **Currency**	Countries Adopting Euro *Currency*
6.	पहले 700 टेस्ट विकेट लेने वाले क्रिकेटर	The First Player to Take 700 Test Wickets	**Shane Warne** The First Player to take 700 Test Wickets	The First Player *Shane Warne* to take 700 Test Wickets
7.	स्टीव इरविन की मृत्यु	Steve Irwin's Death	**Crocodile Hunter** Steve Irwin's Death	*Crocodile Hunter* Steve Irwin's Death
8.	2008 गुवाहाटी बम विस्फोट से क्षति	Guwahati Bombing Damage in 2008	**Casualties** Guwahati Bombing Damage in 2008	Guwahati Bombing Damage *Casualties* in 2008
9.	चामुंडा मंदिर भगदड़	Chamunda Temple Stampede	Chamunda **Devi** Temple Stampede **Jodhpur**	Chamunda *Devi* Temple Stampede *Jodhpur*
10.	आदर्श हाउसिंग सोसाइटी घोटाले इस्तीफा	Adarsh Housing Society Scam Resignation	Adarsh Housing Society Scam **Chief Minister** Resignation	Adarsh Housing Society Scam *Chief Minister* Resignation
11.	ऑस्ट्रेलिया में भारतीय छात्रों पर हमले	The Attacks on Indian Students in Australia	The Attacks on Indian Students in Australia	The Attacks on Indian Students in Australia
12.	दिल्ली मेट्रो सेवा की शुरुआत	Beginning of Delhi Metro Services	Beginning of Delhi Metro **Rail** Services	Beginning of Delhi Metro *Rail* Services
13.	भारतीय नागरिक पाकिस्तानी जासूस	Indian Citizen Pakistani Spy	Indian Citizen **Diplomat** Pakistani Spy	Indian *Diplomat* Citizen Pakistani Spy
14.	शिक्षा अधिकार अधिनियम	Right to Education Act	**Benefits** Right to Education Act	*Benefits* Right to Education Act
15.	बीजेपी से जसवंत सिंह का बहिष्कार	Jaswant Singh Boycott from BJP	Jaswant Singh Boycott from BJP **Controversial Book**	Jaswant Singh Boycott from BJP *Controversial Book*
16.	गोरखालैंड की मांग	Gorkhaland Demand	Gorkhaland Demand by **Bimal Gurung**	Gorkhaland Demand by *Bimal Gurung*
17.	श्रीलंकाई राष्ट्रीय क्रिकेट टीम पर हमला	Attack on Sri Lankan National Cricket Team	Attack on Sri Lankan National Cricket Team **Pakistan**	Attack on Sri Lankan National Cricket Team *Pakistan*
18.	भारत की पहली महिला स्पीकर	India's First Woman Speaker	India's First Woman Speaker in **Lok Sabha**	India's First Woman Speaker in *Lok Sabha*
19.	2001 साहित्य में नोबेल पुरस्कार विजेता	2001 Nobel Prize Winner in Literature	**V.S Naipaul** 2001 Nobel Prize Winner in Literature	*V.S Naipaul* 2001 Nobel Prize Winner in Literature
20.	2003 आशियान कप विजेता	2003 ASEAN Cup Winner	**Indian Team** 2003 ASEAN Cup Winner	*Indian Team* 2003 ASEAN Cup Winner
21.	2001 भारतीय जनगणना	2001 Indian Census	2001 Indian Census **Conducted**	2001 Indian Census *Conducted*
22.	भुज भूकंप	Bhuj Earthquake	Bhuj Earthquake **Gujarat**	Bhuj Earthquake *Gujarat*
23.	धोनी कप्तान भारतीय टीम	Dhoni Captain Indian Team	**Selection** Dhoni Captain Indian Team	*Selection* Dhoni Captain Indian Team
24.	पैगम्बर मोहम्मद कार्टून विवाद	Prophet Mohammad Cartoon Controversy	**Depicting** Prophet Mohammad Cartoon Controversy	*Depicting* Prophet Mohammad Cartoon Controversy
25.	2002 नेटवेस्ट शृंखला का परिणाम	2002 NatWest Series Results	**England** in 2002 NatWest Series Results	2002 *England* NatWest Series Results
26.	इराक का प्रथम चुनाव	Iraq's First Election	Iraq's First **General** Election	Iraq's First *General* Election
27.	प्रतिष्ठित व्यक्तियों पर जूता फेकना	Dignitaries on the Shoe Throwing	**Incident** Dignitaries on the Shoe Throwing	Dignitaries on the Shoe Throwing *Incident*
28.	भारत का पहला मानवरहित चन्द्रमा मशिन	India's First Unmanned Moon Mission	**Chandrayaan-1** India's First Unmanned Moon Mission	*Chandrayaan-1* India's First Unmanned Moon Mission
29.	भारतीय संसद आतंकवादी हमला	Indian Parliament Attack	Indian Parliament **Terrorist** Attack	Indian Parliament *Terrorist* Attack
30.	पोलियो उन्मूलन अभियान	Polio Eradication Campaign	Polio Eradication Campaign, **India**	Polio Eradication Campaign, *India*
31.	अभियुक्त अजमल कसाब	Accused Ajmal Kasab	Accused Ajmal Kasab **Mumbai Attack**	Accused Ajmal Kasab *Mumbai Attack*

continued on following page

Table 4. Continued

Query	Hindi Queries	Translated Queries	Without Term Ordering Algorithm (After OkapiBM25 Ranking)	With Term Ordering Algorithm
32.	सानिया मिर्ज़ा की शादी	Sania Mirza's Marriage	Sania Mirza's Marriage **Shoaib Malik**	Sania Mirza's Marriage *Shoaib Malik*
33.	महेंद्र सहि धोनी राष्ट्रीय पुरस्कार	Mahendra Singh Dhoni National Award	Mahendra Singh Dhoni **Padma Sri** National Award	Mahendra Singh Dhoni *Padma Sri* National Award
34.	वाममोर्चा ने कांग्रेस से समर्थन वापस लिया	Left withdrew Support to the Congress	Left Withdrew Support to the Congress **Government**	Left Withdrew Support to the Congress *Government*
35.	मिग दुर्घटना पश्चिमि बंगाल	MIG crash in West Bengal	MIG **Aircraft** Crash in West Bengal	MIG *Aircraft* Crash in West Bengal
36.	विश्व अहंसिा दविस	World Non-Violence Day	**2nd October** World Non-Violence Day,	World Non-Violence Day *2nd October*
37.	फिल्म सेंसर बोर्ड महिला अध्यक्ष	Film Censor Board Chairperson Woman	Film Censor Board Chairperson **Appointment** Woman	Film Censor Board Chairperson Woman *Appointment*
38.	2010 ऑटो एक्सपो दिल्ली	Delhi Auto Expo 2010	Delhi Auto Expo **Held** 2010	Delhi Auto Exp*o* *Held* 2010
39.	हरभजन सहि ने श्रीसांत को थप्पड़ मारा	Harbhajan Singh Slapped Srisant	**Punishment** Harbhajan Singh Slapped Srisant	*Punishment* Harbhajan Singh Slapped Srisant
40.	भारतीय एनीमेशन फिल्म उद्योग	Indian Animation Film Industry	**Growing** Indian Animation Film Industry	*Growing* Indian Animation Film Industry
41.	ग्रामीण बैंक मुहम्मद यूनुस विवाद	Grameen Bank Muhammad Yunus Dispute	Grameen Bank Muhammad Yunus Dispute, **Bagladeshi Government**	Grameen Bank Muhammad Yunus Dispute, *Bagladeshi Government*
42.	द विन्ची कोड भारत रिलीज़ विवाद	Da Vinci Code India Release Controversy	"Da Vinci Code" India Release Controversy **Religious Group**	"Da Vinci Code" India Release Controversy *Religious Group*
43.	सरवाइकल कैंसर जागरूकता उपचार टीका	Cervical Cancer Awareness, Treatment Vaccine	Cervical Cancer Awareness, Treatment Vaccine	Cervical Cancer Awareness, Treatment Vaccine
44.	पहला फार्मूला 1 सीक्रुटि भारत	India's first Formula 1 Circuit	**Construction** of India's First Formula 1 Circuit	*Construction* of India's First Formula 1 Circuit
45.	स्टीव वॉ अंतर्राष्ट्रीय क्रिकेट सन्यास	Steve Waugh International Cricket Retirement	**Australian** Steve Waugh International Cricket Retirement	*Australian* Steve Waugh International Cricket Retirement
46.	बलि और मेलडिा गेट्स फाउंडेशन परोपकारी क्रियाकलाप भारत	Bill and Melinda Gates Foundation, the Philanthropic Activities in India	**Plans** Bill and Melinda Gates Foundation, the Philanthropic Activities in India	*Plans* Bill and Melinda Gates Foundation, the Philanthropic Activities in India
47.	ग्रीस यूरो कप २००४ विजय	Greece Won the Euro Cup 2004	Greece Won the Euro **Football** Cup 2004	Greece Won the Euro *Football* Cup 2004
48.	इमरान खान कैंसर अस्पताल पाकिस्तान	Imran Khan's Cancer Hospital in Pakistan	Imran Khan's Cancer Hospital **Research Centre** in Pakistan	Imran Khan's Cancer Hospital *Research Centre* in Pakistan
49.	आईफोन आईपैड डिजाइन लोकप्रियता लॉन्च	IPhone iPad Design Popularity Launch	**Apple's** IPhone iPad Design Popularity Launch	*Apple's* IPhone iPad Design Popularity Launch
50.	सैटेनकि वर्सेज विवाद	Satanic Verses Controversy	Satanic Verses Controversy **Fatwa**	Satanic Verses Controversy *Fatwa*

Before Q.E., the value of AP and MAP are 18.5512 and 0.37102 (table 5) respectively. In this case, queries are simply translated into English before being subjected to Google. No ranking of retrieved documents is performed as having in case of Q.E.

When queries are expanded using the proposed approach with no specific term ordering based algorithm as discussed in section 3, the results of AP and MAP are 28.7302 and 0.5746, respectively. While, same approach with the term ordering based algorithm (discussed in section 4), the results of AP and MAP are increased to 30.0926 and 0.6018 respectively. Clearly, these results indicate that Q.E is very effective in improving the retrieval relevancy. Further, where the queries are expanded with the terms placed at the appropriate location in the query using a proposed algorithm, results are further improved. The results are indicating that the MAP in the second case is higher by 4.73%.

On comparing the results obtained before & after Q.E., it is observed that the relevancy in term of the MAP is higher with Q.E. The relevancy of retrieved documents is higher with Q.E are 54.87% (without term ordering based algorithm) and 62.20% (with term ordering based algorithm) as compared to the retrieved documents obtained before Q.E.

Table 5. Precision, AP, MAP with & without term ordering based algorithm

Query	Precision After Q.E.			Average Precision After Q.E.		
	Before Q.E.	After Q.E.		Before Q.E.	After Q.E.	
		Without Term Ordering	With Term Ordering		Without Term Ordering	With Term Ordering
1.	0.5	0.8	0.8	0.3646	0.7067	0.7067
2.	0.4	0.6	0.6	0.2582	0.4546	0.4546
3.	0.5	0.7	0.7	0.4175	0.6565	0.6565
4.	0.7	0.7	0.7	0.6875	0.6365	0.6365
5.	0.4	0.8	0.8	0.355	0.7067	0.7067
6.	0.3	0.7	0.8	0.2266	0.59	0.7003
7.	0.4	0.6	0.6	0.2932	0.513	0.513
8.	0.4	0.5	0.7	0.3171	0.4383	0.6483
9.	0.6	0.7	0.7	0.4546	0.6565	0.6565
10.	0.5	0.8	0.8	0.413	0.8663	0.8663
11.	0.5	0.5	0.5	0.3796	0.3796	0.3796
12.	0.3	0.5	0.5	0.2266	0.4383	0.4383
13.	0.3	0.5	0.6	0.2416	0.3549	0.591
14.	0.5	0.6	0.6	0.413	0.3557	0.3557
15.	0.3	0.5	0.5	0.1766	0.398	0.398
16.	0.4	0.7	0.7	0.3082	0.6732	0.6732
17.	0.4	0.7	0.7	0.3464	0.6115	0.6115
18.	0.4	0.5	0.5	0.2716	0.3915	0.3915
19.	0.6	0.7	0.7	0.569	0.6365	0.6365
20.	0.5	0.8	0.8	0.4291	0.762	0.762
21.	0.5	0.6	0.6	0.4264	0.5133	0.5133
22.	0.6	0.9	0.9	0.5857	0.8353	0.8353
23.	0.4	0.6	0.6	0.3216	0.4957	0.4957
24.	0.4	0.6	0.6	0.355	0.524	0.524
25.	0.5	0.6	0.8	0.4383	0.5133	0.7253
26.	0.6	0.8	0.8	0.4073	0.6817	0.6817
27.	0.6	0.8	0.9	0.5091	0.671	0.9
28.	0.5	0.6	0.6	0.398	0.549	0.549
29.	0.6	0.7	0.7	0.5133	0.616	0.616
30.	0.3	0.4	0.4	0.1766	0.2166	0.2166
31.	0.5	0.7	0.7	0.343	0.5546	0.5546
32.	0.4	0.7	0.7	0.3082	0.6241	0.6241
33.	0.5	0.8	0.8	0.4383	0.7067	0.7067
34.	0.5	0.6	0.6	0.3606	0.3771	0.3771
35.	0.4	0.5	0.5	0.2432	0.2671	0.4264
36.	0.4	0.6	0.7	0.3666	0.5049	0.5323
37.	0.4	0.6	0.8	0.2987	0.524	0.6169
38.	0.5	0.8	0.8	0.4049	0.7267	0.7267
39.	0.4	0.7	0.7	0.2582	0.616	0.616
40.	0.6	0.7	0.7	0.468	0.616	0.616
41.	0.7	0.8	0.8	0.5541	0.762	0.762
42.	0.4	0.6	0.6	0.3082	0.4441	0.4441
43.	0.5	0.5	0.5	0.3057	0.3057	0.3057
44.	0.4	0.7	0.7	0.3321	0.5299	0.6365
45.	0.4	0.6	0.6	0.3082	0.5049	0.5049
46.	0.5	0.8	0.8	0.3707	0.7888	0.7888
47.	0.6	0.9	0.9	0.4612	0.9	0.8788
48.	0.5	0.8	0.8	0.393	0.7267	0.7267
49.	0.5	0.7	0.7	0.3216	0.6467	0.6467
50.	0.5	0.8	0.8	0.4264	0.762	0.762
Total	23.5	33.4	34.4	18.5512	28.7302	30.0926
Mean Average Precision (MAP)				0.37102	0.5746	0.6018

Figure 2. MAP before & after Q.E. (with & without term ordering based algorithm)

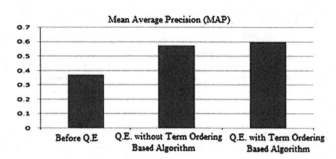

Figure 3. Change in precision value of 6 queries after term ordering based algorithm

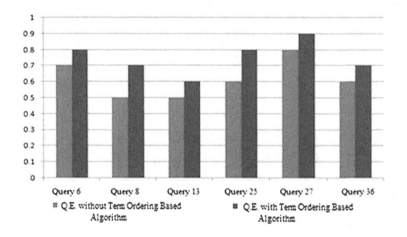

Out of the 50 test queries, the location of 6 queries (as shown in figure 3) i.e. 12% have been changed. By comparing the results of these 12% queries with the expanded queries without term ordering based algorithm, the results indicate an improvement of 30.37% in term of the MAP is recorded. The result is satisfactory and shows the importance & worth of term ordering based algorithm in Q.E. for relevancy improvement.

Among the other contemporary works, Craig Macdonald (Macdonald et al. 2007) worked on TREC 5, 6 datasets to minimize the impact drift query in Q.E and the achieved highest 0.5689 MAP. Bashar Al-Shboul (Al-Shboul et al. 2011a) worked on solving the issue of drift query using Q.E on TREC dataset and achieved highest MAP of 54.34%. In 2014, Bashar Al-Shboul (Al-Shboul et al. 2014 b) again worked on drift query issues using NTCIR dataset and achieved 59.67% MAP. Comparing these results with the result of proposed work, it is observed that MAP (i.e. 0.6018) of proposed work is better.

The overall analysis of this research indicates that Q.E. is an effective technique that increases the relevancy of our Hindi-English CLIR searching. The effectiveness of Q.E. is increased using a proposed term ordering based algorithm and achieved better results.

CONCLUSION AND FUTURE WORK

Q.E. is one of the popular techniques that improved the relevancy of retrieved documents. However, one of the main problems of Q.E. in CLIR is drift query. The issue of drift query can be effectively handled by inserting candidate term(s) at the appropriate location in a query during Q.E. The proposed term ordering based algorithm is found more suitable as it finds the location of terms in the query through searching and matching the pattern in real time retrieved documents.

FIRE dataset has been effectively utilized in proposed work for query expansion. The term ordering based algorithm is based on the frequency of occurrence of terms with respect to query terms in the first retrieved document after an initial search. It is found that proposed work effectively increase the relevancy of CLIR system. However, a more robust way would be to get the expansion term(s) from retrieved Snippets instead of FIRE set as the FIRE test collection cannot provide terms for every user's query.

REFERENCES

Al-Shboul, B., & Myaeng, S. (2014b). Analyzing Topic Drift in Query Expansion for Information Retrieval from a Large-Scale Patent Database. *Big Data and Smart Computing (BIGCOMP), IEEE, 2014 International Conference on,* 177-82.

Al-Shboul, B., & Myaeng, S. (2011a). Query Phrase Expansion Using Wikipedia in Patent Class Search. *Asia Information Retrieval Symposium,* 115-26. 10.1007/978-3-642-25631-8_11

Aljlayl, M., & Frieder, O. (2001). Effective Arabic-English Cross-Language Information Retrieval Via Machine-Readable Dictionaries and Machine Translation. *Proceedings of the tenth international conference on Information and knowledge management ACM,* 295-302. 10.1145/502585.502635

Anastasiu, D. C., Gao, B. J., Jiang, X., & Karypis, G. (2013). A Novel Two-Box Search Paradigm for Query Disambiguation. *World Wide Web (Bussum), 16*(1), 1–29. doi:10.100711280-011-0154-0

Ballesteros, L., & Croft, W. B. (1997b). Phrasal Translation and Query Expansion Techniques for Cross-Language Information Retrieval. *ACM SIGIR Forum, 31,* 84-91.

Ballesteros, L., & Croft, W. B. (1998a). Resolving Ambiguity for Cross-Language Retrieval. *Proceedings of the 21st annual international ACM SIGIR conference on Research and development in information retrieval* 64-71.

Banchs, R. E., & Costa-Jussa, M. (2013). Cross-Language Document Retrieval by Using Nonlinear Semantic Mapping. *Applied Artificial Intelligence, 27*(9), 781–802. doi:10.1080/08839514.2013.835232

Bandyopadhyay, S., Mondal, T., & Naskar, S. K. (2008). Bengali, Hindi and Telugu to English Ad-hoc Bilingual Task. *Proceedings of the 2nd workshop on Cross Lingual Information Access (CLIA) Addressing the Information Need of Multilingual Societies.*

Bertoldi, N., & Federico, M. (2004). Statistical Models for Monolingual and Bilingual Information Retrieval. *Information Retrieval, 7*(1-2), 53–72. doi:10.1023/B:INRT.0000009440.64411.ad

Billerbeck, B. (2005a). *Efficient Query Expansion* (PhD Thesis). RMIT University, Melbourne, Australia.

Billerbeck, B., Scholer, F., & And Williams, H. E. (2003b). Query Expansion Using Associated Queries. *Proceedings of the twelfth international conference on Information and knowledge management*, 2-9.

Buckley, C., Salton, G., Allan, J., & Singhal, A. (1995). Automatic Query Expansion Using SMART: TREC 3. *NIST Special Publication*, 69-80.

Chandra, G., & Dwivedi, S. K. (2014b). A Literature Survey on Various Approaches of Word Sense Disambiguation. *Computational and Business Intelligence (ISCBI), IEEE 2nd International Symposium on*, 106-9.

Chandra, G., & Dwivedi, S.K. (2017a). Query Expansion Based on Term Selection for Hindi–English Cross Lingual IR. *Journal of King Saud University-Computer and Information Sciences*.

Chandra, G., & Dwivedi, S.K. (2017c). Assessing Query Translation Quality Using Back Translation in Hindi-English CLIR. *International Journal of Intelligent Systems and Applications, 9*(3), 51-9.

Chandra, G., & Dwivedi, S. K. (2019d). Query Expansion for Effective Retrieval Results of Hindi–English Cross-Lingual IR. *Applied Artificial Intelligence, 33*(7), 567–593. doi:10.1080/08839514.2019.1577018

Contarctor, D., Kothari, G., Faruquie, T. A., Subramaniam, L. V., & Negi, S. (2010). Handling Noisy Queries in Cross Language FAQ Retrieval. *Proceedings of the 2010 conference on empirical methods in natural language processing*, 87-96.

UAM Corpus, 2012Corpus ToolU. A. M. (2012). Retrieved from http://www.wagsoft.com/CorpusTool/

Daoud, M., & Huang, J. X. (2013). Mining Query-Driven Contexts for Geographic and Temporal Search. *International Journal of Geographical Information Science, 27*(8), 1530–1549. doi:10.1080/1365881 6.2012.756883

Das, S., Seetha, A., Kumar, M., & Rana, J. L. (2010). Post Translation Query Expansion Using Hindi Word-Net for English-Hindi CLIR System. *Proceedings of the Forum for Information Retrieval Evaluation (FIRE'10)*.

Davis, M. (1996). New Experiments In Cross-Language Text Retrieval At NMSU's Computing Research Lab. In *The fifth text Retrieval Conference (TREC-5)*. NIST.

Duque, A., Araujo, L., & Martinez-Romo, J. (2015). CO-Graph: A New Graph-Based Technique For Cross-Lingual Word Sense Disambiguation. *Natural Language Engineering, 21*(5), 743–772. doi:10.1017/S1351324915000091

Dwivedi, S. K. (2012). A Highest Sense Count Based Method for Disambiguation of Web Queries for Hindi Language Web Information Retrieval. *International Journal of Information Retrieval Research, 2*(4), 1–11. doi:10.4018/ijirr.2012100101

Dwivedi, S. K., & Chandra, G. (2016). A Survey on Cross-Language Information Retrieval. *International Journal on Cybernetics & Informatics, 5*, 127–142. doi:10.5121/ijci.2016.5113

Ermakova, L., & Mothe, J. (2016). Document Re-Ranking Based on Topic-Comment Structure. *Research Challenges in Information Science (RCIS), 2016 IEEE Tenth International Conference on*, 1-10.

Flores, E., Barron-Cedeno, A., Moreno, L., & Rosso, P. (2015). Cross-Language Source Code Re-Use Detection Using Latent Semantic Analysis. *J. UCS, 21*(13), 1708–1725.

Gaillard, B., Bouraoui, J., de Neef, E. G., & Boualem, M. (2010). Query Expansion for Cross Language Information Retrieval Improvement. *Research Challenges in Information Science (RCIS), IEEE, Fourth International Conference on,* 337-42.

Grefenstette, G. (Ed.). (2012). *Cross-Language Information Retrieval* (Vol. 2). Springer Science & Business Media.

Gupta, Y., Saini, A., & Saxena, A. K. (2014). A New Similarity Function for Information Retrieval Based on Fuzzy Logic. *Advances in Computing, Communications and Informatics (ICACCI, 2014 IEEE, International Conference on,* 1472-1478.

Harman, D. (1993). Overview of the First TREC Conference. *Proceedings of the 16th annual international ACM SIGIR conference on Research and development in information retrieval,* 36-47.

Hauff, C., & Hiemstra, D., & de Jong. (2008). A Survey of Pre-Retrieval Query Performance Predictors. *Proceedings of the 17th ACM conference on Information and knowledge management,* 1419-20. 10.1145/1458082.1458311

Joshi, H., Bhatt, A., & Patel, H. (2013). Transliterated Search using Syllabification Approach. Forum for Information Retrieval Evaluation.

Jothilakshmi, R., Shanthi, N., & Babisaraswathi, R. (2013). A survey on semantic query expansion. *Journal of Theoretical & Applied Information Technology, 57*(1), 128–138.

Katta, E., & Arora, A. (2015). An Improved Approach to English-Hindi Based Cross Language Information Retrieval System. *Contemporary Computing (IC3), 2015 IEEE Eighth International Conference on,* 354-59.

Kern, D., Mutschke, P., & Mayr, P. (2014). Establishing an Online Access Panel for Interactive Information Retrieval Research. *Digital Libraries (JCDL), 2014 IEEE/ACM Joint Conference on,* 473-74.

Kwok, K. L. (1997). Evaluation of an English-Chinese Cross-Lingual Retrieval Experiment. Working Notes of AAAI-97 Spring Symposiums on Cross-Language Text and Speech Retrieval, 110-14.

Lee, K., Kageura, K., & Choi, K. (2002). Implicit Ambiguity Resolution Using Incremental Clustering in Korean-To-English Cross-Language Information Retrieval. *Proceedings of the 19th International Conference on Computational linguistics,* 1-7.

Levow, G., Oard, D. W., & Resnik, P. (2005). Dictionary-Based Techniques for Cross-Language Information Retrieval. *Information Processing & Management, 41*(3), 523–547. doi:10.1016/j.ipm.2004.06.012

Lin, M., Li, M., Hsu, C., & Wu, S. (2010). Query Expansion from Wikipedia and Topic Web Crawler on CLIR. NTCIR, 101-6.

Liu, Y-H., & Belkin, N.J. (2008). Query Reformulation, Search Performance, And Term Suggestion Devices In Question-Answering Tasks. *ACM Proceedings of the second international symposium on Information interaction in context,* 21-6.

Macdonald, C., & Ounis, I. (2007). Expertise Drift and Query Expansion in Expert Search. *Proceedings of the sixteenth ACM conference on Conference on information and knowledge management*, 341-50. 10.1145/1321440.1321490

Mala, V., & Lobiyal, D. K. (2016, April). Semantic and Keyword Based Web Techniques in Information Retrieval. In *Computing, Communication and Automation (ICCCA), 2016 International Conference on* (pp. 23-26). IEEE.

Mandal, D., Dandapat, S., Gupta, M., Banerjee, P., & Sarkar, S. (2007). Bengali and Hindi to English Cross-Language Text Retrieval under Limited Resources. In *CLEF*. Working Notes.

Manoj, C. K., Sagar, R., Pushpak, B., & Om, D.P. (2007). *Hindi and Marathi to English Cross Language Information Retrieval at CLEF*. Academic Press.

Maxwell, T., & Schafer, B. (2010). Natural Language Processing and Query Expansion in Legal Information Retrieval: Challenges and a Response. *International Review of Law Computers & Technology*, *24*(1), 63–72. doi:10.1080/13600860903570194

Miyabe, M., & Yoshino, T. (2015). Evaluation of the Validity of Back-Translation as a Method of Assessing the Accuracy of Machine Translation. *Culture and Computing (Culture Computing), 2015 IEEE International Conference on*, 145-50.

Oard, D. W. (2003). The Surprise Language Exercises. *ACM Transactions on Asian Language Information Processing*, *2*(2), 79–84. doi:10.1145/974740.974741

Ozolins, U. (2008). Issues of Back Translation Methodology in Medical Translations. *Proceedings, FIT [International Federation of Translators] XVIII Congress*.

Pigur, V. A. (1979). Multilanguage Information-Retrieval Systems: Integration Levels and Language Support. *Automatic Documentation and Mathematical Linguistics*, *13*(1), 36–46.

Pingali, P., Tune, K. K., & Verma, V. (2007). Improving Recall for Hindi, Telugu, Oromo to English CLIR. In *Workshop of the Cross-Language Evaluation Forum for European Languages* (pp. 103–110). Berlin: Springer.

Ponte, J. M., & Croft, W. B. (1998). A Language Modeling Approach to Information Retrieval. *Proceedings of the 21st annual international ACM SIGIR conference on Research and development in information retrieval*, 275- 81. 10.1145/290941.291008

Rahimi, R., Shakery, A., & King, I. (2015). Multilingual Information Retrieval in the Language Modeling Framework. *Information Retrieval Journal*, *18*(3), 246–281. doi:10.100710791-015-9255-1

Raju, B. N. V. N., Raju, M. S. V. S. B., & Satyanarayana, K. V. V. (2014). Translation Approaches in Cross Language Information Retrieval. *Computer and Communications Technologies (ICCCT), 2014 IEEE, International Conference on*, 1-4.

Rapp, R., Sharoff, S., & Zweigenbaum, P. (2016). Recent Advances in Machine Translation Using Comparable Corpora. *Natural Language Engineering*, *22*(4), 501–516. doi:10.1017/S1351324916000115

Rijsbergen, C. J. V. (1979). *Information Retrieval* (2nd ed.). Dept. of Computer Science, University of Glasgow.

Salton, G. (1973). Experiments in Multi-lingual Information Retrieval. *Information Processing Letters, 2*(1), 6–11. doi:10.1016/0020-0190(73)90017-3

Salton, G., & Buckley, C. (1990). Improving Retrieval Performance by Relevance Feedback. *Journal of the American Society for Information Science, 41*(4), 288–297. doi:10.1002/(SICI)1097-4571(199006)41:4<288::AID-ASI8>3.0.CO;2-H

Sanchez-Martinez, F., & Carrasco, R. C. (2011). Document Translation Retrieval Based on Statistical Machine Translation Techniques. *Applied Artificial Intelligence, 25*(5), 329–340. doi:10.1080/08839514.2011.559906

Sari, S., & Adriani, M. (2014). Learning to Rank for Determining Relevant Document in Indonesian-English Cross Language Information Retrieval Using BM25. *Advanced Computer Science and Information Systems (ICACSIS), 2014 IEEE, International Conference on,* 309-14.

Savoy, J. (2012). Authorship Attribution Based on Specific Vocabulary. *ACM Transactions on Information Systems, 30*(2), 12. doi:10.1145/2180868.2180874

Seetha, A., Das, S., & Kumar, M. (2007b). Evaluation of the English-Hindi Cross Language Information Retrieval System Based on Dictionary Based Query Translation Method. *Proceedings of 10th IEEE International Conference on Information Technology (ICIT 2007),* pp. 56-61.

Seetha, A., Das, S., & Kumar, M. (2009a). Improving Performance of English-Hindi CLIR System using Linguistic Tools and Techniques. *Proceedings of the First International Conference on Intelligent Human Computer Interaction,* 261-71. 10.1007/978-81-8489-203-1_26

Sekine, S., & Grishman, R. (2003). Hindi-English Cross-Lingual Question-Answering System. *ACM Transactions on Asian Language Information Processing, 2*(3), 181–192. doi:10.1145/979872.979874

Sheridan, P., & Ballerini, J. P. 1996. Experiments in Multilingual Information Retrieval Using The SPIDER System. *Proceedings of the 19th annual international ACM SIGIR conference on Research and development in information retrieval,* 58-65. 10.1145/243199.243213

Shotk, A., Kurland, O., Carmel, D., Raiber, F., & Markovits, G. (2012). Predicting Query Performance by Query-Drift Estimation. *ACM Transactions on Information Systems, 30*(2), 1–36.

Shukla, S., & Sinha, U. (2015). Categorizing Sentence Structures For Phrase Level Morphological Analyzer For English To Hindi RBMT. *Cognitive Computing and Information Processing (CCIP), IEEE 2015 International Conference on,* 1-6.

Singhal, A. (2001). Modern Information Retrieval: A Brief Overview. *IEEE Data Eng. Bull., 24*(4), 35–43.

Ujjwal, D., Rastogi, P., & Siddhartha, S. (2016). Analysis of Retrieval Models for Cross Language Information Retrieval. *Intelligent Systems and Control (ISCO), 2016 10th International Conference on IEEE,* 1-4.

Varshney, S., & Bajpai, J. (2013). Improving Retrieval Performance of English-Hindi Based Cross-Language Information Retrieval. *Innovation and Technology in Education (MITE), IEEE International Conference in MOOC,* 300-5.

Whissell, J. S., & Clarke, C. L. A. (2011). Improving Document Clustering Using Okapi BM25 Feature Weighting. *Information Retrieval, 14*(5), 466–487. doi:10.100710791-011-9163-y

Xu, J., & Croft, W. B. (2000). Improving the Effectiveness of Information Retrieval With Local Context Analysis. *ACM Transactions on Information Systems, 18*(1), 79–112. doi:10.1145/333135.333138

Xu, X., & Hu, X. (2010). Cluster-Based Query Expansion Using Language Modeling in the Biomedical Domain. *Bioinformatics and Biomedicine Workshops (BIBMW), 2010 IEEE International Conference on,* 185-88.

Zhou, D., Lawless, S., Liu, J., & Zhang, S. (2015). Query Expansion for Personalized Cross-Language Information Retrieval. *Semantic and Social Media Adaptation and Personalization (SMAP), IEEE, 2015 10th International Workshop on,* 1-5.

Zighelnic, L., & Kurland, O. (2008). Query-Drift Prevention for Robust Query Expansion. *Proceedings of the 31st annual international ACM SIGIR conference on Research and development in information retrieval,* 825-26.

KEY TERMS AND DEFINITIONS

Back-Translation: Back-translation is the process of translating, translated query back to original query.

CLIR: Cross-lingual information retrieval provides a convenient way that can solve the problem of language boundaries, where users can submit query in their own language to retrieve the documents of another language.

Drift Query: Drift query is one of the issues that can occur during Q.E., that occurs if new term(s) added to the query at an inappropriate location.

FIRE: Forum for Information Retrieval Evaluation (FIRE) is an evaluation forum and its aim is to encourage South Asian Language Information Access research by providing test collections for experiments as many researchers.

OKapiBM25: The OkapiBM25 measure is an effective method which can be used in Q.E to increase the relevancy of retrieved documents.

Query Expansion: Query Expansion is the process of adding suitable in a query that helps in improving the efficiency of query.

TSV: Term Selection Value(TSV) is the process of selecting a candidate term(s).

Compilation of References

Abbott, R. K., & Molina, H. G. (1992). Scheduling real-time transactions: A performance evaluation. *ACM Transactions on Database Systems*, *17*(03), 513–560. doi:10.1145/132271.132276

Abdalla, H. I. (2012, June). A New Data Re-Allocation Model for Distributed Database Systems. *International Journal of Database Theory and Application*, *5*(2).

Abdelzaher, T. F., Sharma, V., & Lu, C. (2004). A utilization bound for aperiodic tasks and priority driven scheduling. *IEEE Transactions on Computers*, *53*(3), 334–350. doi:10.1109/TC.2004.1261839

Abid, W., Mhiri, M., Salem, M., Bouazizi, E., & Gargouri, F. (2017). A feedback control scheduling architecture for real-time ontology. In *12th International Conference on Intelligent Systems and Knowledge Engineering (ISKE)*. IEEE.

Abuelyaman, E. S. (2008). An Optimized Scheme for Vertical Partitioning of a Distributed Database. *International Journal of Computer Science and Network Security*, *8*(1).

Acharya, S., Alonso, R., Franklin, M., & Zdonik, S. (1995). Broadcast disks: data management for asymmetric communication environments. In *Mobile Computing* (pp. 331–361). Boston, MA: Springer.

Acharya, S., Franklin, M., & Zdonik, S. (1995). Dissemination-based data delivery using broadcast disks. *IEEE Personal Communications*, *2*(6), 50–60. doi:10.1109/98.475988

Acharya, S., Franklin, M., & Zdonik, S. (1997, June). Balancing push and pull for data broadcast. *SIGMOD Record*, *26*(2), 183–194. doi:10.1145/253262.253293

Adi, Baig, Z. A., Hingston, P., & Lam, C.-P. (2016). Distributed denial-of-service attacks against http/2. *Cluster Computing*, *19*(1), 79–86. doi:10.100710586-015-0528-7

Agrawal, S. (2008). *An efficient scheduling algorithm for reliable energy aware real time system with arbitrary deadline* (Ph.D. Thesis). Motilal Nehru National Institute of Technology, Allahabad, India.

Ahmad, M., Chen, Q., & Khan, Z. (2018). Microscopic Congestion Detection Protocol in VANETs. *Journal of Advanced Transportation*. doi:10.1155/2018/6387063

Ahmed, M., & Mahmood, A. N. (2013, June). A novel approach for outlier detection and clustering improvement. In *2013 IEEE 8th Conference on Industrial Electronics and Applications (ICIEA)* (pp. 577-582). IEEE. 10.1109/ICIEA.2013.6566435

Akoum, A. (2017). Automatic Traffic Using Image Processing. *Journal of Software Engineering and Applications*, *10*(09), 765–776. doi:10.4236/jsea.2017.109042

Aksoy, D., & Franklin, M. 1998, March. *Scheduling for large-scale on-demand data broadcasting*. In *Proceedings. IEEE INFOCOM '98, the Conference on Computer Communications. Seventeenth Annual Joint Conference of the IEEE Computer and Communications Societies. Gateway to the 21st Century* (Vol. 2, pp. 651-659). IEEE. 10.1109/INFCOM.1998.665086

Akyildiz, I. F., Lee, W.-Y., & Chowdhury, K. R. (2009). CRAHNs: Cognitive radio ad hoc networks. *Ad Hoc Networks*, 7(5), 810–836. doi:10.1016/j.adhoc.2009.01.001

Akyildiz, I. F., Lee, W.-Y., Vuran, M. C., & Mohanty, S. (2006). NeXt generation/dynamic spectrum access/cognitive radio wireless networks: A survey. *Computer Networks*, 50(13), 2127–2159. doi:10.1016/j.comnet.2006.05.001

Alam & Ferreira. (2016). *Introduction to Intelligent Transportation Systems*. doi:10.1007/978-3-319-28183-4

Alberts, D. S., & Hayes, R. E. (2003). *Power to the edge: Command... control... in the information age. Office of the Assistant Secretary of Defense Washington DC Command and Control Research Program*. CCRP.

Aldarmi, S. A. (1998). *Real-time database systems: concepts and design*. Report-University of York Department of Computer Science YCS.

Aljlayl, M., & Frieder, O. (2001). Effective Arabic-English Cross-Language Information Retrieval Via Machine-Readable Dictionaries and Machine Translation. *Proceedings of the tenth international conference on Information and knowledge management ACM*, 295-302. 10.1145/502585.502635

Alpaydın. (2010). *Introduction to Machine Learning* (2nd ed.). The MIT Press. Retrieved from http://www.britannica.com/EBchecked/topic/1116194/

Al-Shboul, B., & Myaeng, S. (2014b). Analyzing Topic Drift in Query Expansion for Information Retrieval from a Large-Scale Patent Database. *Big Data and Smart Computing (BIGCOMP), IEEE, 2014 International Conference on*, 177-82.

Al-Shboul, B., & Myaeng, S. (2011a). Query Phrase Expansion Using Wikipedia in Patent Class Search. *Asia Information Retrieval Symposium*, 115-26. 10.1007/978-3-642-25631-8_11

Alshehri. (2019). *Effective Mechanism for Selection of Cloud Service Provider Using Cosine Maximization Method. Arabian Journal for Science and Engineering*.

Alzoubi, K. M., Wan, P.-J., & Frieder, O. (2003). Maximal independent set, weakly-connected dominating set, and induced spanners in wireless ad hoc networks. *International Journal of Foundations of Computer Science*, 14(02), 287–303. doi:10.1142/S012905410300173X

Amis, A. D., Prakash, R., Vuong, T. H., & Huynh, D. T. (2000). Max-min d-cluster formation in wireless ad hoc networks. *Proceedings IEEE INFOCOM 2000. Conference on Computer Communications. Nineteenth Annual Joint Conference of the IEEE Computer and Communications Societies*. 10.1109/INFCOM.2000.832171

Amossen, R. (2010). Vertical partitioning of relational OLTP databases using integer programming. *Data Engineering Workshops (ICDEW) of IEEE 5th International Conference on Self Managing Database Systems (SMDB)*. 10.1109/ICDEW.2010.5452739

Anastasiu, D. C., Gao, B. J., Jiang, X., & Karypis, G. (2013). A Novel Two-Box Search Paradigm for Query Disambiguation. *World Wide Web (Bussum)*, 16(1), 1–29. doi:10.100711280-011-0154-0

Andersson, B., & Jonsson, J. (2000). *Fixed-priority preemptive multiprocessor scheduling: To partition or not to partition*. Real-Time Systems and Applications.

Aparna, K., & Nair, M. K. (2016). Effect of outlier detection on clustering accuracy and computation time of CHB K-means algorithm. In *Computational Intelligence in Data Mining—Volume 2* (pp. 25–35). New Delhi: Springer. doi:10.1007/978-81-322-2731-1_3

Attri, U., & Pal, S. (2012). A survey of Performance Evaluation Criteria for Spam E-mail Classifiers. International Journal of IT. *Engineering and Applied Sciences Research, 1*, 65–68.

Azhen, P., Ruifeng, G., Haotian, W., Changyi, D., & Liaomo, Z. (2017). Adaptive real-time scheduling for mixed task sets based on total bandwidth server. *IEEE International Conference on Intelligent Computation Technology and Automation*, 11-15. 10.1109/ICICTA.2017.10

Babamir, S. M. (2012). *Real-Time Systems, Architecture, Scheduling, and Application.* In-Tech. doi:10.5772/2344

Baker, D., & Ephremides, A. (1981). The architectural organization of a mobile radio network via a distributed algorithm. *IEEE Transactions on Communications, 29*(11), 1694–1701. doi:10.1109/TCOM.1981.1094909

Baker, T., & Jose, M. (2018). Greeaodv: an energy-efficient routing protocol for vehicular ad hoc networks. *Proceedings of international Conference on Intelligent Computing*, 670-681. 10.1007/978-3-319-95957-3_69

Ballesteros, L., & Croft, W. B. (1997b). Phrasal Translation and Query Expansion Techniques for Cross-Language Information Retrieval. *ACM SIGIR Forum, 31,* 84-91.

Ballesteros, L., & Croft, W. B. (1998a). Resolving Ambiguity for Cross-Language Retrieval. *Proceedings of the 21st annual international ACM SIGIR conference on Research and development in information retrieval*64-71.

Banchs, R. E., & Costa-Jussa, M. (2013). Cross-Language Document Retrieval by Using Nonlinear Semantic Mapping. *Applied Artificial Intelligence, 27*(9), 781–802. doi:10.1080/08839514.2013.835232

Bandyopadhyay, S., & Coyle, E. J. (2003). *An energy efficient hierarchical clustering algorithm for wireless sensor networks.* Paper presented at the INFOCOM 2003. Twenty-Second Annual Joint Conference of the IEEE Computer and Communications. IEEE Societies. 10.1109/INFCOM.2003.1209194

Bandyopadhyay, S., Mondal, T., & Naskar, S. K. (2008). Bengali, Hindi and Telugu to English Ad-hoc Bilingual Task. *Proceedings of the 2nd workshop on Cross Lingual Information Access (CLIA) Addressing the Information Need of Multilingual Societies.*

Bao, L., & Garcia-Luna-Aceves, J. J. (2003). Topology management in ad hoc networks. *Proceedings of the 4th ACM international symposium on Mobile ad hoc networking & computing.* 10.1145/778415.778432

Baranwal, G. (2018a). *Auction based resource provisioning in cloud computing.* Singapore: Springer Singapore (SpringerBriefs in Computer Science). doi:10.1007/978-981-10-8737-0

Baranwal, G. (2018b). Auction theory. SpringerBriefs in Computer Science, 17–31. doi:10.1007/978-981-10-8737-0_2

Baranwal, G. (2018c). Forward auction-based cloud resource provisioning. In *SpringerBriefs in Computer Science* (pp. 33–51). Singapore: Springer; doi:10.1007/978-981-10-8737-0_3

Baranwal, G., & Vidyarthi, D. P. (2016). A Truthful and Fair Multi-Attribute Combinatorial Reverse Auction for Resource Procurement in Cloud Computing. *IEEE Transactions on Services Computing*, 1–1. doi:10.1109/tsc.2016.2632719

Barbará, D. (1999). Mobile computing and databases-a survey. *IEEE Transactions on Knowledge and Data Engineering, 11*(1), 108–117. doi:10.1109/69.755619

Baruah, S. K. (1998). A general model for recurring real time tasks. *IEEE Real Time Systems Symposium*, 114-122. 10.1109/REAL.1998.739736

Baruah, S., & Fisher, N. (2008). Global fixed-priority scheduling of arbitrary-deadline sporadic task systems. *International Conference on Distributed Computing and Networking*, 215-226. 10.1007/978-3-540-77444-0_20

Basagni & Stefano. (1998). A distance routing effect algorithm for mobility (DREAM). *Proceedings of the 4th annual ACM/IEEE international conference on Mobile computing and networking.*

Basagni, S. (1999). Distributed clustering for ad hoc networks. *Parallel Architectures, Algorithms, and Networks, 1999. (I-SPAN'99) Proceedings.* 10.1109/ISPAN.1999.778957

Basagni, S., Conti, M., & Giordano, S. (2013). *Mobile Ad hoc Networking: cutting edge directions* (2nd ed.). Willey IEEE Press Publisher. doi:10.1002/9781118511305

Basicevic, Ocovaj, S., & Popovic, M. (2015). Use of tsallis entropy in detection of syn flood dos attacks. *Security and Communication Networks*, 8(18), 3634–3640. doi:10.1002ec.1286

Behal, Kumar, K., & Sachdeva, M. (2018). D-face: An anomaly based distributed approach for early detection of ddos attacks and flash events. *Journal of Network and Computer Applications*, 111, 49–63. doi:10.1016/j.jnca.2018.03.024

Bekkerman, R., Bilenko, M., & Langford, J. (2011). *Scaling Up Machine Learning: Parallel and Distributed Approaches.* Cambridge, UK: Cambridge University Press.

Bengio, Y. (2009). *Foundations and Trends in Machine Learning 2.* Boston: Now Publishers.

Bernstein, P. A., Hadzilacos, V., & Goodman, N. (1987). *Concurrency control and recovery in database systems.* Academic Press.

Berrington, J. (2007). Databases. *Anaesthesia and Intensive Care Medicine*, 8(12), 513–515. doi:10.1016/j.mpaic.2007.09.011

Bertoldi, N., & Federico, M. (2004). Statistical Models for Monolingual and Bilingual Information Retrieval. *Information Retrieval*, 7(1-2), 53–72. doi:10.1023/B:INRT.0000009440.64411.ad

Billerbeck, B. (2005a). *Efficient Query Expansion* (PhD Thesis). RMIT University, Melbourne, Australia.

Billerbeck, B., Scholer, F., & And Williams, H. E. (2003b). Query Expansion Using Associated Queries. *Proceedings of the twelfth international conference on Information and knowledge management*, 2-9.

Blake, G., Dreslinski, R. G., & Mudge, T. (2009). A survey of multicore processors. *IEEE Signal Processing Magazine*, 26(6), 26–37. doi:10.1109/MSP.2009.934110

Blum, J. (2003). *Mobility management in IVC networks.* Academic Press.

Boulis, A., & Srivastava, M. (2004). Node-level energy management for sensor networks in the presence of multiple applications. *Wireless Networks*, 10(6), 737–746. doi:10.1023/B:WINE.0000044032.41234.d7

Bowen, T. F., Gopal, G., Herman, G., Hickey, T. M., Lee, K. C., Mansfield, W. H., ... Weinrib, A. (1992). The datacycle architecture. *Communications of the ACM*, 35(12), 71–82. doi:10.1145/138859.138868

Breza, M., Anthony, R., & McCann, J. (2007). Scalable and efficient sensor network self-configuration in bioans. In *First International Conference on Self-Adaptive and Self-Organizing Systems (SASO 2007)*, (pp. 351-354). IEEE. 10.1109/SASO.2007.47

Buckley, C., Salton, G., Allan, J., & Singhal, A. (1995). Automatic Query Expansion Using SMART: TREC 3. *NIST Special Publication*, 69-80.

Burns, A. (1991). Scheduling hard real time systems: A review. *Software Engineering Journal, 6*(3), 116–128. doi:10.1049ej.1991.0015

Burns, A., Tindell, K., & Wellings, A. (1995). Effective analysis for engineering real-time fixed priority schedulers. *IEEE Transactions on Software Engineering, 21*(5), 475–480. doi:10.1109/32.387477

Buttazzo, G. (2006). Special Issue on Major International Initiatives on Real-Time and Embedded Systems. *ACM SIGBED Review, 3*, 1–10. doi:10.1145/1164050.1164052

Calvert, C. L., & Khoshgoftaar, T. M. (2019). Impact of class distribution on the detection of slow HTTP DoS attacks using Big Data. *Journal of Big Data, 6*(1), 67. doi:10.118640537-019-0230-3

Cambiaso. (2017). Slowcomm: Design, development and performance evaluation of a new slow dos attack. *Journal of Information Security and Applications*, (35), 23-31.

Carlow, G. (1984). Architecture of the space shuttle primary avionics software system. *Communications of the ACM, 27*(09), 926–936. doi:10.1145/358234.358258

Castillo-Effer, M. (2004). Wireless sensor networks for flash-flood alerting. In *Proceedings of the Fifth IEEE International Caracas Conference on Devices, Circuits and Systems* (pp. 142-146). IEEE. 10.1109/ICCDCS.2004.1393370

Castle. (2017). Retrieved from Https://Www.Datascience.Com/Blog/Supervised-And-Unsupervised-Machine-LearningAlgorithms

Celik, A., & Kamal, A. E. (2016). Multi-objective clustering optimization for multi-channel cooperative spectrum sensing in heterogeneous green crns. *IEEE Transactions on Cognitive Communications and Networking, 2*(2), 150-161.

Chandra, G., & Dwivedi, S. K. (2014b). A Literature Survey on Various Approaches of Word Sense Disambiguation. *Computational and Business Intelligence (ISCBI), IEEE 2nd International Symposium on,* 106-9.

Chandra, G., & Dwivedi, S.K. (2017a). Query Expansion Based on Term Selection for Hindi–English Cross Lingual IR. *Journal of King Saud University-Computer and Information Sciences.*

Chandra, G., & Dwivedi, S.K. (2017c). Assessing Query Translation Quality Using Back Translation in Hindi-English CLIR. *International Journal of Intelligent Systems and Applications, 9*(3), 51-9.

Chandra, G., & Dwivedi, S. K. (2019d). Query Expansion for Effective Retrieval Results of Hindi–English Cross-Lingual IR. *Applied Artificial Intelligence, 33*(7), 567–593. doi:10.1080/08839514.2019.1577018

Chantem, T., Dick, R. P., & Hu, X. S. (2008). *Temperature-aware scheduling and assignment for hard real-time applications on MPSOCS.* Design, Automation and Test in Europe.

Chantem, T., Wang, X., Lemmon, M. D., & Hu, X. S. (2008). Period and deadline selection for schedulability. *Euromicro Conference on Real-Time Systems,* 168-177.

Chappell & Combs. (2010). *Wireshark network analysis: the official Wireshark certified network analyst study guide.* Protocol Analysis Institute, Chappell University.

Chatterjee, M., Das, S. K., & Turgut, D. (2002). WCA: A weighted clustering algorithm for mobile ad hoc networks. *Cluster Computing, 5*(2), 193–204. doi:10.1023/A:1013941929408

Chaturvedi, V., Huang, H., & Quan, G. (2010). Leakage aware scheduling on maximal temperature minimization for periodic hard real-time systems. *International Conference on Electronic Spectroscopy and Structure,* 1802-1809.

Chen, D., Liu, Z., Wang, L., Dou, M., Chen, J., & Li, H. (2013). Natural disaster monitoring with wireless sensor networks: A case study of data-intensive applications upon low-cost scalable systems. *Mobile Networks and Applications*, *18*(5), 651–663. doi:10.100711036-013-0456-9

Chen, J., Liu, K., & Lee, V. C. (2009, May). Analysis of data scheduling algorithms in supporting real-time multi-item requests in on-demand broadcast environments. In *2009 IEEE International Symposium on Parallel & Distributed Processing* (pp. 1-8). IEEE

Chiang, C.-C., Wu, H.-K., Liu, W., & Gerla, M. (1997). Routing in clustered multihop, mobile wireless networks with fading channel. *Proceedings of IEEE SICON.*

Chowdhury, M., Apon, A., & Dey, K. (2017). *Data Analytics for Intelligent Transportation Systems*. Elsevier.

Cho, Y. J., Lee, H., & Jun, C. H. (2011). Optimization of Decision Tree for Classification Using a Particle Swarm. *IEMS*, *10*(4), 272–278. doi:10.7232/iems.2011.10.4.272

Chunawale, A., & Sirsikar, S. (2017, March). RED: Residual Energy and Distance Based Clustering to Avoid Energy Hole Problem in Self-organized Wireless Sensor Networks. In *International Conference on Information and Communication Technology for Intelligent Systems*, (pp. 155-163). Springer.

Chu, W. W., & Ieong, I. (1993, August). A Transaction-Based Approach to Vertical Partitioning for Relational Database Systems. *IEEE Transactions on Software Engineering*, *19*(8), 804–812. doi:10.1109/32.238583

Clark & Poon. (2003). A Neural Network Based Approach to Automated E-mail Classification. *Proc. of IEEE International Conference on Web Intelligence*, 702-705. 10.1109/WI.2003.1241300

Clausen, T., &Jacquet, P. (2003). *Optimized Link State Routing Protocol (OLSR).* RFC-3626.

Clerk Maxwell, J. (1892). A Treatise on Electricity and Magnetism (vol. 2). Clarendon.

Cloud4SOA. (2016). *Cloud4SOA.* Available at: http://www.cloud4soa.com/

Contarctor, D., Kothari, G., Faruquie, T. A., Subramaniam, L. V., & Negi, S. (2010). Handling Noisy Queries in Cross Language FAQ Retrieval. *Proceedings of the 2010 conference on empirical methods in natural language processing*, 87-96.

Cuff, D., Hansen, M., & Kang, J., (2008). *Urban sensing: out of the woods.* ACM.

Dai, Y., Wu, J., & Xin, C. (2013). Virtual backbone construction for cognitive radio networks without common control channel. *INFOCOM, 2013 Proceedings IEEE.* 10.1109/INFCOM.2013.6566940

Dantas. (2014). A selective defense for application layer ddos attacks. *2014 IEEE Joint Intelligence and Security Informatics Conference*, 75-82. 10.1109/JISIC.2014.21

Daoud, M., & Huang, J. X. (2013). Mining Query-Driven Contexts for Geographic and Temporal Search. *International Journal of Geographical Information Science*, *27*(8), 1530–1549. doi:10.1080/13658816.2012.756883

Das, S., Agrawal, D., & Abbadi, A. E. (2009). ElasTraS: an elastic transactional data store in the cloud. *Proceedings of the conference on Hot topics in cloud computing.*

Das, S., Seetha, A., Kumar, M., & Rana, J. L. (2010). Post Translation Query Expansion Using Hindi Word-Net for English-Hindi CLIR System. *Proceedings of the Forum for Information Retrieval Evaluation (FIRE'10).*

Davis, M. (1996). New Experiments In Cross-Language Text Retrieval At NMSU's Computing Research Lab. In *The fifth text Retrieval Conference (TREC-5).* NIST.

Deb, B., Bhatnagar, S., & Nath, B. (2002). *A topology discovery algorithm for sensor networks with applications to network management*. Academic Press.

Deb, B., Bhatnagar, S., & Nath, B. (2004). STREAM: Sensor topology retrieval at multiple resolutions. *Telecommunication Systems*, *26*(2-4), 285–320. doi:10.1023/B:TELS.0000029043.27689.3f

Del Cid, P. J., Hughes, D., Ueyama, J., Michiels, S., & Joosen, W. (2009, December). DARMA: adaptable service and resource management for wireless sensor networks. In *Proceedings of the 4th International Workshop on Middleware Tools, Services and Run-Time Support for Sensor Networks*, (pp. 1-6). ACM. 10.1145/1658192.1658193

Dhage, M. S. V., Thakre, A. N., & Mohod, S. W. (2014). A review on scalability issue in wireless sensor networks. *International Journal of Innovative Research in Advanced Engineering*, *1*, 463–466.

Dhankhar, S., & Agrawal, S. (2014). VANETs: A survey on routing protocols and issues, *Int. J. Innovative Res. Sci. Eng. Technol.*, (3), 13427-13435.

Divya, K. S., Bhargavi, P., & Jyothi, S. (2018). Machine Learning Algorithms in Big data Analytics. *International Journal of Computer Sciences and Engineering, 6*(1), 64-70.

Douligeris, C., & Mitrokotsa, A. (2004). Ddos attacks and defense mechanisms: Classification and state-of-the-art. *Computer Networks*, *44*(5), 643–666. doi:10.1016/j.comnet.2003.10.003

Driscoll, K., & Hoyme, K. (1992). The airplane information management system: An integrated real time flight-deck control systems. *Real Time Systems Symposium*, 267-270. 10.1109/REAL.1992.242654

Duan, S., Thummala, V., & Babu, S. (2009, August). Tuning Database Configuration Parameters with iTuned. *Proceeding of Very Lagre Data Bases*, *2*(4), 1246–1257.

Duque, A., Araujo, L., & Martinez-Romo, J. (2015). CO-Graph: A New Graph-Based Technique For Cross-Lingual Word Sense Disambiguation. *Natural Language Engineering*, *21*(5), 743–772. doi:10.1017/S1351324915000091

Duy, D., & Tanaka, K. (2017). An effective approach for improving responsiveness of Total Bandwidth server. *International Conference of Information and Communication Technology for Embedded Systems*, 1-6. 10.1109/ICTEmSys.2017.7958777

Dwivedi, S. K. (2012). A Highest Sense Count Based Method for Disambiguation of Web Queries for Hindi Language Web Information Retrieval. *International Journal of Information Retrieval Research*, *2*(4), 1–11. doi:10.4018/ijirr.2012100101

Dwivedi, S. K., & Chandra, G. (2016). A Survey on Cross-Language Information Retrieval. *International Journal on Cybernetics & Informatics*, *5*, 127–142. doi:10.5121/ijci.2016.5113

Dykeman, H. D., & Wong, J. W. (1986, January). Scheduling algorithms for videotex systems under broadcast delivery. In *1986 IEEE International Conference on Communications* (pp. 1861-1865). IEEE.

Eason, G., Noble, B., & Sneddon, I. N. (1955). On certain integrals of Lipschitz-Hankel type involving products of Bessel functions. *Philosophical Transactions of the Royal Society of London. Series A, Mathematical and Physical Sciences*, *247*(935), 529–551. doi:10.1098/rsta.1955.0005

Elejla. (2018). Flow-based ids for icmpv6-based ddos attacks detection. *Arabian Journal for Science and Engineering*, 1–19.

El-sersy & El-sayed. (2015). Survey of Traffic Congestion Detection using VANET. *Communications on Applied Electronics, 1*(4), 14-20.

Erdogan, A., Cayirci, E., & Coskun, V. (2003, October). Sectoral sweepers for sensor node management and location estimation in adhoc sensor networks. In *IEEE Military Communications Conference, 2003. MILCOM 2003* (Vol. 1, pp. 555-560). IEEE.

Ermakova, L., & Mothe, J. (2016). Document Re-Ranking Based on Topic-Comment Structure. *Research Challenges in Information Science (RCIS), 2016 IEEE Tenth International Conference on,* 1-10.

Ewerhart, C., & Schmitz, P. W. (1997). Der Lock in Effekt und das Hold up Problem Der Lock-in Effekt und das Hold-up Problem. *MPRA Paper, 944,* 1–10. Available at: http://mpra.ub.uni-muenchen.de/6944/

Fard, H. M., Prodan, R., & Fahringer, T. (2013). A truthful dynamic workflow scheduling mechanism for commercial multicloud environments. *IEEE Transactions on Parallel and Distributed Systems, 24*(6), 1203–1212. doi:10.1109/TPDS.2012.257

Fayaz, D. (2018). Intelligent Transport System-. *RE:view.*

Fei, Z., Li, B., Yang, S., Xing, C., Chen, H., & Hanzo, L. (2016). A survey of multi-objective optimization in wireless sensor networks: Metrics, algorithms, and open problems. *IEEE Communications Surveys and Tutorials, 19*(1), 550–586. doi:10.1109/COMST.2016.2610578

Firte, L., Lemnaru, C., & Potolea, R. (2010). Spam Detection Filter using KNN Algo-rithm and Resampling. *IEEE International on Conference Intelligent Computer Communication and Processing,* 27-33.

Flores, E., Barron-Cedeno, A., Moreno, L., & Rosso, P. (2015). Cross-Language Source Code Re-Use Detection Using Latent Semantic Analysis. *J. UCS, 21*(13), 1708–1725.

Fok, C. L., Roman, G. C., & Lu, C. (2005, April). Mobile agent middleware for sensor networks: An application case study. In *IPSN 2005. Fourth International Symposium on Information Processing in Sensor Networks,* (pp. 382-387). IEEE.

Forrester. (2019) *The Forrester Wave™: Database-As-A-Service, Q2 2019, The 12 Providers That Matter Most And How They Stack Up.* Available at: https://www.forrester.com/report/The+Forrester+Wave+DatabaseAsAService+Q2+2019/-/E-RES144407

Furthmüller, J., Kessler, S., & Waldhorst, O. P. (2010, February). Energy-efficient management of wireless sensor networks. In *2010 Seventh International Conference on Wireless On-demand Network Systems and Services (WONS),* (pp. 129-136). IEEE. 10.1109/WONS.2010.5437120

Gaillard, B., Bouraoui, J., de Neef, E. G., & Boualem, M. (2010). Query Expansion for Cross Language Information Retrieval Improvement. *Research Challenges in Information Science (RCIS), IEEE, Fourth International Conference on,* 337-42.

Gandomi, A., & Haider, M. (2015, April). Beyond the Hype: Big Data Concepts, Methods, and Analytics. *International Journal of Information Management, 35*(2), 137–144. doi:10.1016/j.ijinfomgt.2014.10.007

Gan, G. (2011). *Data Clustering in C++: an object-oriented approach.* Chapman and Hall/CRC. doi:10.1201/b10814

Gan, G., & Ng, M. K. P. (2017). K-means clustering with outlier removal. *Pattern Recognition Letters, 90,* 8–14. doi:10.1016/j.patrec.2017.03.008

Garcia. (2014). An empirical comparison of botnet detection methods. *Computers & Security,* (45), 100-123. Retrieved from https://stratosphereips.org/new-dataset-ctu-13-extended-now-includes-pcap-files-of-normal-traffic.html

Garcia-Alvarado, C., Raghavan, V., Narayanan, S., & Waas, F. M. (2012)Automatic Data Placement in MPP Databases. *Data Engineering Workshops (ICDEW) of IEEE 28th International Conference on Self-Managing Database Systems (SMDB).*

Garcia-Molina, H., & Lindsay, B. (1990). Research directions for distributed databases. *SIGMOD Record, 19*(4), 98–103. doi:10.1145/122058.122070

Garcia-Molina, H., & Wiederhold, G. (1982). Read-only transactions in a distributed database. *ACM Transactions on Database Systems*, 7(2), 209–234. doi:10.1145/319702.319704

Garg, S., & Patel, R. B. (2017, February). Review of different deployment schemes in wireless sensor networks. In *2017 3rd International Conference on Computational Intelligence & Communication Technology (CICT)*, (pp. 1-8). IEEE. 10.1109/CIACT.2017.7977367

Garg, S. K., Versteeg, S., & Buyya, R. (2011, December). Smicloud: A framework for comparing and ranking cloud services. In *2011 Fourth IEEE International Conference on Utility and Cloud Computing* (pp. 210-218). IEEE. 10.1109/UCC.2011.36

Gayathri, N., & Kumar, S. R. (2015). Critical analysis of various routing protocols in VANET, *Int. J. Adv. Res. Computer Science. Software Engineering, 5*, 619–623.

Giuntini, F. T., Beder, D. M., & Ueyama, J. (2017). Exploiting self-organization and fault tolerance in wireless sensor networks: A case study on wildfire detection application. *International Journal of Distributed Sensor Networks*, 13(4), 1550147717704120. doi:10.1177/1550147717704120

Goli, B., & Govindan, G. (2011). Weka A Powerful Free Software for Implementing Bio-Inspired Algorithms. *CSI Communications*, 9–12.

Golnaraghi, F., & Kuo, B. C. (2017). *Automatic Control Systems*. New York: Mc Grew Hill Education.

Gray, J. N. (1978). Notes on data base operating systems. In *Operating Systems* (pp. 393–481). Berlin: Springer. doi:10.1007/3-540-08755-9_9

Grefenstette, G. (Ed.). (2012). *Cross-Language Information Retrieval* (Vol. 2). Springer Science & Business Media.

Grichi, H., Mosbahi, O., & Khalgui, M. (2014, August). Reconfigurable Wireless Sensor Networks new adaptive dynamic solutions for flexible architectures. In *2014 9th International Conference on Software Engineering and Applications (ICSOFT-EA)*, (pp. 254-265). IEEE. 10.5220/0005005602540265

Grichi, H., Mosbahi, O., Khalgui, M., & Li, Z. (2017). New power-oriented methodology for dynamic resizing and mobility of reconfigurable wireless sensor networks. *IEEE Transactions on Systems, Man, and Cybernetics. Systems*, 48(7), 1120–1130. doi:10.1109/TSMC.2016.2645401

Grozev, N., & Buyya, R. (2014). Inter-Cloud architectures and application brokering: Taxonomy and survey. *Software, Practice & Experience, 44*(3), 369–390. doi:10.1002pe.2168

Gruenwald, L., Banik, S. M., & Lau, C. N. (2007). Managing real-time database transactions in mobile ad-hoc networks. *Distributed and Parallel Databases, 22*(1), 27–54. doi:10.100710619-006-7008-2

Guerrero-Ibáñez, J., Zeadally, S., & Contreras-Castillo, J. (2018). Sensor Technologies for Intelligent Transportation Systems. *Sensors (Basel), 18*(4), 1212. doi:10.339018041212 PMID:29659524

Gulati & Srinivasan. (2019). Image Processing In Intelligent Traffic Management. *International Journal of Recent Technology and Engineering, 8*(2), 213-218.

Gupta, A. K., & Swaroop, V. (2018). Overload Handling in Replicated Real Time Distributed Databases. *International Journal of Applied Engineering Research, 13*(18), 13969-13977.

Gupta, Y., Saini, A., & Saxena, A. K. (2014). A New Similarity Function for Information Retrieval Based on Fuzzy Logic. *Advances in Computing, Communications and Informatics (ICACCI, 2014 IEEE, International Conference on, 1472-1478.*

Gupta, R., & Haritsa, J. (1996). Commit Processing in Distributed Real-Time Database Systems. *Proc. of National Conf. on Software for Real-Time Systems*. 10.1109/REAL.1996.563719

Gupta, R., Haritsa, J., & Ramamritham, K. (1997). Revisiting commit processing in distributed database systems. *SIGMOD Record*, *26*(2), 486–497. doi:10.1145/253262.253366

Gustavsson, S., & Andler, S. F. (2004). Real-time conflict management in replicated databases. In *Proceedings of the Fourth Conference for the Promotion of Research in IT at New Universities and University Colleges in Sweden (PROMOTE IT 2004)* (*Vol. 2*, pp. 504-513). Academic Press.

Gustavsson, S., & Andler, S. R. (2005, April). Continuous consistency management in distributed real-time databases with multiple writers of replicated data. In *19th IEEE International Parallel and Distributed Processing Symposium*. IEEE. 10.1109/IPDPS.2005.152

Gutiérrez, J., Villa-Medina, J. F., Nieto-Garibay, A., & Porta-Gándara, M. Á. (2013). Automated irrigation system using a wireless sensor network and GPRS module. *IEEE Transactions on Instrumentation and Measurement*, *63*(1), 166–176. doi:10.1109/TIM.2013.2276487

Haas, Z. J. (1997, Nov). *The Zone Routing Protocol*. Academic Press.

Habebeh, I. O. (n.d.). A Method for Fragment Allocation Design in Distributed Database System. *The Sixth Annual U.A.E. University Research Conference*.

Hacigümüş, H., Iyer, B., & Mehrotra, S. (2002). Providing database as a service. *Proceedings - International Conference on Data Engineering*, 29–38. 10.1109/ICDE.2002.994695

Haj Said, A., Sadeg, B., Amanton, L., & Ayeb, B. (2008). A Protocol to Control Replication in Distributed Real-Time Database Systems. *Proceedings of the Tenth International Conference on Enterprise Information Systems*, 501-504.

Hameed, S., & Vaidya, N. H. (1999). Efficient algorithms for scheduling data broadcast. *Wireless Networks*, *5*(3), 183–193. doi:10.1023/A:1019194826654

Han, J., Kamber, M., & Pei, J. (2012). *Data Mining Concepts and Techniques* (3rd ed.). Morgan Kaufmann Publishers.

Haritsa, J. R., Canrey, M. J., & Livny, M. (1993). Value-based scheduling in real-time database systems. *The VLDB Journal*, *2*(2), 1993. doi:10.1007/BF01232184

Haritsa, J. R., Carey, M. J., & Livny, M. (1992). Data Access Scheduling in Firm Real-Time Database Systems. *Real-Time Systems*, *04*(03), 203–241. doi:10.1007/BF00365312

Haritsa, J. R., Ramamritham, K., & Gupta, R. (2000). The PROMPT real-time commit protocol. *IEEE Transactions on Parallel and Distributed Systems*, *11*(02), 160–181. doi:10.1109/71.841752

Haritsa, J., Carey, M., & Livny, M. (1990). On being optimistic about real-time constraints. *Proceedings of the ninth ACM SIGACT-SIGMOD-SIGART symposium on Principles of database systems*, 331-343. 10.1145/298514.298585

Harman, D. (1993). Overview of the First TREC Conference. *Proceedings of the 16th annual international ACM SIGIR conference on Research and development in information retrieval*, 36-47.

Hartenstein, H., & Laberteaux, K. P. (2008). A tutorial survey on vehicular ad hoc networks. *Communications Magazine, IEEE*, *46*(6), 164–171. doi:10.1109/MCOM.2008.4539481

Hassan, H. A., Salem, S. A., Mostafa, A. M., & Saad, E. (2016). Harmonic segment-based semi-partitioning scheduling on multi-core real-time systems. *ACM Transactions on Embedded Computing Systems*, *15*(73).

Hauff, C., & Hiemstra, D., & de Jong. (2008). A Survey of Pre-Retrieval Query Performance Predictors. *Proceedings of the 17th ACM conference on Information and knowledge management*, 1419-20. 10.1145/1458082.1458311

Hautamäki, V., Cherednichenko, S., Kärkkäinen, I., Kinnunen, T., & Fränti, P. (2005, June). Improving k-means by outlier removal. In *Scandinavian Conference on Image Analysis* (pp. 978-987). Springer. 10.1007/11499145_99

He, Z., Xu, X., & Deng, S. (2003). Discovering cluster-based local outliers. *Pattern Recognition Letters*, *24*(9-10), 1641–1650. doi:10.1016/S0167-8655(03)00003-5

Hofer, C. N. (2009). Cloud Computing Services: Taxonomy and comparison. *Fifth International Joint Conference on INC, IMS and IDC*, 44-51.

Horowitz, E., & Sahni, S. (1978). *Fundamentals of Computer Algorithms*. Rockville, MD: Computer Science Press.

Hsin, C., & Liu, M. (2006). Self-monitoring of wireless sensor networks. *Computer Communications, 29*(4), 462-476.

Huang, D., He, B., & Miao, C. (2014). A survey of resource management in multi-tier web applications. *IEEE Communications Surveys and Tutorials*, *16*(3), 1574–1590. doi:10.1109/SURV.2014.010814.00060

Huang, H., Guo, W., & Zhang, Y. (2008). A Novel Method for Image Spam Filtering. *9th International Conference for Young Computer Scientists*. 10.1109/ICYCS.2008.440

Huang, Han, J., Zhang, X., & Liu, J. (2019). Automatic Identification of Honeypot Server Using Machine Learning Techniques. *Security and Communication Networks*, *2019*, 1–8. doi:10.1155/2019/2627608

Hui, C. Y., Ng, J. K. Y., & Lee, V. C. S. (2005, August). On-demand broadcast algorithms with caching on improving response time for real time information dispatch systems. In *11th IEEE International Conference on Embedded and Real-Time Computing Systems and Applications (RTCSA'05)* (pp. 285-288). IEEE.

Hu, R., Liu, J., & Liu, X. F. (2011, May). A trustworthiness fusion model for service cloud platform based on DS evidence theory. In *Proceedings of the 2011 11th IEEE/ACM International Symposium on Cluster, Cloud and Grid Computing* (pp. 566-571). IEEE Computer Society. 10.1109/CCGrid.2011.31

Imielinski, T., & Badrinath, B. R. (1994). Mobile wireless computing. *Communications of the ACM*, *37*(10), 18–29. doi:10.1145/194313.194317

Imielinski, T., Viswanathan, S., & Badrinath, B. R. (1997). Data on air: Organization and access. *IEEE Transactions on Knowledge and Data Engineering*, *9*(3), 353–372. doi:10.1109/69.599926

Islam, M. R., & Xiang, Y. (2010). Email Classification Using Data Reduction Method. *5th International ICST Conference on Communications and Networking*, 1-5.

Jacobs, I. S. (1963). Fine particles, thin films and exchange anisotropy. *Magnetism*, 271-350.

Jadhav, P., Kelkar, P., Patil, K., & Thorat, S. (2016). *Smart Traffic Control System Using Image Processing. International Research Journal of Engineering and Technology, 3*, 1207–1211.

Jadon, S., & Yadav, R. S. (2018). Load balancing in multicore systems using heuristics based approach. *International Journal of Intelligent Systems and Applications*, *12*(12), 56–68. doi:10.5815/ijisa.2018.12.06

Jarasuniene. (2007). *Research Into Intelligent Transport Systems (Its) Technologies and Efficiency*. Academic Press.

Jayakumar, G. D. S., & Thomas, B. J. (2013). A new procedure of clustering based on multivariate outlier detection. *Journal of Data Science: JDS, 11*(1), 69–84.

Jazi, Gonzalez, H., Stakhanova, N., & Ghorbani, A. A. (2017). Detecting http-based application layer dos attacks on web servers in the presence of sampling. *Computer Networks*, *121*, 25–36. doi:10.1016/j.comnet.2017.03.018

JH, MK, & JP. (2006). Data Mining: Concepts and Techniques (2nd ed.). Morgan Kaufmann Publication.

Jiang, W., Cui, H., & Chen, J. (2009). *Spectrum-aware cluster-based routing protocol for multiple-hop cognitive wireless network*. Paper presented at the Communications Technology and Applications, 2009. ICCTA'09. IEEE International Conference on.

Jiang, M. F., Tseng, S. S., & Su, C. M. (2001). Two-phase clustering process for outliers detection. *Pattern Recognition Letters*, *22*(6-7), 691–700. doi:10.1016/S0167-8655(00)00131-8

Jiang, S. Y., & An, Q. B. (2008, October). Clustering-based outlier detection method. In *2008 Fifth International Conference on Fuzzy Systems and Knowledge Discovery* (Vol. 2, pp. 429-433). IEEE. 10.1109/FSKD.2008.244

Jinchao Chen, F. X., Du, C., & Lin, B. (2016). *Allocation and scheduling of strictly periodic tasks in multi-core real-time systems*. Embedded and Real-Time Computing Systems and Applications.

Jindal, A., & Dittrich, J. (2011). *Relax and Let the Database Do the Partitioning Online*. Business Intellignce for Real Time Enterprize.

Ji, X., Yu, H., Fan, G., & Fu, W. (2016). SDGR: an SDN-based geographic routing protocol for vanet. *Proceedings of IEEE International Conference on Internet of Things (iThings) and IEEE Green Computing and Communications (GreenCom) and IEEE Cyber, Physical and Social Computing (CPSCom) and IEEE Smart Data (SmartData). IEEE*, 276–281. 10.1109/iThings-GreenCom-CPSCom-SmartData.2016.70

Johnson, D. B., & Maltz, D. A. (1996). *Dynamic Source Routing in Ad Hoc Wireless Networks. In* T. Imielinski & H. Korth (Eds.), *Mobile Computing* (pp. 153–181). Kluwer.

Joshi, H. P., Sichitiu, M., & Kihl, M. (2007, May). *Distributed Robust Geocast Multicast Routing for Inter-Vehicle Communication*. Academic Press.

Joshi, H., Bhatt, A., & Patel, H. (2013). Transliterated Search using Syllabification Approach. Forum for Information Retrieval Evaluation.

Jothilakshmi, R., Shanthi, N., & Babisaraswathi, R. (2013). A survey on semantic query expansion. *Journal of Theoretical & Applied Information Technology*, *57*(1), 128–138.

Jurenoks, A. (2016). Developing the Reconfiguration Method to Increase Life Expectancy of Dynamic Wireless Sensor Network in Container Terminal. *Applied Computer Systems*, *20*(1), 15–20. doi:10.1515/acss-2016-0010

Kadam, N. V., & Pund, M. A. (2013). Joint approach for outlier detection. *International Journal of Computer Science Applications*, *6*(2), 45–4.

Kala, R. (2016). *On-Road Intelligent, Vehicles*. Butterworth-Heinemann Publications.

Kanaka, H.-H., Lee, I., Choi, J.-Y., Sokolsky, O., & Philippou, A. (1998). Symbolic schedulability analysis of real-time systems. *IEEE Real Time Systems Symposium*, 409-418.

Karagiannis, G., Altintas, O., Ekici, E., Heijenk, G., Jarupan, B., Lin, K., & Weil, T. (2011). Vehicular networking: A survey and tutorial on requirements, architectures, challenges, standards and solutions. *IEEE Communications Surveys and Tutorials*, *13*(4), 584–616. doi:10.1109/SURV.2011.061411.00019

Karp, B., & Kung, H. T. (2000). GPSR: Greedy perimeter stateless routing for wireless networks. *Proceedings of the 6th annual international conference on Mobile computing and networking*, 243-254.

Kato, S., & Yamasaki, N. (2008). Portioned Static-Priority Scheduling on Multiprocessors. *IEEE International Symposium on Parallel and Distributed Processing*, 1-12.

Kato, S., & Yamasaki, N. (2008). *Scheduling aperiodic tasks using total bandwidth server on multiprocessors*. IEEE Embedded and Ubiquitous Computing. doi:10.1109/EUC.2008.28

Katta, E., & Arora, A. (2015). An Improved Approach to English-Hindi Based Cross Language Information Retrieval System. *Contemporary Computing (IC3), 2015 IEEE Eighth International Conference on*, 354-59.

Kawadia, V., & Kumar, P. (2003). *Power control and clustering in ad hoc networks*. Paper presented at the INFOCOM 2003. Twenty-Second Annual Joint Conference of the IEEE Computer and Communications. IEEE Societies.

Kellner, A. (2017). Multi-objective Ant Colony Optimisation in Wireless Sensor Networks. In *Nature-Inspired Computing and Optimization* (pp. 51–78). Cham: Springer. doi:10.1007/978-3-319-50920-4_3

Kern, D., Mutschke, P., & Mayr, P. (2014). Establishing an Online Access Panel for Interactive Information Retrieval Research. *Digital Libraries (JCDL), 2014 IEEE/ACM Joint Conference on*, 473-74.

Khan, J. A., Qureshi, H. K., & Iqbal, A. (2015). Energy management in wireless sensor networks: A survey. *Computers & Electrical Engineering*, *41*, 159–176. doi:10.1016/j.compeleceng.2014.06.009

Kihl, M. (2007). *Reliable Geographical Multicast Routing in Vehicular Ad-hoc Networks*. Academic Press.

Kim, H. W., & Cho, H. S. (2017). SOUNET: Self-organized underwater wireless sensor network. *Sensors (Basel)*, *17*(2), 283. doi:10.339017020283 PMID:28157164

Kim, S., Lee, S., & Hwang, C. S. (2003). Using reordering technique for mobile transaction management in broadcast environments. *Data & Knowledge Engineering*, *45*(1), 79–100. doi:10.1016/S0169-023X(02)00155-6

Kim, Y. K. (1996). Towards real-time performance in a scalable, continuously available telecom. *DBMS (Redwood City, Calif.)*.

Klein, S. (2007). Introduction to Electronic Auctions. *Electronic Markets*, *7*(4), 3–6. doi:10.1080/10196789700000041

Kotsiantis, S. B. (2007). Supervised Machine Learning: A Review of Classification Techniques. *Informatica*, *31*, 249–268.

Kraus, S., Shehory, O., & Taase, G. (2003). Coalition Formation with Uncertain Heterogeneous Information. *Proceedings of the International Conference on Autonomous Agents*, 2, 1–8. doi: 10.1145/860576.860577

Krochmal, M., & Husi, H. (2018). Knowledge discovery and data mining. Integration of Omics Approaches and Systems Biology for Clinical Applications, 233-247.

Kumar, S., & Singh, A. K. (2018b). A localized algorithm for clustering in cognitive radio networks. *Journal of King Saud University-Computer and Information Sciences*.

Kumar, D. (2019). Fair mechanisms for combinatorial reverse auction-based cloud market. In *Smart Innovation, Systems and Technologies* (pp. 267–277). Singapore: Springer. doi:10.1007/978-981-13-1747-7_26

Kumar, D., Baranwal, G., Raza, Z., & Vidyarthi, D. P. (2017). A systematic study of double auction mechanisms in cloud computing. *Journal of Systems and Software*, *125*, 234–255. doi:10.1016/j.jss.2016.12.009

Kumar, S., Chow, T. W., & Pecht, M. (2009). Approach to fault identification for electronic products using Mahalanobis distance. *IEEE Transactions on Instrumentation and Measurement*, *59*(8), 2055–2064. doi:10.1109/TIM.2009.2032884

Kumar, S., & Singh, A. K. (2018a). Fault tolerant backbone construction in cognitive radio networks. *AEÜ. International Journal of Electronics and Communications*, *87*, 76–86. doi:10.1016/j.aeue.2018.02.010

Kuo, T.-W., Yang, W.-R., & Lin, K.-J. (2002). A class of rate-based real-time scheduling algorithms. *IEEE Transactions on Computers*, *51*(6), 708–720. doi:10.1109/TC.2002.1009154

Kwok, K. L. (1997). Evaluation of an English-Chinese Cross-Lingual Retrieval Experiment. Working Notes of AAAI-97 Spring Symposiums on Cross-Language Text and Speech Retrieval, 110-14.

Lam, K. Y., Chan, E., & Yuen, J. C. H. (2000). Approaches for broadcasting temporal data in mobile computing systems. *Journal of Systems and Software*, *51*(3), 175–189. doi:10.1016/S0164-1212(99)00122-3

Lam, K. Y., Kuo, T. W., Tsang, W. H., & Law, G. C. (2000). Concurrency control in mobile distributed real-time database systems. *Information Systems*, *25*(4), 261–286. doi:10.1016/S0306-4379(00)00018-1

Lam, K. Y., Lee, V. C., Hung, S. L., & Kao, B. C. (1997). Priority assignment in distributed real-time databases using optimistic concurrency control. *IEE Proceedings. Computers and Digital Techniques*, *144*(5), 324–330. doi:10.1049/ip-cdt:19971496

Langston, J. W., & He, X. (2007). *Multi-core processors and caching: A survey*. Citeseerx.

Larkin, B., & Rose, M. (2015). *2015 Top Markets Report Cloud Computing*. Available at: http://www.export.gov/industry/infocomm/eg_main_086865.asp

Lee, K., Kageura, K., & Choi, K. (2002). Implicit Ambiguity Resolution Using Incremental Clustering in Korean-To-English Cross-Language Information Retrieval. *Proceedings of the 19th International Conference on Computational linguistics*, 1-7.

Lee, W.L., Datta, A., & Cardell-Oliver, R. (2006). *Winms: Wireless sensor network-management system, an adaptive policy-based management for wireless sensor networks*. Academic Press.

Lee, C.-H., & Shin, K. (2004). On-line dynamic voltage scaling for hard real-time systems using the EDF algorithm. *Real Time Systems Symposium*, 319-335.

Lee, S., Hwang, C. S., & Kitsuregawa, M. (2003). Using predeclaration for efficient read-only transaction processing in wireless data broadcast. *IEEE Transactions on Knowledge and Data Engineering*, *15*(6), 1579–1583. doi:10.1109/TKDE.2003.1245294

Lee, V. C. S., Lam, K., Kao, B. C. M., Lam, K., & Hung, S. (1996). Priority Assignment for Sub-transaction in Distributed Real-Time Databases. *First Int. In Workshop on Real-Time Database Systems*.

Lee, V. C., Lam, K. W., & Kuo, T. W. (2004). Efficient validation of mobile transactions in wireless environments. *Journal of Systems and Software*, *69*(1-2), 183–193. doi:10.1016/S0164-1212(03)00084-0

Lee, V. C., Lam, K. W., & Son, S. H. (2002). Concurrency control using timestamp ordering in broadcast environments. *The Computer Journal*, *45*(4), 410–422. doi:10.1093/comjnl/45.4.410

Lee, V. C., Lam, K. W., Son, S. H., & Chan, E. Y. (2002). On transaction processing with partial validation and time-stamp ordering in mobile broadcast environments. *IEEE Transactions on Computers*, *51*(10), 1196–1211. doi:10.1109/TC.2002.1039845

Lee, V. C., Wu, X., & Ng, J. K. Y. (2006). Scheduling real-time requests in on-demand data broadcast environments. *Real-Time Systems*, *34*(2), 83–99. doi:10.100711241-006-7982-5

Lee, V., Ng, J. K., Chong, J. Y., & Lam, K. W. (2004). Reading temporally consistent data in broadcast disks. *Mobile Computing and Communications Review*, *8*(3), 57–67. doi:10.1145/1031483.1031491

Levow, G., Oard, D. W., & Resnik, P. (2005). Dictionary-Based Techniques for Cross-Language Information Retrieval. *Information Processing & Management, 41*(3), 523–547. doi:10.1016/j.ipm.2004.06.012

Li, C., Liu, W., Li, J., Liu, Q., & Li, C. (2013). *Aggregation based spectrum allocation in cognitive radio networks.* Paper presented at the Communications in China-Workshops (CIC/ICCC), 2013 IEEE/CIC International Conference on. 10.1109/ICCChinaW.2013.6670566

Li, Z., Li, S., & Zhou, X. (2009, September). PFMA: Policy-based feedback management architecture for wireless sensor Networks. In *2009 5th International Conference on Wireless Communications, Networking and Mobile Computing* (pp. 1-4). IEEE.

Li, F., & Wang, Y. (2007). Routing in vehicular ad hoc networks: A survey. *IEEE Vehicular Technology Magazine, 2*(2), 12–22. doi:10.1109/MVT.2007.912927

Li, L., & Gruenwald, L. (2012). Autonomous database partitioning using data mining on single computers and cluster computers. *Proceedings of the 16th International Database Engineering & Applications Sysmposium (IDEAS)*, 32-41.

Lin, M., Li, M., Hsu, C., & Wu, S. (2010). Query Expansion from Wikipedia and Topic Web Crawler on CLIR. NTCIR, 101-6.

Lin, C. R., & Gerla, M. (1997). Adaptive clustering for mobile wireless networks. *IEEE Journal on Selected Areas in Communications, 15*(7), 1265–1275. doi:10.1109/49.622910

Lindström, J. (2003). *Optimistic concurrency control methods for real-time database systems* (Ph.D. Dissertation). Department of Computer Science, University of Helsinki, Finland.

Liu, Y-H., & Belkin, N.J. (2008). Query Reformulation, Search Performance, And Term Suggestion Devices In Question-Answering Tasks. *ACM Proceedings of the second international symposium on Information interaction in context,* 21-6.

Liu, H., Shah, S., & Jiang, W. (2004). On-line outlier detection and data cleaning. *Computers & Chemical Engineering, 28*(9), 1635–1647. doi:10.1016/j.compchemeng.2004.01.009

Liu, J. (2000). *Real-Time Systems*. Prentice Hall.

Liu, W., Zhang, Y., Lou, W., & Fang, Y. (2004, October). Managing wireless sensor networks with supply chain strategy. In *First International Conference on Quality of Service in Heterogeneous Wired/Wireless Networks*, (pp. 59-66). IEEE. 10.1109/QSHINE.2004.29

Lokhande, D. B., & Dhainje, P. B. (2019). A Novel Approach for Transaction Management in Heterogeneous Distributed Real Time Replicated Database Systems. *International Journal for Scientific Research and Development, 7*(1), 840-844.

Lo, S. C., & Chen, A. L. P. (2000). An adaptive access method for broadcast data under an error-prone mobile environment. *IEEE Transactions on Knowledge and Data Engineering, 12*(4), 609–620. doi:10.1109/69.868910

Macchelli & Melchiorri. (2002). A real-time control system for industrial robots and control applications based on real-time linux. *IFAC, 35*, 55-60.

Macdonald, C., & Ounis, I. (2007). Expertise Drift and Query Expansion in Expert Search. *Proceedings of the sixteenth ACM conference on Conference on information and knowledge management*, 341-50. 10.1145/1321440.1321490

Macías-Escrivá, F. D., Haber, R., Del Toro, R., & Hernandez, V. (2013). Self-adaptive systems: A survey of current approaches, research challenges and applications. *Expert Systems with Applications, 40*(18), 7267–7279. doi:10.1016/j.eswa.2013.07.033

Madria, S. K., Mohania, M., Bhowmick, S. S., & Bhargava, B. (2002). Mobile data and transaction management. *Information Sciences, 141*(3-4), 279–309. doi:10.1016/S0020-0255(02)00178-0

Mala, V., & Lobiyal, D. K. (2016, April). Semantic and Keyword Based Web Techniques in Information Retrieval. In *Computing, Communication and Automation (ICCCA), 2016 International Conference on* (pp. 23-26). IEEE.

Mallik, S. (2014). Intelligent Transportation System. *International Journal of Civil Engineering Research, 5*(4), 367-372.

Mandal, D., Dandapat, S., Gupta, M., Banerjee, P., & Sarkar, S. (2007). Bengali and Hindi to English Cross-Language Text Retrieval under Limited Resources. In *CLEF*. Working Notes.

Manipriya, S., & Gitakrishnan, V. V. (2015). Grid- Based Real Time Image Processing (GRIP) Algorithm for Heterogeneous Traffic. In *IEEE International conference on Communication Systems and Networks*. IEEE Publications.

Manipriya, S., & Mala, C. (2016). Real Time Multilevel Video Image Processing for VANET. *Proc. 5th international Conference on Computing, Communication and Sensor Network*.

Manoj, C. K., Sagar, R., Pushpak, B., & Om, D.P. (2007). *Hindi and Marathi to English Cross Language Information Retrieval at CLEF*. Academic Press.

Mantas, Stakhanova, N., Gonzalez, H., Jazi, H. H., & Ghorbani, A. A. (2015). Application-layer denial of service attacks: Taxonomy and survey. *International Journal of Information and Computer Security, 7*(2-4), 216–239. doi:10.1504/IJICS.2015.073028

Marsh, S. P. (1994). Formalising trust as a computational concept. Computing, 184.

Mathiason, G., Andler, S. F., & Son, S. H. (2007, August). Virtual full replication by adaptive segmentation. In *13th IEEE International Conference on Embedded and Real-Time Computing Systems and Applications (RTCSA 2007)* (pp. 327-336). IEEE.

Ma, W., Tran, D., & Sharma, D. (2009) A Novel Spam Email Detection System Based on Negative Selection. *4th International Conference on Computer Sciences and Convergence Information Technology*, 987-992. 10.1109/ICCIT.2009.58

Maxwell, T., & Schafer, B. (2010). Natural Language Processing and Query Expansion in Legal Information Retrieval: Challenges and a Response. *International Review of Law Computers & Technology, 24*(1), 63–72. doi:10.1080/13600860903570194

Ma, Y. W., Chen, J. L., Huang, Y. M., & Lee, M. Y. (2010). An efficient management system for wireless sensor networks. *Sensors (Basel), 10*(12), 11400–11413. doi:10.3390101211400 PMID:22163534

McCormick, W. T. Jr, Schweitzer, P. J., & White, T. W. (1972, September). Problem Decomposition and Data Reorganization by A Clustering Technique. *Operations Research, 20*(5), 993–1009. doi:10.1287/opre.20.5.993

Melnykov, I., & Melnykov, V. (2014). On K-means algorithm with the use of Mahalanobis distances. *Statistics & Probability Letters, 84*, 88–95. doi:10.1016/j.spl.2013.09.026

Mihailescu, M., & Teo, Y. M. (2010). Dynamic resource pricing on federated clouds. *CCGrid 2010 - 10th IEEE/ACM International Conference on Cluster, Cloud, and Grid Computing*, 513–517. 10.1109/CCGRID.2010.123

Mills, K. L. (2007). A brief survey of self-organization in wireless sensor networks. *Wireless Communications and Mobile Computing, 7*(7), 823–834. doi:10.1002/wcm.499

Mitola, J., & Maguire, G. Q. (1999). Cognitive radio: making software radios more personal. *IEEE Personal Communications, 6*(4), 13-18.

Miyabe, M., & Yoshino, T. (2015). Evaluation of the Validity of Back-Translation as a Method of Assessing the Accuracy of Machine Translation. *Culture and Computing (Culture Computing), 2015 IEEE International Conference on,* 145-50.

ModaClouds. (2015). *ModaClouds, MOdel-Driven Approach for design and execution of applications on multiple Clouds.* Available at: http://www.modaclouds.eu/

Mok, E., Leong, H. V., & Si, A. (1999, December). Transaction processing in an asymmetric mobile environment. In *International Conference on Mobile Data Access* (pp. 71-82). Springer. 10.1007/3-540-46669-X_7

Moridi, E., & Barati, H. (2017). RMRPTS: A reliable multi-level routing protocol with tabu search in VANET. *Telecommunication Systems, 65*(1), 127–137. doi:10.100711235-016-0219-6

Moylan, P., Betz, R., & Middleton, R. (1993). *The Priority Disinheritance Problem.* Technical Report EE9345, University of Newcastle.

Muñoz-Gea, J. P., Manzanares-Lopez, P., Malgosa-Sanahuja, J., & Garcia-Haro, J. (2013). Design and implementation of a P2P communication infrastructure for WSN-based vehicular traffic control applications. *Journal of Systems Architecture, 59*(10), 923–930. doi:10.1016/j.sysarc.2013.08.002

Murphy, K. (2012). *Machine Learning: A Probabilistic Perspective.* Cambridge, MA: MIT Press.

Narayan, R., Mallikarjunaswamy, B.P., & Supriya, M.C. (2014). *Self-optimization and Self-Protection (Transactional Security) in AODV Based Wireless Sensor Network.* Academic Press.

Navas, J. C., & Imielinski, T. (1997). Geocast - geographic addressing and routing, 1096. *Proceedings of the 3rd annual ACM/IEEE international conference 1097 on Mobile computing and networking, in: MobiCom '97, ACM,* 66–76.

Navathe, S., Ceri, S., Wierhold, G., & Dou, J. (1984, December). Vertical Partitioning Algorithms for Database Design. *ACM Transactions on Database Systems, 9*(4), 680–710. doi:10.1145/1994.2209

Navathe, S., & Ra, M. (1989). Vertical Partitioning for Database Design: A Graph Algorithm. *ACM Special Interest Group on Management of Data (SIGMOD) International Conference on Management of Data.*

Nayyar, A., & Singh, R. (2015). A comprehensive review of simulation tools for wireless sensor networks (WSNs). *Journal of Wireless Networking and Communications, 5*(1), 19–47.

Ndiaye, M., Hancke, G. P., & Abu-Mahfouz, A. M. (2017). Software defined networking for improved wireless sensor network management: A survey. *Sensors (Basel), 17*(5), 1031. doi:10.339017051031 PMID:28471390

Nekovee, M. (2009). *Quantifying the availability of TV white spaces for cognitive radio operation in the UK.* Paper presented at the Communications Workshops, 2009. ICC Workshops 2009. IEEE International Conference on. 10.1109/ICCW.2009.5208035

Nguyen, T. T. T., & Armitage, G. (2008). A survey of techniques for internet traffic classification using machine learning. *IEEE Communications Surveys and Tutorials, 10*(4), 56–76. doi:10.1109/SURV.2008.080406

Nie, T., & Zhang, T. (2009, January). A study of DES and Blowfish encryption algorithm. In Tencon 2009-2009 IEEE Region 10 Conference (pp. 1-4). IEEE.

Nkoro, A. B., & Vershinin, Y. A. (2018). Current and future trends in applications of Intelligent Transport Systems on cars and infrastructure. *17th International IEEE Conference on Intelligent Transportation Systems (ITSC),* 514-519.

Noor, T. H., Sheng, Q. Z., Zeadally, S., & Yu, J. (2013). Trust management of services in cloud environments: Obstacles and solutions. *ACM Computing Surveys, 46*(1), 1–30. doi:10.1145/2522968.2522980

O'hare, G. M. P., Marsh, D., Ruzzelli, A., & Tynan, R. (2005, May). Agents for wireless sensor network power management. In *Proceedings of International Workshop on Wireless and Sensor Networks (WSNET-05)*. IEEE Press.

Oard, D. W. (2003). The Surprise Language Exercises. *ACM Transactions on Asian Language Information Processing*, *2*(2), 79–84. doi:10.1145/974740.974741

Othman, M. F., & Shazali, K. (2012). Wireless sensor network applications: A study in environment monitoring system. *Procedia Engineering*, *41*, 1204–1210. doi:10.1016/j.proeng.2012.07.302

Ouzzani, M., Medjahed, B., & Elmagarmid, A. K. (2009). Correctness criteria beyond serializability. Encyclopedia of database systems, 501-506.

Ouzzani, M., & Bouguettaya, A. (2004). Efficient access to web services. *IEEE Internet Computing*, *8*(2), 34–44. doi:10.1109/MIC.2004.1273484

Ozolins, U. (2008). Issues of Back Translation Methodology in Medical Translations. *Proceedings, FIT [International Federation of Translators] XVIII Congress*.

Padmanabhan, P., Gruenwald, L., Vallur, A., & Atiquzzaman, M. (2008). A survey of data replication techniques for mobile ad hoc network databases. *The VLDB Journal—The International Journal on Very Large Data Bases, 17*(5), 1143-1164.

Padmavathi, B., & Kumari, S. R. (2013). *A survey on performance analysis of DES, AES and RSA algorithm along with LSB substitution*. IJSR.

Pal, S., Kundu, S., Chatterjee, M., & Das, S. (2007). Combinatorial reverse auction based scheduling in multirate wireless systems. *IEEE Transactions on Computers*, *56*(10), 1329–1341. doi:10.1109/TC.2007.1082

Pandey, S., & Shanker, U. (2018a). A One Phase Priority Inheritance Commit Protocol. *Proceedings of the 14th International Conference on Distributed Computing and Information Technology (ICDCIT)*. 10.1007/978-3-319-72344-0_24

Pandey, S., & Shanker, U. (2018b). CART: A Real-Time Concurrency Control Protocol. In *22nd International Database Engineering & Applications Symposium (IDEAS 2018)*. ACM.

Pandey, S., & Shanker, U. (2018c). CART: A Real-Time Concurrency Control Protocol. In *22nd International Database Engineering & Applications Symposium (IDEAS 2018)*. ACM.

Pandey, S., & Shanker, U. (2019b). MDTF: A Contention Aware Priority Assignment Policy for Cohorts in DRTDBS. In Encyclopedia of Organizational Knowledge, Administration, and Technologies, 1st Edition. Academic Press.

Pandey, S., & Shanker, U. (2019c). Transaction Scheduling Protocols for Controlling Priority Inversion: A Review. *Journal of Computer Science Review*.

Pandey, S., & Daniel, A. K. (2016, March). Fuzzy logic based cloud service trustworthiness model. In *2016 IEEE International Conference on Engineering and Technology (ICETECH)* (pp. 73-78). IEEE. 10.1109/ICETECH.2016.7569215

Pandey, S., & Daniel, A. K. (2017). QoCS and cost based cloud service selection framework. *Int. J. Eng. Trends Technol.*, *48*(3), 167–172. doi:10.14445/22315381/IJETT-V48P230

Pandey, S., & Shanker, U. (2016). Transaction Execution in Distributed Real-Time Database Systems. *Proceedings of the International Conference on Innovations in information Embedded and Communication Systems*, 96-100.

Pandey, S., & Shanker, U. (2017a). IDRC: A Distributed Real-Time Commit Protocol. *Procedia Computer Science, 125*, 290–296. doi:10.1016/j.procs.2017.12.039

Pandey, S., & Shanker, U. (2017b). On Using Priority Inheritance Based Distributed Static Two Phase Locking Protocol. *Proceedings of the International Conference on Data and Information System (ICDIS)*, 179-188.

Pandey, S., & Shanker, U. (2018b). Priority Inversion in DRTDBS: Challenges and Resolutions. *Proceedings of the ACM India Joint International Conference on Data Science and Management of Data (CoDS-COMAD '18)*, 305-309. 10.1145/3152494.3167976

Pandey, S., & Shanker, U. (2019a). *EDRC: An Early Data Lending based Real-Time Commit Protocol. Encyclopedia of Organizational Knowledge* (1st ed.). Administration, and Technologies.

Papadomanolakis, S., Dash, D., & Ailamaki, A. (2007, September). Efficient use of the query optimizer for automated physical design. *Proceeding of the 33rd international conference on* Very Large Data Bases *(VLDB)*.

Paradis, L., & Han, Q. (2007). A survey of fault management in wireless sensor networks. *Journal of Network and Systems Management, 15*(2), 171–190. doi:10.100710922-007-9062-0

Parsons, S., Rodriguez-Aguilar, J. A., & Klein, M. (2011). Auctions and bidding: A guide for computer scientists. *ACM Computing Surveys, 43*(2), 1–59. doi:10.1145/1883612.1883617

Pasquier, N., Bastide, Y., Taouil, R., & Lakhal, L. (1999). Efficient mining of association rules using closed itemset lattices. *Information Systems, 24*(1).

Pattanaik, V., Singh, M., Gupta, P. K., & Singh, S. K. (2016). *Smart real-time traffic congestion estimation and clustering technique for urban vehicular roads. In IEEE Region 10 Conference* (pp. 3420–3423). TENCON.

Peddi, P., & DiPippo, L. C. (2002). A replication strategy for distributed real-time object-oriented databases. In *Proceedings Fifth IEEE International Symposium on Object-Oriented Real-Time Distributed Computing. ISIRC 2002* (pp. 129-136). IEEE. 10.1109/ISORC.2002.1003670

Pei, G., Gerla, M., & Chen, T. W. (2000, June). Fisheye State Routing: A Routing Scheme for Ad Hoc Wireless Networks. *Proc. ICC 2000.*

Peng, Leckie, C., & Ramamohanarao, K. (2007). Survey of network-based defense mechanisms countering the dos and ddos problems. *ACM Computing Surveys, 39*(1), 3, es. doi:10.1145/1216370.1216373

Perakovic, Perisa, M., Cvitic, I., & Husnjak, S. (2017). Model for detection and classification of ddos traffic based on artificial neural network. *Telfor Journal, 9*(1), 26–31. doi:10.5937/telfor1701026P

Perillo, M., & Heinzelman, W. B. (2003, May). Providing application QoS through intelligent sensor management. In *Proceedings of the First IEEE International Workshop on Sensor Network Protocols and Applications*, (pp. 93-101). IEEE. 10.1109/SNPA.2003.1203360

Perkins, C., Belding-Royer, E., & Das, S. (2013). *Ad hoc On-Demand Distance Vector (AODV) Routing.* RFC-3561.

Pignaton de Freitas, E. (2008). *A survey on adaptable middleware for wireless sensor networks.* Academic Press.

Pigur, V. A. (1979). Multilanguage Information-Retrieval Systems: Integration Levels and Language Support. *Automatic Documentation and Mathematical Linguistics, 13*(1), 36–46.

Pingali, P., Tune, K. K., & Verma, V. (2007). Improving Recall for Hindi, Telugu, Oromo to English CLIR. In *Workshop of the Cross-Language Evaluation Forum for European Languages* (pp. 103–110). Berlin: Springer.

Pitoura, E., & Chrysanthis, P. K. (1999, June). Scalable processing of read-only transactions in broadcast push. In *Proceedings. 19th IEEE International Conference on Distributed Computing Systems (Cat. No. 99CB37003)* (pp. 432-439). IEEE.

Pitoura, E., & Samaras, G. (2012). *Data management for mobile computing* (Vol. 10). Springer Science & Business Media.

Ponte, J. M., & Croft, W. B. (1998). A Language Modeling Approach to Information Retrieval. *Proceedings of the 21st annual international ACM SIGIR conference on Research and development in information retrieval*, 275- 81. 10.1145/290941.291008

Poonia, R. C., Bhargava, D., & Kumar, B. S. (2015). CDRA: Cluster-based dynamic routing approach as a development of the AODV in vehicular ad-hoc networks. *Proceedings of International Conference on Signal Processing and Communication Engineering Systems (SPACES)*, 397-401. 10.1109/SPACES.2015.7058293

Prakash, U., Thankappan, A., & Balakrishnan, A. (2018). *Density Based Traffic Control System Using Image Processing.* doi:10.1109/ICETIETR.2018.8529111

Prasad. (2014). *Dos and ddos attacks: defense, detection and traceback mechanisms-a survey. Global Journal of Computer Science and Technology.*

Prasad. (2017). Bifad: Bio-inspired anomaly based http-flood attack detection. *Wireless Personal Communications*, *97*(1), 281–308. doi:10.100711277-017-4505-8

Prasad, A. S., & Rao, S. (2014). A mechanism design approach to resource procurement in cloud computing. *IEEE Transactions on Computers*, *63*(1), 17–30. doi:10.1109/TC.2013.106

Pu, C., & Leff, A. (1990). *Replica control in distributed systems: An asynchronous approach.* Academic Press.

Punitha & Mala. (2018). Svm based traffic classification for mitigating http attack. In *Mobile Internet Security (MobiSec 18), 2018 The 3rd International Symposium.* KIISC Research Group on 5G Security, University of San Carlos.

Qin, B., & Liu, Y. (2003). High performance distributed real-time commit protocol. *Journal of Systems and Software*, *68*(02), 145–152. doi:10.1016/S0164-1212(02)00145-0

Quan, G., & Chaturvedi, V. (2010). Feasibility analysis for temperature-constraint hard real-time periodic tasks. *IEEE Transactions on Industrial Informatics*, *6*(3), 329–339. doi:10.1109/TII.2010.2052057

Rahimi, R., Shakery, A., & King, I. (2015). Multilingual Information Retrieval in the Language Modeling Framework. *Information Retrieval Journal*, *18*(3), 246–281. doi:10.100710791-015-9255-1

Rajarajeswari, C. S., & Aramudhan, M. (2015). Ranking Of Cloud Service Providers In Cloud. *Journal of Theoretical & Applied Information Technology*, *78*(2).

Rajkumar, R. (1989). *Task synchronization in real-time systems.* Ph. D. Dissertation.

Raju, B. N. V. N., Raju, M. S. V. S. B., & Satyanarayana, K. V. V. (2014). Translation Approaches in Cross Language Information Retrieval. *Computer and Communications Technologies (ICCCT), 2014 IEEE, International Conference on*, 1-4.

Ramakrishnan, R., & Gehrke, J. (2000). *Database management systems.* McGraw Hill.

Ramamritham, K. (1993). Real-time databases. *Distributed and Parallel Databases*, *1*(2), 199–226. doi:10.1007/BF01264051

Ramanathan, N., Kohler, E., & Estrin, D. (2005). Towards a debugging system for sensor networks. *International Journal of Network Management*, *15*(4), 223–234. doi:10.1002/nem.570

Ramanathan, P., & Hamdaoui, M. (1995). A dynamic priority assignment technique for streams with (m, k)-firm deadlines. *IEEE Transactions on Computers*, *44*(12), 1443–1451. doi:10.1109/12.477249

Rao, J., Zhang, C., Megiddo, N., & Lohman, G. (2002). Automating physical database design in a parallel database. *Proceedings of the* ACM SIGMOD international conference on Management of data, 558-569.

Rao, A. M., & Rao, K. R. (2012). Measuring Urban Traffic Congestion – A Review. *International Journal for Tra-c and Transport Engineering*, 2(4), 286–305. doi:10.7708/ijtte.2012.2(4).01

Rapp, R., Sharoff, S., & Zweigenbaum, P. (2016). Recent Advances in Machine Translation Using Comparable Corpora. *Natural Language Engineering*, 22(4), 501–516. doi:10.1017/S1351324916000115

Ravi. (2012). *Embedded system and its real time applications*. Electronic Hub Tutorial. Retrieved from https://www.electronicshub.org/embedded-system-real-time-applications/

Ray, B. K., Middya, A. I., Roy, S., & Khatua, S. (2017, January). Multi-criteria based federation selection in cloud. In *2017 9th International Conference on Communication Systems and Networks (COMSNETS)* (pp. 182-189). IEEE. 10.1109/COMSNETS.2017.7945375

Raya, M., & Hubaux, J. P. (2007). Securing vehicular ad hoc networks. *Journal of Computer Security*, 15(1), 39–68. doi:10.3233/JCS-2007-15103

Razmara, Asadi, Narouei, & Ahmadi. (2012). A Novel Approach Toward Spam Detection Based on Iterative Patterns. *2nd International eConference on Computer and Knowledge Engineering*, 318-323.

Reeves, G. (1998). What Really Happened on Mars? *Risks Forum, 19*(54).

Regression vs. Classification algorithms webpage on Data Science. (n.d.). Available: https://www.datascience.com/blog/regression-and-classification-machine-learning-algorithms

REMICS. (2016). *REMICS, Reuse and Migration of legacy applications to Interoperable Cloud Services*. Available at: http://www.remics.eu/

Reno. (2016). *Amazon Leads; Microsoft, IBM & Google Chase; Others Trail | Synergy Research Group, Synergy Research Group*. Available at: https://www.srgresearch.com/articles/amazon-leads-microsoft-ibm-google-chase-others-trail

Rijsbergen, C. J. V. (1979). *Information Retrieval* (2nd ed.). Dept. of Computer Science, University of Glasgow.

Rochwerger, B. (2011). An Architecture for Federated Cloud Computing. In *Cloud Computing* (pp. 391–411). Principles and Paradigms. doi:10.1002/9780470940105.ch15

Rodd, S. F., & Kulkarni, U. P. (2010). Adaptive Self-Tuning Techniques for Performance Tuning of Database Systems: A Fuzzy-Based Approach. *International Journal of Computer Science and Information Security*, 8(1).

Romain. (2010). MAWILab: Combining Diverse Anomaly Detectors for Automated Anomaly Labeling and Performance Benchmarking. *ACM CoNEXT '10*. Retrieved from http://mawi.wide.ad.jp/mawi/samplepoint-F/2017/

Rong, H., & Jian-xun, L. (2010, November). Trustworthiness fusion of web service based on DS evidence theory. In *2010 Sixth International Conference on Semantics, Knowledge and Grids* (pp. 343-346). IEEE. 10.1109/SKG.2010.55

Rui, L., Zhang, Y., Huang, H., & Qiu, X. (2018). A New Traffic Congestion Detection and Quantification Method Based on Comprehensive Fuzzy Assessment in Vanet. Ksii Transactions On Internet And Information Systems, 12(1), 41-60.

Ruiz, L. B., Nogueira, J. M., & Loureiro, A. A. (2003). Manna: A management architecture for wireless sensor networks. *IEEE Communications Magazine*, 41(2), 116–125. doi:10.1109/MCOM.2003.1179560

Russell & Norvig. (2003). *Artificial Intelligence A Modern Approach* (2nd ed.). Pearson Education Inc.

Saini, M., & Rao, S. (2007). Fairness in combinatorial auctioning systems. *AAAI Spring Symposium - Technical Report*, 61–67. Available at: http://www.aaai.org/Papers/Symposia/Spring/2007/SS-07-02/SS07-02-009.pdf

Sajid, M., & Raza, Z. (2013). Cloud computing: Issues & challenges. In *International Conference on Cloud* (pp. 34–41). Big Data. Available at https://www.researchgate.net/profile/Mohammad_Sajid4/publication/278117154_Cloud_Computing_Issues_Challenges/links/557c12a908ae26eada8c7097/Cloud-Computing-Issues-Challenges.pdf

Salem, R., Saleh, S. A., & Abdul-kader, H. (2016). Scalable data-oriented replication with flexible consistency in real-time data systems. *Data Science Journal*, 15.

Salton, G. (1973). Experiments in Multi-lingual Information Retrieval. *Information Processing Letters*, 2(1), 6–11. doi:10.1016/0020-0190(73)90017-3

Salton, G., & Buckley, C. (1990). Improving Retrieval Performance by Relevance Feedback. *Journal of the American Society for Information Science*, 41(4), 288–297. doi:10.1002/(SICI)1097-4571(199006)41:4<288::AID-ASI8>3.0.CO;2-H

Sanchez-Martinez, F., & Carrasco, R. C. (2011). Document Translation Retrieval Based on Statistical Machine Translation Techniques. *Applied Artificial Intelligence*, 25(5), 329–340. doi:10.1080/08839514.2011.559906

Sankaranarayanan, M., Mala, C., & Samson, M. (2017). Congestion Rate Estimation for VANET Infrastructure using Fuzzy Logic. In *International Conference on Intelligent Systems, Metaheuristics & Swarm Intelligence*. ACM Digital Library.

Sankaranarayanan, Mala, & Samson. (2014). *Performance Analysis of Spatial Color Information for Object Detection Using Background Subtraction*. Elsevier Publications.

Sari, S., & Adriani, M. (2014). Learning to Rank for Determining Relevant Document in Indonesian-English Cross Language Information Retrieval Using BM25. *Advanced Computer Science and Information Systems (ICACSIS), 2014 IEEE, International Conference on*, 309-14.

Sarkar, S. K., Basavaraju, T. G., & Puttamadappa, C. (2016). *Ad Hoc Mobile Wireless Networks: Principles, Protocols and Application* (2nd ed.). CRC Press. doi:10.1201/b13094

Savoy, J. (2012). Authorship Attribution Based on Specific Vocabulary. *ACM Transactions on Information Systems*, 30(2), 12. doi:10.1145/2180868.2180874

Schnaitter, K., Abiteboul, S., Milo, T., & Polyzotis, N. (2012). On-line index selection for shifting workloads. International workshop of self-managing database systems, 459-468.

Schnaitter, K., & Polyzotis, N. (2012). Semi-Automatic Index Tuning: Keeping DBAs in the Loop. *Proceeding of Very Lagre Data Bases*, 5(5), 478–489.

Schorr, S. (2015). *Adaptive real-time scheduling and resource management on multicore architectures* (Ph.D. Thesis). Technische Universität Kaiserslautern.

Seetha, A., Das, S., & Kumar, M. (2007b). Evaluation of the English-Hindi Cross Language Information Retrieval System Based on Dictionary Based Query Translation Method. *Proceedings of 10th IEEE International Conference on Information Technology (ICIT 2007)*, pp. 56-61.

Seetha, A., Das, S., & Kumar, M. (2009a). Improving Performance of English-Hindi CLIR System using Linguistic Tools and Techniques. *Proceedings of the First International Conference on Intelligent Human Computer Interaction*, 261-71. 10.1007/978-81-8489-203-1_26

Seh & Chaurasia. (2019). A Review on Heart Disease Prediction Using Machine Learning Techniques. *International Journal of Management, IT & Engineering, 9*.

Sekine, S., & Grishman, R. (2003). Hindi-English Cross-Lingual Question-Answering System. *ACM Transactions on Asian Language Information Processing, 2*(3), 181–192. doi:10.1145/979872.979874

Severance, D. J., & Hoffer, J. A. (1975). The use of cluster analysis in physical database design. *Proceedings of the 1st International Conference on Very Large Data Bases.*

Sha, L., Rajkumar, R., & Lehoczky, J. P. (1990). Priority Inheritance Protocols: An Approach to Real-Time Synchronization. *IEEE Transactions on Computers, 39*(9), 1175–1185. doi:10.1109/12.57058

Shanker, U., Agarwal, N., Tiwari, S., Goel, P., & Srivastava, P. (2010). ACTIVE-a real time commit protocol. *Wireless Sensor Network, 2*(3).

Shanker, U., Misra, M., & Sarje, A. K. (2005, July). Priority assignment heuristic to cohorts executing in parallel. In *Proceedings of the 9th WSEAS International Conference on Computers* (pp. 1-6). World Scientific and Engineering Academy and Society (WSEAS).

Shanker, U., Vidyareddi, B., & Shukla, A. (2012). PERDURABLE: A real time commit protocol. *Recent Trends in Information Reuse and Integration*, 1-17.

Shanker, U., Misra, M., & Sarje, A. K. (2006). SWIFT - A new real time commit protocol. *Distributed and Parallel Databases, 20*(01), 29–56. doi:10.100710619-006-8594-8

Shanker, U., Misra, M., & Sarje, A. K. (2008). Distributed real time database systems: Background and literature review. *Distributed and Parallel Databases, 23*(2), 127–149. doi:10.100710619-008-7024-5

Shanmugasundaram, J., Nithrakashyap, A., Sivasankaran, R., & Ramamritham, K. (1999, June). Efficient concurrency control for broadcast environments. *SIGMOD Record, 28*(2), 85–96. doi:10.1145/304181.304190

Sharma, U., & Reddy, S. R. N. (2012). Design of home/office automation using wireless sensor network. *International Journal of Computers and Applications, 43*(22), 46–52. doi:10.5120/8428-2195

Sheridan, P., & Ballerini, J. P. 1996. Experiments in Multilingual Information Retrieval Using The SPIDER System. *Proceedings of the 19th annual international ACM SIGIR conference on Research and development in information retrieval*, 58-65. 10.1145/243199.243213

Shigiltchoff, O., Chrysanthis, P. K., & Pitoura, E. (2004, January). Energy efficient access in multiversion broadcast environment. In *IEEE International Conference on Mobile Data Management, 2004. Proceedings. 2004* (p. 168). IEEE. 10.1109/MDM.2004.1263058

Shirke, N., Patil, K., Kulkarni, S., & Markande, S. (2014). *Energy efficient cluster based routing protocol for distributed Cognitive Radio Network.* Paper presented at the Networks & Soft Computing (ICNSC), 2014 First International Conference on. 10.1109/CNSC.2014.6906712

Shotk, A., Kurland, O., Carmel, D., Raiber, F., & Markovits, G. (2012). Predicting Query Performance by Query-Drift Estimation. *ACM Transactions on Information Systems, 30*(2), 1–36.

Shrivastava, P., & Shanker, U. (2018, August). Replica update technique in RDRTDBS: issues & challenges. In *Proceedings of the 24th International Conference on Advanced Computing and Communications (ADCOM-2018), Ph. D. Forum* (pp. 21-23). Academic Press.

Shrivastava, P., Jain, R., & Raghuwanshi, K. S. (2014, January). A Modified Approach of Key Manipulation in Cryptography Using 2D Graphics Image. In *2014 International Conference on Electronic Systems, Signal Processing and Computing Technologies* (pp. 194-197). IEEE. 10.1109/ICESC.2014.40

Shrivastava, P., & Shanker, U. (2018). Replica control following 1SR in DRTDBS through best case of transaction execution. In *Advances in Data and Information Sciences* (pp. 139–150). Singapore: Springer. doi:10.1007/978-981-10-8360-0_13

Shrivastava, P., & Shanker, U. (2018). Replication protocol based on dynamic versioning of data object for replicated DRTDBS. *International Journal of Computational Intelligence & IoT, 1*(2).

Shrivastava, P., & Shanker, U. (2019, January). Real time transaction management in replicated DRTDBS. In *Australasian Database Conference* (pp. 91-103). Springer. 10.1007/978-3-030-12079-5_7

Shrivastava, P., & Shanker, U. (2019, January). Supporting transaction predictability in replicated DRTDBS. In *International Conference on Distributed Computing and Internet Technology* (pp. 125-140). Springer. 10.1007/978-3-030-05366-6_10

Shrivastava, P., & Shanker, U. (2020). Secure System Model for Replicated DRTDBS. In *Security and Privacy Issues in Sensor Networks and IoT* (pp. 264–281). IGI Global. doi:10.4018/978-1-7998-0373-7.ch011

Shukla, S., & Sinha, U. (2015). Categorizing Sentence Structures For Phrase Level Morphological Analyzer For English To Hindi RBMT. *Cognitive Computing and Information Processing (CCIP), IEEE 2015 International Conference on,* 1-6.

Singh, P. K., & Shanker, U. (2017, September). Priority heuristic in mobile distributed real time database using optimistic concurrency control. In *2017 23RD Annual International Conference in Advanced Computing and Communications (ADCOM)* (pp. 44-49). IEEE. 10.1109/ADCOM.2017.00014

Singh, P.K., & Shanker, U. (2019). Transaction Scheduling Heuristics in Mobile Distributed Real Time Database System. *Recent Advances in Computer Science and Communications.* doi:10.2174/2213275912666190809120654

Singh, P.K., & Shanker, U. (2019a). Transaction Scheduling Heuristics in Mobile Distributed Real Time Database System. *Recent Advances in Computer Science and Communications.*

Singh, P.K., & Shanker, U. (2019b). Priority Heuristic in MDRTDBS. *International Journal of Sensors, Wireless Communications and Control.*

Singh, A., & Kad, S. (2016). A Review on the various security techniques for VANETs. *Procedia Computer Science, 78,* 284–290. doi:10.1016/j.procs.2016.02.055

Singhal, A. (2001). Modern Information Retrieval: A Brief Overview. *IEEE Data Eng. Bull., 24*(4), 35–43.

Singh, P. K., & Shanker, U. (2018a). A New Priority Heuristic Suitable in Mobile Distributed Real Time Database System. In *International Conference on Distributed Computing and Internet Technology* (pp. 330-335). Springer. 10.1007/978-3-319-72344-0_29

Singh, P. K., & Shanker, U. (2018b). A Priority Heuristic Policy in Mobile Distributed Real-Time Database System. In *Advances in Data and Information Sciences* (pp. 211–221). Singapore: Springer. doi:10.1007/978-981-10-8360-0_20

Singh, P. K., & Shanker, U. (2019). *Priority Heuristic in MDRTDBS. International Journal of Sensors, Wireless Communications and Control.* doi:10.2174/2210327909666191119104550

Singh, Singh, P., & Kumar, K. (2018). User behavior analytics-based classification of application layer http-get flood attacks. *Journal of Network and Computer Applications, 112,* 97–114. doi:10.1016/j.jnca.2018.03.030

Son, S. H., & Zhang, F. (1995, April). Real-Time Replication Control for Distributed Database Systems: Algorithms and Their Performance. In DASFAA (Vol. 11, pp. 214-221). Academic Press.

Song, H., Kim, D., Lee, K., & Sung, J. (2005, April). UPnP-based sensor network management architecture. *Proc. International Conference on Mobile Computing and Ubiquitous Networking.*

Song, Wang, X., Jin, L., & You, J. (2018). Malicious behaviour classification in web logs based on an improved Xgboost algorithm. *International Journal of Web Engineering and Technology, 13*(4), 334–362. doi:10.1504/IJWET.2018.097560

Song, X., & Liu, J. W. S. (1995). Maintaining temporal consistency: Pessimistic vs. optimistic concurrency control. *IEEE Transactions on Knowledge and Data Engineering, 7*(5), 786–796. doi:10.1109/69.469820

Son, S. H., & Kouloumbis, S. (1993). A token-based synchronization scheme for distributed real-time databases. *Information Systems, 18*(6), 375–389. doi:10.1016/0306-4379(93)90014-R

Son, S. H., Zhang, F., & Hwang, B. (1996). Concurrency control for replicated data in distributed real-time systems. *Journal of Database Management, 7*(2), 12–23. doi:10.4018/jdm.1996040102

Spuri, M., & Buttazzo, G. (1996). Scheduling aperiodic tasks in dynamic priority systems. *Real-Time Systems, 10*(2), 179–210. doi:10.1007/BF00360340

Sreeram & Vuppala. (2017). *Http flood attack detection in application layer using machine learning metrics and bio inspired bat algorithm.* Applied Computing and Informatics.

Srivastava, A., Shankar, U., & Tiwari, S. K. (2012). A protocol for concurrency control in real-time replicated databases system. *IRACST—International Journal of Computer Networks and Wireless Communications, 2*(3).

Srivastava, R., & Daniel, A. K. (2019). Efficient Model of Cloud Trustworthiness for Selecting Services Using Fuzzy Logic. In *Emerging Technologies in Data Mining and Information Security* (pp. 249–260). Singapore: Springer. doi:10.1007/978-981-13-1951-8_23

Srivastava, S., & Ghosh, R. (2002). Cluster based routing using a k-tree core backbone for mobile ad hoc networks. *Proceedings of the 6th international workshop on Discrete algorithms and methods for mobile computing and communications.* 10.1145/570810.570813

Stankovic, J. A., Spuri, M., Ramamritham, K., & Buttazzo, G. (1998). *Deadline scheduling for Real-Time* (Vol. 460). Systems, The Springer International Series in Engineering and Computer Science. doi:10.1007/978-1-4615-5535-3

Su, C. J., Tassiulas, L., & Tsotras, V. J. (1999). Broadcast scheduling for information distribution. *Wireless Networks, 5*(2), 137–147. doi:10.1023/A:1019134607998

Sumalee, A., & Ho, H. W. (2018). Smarter and more connected: Future intelligent transportation system. *IATSS Research, 42*(2), 67–71. doi:10.1016/j.iatssr.2018.05.005

Supervised and Unsupervised Machine Learning Algorithms Webpage on Machine Learning Mastery. (n.d.). Available: https://machinelearningmastery.com/ supervised-and-unsupervised-machine-learning-algorithms/

Supriya, M., Sangeeta, K., & Patra, G. K. (2014, October). Estimation of Trust values for Varying Levels of Trustworthiness based on Infrastructure as a Service. In *Proceedings of the 2014 International Conference on Interdisciplinary Advances in Applied Computing* (p. 16). ACM. 10.1145/2660859.2660921

Syberfeldt, S. (2007). *Optimistic replication with forward conflict resolution in distributed real-time databases* (Doctoral dissertation). Institutionen för datavetenskap.

Syed, A., Pérez, D. G., & Fohler, G. (2018). Job-Shifting: An algorithm for online admission of non-preemptive aperiodic tasks in safety critical systems. *Journal of Systems Architecture, 85*, 14–27. doi:10.1016/j.sysarc.2018.01.005

Taleb, A. A. (2018). VANET Routing Protocols and Architecture: An Overview. *Journal of Computational Science, 14*(3), 423–434. doi:10.3844/jcssp.2018.423.434

Talukder, S. (2010). *Mathematical Modelling and Applications of Particle Swarm Optimization.* Masters Thesis on Mathematical Modelling and Simulation, Thesis no: 2010:8.

Tanaka, K. (Ed.). (2013). Adaptive total bandwidth server: Using Predictive execution time. In Embedded Systems: Design, Analysis and Verification. Berlin: Springer.

Tclouds-project. (2016). *Tclouds-project.* Available at: http://www.tclouds-project.eu/

Tembhurne, D.S., Adhikari, J., & Babu, R. (2019). *A Review study on Application of Data Mining Techniques in CRM of Pharmaceutical Industry.* Academic Press.

Theis, J. (2015). *Certification-cognizant mixed-criticality scheduling in time-triggered systems.* Ph.D. Thesis.

Thomadakis, M. E., & Liu, J.-C. (1999). On the efficient scheduling of non-periodic tasks in hard real-time *systems. IEEE Real Time Systems Symposium,* 148-151. 10.1109/REAL.1999.818836

Times, E. (2017). Subsidy for MSMEs deploying cloud computing. *The Hindu.* Available at: http://economictimes. indiatimes.com/small-biz/sme-sector/government-proposes-subsidy-for-msmes-deploying-cloud-computing/article-show/57604194.cms

Tolle, G., & Culler, D. (2005, February). Design of an application-cooperative management system for wireless sensor networks. In *Proceedings of the Second European Workshop on Wireless Sensor Networks,* (pp. 121-132). IEEE. 10.1109/EWSN.2005.1462004

Tom, V. (2014). Design Principles of Traffic Signal. *Transportation System Engineering,* 34.1-34.13.

Tonguz, O. K., Wisitpongphan, N., Bai, F., Mudalige, P., & Sadekar, V. (2007, May), Broadcasting in VANET. *Proc. IEEE INFOCOM MOVE Workshop.*

Turon, M. (2005, May). Mote-view: A sensor network monitoring and management tool. In *The Second IEEE Workshop on Embedded Networked Sensors, 2005. EmNetS-II* (pp. 11-17). IEEE. 10.1109/EMNETS.2005.1469094

UAM Corpus, 2012 Corpus ToolU. A. M. (2012). Retrieved from http://www.wagsoft.com/CorpusTool/

Ujjwal, D., Rastogi, P., & Siddhartha, S. (2016). Analysis of Retrieval Models for Cross Language Information Retrieval. *Intelligent Systems and Control (ISCO), 2016 10th International Conference on IEEE,* 1-4.

Ullman, J. D. (1984). *Principles of database systems.* Galgotia Publications.

Ulusoy, Ö. (1994). Processing real-time transactions in a replicated database system. *Distributed and Parallel Databases,* 2(4), 405–436. doi:10.1007/BF01265321

Ulusoy, Ö. (1995). A study of two transaction-processing architectures for distributed real-time database systems. *Journal of Systems and Software, 31*(2), 97–108. doi:10.1016/0164-1212(94)00090-A

Urgaonkar, B. (2007). Analytic modeling of multitier Internet applications. *ACM Transactions on the Web, 1*(1). doi:10.1145/1232722.1232724

Vaidya, N. H., & Hameed, S. (1999). Scheduling data broadcast in asymmetric communication environments. *Wireless Networks, 5*(3), 171–182. doi:10.1023/A:1019142809816

Van Roy, P., Haridi, S., Reinefeld, A., Stefani, J. B., Yap, R., & Coupaye, T. (2007, October). Self- management for large-scale distributed systems: An overview of the selfman project. In *International Symposium on Formal Methods for Components and Objects,* (pp. 153-178). Springer.

Vanajakshi, L., Ramadurai, G., & Anand, A. (2010). *Centre of Excellence in Urban Transport IIT Madras Intelligent Transportation Systems Synthesis Report on ITS Including Issues and Challenges in India.* Tamil Nadu, India: IIT Madras.

Varshney, S., & Bajpai, J. (2013). Improving Retrieval Performance of English-Hindi Based Cross-Language Information Retrieval. *Innovation and Technology in Education (MITE), IEEE International Conference in MOOC, 300-5.*

Venkata Lakshmi & Shivsankar. (2014). Heart Disease Diagnosis Using Predictive Data Mining. *International Journal of Innovative Research in Science, Engineering and Technology, 3*(3).

Vestal, S. (2007). *Preemptive scheduling of multi-criticality systems with varying degrees of execution time assurance.* Real Time Systems Symposium. doi:10.1109/RTSS.2007.47

Wang, F., Yao, L. W., & Yang, Y. L. (2011). Efficient verification of distributed real-time systems with broadcasting behaviors. *Real-Time Systems, 47*(4), 285–318. doi:10.100711241-011-9122-0

Wang, J., Han, S., Lam, K., & Mok, A. K. (2011). On least idle slot first co-scheduling of update and control tasks in real-time sensing and control systems. *IEEE International Conference on Parallel and Distributed Systems*, 684-691. 10.1109/ICPADS.2011.86

Wang, L. L., & Wang, C. (2017). A self-organizing wireless sensor networks based on quantum ant Colony evolutionary algorithm. *International Journal of Online Engineering, 13*(07), 69–80. doi:10.3991/ijoe.v13i07.7284

Wang, Miu, T. T. N., Luo, X., & Wang, J. (2018). Skyshield: A sketch-based defense system against application layer ddos attacks. *IEEE Transactions on Information Forensics and Security, 13*(3), 559–573. doi:10.1109/TIFS.2017.2758754

Wellings, A., Burns, A., Santos, O., & Brosgol, B. (2007). Integrating priority inheritance algorithms in the real-time specification for java. *Proceedings of the 10th IEEE International Symposium on Object and Component-Oriented Real-Time Distributed Computing (ISORC' 07)*, 115-123. 10.1109/ISORC.2007.40

Wen-Jiang, F., Di, W., Wei-Heng, J., & Nian-Long, J. (2011). *The Formation of Virtual Backbone Network in MANETs Based on Cognitive Radio. In Advanced Electrical and Electronics Engineering* (pp. 451–458). Springer.

Whang, J. J., Dhillon, I. S., & Gleich, D. F. (2015, June). Non-exhaustive, overlapping k-means. In *Proceedings of the 2015 SIAM International Conference on Data Mining* (pp. 936-944). Society for Industrial and Applied Mathematics. 10.1137/1.9781611974010.105

Whissell, J. S., & Clarke, C. L. A. (2011). Improving Document Clustering Using Okapi BM25 Feature Weighting. *Information Retrieval, 14*(5), 466–487. doi:10.100710791-011-9163-y

Williamson, O. E. (1975). *Markets and Hierarchies: Analysis of Antitrust and Implications.* New York: The Free Pres.

Winkler, M., Tuchs, K.D., Hughes, K., & Barclay, G. (2008). Theoretical and practical aspects of military wireless sensor networks. *Journal of Telecommunications and Information Technology*, 37-45.

Wong, J. W. (1988). Broadcast delivery. *Proceedings of the IEEE, 76*(12), 1566–1577. doi:10.1109/5.16350

Wu, J., & Li, H. (1999). On calculating connected dominating set for efficient routing in ad hoc wireless networks. *Proceedings of the 3rd international workshop on Discrete algorithms and methods for mobile computing and communications.* 10.1145/313239.313261

Xie, Tang, S., Xiang, Y., & Hu, J. (2013). Resisting web proxy-based http attacks by temporal and spatial locality behaviour. *IEEE Transactions on Parallel and Distributed Systems, 24*(7), 1401–1410. doi:10.1109/TPDS.2012.232

Xing, Z., & Gruenwald, L. (2007). *Issues in designing concurrency control techniques for mobile ad-hoc network databases. Technical Report.* School of Computer Science.

Xiong, M., Ramamritham, K., Haritsa, J. R., & Stankovic, J. A. (2002). MIRROR: A state-conscious concurrency control protocol for replicated real-time databases. *Information Systems*, 27(4), 277–297. doi:10.1016/S0306-4379(01)00053-9

Xu, X., & Hu, X. (2010). Cluster-Based Query Expansion Using Language Modeling in the Biomedical Domain. *Bioinformatics and Biomedicine Workshops (BIBMW), 2010 IEEE International Conference on,* 185-88.

Xuan, P., Sen, S., Gonzalez, O., Fernandez, J., & Ramamritham, K. (1997, June). Broadcast on demand: Efficient and timely dissemination of data in mobile environments. In *Proceedings Third IEEE Real-Time Technology and Applications Symposium* (pp. 38-48). IEEE. 10.1109/RTTAS.1997.601342

Xu, C., Song, L., Han, Z., Zhao, Q., Wang, X., Cheng, X., & Jiao, B. (2013). Efficiency resource allocation for device-to-device underlay communication systems: A reverse iterative combinatorial auction based approach. *IEEE Journal on Selected Areas in Communications*, 31(9), 348–358. doi:10.1109/JSAC.2013.SUP.0513031

Xu, G., Shen, W., & Wang, X. (2014). Applications of wireless sensor networks in marine environment monitoring: A survey. *Sensors (Basel)*, 14(9), 16932–16954. doi:10.3390140916932 PMID:25215942

Xu, J., & Croft, W. B. (2000). Improving the Effectiveness of Information Retrieval With Local Context Analysis. *ACM Transactions on Information Systems*, 18(1), 79–112. doi:10.1145/333135.333138

Xu, J., Tang, X., & Lee, W. C. (2005). Time-critical on-demand data broadcast: Algorithms, analysis, and performance evaluation. *IEEE Transactions on Parallel and Distributed Systems*, 17(1), 3–14.

Yan, C., & Ji-Hong, Q. (2010, October). Application analysis of complex adaptive systems for WSN. In *2010 International Conference on Computer Application and System Modeling (ICCASM 2010),* (Vol. 7, pp. V7-328). IEEE.

Yang, F., Tang, Y. L., & Huang, L. F. (2013). A novel cooperative MAC for broadcasting in clustering VANETs. *Proceedings of International Conference on Connected Vehicles and Expo*, 893–897. 10.1109/ICCVE.2013.6799922

Yao, F., Demers, A., & Shenker, S. (1995). A scheduling model for reduced CPU energy. *IEEE Symposium on Foundations of Computer Science*, 374-382. 10.1109/SFCS.1995.492493

Yeh, C.-H., Hsieh, M.-Y., & Li, K.-C. (2012). *An Efficient Clustering Authentication Mechanism for Mobile Ad Hoc Networks*. Paper presented at the Ubiquitous Intelligence & Computing and 9th International Conference on Autonomic & Trusted Computing (UIC/ATC), 2012 9th International Conference on. 10.1109/UIC-ATC.2012.134

Ye, M., Guan, L., & Quddus, M. (2019). MPBRP- Mobility Prediction Based Routing Protocol in VANETs. *2019 International Conference on Advanced Communication Technologies and Networking (CommNet)*. 10.1109/COMMNET.2019.8742389

Yilmaz, H. B., & Tugcu, T. (2015). *Energy efficient MAC protocol for cluster formation in mobile cooperative spectrum sensing*. Paper presented at the Wireless Communications and Networking Conference Workshops (WCNCW).

Ying, Z., & Debao, X. (2005, September). Mobile agent-based policy management for wireless sensor networks. In *Proceedings. 2005 International Conference on Wireless Communications, Networking and Mobile Computing*, (Vol. 2, pp. 1207-1210). IEEE. 10.1109/WCNM.2005.1544270

Yodaiken, V. (2004). *Against Priority Inheritance*. Technical report, Finite State Machine Labs (FSMLabs).

Youssef, M., Youssef, A., & Younis, M. (2009). Overlapping multihop clustering for wireless sensor networks. *IEEE Transactions on Parallel and Distributed Systems*, 20(12), 1844–1856. doi:10.1109/TPDS.2009.32

Zhang, H., Zhao, W., Moser, L. E., & Melliar-Smith, P. M. (2011). Design and Implementation of a Byzantine Fault Tolerance Framework for Non-Deterministic Applications. *IET Software*, 5(3), 342–356. doi:10.1049/iet-sen.2010.0013

Zhang, X., Urban, C., & Wu, C. (2012). Priority inheritance protocol proved correct. *Proceedings of the 3rd Conference on Interactive Theorem Proving (ITP)*, 7406, 217–232. 10.1007/978-3-642-32347-8_15

Zhang, Y., Zhang, Y., & Hai, M. (2012, August). An evaluation model of software trustworthiness based on fuzzy comprehensive evaluation method. In *2012 International Conference on Industrial Control and Electronics Engineering* (pp. 616-619). IEEE. 10.1109/ICICEE.2012.167

Zhan, Z. H., Zhang, J., Li, Y., & Chung, H. S. H. (2009). Adaptive Particle Swarm Opti-mization. *IEEE Transactions on Systems, Man, and Cybernetics. Part B, Cybernetics*, 39(6), 1362–1380. doi:10.1109/TSMCB.2009.2015956 PMID:19362911

Zhao, W. (2014). *Building dependable distributed systems*. John Wiley & Sons; doi:10.1002/9781118912744

Zhao, Z., Huangfu, W., Liu, Y., & Sun, L. (2011, December). Design and Implementation of Network Management System for Large-Scale Wireless Sensor Networks. In *Seventh International Conference on Mobile Ad-hoc and Sensor Networks*, (pp. 130-137). IEEE. 10.1109/MSN.2011.33

Zhong, S., Huang, H., & Pan, L. (2010). An Effective Spam Filtering Technique Based on Active Feedback and Maximum Entropy. *7th International Conference on Fuzzy Systems and Knowledge Discovery*, 5, 2437-2440. 10.1109/FSKD.2010.5569301

Zhou, D., Lawless, S., Liu, J., & Zhang, S. (2015). Query Expansion for Personalized Cross-Language Information Retrieval. *Semantic and Social Media Adaptation and Personalization (SMAP), IEEE, 2015 10th International Workshop on*, 1-5.

Zhou, Jia, W., Wen, S., Xiang, Y., & Zhou, W. (2014). Detection and defense of application-layer ddos attacks in backbone web traffic. *Future Generation Computer Systems*, 38, 36–46. doi:10.1016/j.future.2013.08.002

Zhou, M., Zhang, R., Xie, W., Qian, W., & Zhou, A. (2010, November). Security and privacy in cloud computing: A survey. In *2010 Sixth International Conference on Semantics, Knowledge and Grids* (pp. 105-112). IEEE. 10.1109/SKG.2010.19

Zhou, Y., Yu, H., & Cai, X. (2009, December). A novel k-means algorithm for clustering and outlier detection. In *2009 Second International Conference on Future Information Technology and Management Engineering* (pp. 476-480). IEEE. 10.1109/FITME.2009.125

Zighelnic, L., & Kurland, O. (2008). Query-Drift Prevention for Robust Query Expansion. *Proceedings of the 31st annual international ACM SIGIR conference on Research and development in information retrieval*, 825-26.

About the Contributors

Udai Shankar is presently Professor in the Department of Computer Sc. & Engineering of M. M. M. University of Technology, Gorakhpur-273010. For his imitation of the most modern of approaches and also for his exemplary devotion to the field of teaching, and sharing his profound knowledge with students to make better future citizen of India, he has been a role model for the new generation of academicians. Besides introduced radical and revolutionary changes that have positively impacted the database world and student community, he is a man well versed with all the intricacies of academics.

Sarvesh Pandey is presently working as a Senior Research Fellow in the Computer Science & Engineering Department of Madan Mohan Malaviya University of Technology, Gorakhpur, India. His broad area of research includes distributed real-time database systems, cloud computing and advanced networks. He is associated as a review expert for some reputed journals, conferences and book series.

* * *

Umamakeswari A. pursued doctorate degree from SASTRA Deemed to be University, Thanjavur, India. and currently designated as Dean School of Computing, SASTRA Deemed to be University. Her research area includes security in Wireless Sensor Network, Cloud computing, embedded system and Internet of Things. She has published many research papers over the last years in refereed journals and conferences.

Neelendra Badal is a Professor in the Department of Computer Science & Engineering at Kamla Nehru Institute of Technology, (KNIT), at Sultanpur (U.P.), INDIA of Dr. A.P.J. Abdul Kalam Technical University (AKTU), UP Lucknow INDIA (Formerly Uttar Pradesh Technical University, (UPTU), Lucknow). He received B.E. (1997) from Bundelkhand Institute of Technology (BIET), Jhansi (U.P.), INDIA, in Computer Science & Engineering, M.E. (2001) in Communication, Control and Networking from Madhav Institute of Technology and Science (MITS), Gwalior (M.P.), INDIA and PhD (2009) in Computer Science & Engineering from Motilal Nehru National Institute of Technology (MNNIT), Allahabad (U.P.), INDIA. He is Chartered Engineering (CE) from Institution of Engineers (IE), India. He is a Life Member of IE, IETE, ISTE, CSI, India. He has published more than 75 papers in International/ National Journals, conferences and seminars. His research interests are Distributed System, Parallel Processing, GIS, Data Warehouse & Data mining, Software engineering and Networking.

Gaurav Baranwal is faculty in Department of Computer Science, Banaras Hindu University, Varanasi, UP, India. He did his M.Tech and Ph.D. in Computer Science from Jawaharlal Nehru University, India. He has published research papers in various peer reviewed International Journals (including IEEE, Elsevier, Springer, Wiley etc.) and in proceedings of various peer-reviewed conferences. His research interests include resource provisioning and service coordination in cloud computing and Internet of Things.

Mala C. is an Associate Professor in the Department of Computer Science and Engineering, National Institute of Technology, Tiruchirappalli, Tamil Nadu, India – 620 015. Her research area of interest includes Data Structures & Algorithms, Computer Networks, Parallel Algorithms, Computer Architecture, Sensor Networks, Soft Computing Techniques, Image Processing, Intelligent Transportation Systems and Vehicular Adhoc Networks.

Ganesh Chandra received his Ph.D. degree from Department of Computer Science at Babasaheb Bhimrao Ambedkar Central University, Lucknow, India. His major research interests include Information Retrieval, WSD and Machine Translation. He has published papers in various international journals and conferences.

Pawan Chaurasia is presently working as an Associate Professor in Department of Computer Science and Information Technology, Mahatma Gandhi Central University, Motihari, Bihar more than 15 years teaching experience and 6 years research, more than 20 research journal papers and published one book.

A. Joy Christy is working as an Assistant Professor in School of Computing at SASTRA Deemed University, Thanjavur. She completed her Ph.D., during the year 2018 in the broad area of data mining. She has presented papers at conferences and published research articles in the field of data mining. Her areas of interest are Big Data, Data Mining and Software Metrics.

A. K. Daniel is currently a Professor in the Department of Computer Science and Engineering at M.M.M. University of Technology Gorakhpur, Uttar Pradesh India. He is a member of various academic bodies like ACM, IEEE CSI, IETE, ISTE and Institute of Engineer member. He has served as reviewer of leading journals, conferences and book series. His research interest include wireless sensor network, artificial intelligence, fuzzy logic based system design, and cloud computing. He has published more than 170 `research papers in leading journals and conferences.

Sanjay K. Dwivedi is working as Professor & Head, Department of Computer Science at Babasaheb Bhimrao Ambedkar University (A Central University), Lucknow, India. His research interest includes Artificial Intelligence, Information Retrieval, Web Mining, NLP and WSD. He has published number of research papers in reputed journals and conferences.

Ajay Kr. Gupta is presently a Ph.D Research Scholar in the Department of Computer Sc. & Engineering of M. M. M. University of Technology, Gorakhpur 273010. His current research areas are Spatio-Temporal Database, Location Dependent Database, and Mobile Distributed Database.

Shruti Jadon is working as Assistant Professor(CSE) in Nirma University, Ahmedabad, India. She received her B. Tech degree in Computer Science and Engineering from Uttar Pradesh Technical University, Lucknow (U.P.), India in 2011 and M.Tech in Computer Science from Banasthali University, Banasthali (Rajasthan) India in 2013. Presently, she is pursuing PhD from Motilal Nehru National Institute of Technology Allahabad (U.P.), India since July, 2013. She has also worked with Dr. Amey Karkare, Computer Science and Engineering Department, IIT Kanpur (U.P.), India from July 2012 to June 2013. Her area of interest includes real time embedded systems and parallel and distributed systems.

Dinesh Kumar is faculty in Department of Computer Science and Engineering, Motilal Nehru National Institute of Technology, Allahabad, UP, India. He did his M.Tech and Ph.D. in Computer Science from Jawaharlal Nehru University, India. He has published research papers in various peer reviewed International Journals and in proceedings of various peer-reviewed conferences. His research interests include resource provisioning in cloud computing and Internet of Things.

Santosh Kumar received his Bachelor degree, B.Tech. in Computer Science and Engineering from Institute of Engineering and Technology, Lucknow, Uttar Pradesh, India, his M.Tech. degree in Computer Science and Engineering from NIT Jalandhar, Punjab, India, and Ph.D degree from NIT Kurukshetra, Haryana, India. He is working as an Assistant Professor in the Department of Computer Engineering (COE) at the National Institute of Technology, Kurukshetra, India. His research interests include distributed computing, mobile computing, ad hoc networks, and cognitive radio networks.

Samson Mathew is the Professor of Civil Engineering Department, National Institute of Technology, Tiruchirappalli, Tamil Nadu, India – 620 015. His area of expertise include Remote Sensing and GIS, Pavement Management System, Geographical Information System, Landuse planning.

Ashish Ranjan Mishra is working as an assistant professor in Department of Computer Science and Engineering at Rajkiya Engineering College Sonbhadra. He has pursued Master of Technology in Computer Science & Engineering at Kamla Nehru Institute of Technology (KNIT), Sultanpur, India. He has received his Bachelor of Technology degree in 2012 from College of Science and Engineering (CSE), Jhansi, India in Computer Science & Engineering. His core academics teaching include Distributed database systems, Data structures and Algorithms, Principle of Programming. He has 4 years of teaching experience at undergraduate level.

Pavan Pandey has received his M.Tech Degree from IIT (ISM) Dhanbad and he is pursuing research from Dr. A.P.J. Abdul Kalam Technical University, Lucknow in field of VANETs. He has around 10 years of IT experience and worked with multiple MNCs since 2010. Currently He is working in Oracle India Pvt. Ltd., Gurugram.

Ram Bahadur Patel received PhD from IIT Roorkee in Computer Science & Engineering, PDF from Highest Institute of Education, Science & Technology (HIEST), Athens, Greece, MS (Software Systems) from BITS Pilani and B. E. in Computer Engineering from M. M. M. Engineering College, Gorakhpur, UP. Dr. Patel is in teaching and Research & Development since 1991. He has supervised several M. Tech, and M. Phil and PhD Thesis. He is currently supervising several M. Tech, and PhD students. He has published more than 100 research papers in International/National Journals and Refereed International

Conferences. Dr. Patel received several research awards. He is working as a professor in the department of Computer engineering in Chandigarh College of Engineering and Technology, Chandigarh, INDIA.

Manipriya Sankaranarayanan is a Research Scholar in the Department of Computer Science and Engineering, National Institute of Technology, Tiruchirappalli, Tamil Nadu, India – 620 015. She has completed her Bachelors and Master degree in Computer Science from Anna University, Chennai, India – 600041.Her research area includes Video Image Processing, Intelligent Transportation Systems and Vehicular Adhoc Networks.

Pratik Shrivastava is a research scholar at M.M.M.U.T., Gorakhpur - Department of Computer Science & Engineering. Her research interests include Replication Technique, Distributed Real Time Database System, Cryptography.

Awadhesh Kumar Singh received his Bachelor of Technology (B.Tech.) degree in Computer Science from Madan Mohan Malaviya University of Technology, Gorakhpur, India, in 1988, and his MTech and Ph.D. degrees in Computer Science from Jadavpur University, Kolkata, India, in 1998 and 2004, respectively. He is working as a Professor in the Department of Computer Engineering at the National Institute of Technology, Kurukshetra, India, since 1991. Earlier, he also served as head of the Computer Engineering Department during 2007–2009 and 2013-2015. His research interests include distributed algorithms, mobile computing and radio networks.

Punitha Victor has completed her Master of Engineering in Computer Science and Engineering from National Institute of Technology, Tiruchirappalli, Tamil Nadu, India – 620 015, in 2003. Currently she is pursuing Ph.D degree in the same Institute in Department of Computer Science and Engineering. Her research area of interest includes Parallel and Distributed Systems, Cloud Computing, Computer Networks, Wireless Networking, Security, Quality of Service and Soft Computing Techniques.

Deo Prakash Vidyarthi is Professor in the School of Computer and Systems Sciences, Jawaharlal Nehru University, New Delhi, India. Dr. Vidyarthi has published around 100 research papers in various International Journals and Transactions (including IEEE, Elsevier, Springer, Wiley, World Scientific etc.) and around 45 research papers in the proceedings of various peer-reviewed conferences in India and abroad. He has contributed many chapters and articles in various edited volumes/magazines. He is in the editorial board of few International Journals and also in the reviewer's panel of some International Journals. Dr. Vidyarthi has co-authored three books. First one, a research monograph, entitled "Scheduling in Distributed Computing Systems: Design, Analysis and Models" was published by Springer, USA in 2009. Second book (edited) by Dr. Vidyarthi is "Technologies and Protocols for the Future Internet Design: Reinventing the Web", by IGI-Global (USA) released in the year 2012. The third research monograph by Dr. Vidyarthi is "Auction Based Resource Provisioning in Cloud Computing" published by Springer in the year 2018. Dr. Vidyarthi is the member of the IEEE, ACM, International Society of Research in Science and Technology (ISRST), USA, Senior member of the International Association of Computer Science and Information Technology (IACSIT), Singapore and International Association of Engineers (IAENG). His research interest includes Parallel and Distributed System, Grid and Cloud Computing, Mobile Computing, Internet of Things, Evolutionary Computing.

Rama Shankar Yadav is currently a professor at Motilal Nehru National Institute of Technology, Allahabad, India. He received his Ph.D. degree from the Indian Institute of Technology (IIT) Roorkee, M.S. degree from Birla Institute of Technology and Science (BITS) Pilani, and B. Tech. degree from the Institute of Engineering and Technology (I.E.T.), Lucknow, India. Dr. Yadav has extensive research and academic experience. He has worked in leading institutions such as Govind Ballabh Pant Engineering College (GBPEC), Pauri, Garhwal, and Birla Technical Training Institute (BTTI), Pilani. He has authored more than 70 research papers in national/international conferences, refereed journals, and book chapters. Dr. Yadav's areas of interest are real time systems, embedded systems, fault-tolerant systems, energy aware scheduling, network survivability, computer architecture, distributed computing, and cryptography.

Index

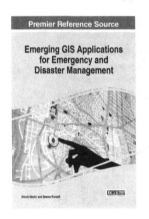
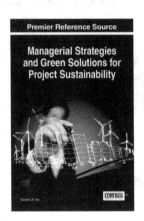

Printed in the United States
By Bookmasters